DATE DUE

Conflict
of Interest
and
Federal
Service

Conflict
of Interest

and

Federal

Service

The Association of the Bar of the City of New York
Special Committee on the Federal
Conflict of Interest Laws.

HARVARD UNIVERSITY PRESS

Cambridge, Massachusetts

1 9 6 0

Distributed in Great Britain by Oxford University Press, London

Typography by Burton J. Jones

Manufactured in the U.S.A. by The Riverside Press, Cambridge

Library of Congress Catalog Card Number 60-13195

THE COMMITTEE

[On this and the succeeding page are listed the ten members of the Committee and its principal staff, together with public positions the members have held.]

ROSWELL B. PERKINS, CHAIRMAN · *Partner: Debevoise, Plimpton & McLean, New York City; former Assistant Secretary of Health, Education and Welfare; former Counsel to the Governor of the State of New York.*

HOWARD F. BURNS · *Partner: Baker, Hostetler & Patterson, Cleveland, Ohio; member of the Council of the American Law Institute.*

CHARLES A. COOLIDGE · *Partner: Ropes, Gray, Best, Coolidge & Rugg, Boston, Massachusetts; former Deputy Director of Internal Security Affairs, Department of State; former Assistant Secretary of Defense for Legal and Legislative Affairs; former Special Assistant to the Secretary of Defense to recommend on the Hoover Commission Reports; former Special Assistant to the Secretary of Defense to recommend on classified information; former Special Assistant to the Secretary of Defense to recommend on reorganization; former Director, Joint Disarmament Study by the Departments of State and Defense.*

PAUL M. HERZOG · *Executive Vice President of the American Arbitration Association, New York; former Chairman of the National Labor Relations Board; former Associate Dean of the Graduate School of Public Administration, Harvard University.*

ALEXANDER C. HOAGLAND, JR. · *Practicing lawyer associated with Curtis, Mallet-Prevost, Colt & Mosle, New York City; former Fellow, The Association of the Bar of the City of New York.*

EVERETT L. HOLLIS · *Corporate Counsel, General Electric Company, New York City; former General Counsel, Atomic Energy Commission.*

CHARLES A. HORSKY · *Partner: Covington & Burling, Washington, D.C.; former assistant prosecutor at Nurnberg with the Chief of Counsel for War Crimes.*

JOHN V. LINDSAY · *United States Congressman from the 17th Congressional District, New York; partner: Webster, Sheffield & Chrystie, New York City; former executive assistant to the Attorney General of the United States.*

JOHN E. LOCKWOOD · *Partner: Milbank, Tweed, Hope & Hadley, New York City; former General Counsel, Office of Inter-American Affairs, Deputy Director, Latin American Division, Department of State.*

SAMUEL I. ROSENMAN · *Partner: Rosenman, Goldmark, Colin & Kaye, New York City; former Special Counsel to Presidents Roosevelt and Truman; former Justice of the Supreme Court of the State of New York.*

THE STAFF

STAFF DIRECTOR

BAYLESS MANNING · *Professor of Law, Yale University.*

ASSOCIATE STAFF DIRECTOR

MARVER H. BERNSTEIN · *Professor of Politics, Princeton University.*

Foreword by the Committee

This book is a report by private citizens on a public problem. The studies upon which it rests were begun some five years ago at The Association of the Bar of the City of New York. It had become apparent by then that the nation's nineteenth-century system of conflict of interest law was totally inadequate to the needs of the twentieth century, and the problem had begun to attract the attention not only of lawyers, scholars, and government administrators, but also of the press and the public. Gradually there had developed a body of serious criticism and a responsible demand for reform. Some observers charged that the law was no longer sufficient to protect the government against venality; others argued that whatever other disadvantages it might have, the law clearly discouraged able men and women from taking jobs in the federal government. In the Congress there were pending a number of bills to remedy specific shortcomings.

Among those who had personally observed the shortcomings of the law were members of The Association of the Bar of the City of New York. The Association, founded in 1870, has always counted among its members a substantial number who are active in public service, including its former presidents Elihu Root, Charles Evans Hughes, Henry L. Stimson, and Robert P. Patterson. It was another former president of the Association, Bethuel M. Webster of New York, who after a period of government service suggested that the Association undertake a study of the conflict of interest laws. President Allen T. Klots assigned the task to the Committee on Law Reform, then under the chairmanship of Robert B. von Mehren; it is one of some seventy committees of the Association constantly engaged in the review of, and the effort to improve, all aspects of the law, state and federal.

At that time Alexander C. Hoagland, Jr., a member of the present Special Committee, was, as the Fellow of the Association, a full-time assistant to its officers. It was he who over a two-year period did the extensive research that laid the groundwork for this study, and it was he who exposed the full magnitude of the problem both in national significance and in scope, and who recommended a comprehensive investigation of the subject under the auspices of a special committee financed independently and assisted by a professional staff. (Indeed, if the study claims parentage, Mr. Hoagland must certainly be deemed the putative father.)

Early in 1958 the Association applied for and was given a grant of $47,500 (later supplemented with an additional grant of $25,000) by the Ford Foundation to help finance a full-scale examination of the subject, and in May of that year Louis M. Loeb, Mr. Klots's successor as President, appointed this Special Committee to undertake the work.

The Association has often obtained foundation grants and established special committees, assisted by professional staffs, to undertake long-term projects of research into problem areas of the law and the administration of justice. Their publications include reports on the family laws of New York City, on the administration of the court system in the State of New York, and, on the national level, on the federal loyalty-security programs, the right to travel, and the public defender systems. In all such studies, the Association has selected the members of the special committees and their staffs. The institutions providing financial support have neither sought nor been granted any part in the selection of members, the conduct of the studies, the findings, or the conclusions. This Committee has adhered to that principle. Furthermore, whenever such studies have been national in scope, the Association has included on the special committees some of its associate members who live and practice law in parts of the country other than New York. That practice was followed in the appointment to this Special Committee of members from Boston, Cleveland, and Washington, D.C.

For its professional staff, the Committee needed experts both in the law and in government and public administration — the two basic disciplines bearing upon the problem. Professor Bayless Manning of the Yale Law School agreed to serve as Staff Director, and Professor Marver H. Bernstein of the Department of Politics, Princeton University, joined the project as Associate Staff Director.

The mandate of the Special Committee was expressed by President Loeb: its task was "bringing order into this highly confused state of the law [of conflict of interest]; determining in what way the law fails to guard against corrupt practices; evaluating the impact of these laws upon the recruitment of personnel by the federal government and publicizing the findings for the benefit of the public." The study was to be balanced, comprehensive, scholarly, nonpartisan, and constructive. The Committee was not interested in raking over old examples of corruption in government or digging up new ones.

The Committee and staff moved forward simultaneously on two fronts. On one, it had to find out what the conflict of interest law actually provided; that required reducing to orderly, intelligible form the bramblebush of statutes, exemptions, exceptions, regulations, decisions, and rulings that had grown up during the past hundred years. This phase of the work began as a continuation of the earlier research done by Mr. Hoagland, and he temporarily served in a staff role by helping Professor Manning to launch the legal research program. The report of the research program provided a foundation upon which the Committee proceeded to the task of evaluation of the law. That report will be published in 1961 as a companion to this book; it is intended to provide lawyers, government officials, and other interested persons with the first detailed, comprehensive, and reliable guide to the federal law of conflict of interest.

On its second front, the Committee sought to find out how the law worked in practice. Almost no facts were available in consolidated form, and statements in the limited literature on the subject were largely anecdotal. The staff, therefore, worked out an extensive interview program (described in Appendix C) to meet the demands of factual research in the area. This involved, among other things, conducting interviews in selected governmental agencies and with the staffs and members of certain congressional committees. The Committee interviewed other persons having knowledge of the subject or having had experience relevant to the study, including present and former officials of the government, members of Congress, lawyers, scientists, and businessmen. The interviews numbered over two hundred. In addition, many officials, members of Congress, and private individuals set forth their views at meetings of the Committee. All gave freely of their time, and without their cooperation and the cooperation of the governmental establishment as a whole, the crucial factual research could never have been completed. All conferences and interviews, whether with officials or private individuals, were conducted on the understanding that although the Committee was free to make whatever use it chose of the information elicited, the sources would remain confidential.

Upon completion of the research and evaluation, the Committee undertook, again simultaneously, its two final tasks — the preparation of its report and the drafting of a new, unified, and comprehensive system of conflict of interest law. An initial draft of the report, provided by Professors Manning and Bernstein, was scrutinized and discussed extensively by the Committee members and substantially revised in subsequent drafts in accordance with their decisions. The proposed statute was likewise a Committee enterprise. Proceeding from a bare outline of concepts, it went through some fifteen drafts, which were debated in great detail in monthly two-day Committee meetings during the spring, summer, and fall of 1959. That statute, along with a detailed explanation, is presented in Chapter XI.

The report and the statute are therefore the work of the entire Committee, and they have been adopted unanimously; the few compromises they bear have been minor compared to the vast areas of complete agreement on the part of all the members. Together they provide a critique of the existing federal conflict of interest restraints and a proposed new program of controls designed for modern needs. Whether or not the program is adopted in all its particulars, the Committee hopes that its study will contribute to recognition of the importance and complexity of the problem and the need for a balanced and integrated approach to it.

This book stands upon the shoulders of many men and women who have given their time and labor to the problem. We owe a great debt to the students, both private and governmental, who have preceded us in this field. It was our good fortune that one who had given much thought to this subject, William Pincus, was the representative of the Ford Foundation to whom the idea of the study was first submitted. We gained much from his advice and wise counsel.

Miss Ruth D. Carter, the Committee's secretary, loyally and devotedly performed the formidable task of handling mountains of reports, summaries, drafts, and correspondence, and of preparing this report for publication. At the same time, she transcended that job by acting, in effect if not in title, as the Committee's administrative assistant and chargé d'affaires. Without her, the project would surely have ground to a calamitous halt as its magnitude increased.

Near the study's close, Mr. Hoagland again added to his duties as a Committee member by assuming the extra burdens of detailed editorial work on the report and of supervision of the production, preparation, and handling of the Committee's press releases.

We are also indebted to the library of The Association of the Bar of the City of New York. Arthur Charpentier, the Librarian, and Joseph L. Andrews, the Reference Librarian, not only gave us every assistance, but early in the study compiled an exhaustive bibliography upon which we have relied heavily.

Invaluable legal research was performed by Mrs. Molly Epstein Cohen, William Kass, Robert Higgins, and Edward Fowler in the summer of 1958. Donald L. Godiner, working under the supervision of Professor Manning, pushed the legal research to completion and deserves substantial credit for the legal report that will be published as a companion to the present volume. A. Edward Gottesman, as Staff Secretary to the Committee in its early months, contributed significantly to the organizational phase.

Paul B. De Witt, Executive Secretary of the Association, helped to launch the study of the subject five years ago, and later was instrumental in obtaining the grant from the Ford Foundation and helped to set up this Committee. Not only has he been an invaluable support in our work, but he and Gerald MacDonagh, Administrative Manager of the Association, made our meetings pleasant as well as productive.

Our particular thanks go to Dudley B. Bonsal, President of the Association for two years past. Faithfully attending our many prolonged sessions, he gave us the encouragement of his leadership and the benefit of his wide experience and learning.

Our final expression of gratitude goes to Bayless Manning and Marver H. Bernstein. They planned and carried out the enormous task of research with vigor, imagination, tact, and thoroughness. And they brought to our conference table not only the results of their researches; they also brought their own wide knowledge, sound judgment, and rigorous professional standards. They were our intellectual leaders, and the work of their minds is everywhere in this book.

As the individual responsible for the staff work on the entire project, for fitting all its pieces together and guiding the Committee's deliberations, Professor Manning has rendered a truly outstanding performance both as a legal scholar and as a practical administrator. His work on this project, superimposed on a full teaching schedule and major commitments to several other projects, could easily have required full-time labors of several years' duration on the part of anyone of lesser capacity and diligence.

Howard F. Burns	Charles A. Horsky
Charles A. Coolidge	John V. Lindsay
Paul M. Herzog	John E. Lockwood
Alexander C. Hoagland, Jr.	Roswell B. Perkins
Everett L. Hollis	Samuel I. Rosenman

Postscript by the Chairman

A prerogative of a chairman is — or should be — to have the last word. In this case it will be brief. In my judgment, no group of nine men ever served more loyally and diligently on a project of major public concern than the members of this Special Committee on the Federal Conflict of Interest Laws. All of them served while busy with their regular jobs, and the hours stolen from office and family to perform the task constitute a massive total. Their reward was and will be nothing but the satisfaction derived from the Committee's work and its pleasant and stimulating associations. My gratitude to the members is overwhelming, as is my personal admiration for the capacities that each brought to bear on the project.

I want to add a personal note to express my great debt to the Association's President, Dudley B. Bonsal, who earlier chaired the Association's Special Committee on the Federal Loyalty-Security Program. Throughout this study his guidance and support have been of inestimable value.

ROSWELL B. PERKINS, *Chairman*

Contents

Contents

Contents

Part One
The Study

I

Thesis

This book has two themes. The first is that ethical standards in the United States federal government must be beyond reproach. The second is that the federal government must be in a position to obtain the personnel and information it needs to meet the demands of the twentieth century. These themes are coequal. Neither may be safely subordinated to the other.

The book proposes an integrated program for advancing both these objectives in an important area where neither is being satisfactorily furthered today. That area is the regulation of conflicts of interest in the executive branch.

The term "conflict of interest," with related terms, has a limited meaning in this study. Any interest of an individual may conflict at times with any other of his interests. This book, however, is concerned with only two interests: one is the interest of the government official (and of the public) in the proper administration of his office; the other is the official's interest in his private economic affairs. A conflict of interest exists whenever these two interests clash, or appear to clash.

A conflict of interest does not necessarily presuppose that action by the official favoring one of these interests will be prejudicial to the other, nor that the official will in fact resolve the conflict to his own personal advantage rather than the government's. If a man is in a position of conflicting interests, he is subject to temptation however he resolves the issue. Regulation of conflicts of interest seeks to prevent situations of temptation from arising. An Internal Revenue agent auditing his own tax return would offer a simple illustration of such a conflict of interest. Perhaps the agent's personal interest in the matter would not affect his discharge of his official duty; but the experience of centuries indicates that the contrary is more likely, and that affairs should be so arranged as to prevent a man from being put in such an equivocal position.

The danger of such conflicts of interest was noted long ago; even before the Sermon on the Mount warned against serving two masters, Plato had forbidden his philosopher kings to hold any personal economic interests whatever.[1] In America the problem was recognized early. When the United States was new, its first Congress forbade the holder of the office of Secretary of the Treasury to invest in government securities;[2] and the bulk of our present conflict of interest statutes dates from the nineteenth century. But since the end of World War II the attention of the American public has been drawn to conflict of interest problems with a new frequency and intensity.

The last days of the New Deal–Fair Deal era were marred by scandals, investigations, and indictments of federal officials; ethics in government was an important campaign topic in 1952.[3] Following a general study of ethics in government in 1951, a Senate subcommittee under Senator Douglas of Illinois recommended, among other things, a tightening of conflict of interest restraints.[4] In 1953, the advent of the first Republican administration in twenty years was accompanied by a sweeping personnel turnover at executive levels and generally increased recruitment of business executives. Conflict of interest problems as such moved to stage center. Charles Wilson,

[1] PLATO, THE REPUBLIC 543C.

[2] See Chapter III, note 3 infra.

[3] See, e.g., Hearings Before the Senate Committee on Banking and Currency Concerning an Investigation of the Federal Housing Administration, 83d Cong., 2d Sess. (1954); Hearings Before the Special Subcommittee of the House Committee on the Judiciary Concerning an Investigation of the Department of Justice, 82d Cong., 2d Sess. (1952) and 83d Cong., 1st Sess. (1953); Hearings Before the Subcommittee on Administration of the Internal Revenue Laws of the House Committee on Ways and Means Concerning an Internal Revenue Investigation, 82d Cong., 1st Sess. (1951); Hearings Before the Senate Committee on Agriculture and Forestry Concerning an Investigation of the Commodity Credit Corporation, 81st Cong., 1st Sess. (1949); Hearings Before the Senate Committee on Banking and Currency Concerning an Investigation of the Loan Policy of the Reconstruction Finance Corporation, 81st Cong., 1st Sess. (1949).

[4] SUBCOMM., SENATE COMM. ON LABOR AND PUBLIC WELFARE, 82D CONG., 1ST SESS., REPORT ON ETHICAL STANDARDS IN GOVERNMENT 45–65 (Comm. Print 1951).

president of General Motors, named Secretary of Defense as President Eisenhower's first Cabinet appointee, ran head-on into the issue when, with much publicity, the Senate Armed Services Committee forced him to dispose of his GM holdings as the price of confirmation.[5]

Subsequent appointees coming before the same Committee found it increasingly sensitive to conflicts of interest. Correspondingly, emphasis in congressional investigation and in the press shifted from overt misconduct to the more subtle concerns of conflicting interests. Over a period of years, several highly placed officials in the Eisenhower Administration came to grief on this score.[6]

By 1958, conflicts of interest had become sufficiently identified as an independent issue separate from other ethical problems to merit a special study by a subcommittee of the House Judiciary Committee.[7] In 1958 no fewer than seventeen bills and resolutions were introduced to curb ex parte communications and other aspects of executive conduct involving, or closely related to, conflict of interest issues.[8] In January of 1960 a subcommittee of the House Armed Services Committee brought in its report after hearings on the alleged impropriety of defense contractors' hiring senior military officers immediately after their retirement.[9] And the Antitrust Subcommittee of the House Judiciary Committee opened hearings in February 1960 on proposals for reform of the conflict of interest statutes.

It is interesting, and significant, that contemporary America has

[5] See Chapter V *infra.*

[6] The instances are discussed in Chapter V.

[7] STAFF OF SUBCOMM. NO. 5, HOUSE COMM. ON THE JUDICIARY, 85TH CONG., 2D SESS., REPORT ON FEDERAL CONFLICT OF INTEREST LEGISLATION, pts. I & II (Comm. Print 1958).

[8] For example, on June 11, 1958, Senator Neuberger introduced S. 3979, designed to include members of Congress within certain of the statutes on conflicts of interest currently applicable only to the executive branch, namely, 18 U.S.C. §§ 283, 284, 1914 (1958) and REV. STAT. § 190 (1875), 5 U.S.C. § 99 (1958). On June 30, 1958, Senator Javits and Representative Keating introduced bills which would have established an employees' code of ethics. See S. 4078 and H.R. 13216. Senator Case, on August 1, 1958, introduced S. 4223, a bill to require members of Congress and other employees earning more than $12,500 a year to file an annual report of income and gifts in excess of $100. None of these bills was passed. See Chapter V, note 64 *infra.*

[9] See *Hearings Before the Subcommittee for Special Investigations of the House Committee on Armed Services Pursuant to H. Res. 19,* 86th Cong., 1st Sess. (1959). See also SUBCOMM. FOR SPECIAL INVESTIGATIONS, HOUSE COMM. ON ARMED SERVICES, 86TH CONG., 1ST SESS., REPORT ON EMPLOYMENT OF RETIRED COMMISSIONED OFFICERS BY DEFENSE DEPARTMENT CONTRACTORS (Comm. Print 1960).

shown itself keenly aware of the conflict of interest problem. In a sense conflict of interest is a luxury issue — a matter that only an otherwise secure and established society can afford to worry about. Only when grosser larcenies in government have been reduced to tolerable limits — only when overt venality is uncommon enough to shock — is it possible for a government to concentrate on potentials for evil and to try to head off corruption at its sources. In periods and societies where reformers have all they can do to raise public ire at blatant dishonesty, it is impossible to generate much alarm at the mere demonstration that an official is in a position of possible conflicting interests. Indignation at conflicting interests requires a more sensitive ethic. In a backhanded way, it is a tribute to the general moral health of American government today that headlines can be made of potential evil.

But though bribery and other such heinous official misconduct are dangers of more primitive concern, conflicts of interest on the part of government officials are serious matters. Water is a more immediate human need than vitamin C, but in time scurvy will kill as permanently as thirst. Particularly in a democracy, several basic policies are at risk of erosion from official conflicts of interest. It is worth while to isolate these and state them explicitly. All are predicated on the tendency of men to act toward their personal ends, but, as will be seen, the policy objectives at stake are not identical and may, in varying circumstances, call for different courses of action, protections, or remedies. Five such policy objectives may be listed.

Government efficiency. A corrupt government is an inefficient government. The official who throws a government contract to his own firm is apt to throw away the government's chance to have the job done better and cheaper.

Equal treatment of equal claims. A government that plays favorites among its citizens is fundamentally objectionable to American conceptions of the equality of men under the law, notions of fair play, and the assumptions of free competition. Few things make an American citizen angrier than to find out that he did not get a fair shake; and a secret personal interest of a deciding official is a kind of dice loading.

Public confidence. Ultimately every government depends upon the confidence of its people. This is most obviously the case in a democracy. If the people are persuaded that government officials use their office unfairly and for personal rather than public advantage, government by consent of the governed and voluntary compliance with government orders become virtually unattainable. This element of confidence in the government's integrity is simultaneously idealistic and intensely pragmatic. It must be preserved.

Preventing the use of public office for private gain. When public officials use their office for private gain, they usually undermine one or more of the three objectives just listed. However, it is possible to imagine the case of an official who acts impartially, does not play favorites, and is a model of public decorum, but who, for example, speculates on the grain market on the basis of inside government information. The universal condemnation of such action indicates that the prevention of the use of public office for private gain is an independent and separate objective involved in the field of official conflicts of interest.

Preserving the integrity of government policy-making institutions. Our governmental structure and democratic processes provide an elaborate complex of institutions for making government decisions. The institutions and procedures are, in varying degrees, sensitive to the wishes of different interests in ways that are acceptable and indeed necessary in a democracy. But these open and known channels for decision-making are frustrated when a government official appears to perform an ordinary role but is in fact responding to the demands of others to whom he is secretly economically tied. It is not simply that he or the outside group makes money out of it. They may not. It is that the public processes of government are being subverted while policy is made silently by forces not known or responsive to the electorate.

Each of these policy considerations will be seen to play a part from time to time in discussions and proposals concerning official conflicts of interest. Together they present an array of formidable consequence. The first theme of this study is, therefore, that conflicts of interest in federal service must be effectively controlled.

The second theme is the need for adequate staffing of the federal government. The United States as a whole has long been fortunate in its resources of trained talent, but since World War II the problem of providing the federal government with qualified personnel has come to be recognized as a serious matter too long minimized. Fundamental changes have overtaken the federal establishment in the past twenty years. These changes have brought with them a governmental demand for general and executive personnel on a scale and at a level of competence not before known in this country.

The most obvious development in the federal government in the twentieth century has been its sheer growth. It costs more today to pay the annual interest on the national debt than it did to finance the total federal budget in 1933. Spending about $80 billion per year (about one-fifth of the national income), the federal government employs 2.4 million civilian employees and operates 1800 departments, agencies, bureaus, commissions, and other units. The armed services account for another 2.5 million persons at the present time. As the first Hoover Commission concluded in 1949, "It is almost impossible to comprehend the . . . problems of the Federal Government unless one has some concept of its hugeness and complexity. The sheer size, complexity, and geographical dispersion . . . almost stagger the imagination. As a result of depression, war, new needs for defense, and our greater responsibilities abroad, the Federal Government has become the largest enterprise on earth." [10]

Mere growth is not the only source of the heightened demand for governmental personnel. Governmental functions have ramified in kind as well as in size, and the need for experts and trained top executives has grown commensurately. The soaring rate of scientific development and the nation's reliance on federal programs in this field are creating an increasing governmental need for technical specialists. In the world of international affairs the same picture emerges. The United States stands today in a position of preeminence. This has not come about through a slow process of growth or long-range planning. World leadership has been thrust upon it in a generation — against the bitter resistance of many Americans. With it have come large new commitments and responsibilities for overseas establishments and programs — all demanding special staffs in numbers and kinds not before envisioned.

Increasingly the government has found that it can meet its personnel needs only by going outside for talent. The government has

[10] THE COMMISSION ON ORGANIZATION OF THE EXECUTIVE BRANCH OF THE GOVERNMENT (First Hoover Commission), CONCLUDING REPORT 3–4 (1949).

devised in recent years new techniques and devices for enlisting the services of persons outside its regular employees. Intermittent and quasi employment arrangements, involving consultants, part-time experts, advisers with or without compensation, advisory committees, and independent study contractors, have become widespread. The features of the government's personnel system itself have to some extent adjusted to the new demands put upon it.

What has been said so far has been said without reference to the Cold War. But its chill shadow is upon us. The Soviet Union is able to attract or mobilize all its human resources to the services of the government. Holding an international world view receptive to long-range planning, our adversary is playing the national power game with resourceful staffs, long trained for the occasion. Under these circumstances, it is vital to ask whether the United States is doing enough to assure itself of needed talent for government service, to inquire what policy changes could improve its position. The stakes riding on the issue of government manpower today do not permit chances to be taken.

At this point the two themes of this book intersect. As always, pursuit of one desirable policy leads to conflict with another. The relation between controls on conflicts of interest and government staffing is most evident wherever the demand for trained talent is most desperate. A society not yet industrialized or fully developed may find itself with one engineer capable of designing and supervising the construction of a steel mill; when matters arise involving steel mills, the government has no recourse but to turn to its one expert for guidance, regardless of what his personal economic activities or affiliations may be. Vigorous enforcement of conflict of interest restrictions implies either the availability of alternative experts equally capable, or a deliberate choice to get along with the less capable. Most nations do not have the first and are unwilling to risk the second.

The question is whether existing restraints on conflicts of interest are substantially adding to the difficulties of operating the United States government. Are present restrictions, aimed at the worthy goal of higher ethics, hobbling the government's efforts to get needed manpower?

The Second Hoover Commission thought so: "A particular ob-

stacle to attracting competent men into political service is the
problem caused by those portions of the conflict of interest laws
requiring divestment of personal investments and industrial pension
and other rights. While competent men may be willing . . . to accept
lower pay in public service, increasingly they are becoming reluctant
to give up their lifetime accumulations of investments and pension
and other rights of private industry and life. We must develop a
fresh approach to this matter." [11] Strong statements to the same
effect were also made by the Task Force on Business Organization of
the Department of Defense.[12] Others who have investigated the area
have agreed.[13] An important conclusion of the present study, and of
the research on which it is based, is that these views are, in general,
supported by the evidence. With certain refining qualifications described later, existing conflict of interest restraints have worked to
hamper the government's recruiting efforts.

If this conclusion is correct, what can be done about it — what
remedies can be found? Whatever the remedies may be, they cannot
be allowed to undermine public protections against unethical practices in government. The risk from inadequate staffing is immediate;
the risk of corruption and loss of public confidence in governmental
integrity is longer range. Neither risk can be tolerated.

What is needed is balance in the pursuit of two objectives. The
national interest demands an integrated policy for the long and for
the short run. We need a policy that neither sacrifices integrity for
opportunism nor drowns practical staffing needs in moralism. We

---

11 The statement continues: "Recommendation #5 — We recommend that the
President and the appropriate Committees of the Congress review the conflict of interest laws to determine whether the intent of such laws can be better achieved by
other and more positive means which would encourage rather than discourage entry of
competent men into public life." COMMISSION ON ORGANIZATION OF THE EXECUTIVE
BRANCH OF THE GOVERNMENT (Second Hoover Commission), REPORT TO THE CONGRESS ON
PERSONNEL AND CIVIL SERVICE 36 (1955). No evidence on the conflict of interest point
was adduced by the Commission. The problem was discussed by the President's Committee on Governmental Organization, headed by Nelson Rockefeller, but on December
5, 1955, the Committee "deferred indefinitely" any action on the Hoover Commission
proposal.

12 See COMMISSION ON ORGANIZATION OF THE EXECUTIVE BRANCH OF THE GOV-
ERNMENT (Second Hoover Commission), REPORT ON BUSINESS ORGANIZATION OF THE
DEPARTMENT OF DEFENSE 58–59 (1955).

13 See Davis, *The Federal Conflict of Interest Laws*, 54 COLUM. L. REV. 893, 898
(1954). See also HARVARD BUSINESS SCHOOL CLUB OF WASHINGTON, D.C., BUSINESSMEN
IN GOVERNMENT 26 (1958).

need a careful regulatory scheme that restrains official conflicts of interest without creating pernicious side effects.

The optimistic thesis of this book is that such a scheme can be worked out. The concluding chapters propose a new program believed to achieve this result.

I I

Scope

This is not a book about general ethics in the federal government, though the topics overlap. Beyond even the broadest definition of conflict of interest lies a vast range of activities that all would agree to be unethical if practiced by government officials. On the other hand, as will be seen, some actions that fall within the ban of conflict of interest regulation do not strike us as immoral or improper in a personal or subjective sense. Similarly, the book is not the product of an investigation calculated to expose the delinquencies of individual officials. Individual past instances of misconduct are referred to here for illustrative purposes only; no new instances are discovered to public eye. The focus of interest of the book is upon a permanent and endemic problem of all government — the continuing problem posed by the clash between the personal and public life of officials.

The scope of the concept "conflict of interest" proves to be highly particular and somewhat elusive. Its outlines will sharpen as the book progresses, but a first approximation must be sketched at the outset.

LIMITATION TO THE FEDERAL EXECUTIVE BRANCH

This book deals solely with the conflict of interest problem of the executive branch of the federal government.[1] The judicial and legis-

[1] State and local regulation is beyond the scope of this book. The conflict of interest problem often arises in this context, however. See Appendix A, "A Note on State, Local, and Foreign Government."

lative branches are touched upon only peripherally. Ideally, perhaps, all three coordinate branches should be studied at once, even as, ideally, conflicts of interest should be studied simultaneously with all other aspects of ethical behavior in government. But the conflict of interest problems of the judiciary and members of Congress are very different in character from each other and from those of the executive branch. The decision to limit this study to one branch does not imply that the conflict of interest problems of the other branches are unimportant. It is a decision to treat one topic in depth rather than three related, but different, topics more thinly.

The special position of the judiciary is easily seen. Probably no other institution in our society has been as sensitive to the conflict of interest problem as the judiciary, with its ancient and scrupulous practice of self-disqualification. But, by the same token, unique elements in the federal judicial institution, such as life tenure, professional traditions, and the limited scale and special character of the business of the courts, create unique conflict of interest problems and call for unique machinery for their solution.[2] In addition, no special public concern about the ethical standards of the federal judiciary is currently observable.

The congressional conflict of interest problem, on the other hand, is current, complex, and controversial.[3] It is also largely unsolved. How far should a congressman or senator go in voting on matters in which he has some personal stake? What are the proper limits on the power of a member of Congress to appoint his staff from among his family? What kinds of outside employment and income

---

[2] Thus the most directly applicable statutory conflicts restraints upon members of the federal judiciary, 28 U.S.C. § 455 (1958) and 28 U.S.C. § 144 (1958), reflect a less rigorous set of conflicts standards than those imposed upon executive officials. These statutes are pointed primarily toward the protection of a litigant's right to an impartial trial, rather than to possible conflicts between a personal economic interest and an official duty to the United States. See also FED. R. CRIM. P. 42(b). Another relevant statute is 28 U.S.C. § 454 (1958), reading: "Any justice or judge appointed under the authority of the United States who engages in the practice of law is guilty of a high misdemeanor."

[3] The Douglas Committee touched on the problem of conflicts of interest of members of Congress. SUBCOMM., SENATE COMM. ON LABOR AND PUBLIC WELFARE, 82d CONG., 1ST SESS., REPORT ON ETHICAL STANDARDS IN GOVERNMENT 55–59 (Comm. Print 1951). See also N.Y. Times, March 31, 1959, p. 1, col. 1 (Senator disposing of stock as a duty); Neuberger, *When Influence is Good — and Bad*, N.Y. Times, July 27, 1958, p. 9 (Magazine); Neuberger, *Who Polices the Policeman (Congress)?*, N.Y. Times, Feb. 23, 1958, p. 18 (Magazine). For examples of bills introduced in 1958 and 1959 see Chapter I, note 8 *supra* and Chapter V, note 64 *infra*.

are compatible with what kinds of committee assignments? Which campaign contributions are properly acceptable and which are not? The questions are easily multiplied.

Neither law nor custom provides many answers. A rule of the House of Representatives calls for congressmen to disqualify themselves from voting in certain limited situations of personal interest, but disqualification is seldom invoked and virtually unenforcible.[4] The Senate has no corresponding formal rule, but appears to occupy about the same position as the House.[5] Of late years, legislation has been proposed to deal with the checkered state of campaign financing, but the issue is apparently not yet ready for serious assault or solution.[6] Two of the seven conflict of interest statutes examined in the next chapter are applicable to members of Congress, and, of course, the bribery laws cover them.[7] But by and large the law is undeveloped on the conflict of interest problems of members of Congress.[8]

In fundamental respects, however, the congressional problem differs from that of the executive. It is too easy to say glibly that rules governing the administrator should govern the legislator. The congressman's representative status lies at the heart of the matter. As a representative, he is often supposed to represent a particular economic group, and in many instances his own economic self-interest is closely tied to that group. That is precisely why it selected him. It is common to talk of the Farm Bloc, or the Silver Senators. We would think odd a fishing state congressman who was not mindful of the interests of the fishing industry — though he may be in the fishing business himself, and though his campaign funds come in part from this source. This kind of representation is considered inevitable and, indeed, generally applauded. Sterile application of an abstract rule against acting in situations involving self-interest would prevent the farmer senator from voting on farm legislation

4 See H.R. Doc. No. 474, 84th Cong., 2d Sess. 318–19 (1957).

5 See H.R. Doc. No. 474, 84th Cong., 2d Sess. 171–72 (1957).

6 The problem of campaign contributions and expenses has been the subject of congressional concern in recent years. See 104 CONG. REC. 8247–51 (1958), and 105 CONG. REC. 722–23 (1959) for examples of recently proposed bills on this subject.

7 See the discussions of 18 U.S.C. §§ 281 and 216 in Chapter III. See, on bribery, note 12 *infra*.

8 18 U.S.C. § 282 (1958) does, however, forbid members of Congress to practice law before the Court of Claims, and 18 U.S.C. § 431 (1958) forbids them to enter into contracts with the government.

or the Negro congressman from speaking on civil rights bills. At some point a purist attitude toward the evils of conflicts of interest in Congress runs afoul of the basic premises of American representative government.

Furthermore, no member of Congress can subsist on his government salary. Forced to keep his base and to spend time in his home district, he unavoidably incurs heavy and regular travel expenses.[9] Campaign costs soar as campaign techniques turn to mass communication media.[10] And the congressman must always be prepared to sail on the next ebb of the political tide. These facts, taken together with the myth that membership in Congress is still a part-time job, ensure that congressmen will keep up their outside economic connections, and that they will insist upon the necessity and justice of their doing so.

Other special circumstances mark the congressional conflict of interest problem. Congressional elections and primaries can often be relied upon to smoke out an elected official's improprieties; they provide a source of public protection not existing in the case of members of the executive branch. In addition, if the constituency continues to elect a man in spite of improprieties, some leeway must be left for the principle that the people get the kind of government they deserve. Congress' distinctive governmental function, and the special role of party affiliation and discipline in congressional operations also serve to set Congress apart as unique.

The anaylsis and research required for a study of the congressional conflict of interest problem would differ materially from that

9 While salaries and expense allowances for congressmen and senators have been increased in recent years, costs of operating congressional offices have increased even more. Some allowances appear to be generally adequate, while others fall far short of meeting legislators' needs. For example, each congressman is granted a travel allowance for only one round trip per legislative session between Washington and his district. See generally, U.S. News & World Report, Oct. 3, 1952, pp. 21–24; N.Y. Times, March 2, 1955, p. 1, col. 8.

10 In recent statewide elections up to a third or more of all campaign funds have been spent for television. During the 1956 election season, fifteen-minute local telecasts on leading stations in early evening hours cost about $1600 in Chicago, $1000 in Philadelphia, and up to $3360 in New York City. The cost of getting elected to the Senate in a fairly large state runs about $200,000. U.S. News and World Report, Feb. 17, 1956, pp. 42–44. See also HEARD, THE COSTS OF DEMOCRACY (to be published in June 1960); THOMSON, TELEVISION AND PRESIDENTIAL POLITICS (1956); SHANNON, MONEY AND POLITICS (1959); Thomson, Television, Politics and Public Policy, 8 PUBLIC POLICY 368–406 (1958). See also Heard, Money and Politics, Public Affairs Pamphlet No. 242 (1956); N.Y. Times, Oct. 28, 1954, p. 30, col. 3.

of the present study, and any effort to apply conclusions drawn from
the one to the other would be certain to be dangerous and at least
in part unworkable.

But though the position of Congress is necessarily a separate topic
of study, it must be recognized that in the actual operation of American government, the executive and legislative branches continually
affect each other. For example, interest groups frequently work
through the legislature in order to affect action in the executive
branch. Confronted with the staggering complexity and bureaucratic
maze of modern government, the citizen often turns to his congressman as the only federal official known to him who can deal with all
federal agencies and as the only federal official over whom he has
any direct influence. A congressman is expected by his constituents
to intercede on their behalf to get a son transferred from one military
post to another, to put in a good word with procurement officials for
a local company, or to get the Bureau of Reclamation to step up an
irrigation program. Often such congressional intervention is a useful
stimulus to counteract administrative inaction, indecision, or red
tape. Yet such intervention through congressional channels constitutes a significant part of the problem of ex parte communications
to administrative agencies, a problem that edges closely toward the
conflict of interest field.[11] In other less obvious ways as well, executive conduct is conditioned by congressional conduct. The general
ethical atmosphere surrounding the behavior of members of Congress will have an inevitable influence upon the level of conduct in
the executive branch.

Thus an important by-product of a serious examination of the
conflict of interest problems of Congress, with such improvements in
law as are found to be needed, would be a contribution toward the
resolution of conflict of interest problems in the executive branch.
It is therefore strongly recommended here that an independent and
thorough study be undertaken, devoted specifically to the subject of
conflict of interest problems of members of Congress.

THE PRESIDENT AND THE VICE PRESIDENT

The role of the Presidency is a vital aspect of the administration
of conflict of interest restrictions in the executive branch, and the

11 See discussion in this chapter *infra,* and Chapter V, note 6o *infra.*

proper function of the Chief Executive in this field is a major center of consideration in this study. But the conflict of interest problems of the President and the Vice President as individual persons must inevitably be treated separately from the rest of the executive branch. For example, as Chief of State, the President is the inevitable target of a running stream of symbolic gifts pouring in from all over the world, for reasons ranging from the best to the worst. The uniqueness of the President's situation is also illustrated by the fact that disqualification of the President from policy decisions because of personal conflicting interests is inconceivable. Personal conflict of interest problems of the Presidency and the Vice Presidency are unique and are therefore not within the scope of this book.

LIMITATION TO ECONOMIC INTERESTS

It has been pointed out earlier that this inquiry is limited to conflicts between the official's duties and his personal economic interests. But man is driven by many motivations. What of conflicts between his official duties and, for example, his religious or family affiliations? In preference to his business associates, an official may choose to favor his old college roommate with a contract or his mother with a market tip. Job appointments in government are often made in accord with political debts; and intangible loyalties to an institution, such as a school, company, or law firm, may long survive resignation, sale of stock, or severance from a payroll. Then why single out simple economic ties for study and regulation?

The simplest reason is that it is better to control whatever fraction of improper behavior is attributable to economic motives than to control none. The second reason is that regulatory schemes have to be administered. Restrictions on outside economic affiliations can be written with reasonable particularity and enforced with moderate predictability; no one has yet devised a method for sorting out acquaintances, friends, relations, and lovers for purposes of a rule permitting official dealings with some and not with the others.

Finally — and this is the first statement of a point that will appear again in this book — where public confidence is at issue, what people think is true may be as important as what is true. There is little doubt that in the mind of much of the public, personal financial interest is considered a dominant factor in determining human conduct. A variety of elements deep in the culture and history of the United States — the "Protestant ethic," moral elevation of the profit motive, a frontier psychology, the emphasis on material standards of living, the low prestige status of government service — magnify the acquisitiveness of man and make it appear bigger than it is. Non-Americans often believe that we are unregenerate materialists, and Americans half believe it themselves. An instance is their readiness to assume that a man in political office will leap at an opportunity to pick up a dollar. American political history provides ample evidence to support this theory to the satisfaction of those who already believe it. So long as a prevailing ethical concern of the populace is economic, conflict of interest restraints must emphasize economics, for public confidence is the single most important goal at stake in the field of governmental ethics.

OTHER BOUNDARIES

Even with the stipulation that only economic interests will be considered, the subject of conflict of interest will be found to remain open-ended. More than most, the present subject requires clear statement of the outer limits of inquiry, for it has some odd features.

BRIBERY

To raise the issue of conflicting interest, in the sense used here, we need first an employee of the federal executive branch. The kind of employee he must be will engage our attention often in later pages, but need not now be raised. What kinds of acts by this hypothetical employee bring him within the range of the present study?

Many possible acts that can put him into a position where his personal economic interests conflict with his official duties are outside the scope of this book. The mint worker who takes home part of the daily product is an example. In a rather elemental way he is involved in a conflict of interest, but we call him a thief, not an offender against conflict of interest principles. His offense is an act of commission. Its criminal character depends entirely on what he does, not who he is. And his act — the taking of the money — is itself the evil consequence that the law seeks to prevent.

Similarly, the government contracting officer who accepts money from a contractor in exchange for granting him a contract puts himself in an extreme position of conflict between his official duty and personal economic interest. Again we have a specialized name for this offense, and again it is beyond the scope of this book. This offense is bribery. Unlike theft, it must involve an official. Its essential element is a payment to influence official action. It assumes a *quid* for a *quo;* the official is to do something in his official character in return for the payment.[12]

But now assume that the same contracting officer simply receives a large gift from the contractor. There is no agreement or discussion about any contract, and the officer in fact does not give the contract to the donor. If this act is to be forbidden, it cannot be on a theory of theft or bribery. It must be on the theory that the conflict of interest set up by the gift is *likely* to lead to a warping of the official's judgment, or is likely to create the appearance of improper influence. If the official were not an official, the gift would be unexceptionable under federal law. The wrong arises entirely out of the undesirably inconsistent position of the official, first in his relationship to the outside party, and second in his relationship to his federal employer. The offense is an offense arising out of special status. The whole is greater than the sum of the parts: a subjectively innocent gift combined with a subjectively innocent official performing an innocent act can combine to constitute an offense against conflict of interest principles.

Regulation of conflicts of interest is regulation of evil before the event; it is regulation against potential harm. These regulations are in essence derived, or secondary — one remove away from the ulti-

12 Federal bribery law is made up of scraps and rag tags. The first general federal bribery statute was enacted in 1853. Until then, except for special statutes on judicial bribery passed in 1790 REV. STAT. §§ 5449, 5499 (1875) as amended, 18 U.S.C. §§ 206, 207 (1958), the government had relied upon the common law of the crime. See United States v. Worrall, 28 Fed. Cas. 774 (No. 16766) (C.C.D. Pa. 1798). Today at least twenty-three separate statutes must be considered bribery statutes, and, depending upon the definition of bribery adopted, other provisions would have to be included under this heading. The basic statutes are: 18 U.S.C. §§ 201–02 (1958) (general); 18 U.S.C. §§ 204–05 (1958) (members of Congress); 18 U.S.C. §§ 206–08 (1958) (judges and judicial officers); 18 U.S.C. §§ 203, 209–10, 1503–05 (other persons in legal administration); 18 U.S.C. §§ 211–13 (1958), INT. REV. CODE OF 1954 § 7214 (revenue and customs officers); 18 U.S.C. §§ 214–15 (1958) (procuring public office); 18 U.S.C. §§ 217–23 (1958) (government banking and lending operations).

mate misconduct feared. The bribe is forbidden because it subverts the official's judgment; the gift is forbidden because it may have this effect, and because it looks to others as though it does have this effect. This potential or projective quality of conflict of interest rules is peculiar and important. We are not accustomed to dealing with law of this kind. It is as though we were to try to prevent people from acting in a manner that may lead them to rob a bank, or in a manner that looks to others like bank robbery.

One outer boundary to the present inquiry is the point at which the government employee's conduct can be identified as the distinguishable overt offense of bribery.

CONFLICTS OF POLICY

At the opposite extreme from the overt offense of bribery, conflict of interest problems blend into differences over public policy — and at this point lies the other limit to this study.

In a senatorial confirmation proceeding, a senator may use the vocabulary of conflict of interest to express reservations about an appointment. But the alleged conflict of interest and the senator's policy differences with the appointee are very close to identical. A public power proponent on a Senate committee may, for example, be expected to balk at the confirmation of the president of a private utility company as a Federal Power Commissioner. He asks how such a man, even after he resigns his corporate position, can be expected, in conflict with his own interests, to carry out a congressional decision favoring public power. What the senator is really saying is that he disagrees with the policy predispositions of the appointee. He fears that the appointee's background will have given him an emotional and intellectual set that will lead him to run the agency in a manner counter to the senator's view of how it should be run. No demonstration of the appointee's severance with his old company and no stock divestment will make the senator happy, for personal economic holdings are not at the root of his concern; yet it is from the appointee's connections in private industry that the senator infers him to be an "industry man" and suspect. Personal interests, which can be effectively regulated by law, shade off into policy interests, amenable to political resolution only. The division point is difficult to locate.

This transmutation from personal interest questions to policy questions sometimes appears on a broad scale. A number of major governmental programs and agencies may be viewed as the result of the successful efforts of particular interest groups to harness the power of government to their own purposes. The Department of Agriculture, the Department of Labor, and the Department of Commerce are examples of agencies that were set up to serve — and are expected to serve — a particular segment of the economy and represent it in the executive branch. They are in some respects promotional agencies, promoting a particular outside interest through government action. Some bureaus and offices became identified with specific interest groups — mine workers and mine owners with the Bureau of Mines in the Department of the Interior, the railroads with the Interstate Commerce Commission, the natural gas industry with the Federal Power Commission, defense contractors with the Business and Defense Services Administration in the Department of Commerce. An agency — especially a promotional or regulatory agency — is apt to develop close working relations with the particular industries and firms to which its program relates, and to find itself negotiating continuously with this interest group constituency. On occasion, the voice of this constituency becomes very strong, and opposition voices begin to refer to the agency as a "captive agency" — a crypto-representative within government of an interest outside it. In a sense, the whole agency and its executives can become caught up in one big conflict of interest.

Still it is a mistake — or at least a usage outside that of this book — to talk of such problems as problems of conflict of interest. Of course private economic interests are being represented by the promotional agencies. Certainly there is a constant struggle by regulated industries to gain a voice in the regulating agency. The Secretary of Agriculture may well be a farmer, perhaps he should be. It would not be surprising if the Department of Commerce were found to reflect a pro-business bias; in large part that is its job. And it might be a supportable view that the farmers, or labor, or business, wield too much power in the federal government through their men in the Department of Agriculture, Labor, or Commerce. But these statements are statements about political policy, not ethics.

In analyzing the problem of personal conflicts of interest, and in constructing a set of conflict of interest restraints, great care must be taken not to be drawn into the deceptively related — but separate — political problem of the alleged undue influence of interest group X over agency Y or over general government policy.

EX PARTE COMMUNICATIONS

In 1958 it was discovered that a Federal Communications Commissioner had had continuous and improper dealings with a successful applicant for valuable television channel rights.[13] Much congressional and public attention has since been given to the problem of ex parte communications — undisclosed, extracurricular contacts with agency officials by or on behalf of an interested party in an administrative proceeding.

A telephone call by an interested party to a commissioner, urging special treatment of his case, is objectionable on the ground of unfairness to other interested parties, and on other grounds. Ex parte communications represent a fundamental and difficult problem in federal administrative procedure. The basic problem is how to provide for fair hearing and adjudicatory procedures in quasi-judicial agencies.[14] That problem is, however, separate from the subject of conflicts of interest.

Ex parte communications may in some cases form part of a pat-

---

13 See Chapter V, note 84 *infra* and accompanying text.

14 A proposed code of ethics and a report on this subject were prepared by a five-man special committee of the Administrative Law Section of the American Bar Association, headed by Judge David W. Peck, presiding justice of the appellate division of the New York Supreme Court. In general, the code was designed to establish for the administrative agencies standards of conduct comparable to the Canons of Judicial Ethics, which apply to judges. See American Bar Association Press Release 4–59, Feb. 12, 1959.

The Council of the Section on Administrative Law of the American Bar Association redrafted this proposed code in order to confine it more closely to the judicial functions of the agencies. The final proposed code therefore covered only agency personnel engaged in the decisional process. See American Bar Association, Supplemental Report of the Section on Administrative Law, February 1959. The Bar Association sought but failed to obtain congressional enactment of its code.

During 1958 several bills were introduced on this subject. For example, H.R. 13036, introduced by Representative Derounian in the second session of the 85th Congress, would have made it unlawful for any party to consult with any agency employee as to any pending case except upon notice and opportunity to all parties to participate. S. 4223, introduced by Senator Case in the same session, would have required that all communications, including those from Congress and the executive branch, with respect to any case pending before a federal agency, be made a part of the public record of the case in question. No legislation was enacted in this field, however.

tern of improper influence through bribery, favors, or other means. To the extent that an agency official permits himself to be drawn into a compromising position with a party to a proceeding, as through the receipt of favors, a conflict of interest problem is created of the kind under consideration here. But the ex parte communication in itself does not have this effect. The topic is, therefore, only collaterally discussed in this study.

INFLUENCE PEDDLING

Periodically the "influence peddler" or "fixer" appears on the governmental scene. The influence peddler is one who, for a fee, undertakes to see to it that things are done by the government that the client wants done. He achieves his results, if he does, by whatever means are available, from personal friendship to bribery or worse.

Sometimes the influence peddler is an employee or former employee of the government; if so he will run afoul of the conflict of interest statutes or regulations. He may encounter them in other ways as well, for example, if he showers a government employee with gifts. But the over-all problem of regulating the influence peddler as such is not within the scope of this study.[15]

WOCS AND ADVISORY COMMITTEES

It is a general rule that employees of the United States must be on the government payroll. Congress sometimes grants exceptions to this rule. Those who are appointed to these positions are colloquially called WOCs, since they serve "without compensation." WOCs normally continue to draw their pay from their regular employers. The WOC's dual status as a government employee on a private payroll raises many aspects of the conflict of interest question with which

---

15 Influence peddling is a separate problem, exceedingly difficult to define, and more difficult to regulate sensibly: if the peddler is merely capitalizing on old friendships, all the definitional problems discussed pp. 17–18 *supra* are raised; there is only the vaguest of lines between the improper sale of personal know-who and the legitimate use of experience and know-how; and an experienced Washington hand can often perform a useful social function as marriage broker between government and private parties not familiar with government practices. The subject merges, too, with the whole complex subject of lobbying. The Defense Department seeks to handle part of one problem by regulation. See 32 C.F.R. §§ 1.500–1.509 (1953). And at least two statutory sections select out one specific act of influence peddling and make it criminal to accept money for obtaining a public office for another. 18 U.S.C. §§ 214, 215 (1958). There are few cases under these sections.

this book is concerned and the WOC appears often in these pages. But the general problem whether employment of WOCs should ever be permitted, and if so under what circumstances, is a vast subject in itself, the topic of perennial congressional debate, and beyond the scope of this study.

Similarly the propriety of the use of public advisory committees and the problem of the conditions under which they operate do not in themselves fall within the limits of this study. However, the issues of conflicting interests of those who serve on such committees are clearly within the bounds of this inquiry.[16]

With the metes and bounds of the study thus set, it is possible to proceed to the problem itself. The seven chapters that follow present an examination of the existing system of conflict of interest restraints and an assessment of its effects — a review and analysis of the present situation.

[16] WOCs are discussed further in Chapters III and V, advisory committees in Chapters IV and VI.

Part Two
The Situation

III

The Conflict
of Interest Statutes

The companion volume to this book is devoted to a detailed legal
analysis of federal law on conflict of interest. It is designed for the
specialized reader. This chapter, by contrast, is intended to give the
general reader a broad working familiarity with this body of statutory law and its sources. The chapter also includes some critical
commentary upon the statutes, on matters appearing on their face.
Major substantive evaluation of the statutes must be deferred until
later chapters can provide a perspective for it.

The law in this field is not widely known, and relatively little
has been written about it.[1] Indeed, there is considerable room for
choice in deciding what statutes to group together as conflict of interest laws. The present study puts seven general statutes into this
category, though the term "conflict of interest" appears in no one of
them.[2] This classification excludes the cluster of statutes dealing with
bribery, and provisions applicable only to members of Congress;
and spot provisions pertaining only to particular executive offices
are omitted as wanting in general interest.[3] The seven statutes chosen

---

[1] For general treatments of the subject see STAFF OF SUBCOMM. NO. 5, HOUSE COMM.
ON THE JUDICIARY, 85TH CONG., 2D SESS., REPORT ON FEDERAL CONFLICT OF INTEREST
LEGISLATION, pts. I & II (Comm. Print 1958). See also Davis, *The Federal Conflict of
Interest Laws*, 54 COLUM. L. REV. 893 (1954); McElwain & Vorenberg, *The Federal
Conflict of Interest Statutes*, 65 HARV. L. REV. 955 (1952).

[2] Some writers would include only six, excluding 18 U.S.C. § 216.

[3] A good example of this kind of legislation is the act passed at the first Congress
establishing the Treasury Department. In its present version this statute states: "No
person appointed to the office of Secretary of the Treasury, or Treasurer, or Register,

form the core of legislation of general application dealing with the conflict of interest problem among executive branch employees — the legislation that affects most of them directly and is the focal point of controversy in the field.

In general, what do these seven statutes do? Three of them restrict government employees or former employees from assisting others in the "prosecution of claims" against the United States.[4] A fourth is sighted essentially on the same target but is focused a little differently: it forbids government employees to assist others for pay before a forum of the executive branch in any matter in which the United States is interested.[5] The fifth statute prohibits a government official from acting for the government in transactions with a business entity in which he has an economic interest.[6] The sixth forbids the official to receive pay from non-government sources "in connection with" his official services.[7] And the seventh forbids the official to receive pay for assisting another in obtaining a government contract.[8]

Most tersely, five of the seven provisions forbid officials to assist

---

shall directly or indirectly be concerned or interested in carrying on the business of trade or commerce, or be owner in whole or in part of any sea vessel, or purchase by himself, or another in trust for him, any public lands or other public property, or be concerned in the purchase or disposal of any public securities of any State, or of the United States, or take or apply to his own use any emolument or gain for negotiating or transacting any business in the Treasury Department, other than what shall be allowed by law; and every person who offends against any of the prohibitions of this section shall be deemed guilty of a high misdemeanor and forfeit to the United States the penalty of three thousand dollars, and shall upon conviction be removed from office, and forever thereafter be incapable of holding any office under the United States; and if any other person than a public prosecutor shall give information of any such offense, upon which a prosecution and conviction shall be had, one-half the aforesaid penalty of three thousand dollars, when recovered, shall be for the use of the person giving such information." 1 Stat. 67 (1789), as amended, REV. STAT. § 243 (1875), 5 U.S.C. § 243 (1958). Special provisions restricting outside interests of employees of regulatory agencies include 46 Stat. 797 (1930), 16 U.S.C. § 792 (1958) (FPC); 38 Stat. 717 (1914), as amended, 15 U.S.C. § 41 (1958) (FTC); 24 Stat. 383 (1887), as amended, 49 U.S.C. § 11 (1958) (ICC); 52 Stat. 980 (1938), as amended, 49 U.S.C. § 421 (1958) (CAB); 48 Stat. 1066 (1934), 66 Stat. 711 (1952), as amended, 70 Stat. 738, 47 U.S.C. § 154(b) (1958) (FCC). See, for other examples, 18 U.S.C. § 440 (1958) forbidding postal employees from contracting or acting as agents for contracting with the Post Office Department; and REV. STAT. § 452 (1875), 43 U.S.C. § 11 (1958) prohibiting Bureau of Land Management officials from buying public land.

  [4] 18 U.S.C. §§ 283, 284 (1958); REV. STAT. § 190 (1875), 5 U.S.C. § 99 (1958).
  [5] 18 U.S.C. § 281 (1958).
  [6] 18 U.S.C. § 434 (1958).
  [7] 18 U.S.C. § 1914 (1958).
  [8] 18 U.S.C. § 216 (1958).

outsiders in their dealings with the government; one requires officials to disqualify themselves from acting in government matters in which they have a conflicting personal economic interest; and one prohibits outside pay for government work.

Some incidental facts about these statutes are of preliminary interest. Five of the seven were enacted between 1853 and 1872. Three were responses to the venalities of the Civil War. All but one are criminal statutes, in the style of the nineteenth century, with differing penalties ranging from $1,000 to $10,000 and from six months' to two years' imprisonment. It is the executive branch that feels the main sting of the provisions, with members of Congress expressly covered by only two of them, and the judiciary by none. Five apply to employees when in government service; the other two (both of them "prosecution of claims" statutes) restrict the activities of former government employees for a period of two years. No two of the provisions use the same drafting language in defining the scope of their application or the offense proscribed, though three of them refer expressly to prosecution of government claims.

The most symmetrical way to group the statutes for inspection would be either by chronology or by the subject problem treated. But a more manageable way seems to be a combination of these, with the four earliest statutes considered first as a group, the two statutes on post-employment restrictions next, and the statute on outside compensation last.

THE MID-NINETEENTH-CENTURY STATUTES

HISTORICAL BACKGROUND

Judged by almost any standard, the level of public morality in federal office during the mid-1800's was low. Every change of administration brought into office a new, untrained mass of workers, from Cabinet secretaries to clerks. These beneficiaries of the spoils system tended to regard their jobs as legitimate rewards for service to the party. The concept of the "public servant" was hardly born, and a professional spirit was unknown in the ranks of government employees. Self-aggrandizement was common and took many forms.

Conscious venality was not the only problem, however. Among men of the highest motives and reputation there was considerable disagreement over what could and what could not properly be done from a station of public office. Some practices were condoned which today seem almost incredible. The different standards of a different era glint through the well-known correspondence between Senator Daniel Webster and Nicholas Biddle, President of the National Bank. On October 29, 1833, the Senator suggested in a letter written "as a private one" that Biddle might wish him to bring before Congress the matter of President Jackson's proposed withdrawal of United States deposits from the bank. A letter of December 21 reveals that Webster's interest in the bank's fortunes was more than political:

Sir

Since I have arrived here, I have had an application to be concerned, professionally, against the Bank, which I have declined, of course, although I believe my retainer has not been renewed, or *refreshed* as usual. If it be wished that my relation to the Bank should be continued, it may be well to send me the usual retainers.[9]

Representative Stephens of Georgia recalled in 1853 that it had been a common thing "from the beginning of this Government, for Senators and members of this House to appear as counsel for fee and reward or compensation before the Supreme Court of the United States, to appear before any of the courts of the Union, and before commissioners appointed to adjudicate claims" against the government.[10] Members of Congress appeared on behalf of claimants before the claims commission established under the Jay Treaty. At the end of the War of 1812, Senator Pinkney of Maryland appeared before the claims commission, and Vice President Dallas, with others, including members of Congress, received fees for prosecuting a claim before one of the departments. Senators Benton of Missouri, Soule of Louisiana, Webster of New Hampshire, and others represented claimants before the Mexican Claims Commission. Congressman Stephens, in the speech just quoted, went on:

Now, my point was, to show from the whole legislative history of the country, that such a connection has never been deemed improper, that

9 See Letters From Daniel Webster to Nicholas Biddle, October 29, 1833, December 21, 1833, in McGrane, The Correspondence of Nicholas Biddle 216–17, 218 (1919).
10 Cong. Globe, 32d Cong., 2d Sess. 289 (1853).

there is no legislation against it. . . . The only Department of the Government in relation to which such a connection is prohibited by law, is that of the Treasury.[11] That is the only Department in which public officers are prohibited from holding such a relationship. In the War Department there is no law against either the head of it or any subordinate being interested in a claim, or prosecuting a claim pending before the Treasury. In the State Department there is no such prohibition, or in any other Department. Here, and in this connection, I beg to call the attention of the House to the investigation which was had in 1837, before the memorable committee of Mr. Wise. You recollect, perhaps, that amongst other charges of impropriety preferred by Mr. Wise, was, that the heads of some of the Departments were speculating in the public lands, and with having interest in, and with prosecuting claims against the Government. The position of General Jackson, and of the party then in power, of which he was emphatically the head, was, that *there was no law against it,* and that if the head of any of the Departments, except the Treasury, or any of the officers of the Government, had a claim against the Government, or was disposed to invest his money in speculating in the public lands, that it was no well-grounded charge against the integrity of such officer. . . .

The Secretary of State was charged at that time with being largely interested in a land company in the State of Alabama. . . . There was no law against it, and the question was not permitted to be propounded touching the matter without this modification. The inference was clear that he was, or if he was, that it was his legal right to be so interested. . . .

It was freely admitted by the then Secretary of State — Mr. Forsyth — that he had been employed as attorney, and was so employed while Secretary of State, to prosecute against the Government what is well known as the Galphin claim. General Jackson knew, and the country knew, that Mr. Forsyth admitted this. It was not denied. He was Secretary of State, and admitted the fact before the committee. . . . Yet no one censured Mr. Forsyth; and no one then dared to impugn his honor for it. That then and now stands above reproach — because it was his legal right to do so.[12]

A special sore spot was this matter of prosecuting claims against the United States. The Court of Claims was not established until 1855. Until then, and in major part even after its creation, private claims against the government were handled through private acts of Congress or were handled directly by the relevant department. Claim proceedings before the departments were often inside affairs,

[11] See note 3 *supra.*
[12] CONG. GLOBE, 32d Cong., 2d Sess. 289–90 (1853).

conducted ex parte and with no adversary practice.[13] The combination of this system and the spoils concept of government office produced its inevitable results of influence peddling, information selling, and dissipation of public funds. Not only were some high-ranking members of the executive and legislative branches willing to hire out to claimants, but some members of Congress went so far during the Civil War period as to advertise their availability for such services in the Washington newspapers.[14] Among the villains of the piece were the professional claims agents who swarmed to Washington like ants to a picnic. Government employees were assisting private parties in bringing claims against the government for Mexican War damage, for unpaid salaries for military service, and even for government salaries presently accruing. [15] Some more enterprising employees did not wait for the claimant to request aid, but combed the government files for overlooked or unmatured claims which they then purchased at a fraction of full value and prosecuted on their own.

It is difficult to say how widespread the abuses of the government claims procedures were and how many government employees were actually involved. It is also a question how much of the record that remains is politically colored, as it clearly is in part in the notorious Gardiner incident. Senator Corwin of Ohio undertook to represent before the Mexican Claims Commission the cause of one Dr. Gardiner in his claim for damages arising from the destruction of a silver mine during the Mexican War. The Senator acquired a fractional interest in the claim. His success in recovering $500,000 for his client produced no public attention. But in 1852 it developed that Dr. Gardiner was an itinerant quack and that the silver mine had never existed. The ensuing public explosion was intensified by the fact

13 For problems in handling claims, see RICHARDSON, HISTORY, JURISDICTION, AND PRACTICE OF THE COURT OF CLAIMS (2d ed. 1885); S. REP. No. 1, 33d Cong., 1st Sess. (1853). From 1855 to 1863, the court received cases directly from Congress or by petition from claimants. All decisions of the court were referred to Congress and placed on the legislative calendars. Favorable decisions of the court were accompanied by bills for congressional consideration. After March 3, 1863, the judgment of the court became final, subject to appeal to the Supreme Court. 12 Stat. 765. See WHITE, THE JACKSONIANS 159–61 (1954).

14 CONG. GLOBE, 38th Cong., 1st Sess. 559 (1864).

15 See CONG. GLOBE, 32d Cong., 2d Sess. 392 (1853). Some executive departments went so far as to pay the fee of the claims agent directly out of the compensation that was due to the claimant. See CONG. GLOBE, 32d Cong., 1st Sess. 1259 (1852). Other aspects of the claims agent situation are referred to at CONG. GLOBE, 32d Cong., 1st Sess. 1337–40 (1852).

that Corwin, having resigned from the Senate, was President Fillmore's Secretary of the Treasury at the time the fraud was discovered. Political foes of the administration went after the Secretary with the elan to be expected, and friends of the administration rallied to the defense of Corwin's personal innocence.[16] Apparently Corwin was ignorant of the fraudulence of the claim, and, fortunately for him, had sold his fractional interest in the claim upon entering the Treasury office. But during 1852 and 1853 the Gardiner affair was front page news, and the congressional debate fills many pages in the *Globe*.[17]

Whatever the political overtones of the Gardiner incident, there is no doubt that it turned congressional and public attention to the whole system of claims agents and of prosecuting claims against the United States. The situation was at least sufficiently serious to excite some pungent oratory. Hear Senator Hale of New Hampshire, speaking in 1853:

Our influence, our contenance, our affection, everything is bartered away and sold by these agents, who block up the Capitol, and block up the avenues to the Departments, and it has got to such a state now that a sailor cannot get his pay for his services unless he procures the service of an agent to get his claim through. . . .

The claim agents by whom we are surrounded, when we walk and when we sit, have a practice of representing to sailors in our ships-of-war on foreign coasts, that it is necessary to employ them to get their pay. I am informed by the Secretary of the Navy that he has had orders presented to him, and that sixty dollars has been charged and received for procuring the signature of the Secretary to a paper which it was just as much a matter of course for him to affix as for the Secretary of the Senate to read the daily Journal.[18]

Or Senator Underwood of Kentucky, in 1852: "There are those who go through the country, hunting up claims against the Government, which are not well-founded; and, having sought and found them, they set up and support the claims by subornation . . ."[19] In

16 For example, the speech of Representative Stephens, quoted *supra,* was delivered in defense of Secretary Corwin. See CONG. GLOBE, 32d Cong., 2d Sess. 289–90 (1853).

17 See CONG. GLOBE, 32d Cong., 2d Sess. 242–43, 273–74, 288–96 (1853); CONG. GLOBE, 32d Cong., 1st Sess. 2301–05, 2413–14, 2418 (1852).

18 CONG. GLOBE, 32d Cong., 2d Sess. 392 (1853).

19 CONG. GLOBE, 32d Cong., 1st Sess. 1338 (1852).

support of an 1853 bill restricting government officials in assisting claimants against the United States, Representative Andrew Johnson of Tennessee perorated:

I cannot conclude without making an earnest appeal to the House to come forward and sustain this bill, as one step towards arresting and condemning this system of high-handed plundering and swindling, which has been and is being carried on, about Congress and the various departments of the Government. Sound morality, common honesty, justice, an eviscerated Treasury, all demand that something should be done to separate these vampires from the body politic. There must be something done to restore public confidence, for it is going very fast, if not already gone. The Government and the functionaries of Government are beginning to stink in the very nostrils of the nation; it is now dead and rotten in many of its parts, while the disease is rapidly making its way into the others less accessible. Its putrid stench is sent forth upon every wind and is arresting the attention of the voracious vultures throughout the land, and they have gathered, and are still gathering, around the carcass, ready to begin their foul work.[20]

The spoils system and an undisciplined claims procedure created serious ethical problems for the federal government in time of peace. In time of war the administrative immaturity of the governmental establishment invited outright fraud, dishonesty, and theft. The sudden flood of Civil War contracts offered temptation to profiteers, and they were not slow to succumb to it. The sordid history of military procurement frauds is familiar; [21] the important fact for present purposes is that frequently government officials, employees, or former employees were among the participants.

For example, there was the famous Hall carbine affair. It appears that the aides-de-camp to General Fremont, and others, were able to arrange, to their own profit, for the government to purchase at $22 apiece a large number of carbines which not six months earlier the government itself had sold as defective weapons at $3.50 each. A House investigating committee reported on December 17, 1861,

20 CONG. GLOBE, 32d Cong., 2d Sess. 67 (App. 1853).
21 See generally SHANNON, THE ORGANIZATION AND ADMINISTRATION OF THE UNION ARMY, 1861–1865 (2 vols. 1928); RANDALL, THE CIVIL WAR AND RECONSTRUCTION (1937); MENEELY, THE WAR DEPARTMENT, 1861: A STUDY IN MOBILIZATION AND ADMINISTRATION (1928). See also H.R. EXEC. DOC. No. 151, 37th Cong., 2d Sess. (1862); H.R. MISC. DOC. No. 34, 37th Cong., 2d Sess. (1862); H.R. REP. No. 2, 37th Cong., 2d Sess. (1861).

that the affair was "remarkable in illustrating the improvidence of gentlemen prominently connected with the public service, the corrupt system of brokerage by which the treasury has been plundered, and the prostitution of public confidence to purposes of individual aggrandizement." [22]

Another notorious incident of the period was that of a manufacturer, one Schubarth, who solicited the aid of a member of Congress in his efforts to obtain a government contract. Senator Simmons of Rhode Island was promised a $10,000 commission in return for introducing Schubarth to the Secretary of War. The Congressional Commission on Ordnance Stores, on January 2, 1862, after investigating the matter, stated that Schubarth's conduct was "chargeable to a vicious system of administration, which in abandoning the law, forces the citizen to seek the patronage of his government by purchase through mercenary agencies, instead of obtaining it by open and honorable competition." [23] The Commission concluded, however, that neither the Senator nor Schubarth had violated the law.

A further issue of public propriety debated during the Civil War was the question whether members of Congress should be free to represent clients before courts martial. The jurisdiction and activity of these courts had expanded greatly during the war, and opportunities for law practice before them had correspondingly increased. Some members of Congress accepted clients for the purpose; but some argued that congressional representation would improperly influence the judgment of the military judges, since their personal careers and promotions hung on congressional approval. "Taking human nature as it is," said Senator Foster of Connecticut, "it is utterly inconceivable that members of these military courts should not have this fact in their mind while they are trying cases brought before them." He added that he had heard of an occasion on which a member of Congress who appeared as counsel before a court-martial, dissatisfied with some preliminary decisions made by the tribunal, was reported to have said to a member of the court: "You expect soon to be promoted and I give you to understand that your

22 See H.R. REP. No. 2, pt. 1, 37th Cong., 2d Sess. 40 (1861). See also H.R. REP. No. 2, pt. 2, 37th Cong., 2d Sess. lxvi–lxviii and *passim* (1861).
23 H.R. EXEC. DOC. No. 151, 37th Cong., 2d Sess. 2–5, 6 (1862).

confirmation will not get through the Senate without some difficulty." [24]

Perhaps the temper of the times and the gravity of the problem of
procurement fraud are best shown by the anguished resolutions
passed by the New York, Ohio, and Michigan legislatures beseeching
Congress to take some action to "prevent peculation and frauds in
providing supplies for our armies, . . . and also provide safeguards
so that soldiers in the field and camp shall be protected from the
extortion of army sutlers." [25]

This is the general background against which Congress enacted
four of the seven statutes under review here, one in 1853, and one
each in 1862, 1863, and 1864. Although today we often call these
statutes "conflict of interest statutes," the environment of their conception and birth was not that of a nice calculated concern at potential dangers; it was an environment of actual fraudulent claims,
sale of information, claim chasing, overt sale of influence, improper
diversion of public funds, corruption in public office, and wartime
contract frauds and favoritism.

18 U.S.C. § 283: UNCOMPENSATED ASSISTANCE TO CLAIMANTS (1853)

In 1850, 1851, and again in 1852, President Millard Fillmore requested Congress to improve procedures for handling claims against
the government by creating a claims commission or tribunal.[26] In
1852 he also called for further legal protection against the theft and
destruction of public documents and against bribery.[27] As a result of
administration pressures, the Gardiner scandal, and a series of congressional investigations and debates, Congress passed in 1853 an
omnibus reform bill captioned "An Act to Prevent Frauds on the
Treasury of the United States." [28] It contained the predecessor of

24 CONG. GLOBE, 38th Cong., 1st Sess. 557 (1864).

25 The quotation is taken from the New York resolution. H.R. MISC. DOC. No. 34,
37th Cong., 2d Sess. (1862). See S. MISC. DOC. No. 34, 37th Cong., 2d Sess. (1862) (Michigan); H.R. MISC. DOC. No. 44, 37th Cong., 2d Sess. (1862) (Ohio).

26 He covered the point in his first annual message to Congress. 5 RICHARDSON,
MESSAGES AND PAPERS OF THE PRESIDENTS 91–92 (1897).

27 Id. at 178–79. He paid tribute to the integrity of the government's employees,
but pointed out that "they are appointed to guard the approaches to the public
Treasury, and they occupy positions that expose them to all the temptations and
seductions which the cupidity of peculators and fraudulent claimants can prompt
them to employ." Ibid.

28 10 Stat. 170 (1853), as amended 18 U.S.C. § 283 (1958).

present Section 283, the oldest of the statutes on conflict of interest.

Of the eight sections of the original omnibus bill, only Section 2 is reflected in present Section 283. The other sections either have been repealed or dealt with matters other than conflict of interest, such as bribery, assignment of claims against the United States, and the purloining of public documents. Since its enactment Section 2 has undergone technical revisions, and minor exemptions have been carved out from it. Otherwise, present Section 283 is substantially identical to Section 2 of the 1853 statute.

The section is short and direct.[29] It is aimed at the employee who works for the government and simultaneously works against it by assisting others in claims against the United States. In substance Section 283 forbids a government employee (other than in the discharge of his duties) to assist, or act as agent or attorney, in the prosecution of any claim against the United States. The prohibition applies whether or not the employee receives compensation for his services to the claimant, but it also forbids the employee to receive any gratuity or interest in a claim in return for assisting in prosecuting it. Members of Congress are not covered by Section 283.[30] Originally the section was subject to an exception making it clear that it did not bar employees from prosecuting claims against the government in the courts, but in 1873 this exception was deleted.[31] The penalty of the section is criminal.

Little debate attended Section 2 of the 1853 act. Most of the floor discussion related to the general purpose of the bill as a whole and to Section 3 (subsequently repealed), forbidding members of Con-

---

[29] In its present form the section reads: "Whoever, being an officer or employee of the United States or any department or agency thereof, or of the Senate or House of Representatives, acts as an agent or attorney for prosecuting any claim against the United States, or aids or assists in the prosecution or support of any such claim otherwise than in the proper discharge of his official duties, or receives any gratuity, or share of or interest in any such claim in consideration of assistance in the prosecution of such claim, shall be fined not more than $10,000 or imprisoned not more than one year, or both." 18 U.S.C. § 283 (1958).

[30] A separate section of the 1853 Act, section 3, did apply to members of Congress. See 10 Stat. 170 (1853). That section forbade Congressmen to prosecute claims against the government for a fee. The section was repealed in 1873.

[31] See 10 Stat. 171 (1853). In the general recodification and revision of federal statutes in 1873–74 this exception was dropped from the new REV. STAT. § 5498 (1875) by operation of the general repeal language in REV. STAT. § 5596 (1875). It seems odd that Congress should have made so great a substantive change by general repealer language.

gress from prosecuting claims against the government for a fee. Senator Badger of North Carolina, chairman of the committee that reported the bill and its chief proponent throughout the debates, outlined the purpose of Section 2 as follows:

> It was confined to one or two specific purposes. It was intended for the benefit of a class of men who are entitled to the aid and assistance of the Government — for the benefit of the poor and ignorant, who have claims against the United States, and who are put under the necessity, as the law now exists, of submitting to the most grinding oppression — the most cruel and merciless oppression — for the purpose of getting their claims brought forward and sanctioned here in Congress, or before the Executive Departments.
>
> It was intended, in the second place, to protect the United States, because, as the law stands at present, the largest inducements are held out to crafty or dishonest men to get up, by whatever means, maintain, and carry through before the Departments, or before Congress, claims that are really unfounded, or claims that are greatly exaggerated.
>
> The next object was to protect the Government, by preventing the Executive officers of the Government from employing themselves, while they hold office under the Government of the United States, and are paid by the Government of the United States, from availing themselves of their opportunities to hunt up and to prosecute claims against the Government. It is needless for me to say to what crying abuses such a privilege has already led, and must continue to lead, unless it is put an end to.[32]

Though Section 283 is over a hundred years old, only about four judicial cases and a handful of opinions of the Attorney General have arisen under it. The section is deceptive in its apparent simplicity. What does it mean, for example, to "assist" another in a claim? Does a government employee violate this criminal statute if he appears voluntarily as a witness for another employee in a suit for back pay? Perhaps the government employee can violate the section while doing nothing; the Attorney General has published his opinion that the employee is subject to the penalties of the statute if one of his law partners prosecutes a claim against the government even though the employee does not participate at all.[33] As it stands,

[32] CONG. GLOBE, 32d Cong., 1st Sess. 1339 (1852).

[33] 40 OPS. ATT'Y GEN. 289 (1943). It is not possible to tell from the opinion, however, whether the Attorney General would have reached the same result if the government employee had remained a partner in his partnership, but had insulated himself from

Section 283 is a sweeping statement of policy, applying to all employees of the executive branch alike, striking with criminal sanctions at abuses of government claims procedures that were common in the mid-nineteenth century.

18 U.S.C. § 281: COMPENSATED ASSISTANCE TO OTHERS IN EXECUTIVE FORUM (1864)

Similar in spirit and technique to Section 283 was a statute enacted in 1864.[34] The section is the conflict of interest statute now codified as 18 U.S.C. § 281. It may for present purposes be regarded as substantially identical with its Civil War ancestor.[35]

Section 281 is pointed again at the problem of preventing government employees from assisting outsiders in their dealings with the government, but its scope of coverage is appreciably different. It is broader than Section 283 in two important respects. It extends the prohibition against assisting outsiders far beyond "claims," for it forbids the government employee to render services in relation to any matter in which the United States is a party or is directly or indirectly interested. And it not only covers the personnel of the executive branch but also expressly applies to members of Congress. On the other hand it is narrower than Section 283 in two significant respects. It forbids only services rendered for compensation. And it applies only to proceedings or other matters before a department, agency, court-martial, officer, or commission; thus it is limited to proceedings in an executive forum, and does not apply to court proceedings.[36]

---

sharing in any partnership proceeds derived from prosecuting claims against the government.

[34] 13 Stat. 123 (1864).

[35] In its present form the section reads: "Whoever, being a Member of or Delegate to Congress, or a Resident Commissioner, either before or after he has qualified, or the head of a department, or other officer or employee of the United States or any department or agency thereof, directly or indirectly receives or agrees to receive, any compensation for any services rendered or to be rendered, either by himself or another, in relation to any proceeding, contract, claim, controversy, charge, accusation, arrest, or other matter in which the United States is a party or directly or indirectly interested, before any department, agency, court martial, officer, or any civil, military, or naval commission, shall be fined not more than $10,000 or imprisoned not more than two years, or both; and shall be incapable of holding any office of honor, trust, or profit under the United States." 18 U.S.C. § 281 (1958).

[36] As noted above, the predecessor to section 283 also made exception for judicial proceedings until 1873. See note 31 *supra*.

The necessity for the enactment of the statute in 1864 is not very clear from the record. It might be thought that it was needed mainly to cover members of Congress, since they were not covered by Section 2 of the 1853 act. But, it will be recalled, Section 3 of that statute did apply to compensated services on behalf of claimants by members of Congress — a direct response to the Gardiner affair.[37] Thus there was no great loophole in the 1853 act requiring remedial legislation in 1864, though it is true that the 1864 act extended the 1853 restrictions to a wider group of matters than just "claims," and expressly covered court-martial proceedings, the major topic of debate. In any case, it is interesting that little mention was made of the similar 1853 statute already on the books.[38] The likely reason for the enactment of the 1864 act was that abuses had continued and grown worse with the war, scandal was in the air, public opinion was aroused, and action was the order of the day.

The new 1864 act and Section 3 of the 1853 act remained side by side on the books until 1873. In that year a general codification and revision of the federal statutes were undertaken. In the course of the revision, the revisers apparently concluded that Congress had intended by the 1864 act to repeal the partially overlapping Section 3 of the 1853 act. The 1853 section on members of Congress quietly disappeared, and the 1864 predecessor of the present Section 281 was left standing alone.

Section 281, proscribing compensated services by government employees before an executive forum, has been by far the most litigated of the laws on conflict of interest and is said to be the keystone of the statutes in the field. Even so, in its lifetime of nearly a century, only about ten reported cases and a few opinions of the Attorney General have arisen under it. Two decisions deserve mention here, each an illustration of the broad reach of the section. The first indicates that a government employee violates Section 281 if he receives income, with knowledge of its source, arising from activities listed in the section but performed solely by his nongovernmental partners.[39] This interpretation, taken together with the breadth of activities to which Section 281 applies, makes it difficult for any

[37] See note 30 *supra*.

[38] At least one Senator flagged this point, however. See CONG. GLOBE, 38th Cong., 1st Sess. 561 (1864).

[39] See United States v. Quinn, 141 F. Supp. 622 (S.D.N.Y. 1956).

person to serve as a government employee at the same time that he is a member — even an inactive member — of a partnership engaged in representative work, such as a law firm. The other decision expands the scope of the section in another direction. It held, in the context of a Post Office fraud-order proceeding, that the United States may be "directly or indirectly interested" for purposes of Section 281 even though the government has no pecuniary interest in the matter.[40] Altogether, Section 281, even more than Section 283, cuts with a long blade.

18 U.S.C. § 216: COMPENSATION FOR ASSISTING IN PROCUREMENT OF GOVERNMENT CONTRACTS (1862)

The Hall carbine affair, the Schubarth episode, and the general topic of contract procurement scandals recurrently made headlines during the Civil War. Pressed by the states, public opinion, and its own concern, after almost a year of continuous investigation and resolutions voicing alarm, Congress took action in June of 1862 to do something about government contracting practices. It passed a bill requiring each War, Navy and Interior contract to be filed in a special office along with an affidavit of the contracting officer that he had made the contract "fairly without benefit or advantage to [himself], or allowing any such benefit or advantage corruptly to the [other party]." [41] This statute proved administratively unworkable for a nation engaged in a war, and on July 17, 1862, the operation of the Act was suspended.[42] One day earlier, a more general criminal act went into effect, entitled "An Act to prevent Members of Congress and Officers of the Government of the United States from taking Consideration for procuring Contracts, Office or Place from the United States . . ." [43] This is the parent of the present Section 216, third of the conflict of interest statutes under study.[44]

Like Sections 283 and 281, the 1862 statute was pointed squarely

40 See Burton v. United States, 202 U.S. 344 (1906).
41 See 12 Stat. 412 (1862).
42 See CONG. GLOBE, 37th Cong., 2d Sess. 2915, 3403 (1862). See also 12 Stat. 600 (1862).
43 See 12 Stat. 577 (1862). See also CONG. GLOBE, 37th Cong., 2d Sess. 3378 (1862).
44 As originally enacted, the 1862 statute also contained criminal provisions forbidding payments and receipt of payments to obtain public office or for the attention of a member of Congress to any matter officially before him. These provisions are direct bribery statutes and are now contained in substance in 18 U.S.C. §§ 204, 205 (1958).

at the government official who was aiding an outside private party in his dealings with the government. Section 216 is simple and quite specific.[45] It forbids a government employee to accept payment for procuring a government contract for any person, or for helping him to procure such a contract. Conversely, it penalizes any person who makes such a payment. As would be expected in view of its origin, Section 216, like Section 281, expressly applies to members of Congress as well as to executive officials. Limited in scope to contracts only, Section 216 is much less broad in substantive application than Section 281. In addition to criminal sanction, Section 216 authorizes the President to void any contract made in violation of the section.

Though included here as a conflict of interest statute, Section 216 is in fact a hybrid, for it is half a bribery statute. If an employee who does not work on government contracts accepts payment to help a private party get a government contract, he violates Section 216. If the contracting officer himself accepts the payment for the same purpose he too violates Section 216, but in so doing he is also guilty of taking a bribe. For employees whose official duties relate to the contracting process, therefore, Section 216 operates as a bribery statute, independent of, and supplementary to, the general bribery laws.

There is very little case law under Section 216. That part of the section that is not covered by the bribery statutes is blanketed, though in much different language, by the broad prohibitions of Section 281. As a result, Section 216 has been neither a source of trouble nor a source of assistance in the administration of governmental ethics.

18 U.S.C. § 434: DISQUALIFICATION (1863)

Last of the four statutes grouped here as products of the

---

[45] In its present form, the section reads:

"Whoever, being a Member of or Delegate to Congress, or a Resident Commissioner, either before or after he has qualified, or being an officer, employee or agent of the United States, directly or indirectly takes, receives, or agrees to receive, any money or thing of value, for giving, procuring or aiding to procure to or for any person, any contract from the United States or from any officer, department or agency thereof; or

"Whoever, directly or indirectly, offers, gives, or agrees to give any money or thing of value for procuring or aiding to procure any such contract —

"Shall be fined not more than $10,000 or imprisoned not more than two years, or both; and be disqualified from holding any office of honor, profit, or trust under the United States.

"The President may declare void any such contract or agreement." 18 U.S.C. § 216 (1958).

mid-nineteenth century is present-day Section 434 of Title 18.

Enacted in 1863, the ancestor of Section 434 sprang from the same environment of wartime procurement frauds as the ancestors of Sections 216 and 281. The record reveals almost no specific legislative history to Section 434. In 1863 Congress was again, or still, considering omnibus legislation to curb claims and contract abuses.[46] It seems likely that instances had come to light of government employees' dealing in their official capacity with concerns in which they held a personal interest; indeed, in the same session of Congress a select committee had been appointed to "inquire whether any employés of the government are interested in the banks or government contracts." [47] To meet this matter of dual interests, Senator Howard of Michigan introduced a floor amendment that was agreed to without discussion and is now Section 434.[48]

From the outset, the provision now contained in Section 434 has been distinguished by its technique of regulation. In a sense, it is the most crystallized expression of the concept of conflict of interest. Unlike all the other statutes under consideration here, it does not restrict what a government employee does outside his official duties; instead it limits the official activities of the employee. In substance it provides that an employee may not act as an officer or agent for the government in the transaction of business with any business entity of which he is an officer or in which he has a pecuniary interest. Thus it is essentially, though not in words, a disqualification statute, not forbidding the employee to hold the outside interest, but requiring him to step aside from any official dealings with the entity in which he has the interest. In its original form, the act was limited in its application to outside interests in banks, commercial corpora-

---

[46] The 1863 omnibus legislation contained seven sections dealing with false claims, false vouchers, false oaths, signature forgeries, conspiracy to cheat the government, embezzlement of United States military property, use of military property with intent to defraud, delivery of arms receipts without knowledge of the facts, and purchase of arms and equipment from soldiers having no right to sell them. See 12 Stat. 696–97 (1863). See also CONG. GLOBE, 37th Cong., 3d Sess. 952 (1863).

[47] H.R. REP. NO. 64, 37th Cong., 3d Sess. (1863).

[48] In its present form, the section reads: "Whoever, being an officer, agent or member of, or directly or indirectly interested in the pecuniary profits or contracts of any corporation, joint-stock company, or association, or of any firm or partnership, or other business entity, is employed or acts as an officer or agent of the United States for the transaction of business with such business entity, shall be fined not more than $2,000 or imprisoned not more than two years, or both." 18 U.S.C. § 434 (1958).

tions, and mercantile or trading firms, but subsequent amendments altered the phraseology of the statute somewhat and, among other things, extended it to any "business entity." [49] Members of Congress are not expressly covered, and the executive nature of the activities with which the section is concerned probably negatives any argument that they are included within the general language "officer or agent of the United States."

There are almost no cases reported under Section 434. An opinion of the Supreme Court arising in unique circumstances suggests that an officer or member of an outside entity is not covered by the section unless he has a pecuniary interest in the entity.[50] At this writing another case calling for interpretation of Section 434 is before the Supreme Court on petition of certiorari.[51]

These, then, are the four conflict of interest statutes arising out of the middle of the last century. Sections 283, 281, 216, and 434 differ among themselves in coverage, regulatory technique, penalty, and other details. Still they bear a strong family resemblance, and were born alike out of a primitive personnel system, a poorly controlled disbursement procedure, and the wastes of war.

THE POST-EMPLOYMENT STATUTES

In two statutes, enacted in 1872 and 1944, Congress grappled with the problem of regulating the activities of former government employees.[52] These two post-employment statutes make up two of the seven conflict of interest laws.

5 U.S.C. § 99: THE CIVIL POST-EMPLOYMENT STATUTE (1872)

In 1853 and again in 1864, as we have seen, Congress had legis-

---

[49] See H.R. REP. No. 304, 80th Cong., 1st Sess. A32 (1947).

[50] Cf. United States v. Chemical Foundation, Inc., 272 U.S. 1 (1926).

[51] The case arises out of the celebrated Dixon-Yates electric utility contract, canceled by the government in 1955, in part on grounds of alleged conflict of interest of a government adviser. The incident is discussed in Chapter V.

[52] The problem has indeed been perennial. For example, in the summer of 1959 a special subcommittee of the House held hearings and undertook an investigation into the alleged practice of defense contractors' hiring retired military officers because of their asserted influence in the Department of Defense. See Chapter V, note 59, and accompanying text.

lated against officials' assisting outside claimants against the government (present Sections 283 and 281 of Title 18). It soon became clear, however, that many of the evils feared from this practice were equally present in the case of the claimant's attorney who until the day before had been a government official. In 1872 Congress enacted legislation on the matter, introduced by Representative James Garfield of Ohio.[53] In substance, it forbade an employee of an executive department to act as counsel, attorney, or agent, for a period of two years after leaving office, in the prosecution of claims pending in a department while he was in office. The substance of the provision is today contained in Section 99 of Title 5.[54]

Considerable debate attended the course of the Garfield bill through Congress. Opinions varied on who should be covered: all employees, only high-ranking employees, members of Congress? Was two years the best quarantine period? Should the employee be barred from prosecuting all claims, or claims pending in any department while he was in service, or claims pending in his own department, or claims on which he had worked? What should be the penalty? Differing answers to these questions reflected differing conceptions of the need for the legislation and of its purpose.

Three main themes appear from the congressional debate in support of the bill. Some supporters were still concerned about fraudulent claims — especially about the former employee with inside knowledge about a claim and its weaknesses. "The trouble in allowing these Departments to be open to everybody," said Senator Edmunds of Vermont, "is not the disclosure of the facts that are there, but it is the disclosure of facts that are not there . . . ; it is to enable people who are sharp and unscrupulous to see exactly what facts are wanting to make out a case, and then to find the witness who will swear to a lie to make up on the record . . . "[55]

Others, exhibiting an essentially adversary notion of the claims

[53] 17 Stat. 202 (1872), as amended 5 U.S.C. § 99 (1958).

[54] In its present form, the section reads: "It shall not be lawful for any person appointed as an officer, clerk, or employee in any of the departments, to act as counsel, attorney, or agent for prosecuting any claim against the United States which was pending in either of said departments, while he was such officer, clerk, or employee, nor in any manner, nor by any means, to aid in the prosecution of any such claim, within two years next after he shall have ceased to be such officer, clerk, or employee." REV. STAT. § 190 (1875), 5 U.S.C. § 99 (1952).

[55] CONG. GLOBE, 42d Cong., 2d Sess. 3133 (1872).

process, were concerned to save money for the Treasury and to scotch the treachery of switching sides. Senator Cragin of New Hampshire, for example, was worried at the financial success of a clerk in the Post Office Department who, having access to the files, discovered that many former postmasters were owed back pay by the government, though few of them knew it, and who circularized the potential claimants offering his collection services.[56] The counterview was, "If the Government owes, let the Government pay, and let all the facts favorable to the claimant be open to his agent and to the public." [57] But the adversary conception had a strong grip on the mind of Congress, preponderantly made up of lawyers. By analogy to the ethical ideas of the legal profession, many apparently saw an absolute immorality in the behavior of a former government employee who had switched sides.

Finally, there were those who thought the question was one of continuing personal influence. Senator Edmunds put the hypothetical case of an official on a salary of $3,000 a year who had control of the conduct of the government's side of a controversy and was aware that particular clerks in the department could be persuaded, either from ignorance or interest, to approve a claim. Often such an official, said the Senator, would quit his job and appear the next day as attorney for the other side with a contingent fee of $10,000: "he goes right back into the Department, hunts up the proper clerk in that bureau, and uses his influence upon him; I do not say always corruptly in the sense of using money, but uses the influence which naturally could be exercised by a man of capacity upon people with whom he had been associated . . ." [58]

These three arguments have continued in the years since to be the themes of proponents of different kinds of restrictive regulation for former employees.[59]

In the course of the debate on Section 99, Senators Nye of Nevada and Sprague of Rhode Island displayed another attitude perhaps not yet totally dead. Said Nye: "I am a little slow to say that if I go into

56 *Id.* at 3112.
57 *Id.* at 3111.
58 *Id.* at 3109.
59 In the 1959 hearings on employment of retired military personnel, primary attention was given by the House subcommittee to the argument of continuing influence. See note 52 *supra.*

any Department and acquire a knowledge which enables me to perform duties that others cannot perform by that knowledge that I have accumulated, I shall incur a penalty if I use it." [60] The Senator liked a man who "has pluck enough to get out of these departments." [61] Senator Sprague added his view that a position in government was a "demeaning one," and if a clerk "can gain a more independent livelihood by the use of the knowledge which he acquired in Government employ . . . , one person at least would be saved from its pernicious influence." [62]

Out of the heated congressional debate, the 1872 post-employment statute — present Section 99 — took shape. Its most noticeable feature was that it provided no penalty for violation. It read only that "it shall not be lawful" for ex-officers to engage in the prosecution of certain claims for two years after separation. In answer to those who wished to tack a criminal penalty onto the 1872 bill, Senator Bayard of Delaware argued that the real cure of the evils of improper claims prosecution "after all will be found in the integrity and intelligence of the officers of the Departments." A mere policy declaration by Congress would be enough, without "this continual addition of crimes and penalties to our laws." [63] Asked what would be done if anyone violated the statute, Mr. Bayard replied that he could not imagine that a person would attempt to act in the face of an official pronouncement of illegality. "That," retorted Mr. Edmunds of Vermont, "is a very millennial argument." [64] Millennial or no, the bill went through in the noncriminal declaratory form in which it had been introduced by Mr. Garfield. And so it remains today in Section 99, the only one of the seven conflict of interest statutes not bearing a criminal penalty.

The other main item of interest about the ancestor to Section 99 is its resolution of the problem of substantive scope — from what claims should the former officer be barred. Though the language was hardly exemplary, it seems reasonably certain that the statute in its 1872 version was intended to forbid participation by the ex-officer if, but only if, the claim involved was pending while he was in office

[60] CONG. GLOBE, 42d Cong., 2d Sess. 3110 (1872).
[61] Ibid.
[62] Id. at 3111.
[63] Id. at 3110–11.
[64] Id. at 3111.

and was pending before *his* Department.[65] When the general revision
of the federal statutes was made in 1873–1874, however, the revisers,
in pursuit of the ever elusive goal of clarity, slightly altered the
critical language defining the scope of the 1872 statute. As often
occurs, the revised form was less comprehensible than the original.[66]
But the 1874 amended form remains the language of Section 99 today. And it is now the generally accepted interpretation of the provision that it forbids the ex-officer to participate in the prosecution
of the claim if it was pending before *any* department while he was
in office.[67] Yet a claim that becomes pending the day after the officer's
separation is not within the statute.

In another respect the coverage of Section 99 is peculiarly trun-
cated. Literally read, the section refers to former employees of, and
claims before, "departments" only. This is not surprising, since the
federal establishment in 1872 consisted entirely of executive departments, seven of them. At the time the statute was passed, the first of
the independent agencies — the Civil Service Commission — was still
eleven years in the future, and the second — the Interstate Commerce Commission — was fifteen years ahead. When the inevitable
question arose whether Section 99 applied to an independent agency,
the Attorney General in 1903 answered, "No, it reads 'department'
and it means 'department.' " [68] Thus today this conflict of interest
statute is considered to apply to former employees of, and claims
before, any of the present ten executive Cabinet departments, such
as State or Agriculture, but to have no application to employees of,
or claims before, any of the dozens of federal agencies, commissions,
or other organizations that are not Cabinet departments. The section thus irrationally imposes a legal post-employment obligation on
one large group of executive branch employees, but not on all the
others.

Of fearsome mien, but toothless, Section 99 has slunk to an
obscure corner. Never the subject of a reported federal case, the

---

65 *Id.* at 3109–10.

66 The reader is invited to guess the meaning of the words "either of said departments" in the text of section 99 set forth at note 54 *supra*.

67 20 Ops. Att'y Gen. 696 (1894).

68 25 Ops. Att'y Gen. 6 (1903). The opinion was less stubbornly literal than appears
on the surface. In the 1873–1874 Revision the section had been quite specifically tied
to a statutory definition of "Department" which listed the departments by name. See
Rev. Stat. §§ 158, 159, 190 (1875).

section has received a little attention in two state cases on the question of when a claim becomes "pending." [69] Beyond this the interpretive material on the section is limited to a scattering of opinions of the Attorney General. Traceable to one of these opinions is one thread in the rather tangled history of the present companion piece to Section 99, the other post-employment conflict of interest statute, Section 284.

18 U.S.C. § 284: THE CRIMINAL POST-EMPLOYMENT STATUTE (1944)

In 1919 Secretary of War Newton D. Baker asked the Attorney General for an opinion on the applicability of Section 99 to officers of the Army. A wartime procurement crisis had again produced thousands of contract claims against the government, and former Army contracting officers had gone into business as attorneys and agents in the prosecution of these supply contract claims. The Secretary of War hoped to find a weapon of control in Section 99, but Attorney General Palmer was not helpful. In his opinion, the Army was not a part of the War Department. It was a separate establishment supervised by the War Department. Army officers as such were not employees of a "department" and were not, therefore, covered by Section 99.[70] Disappointed, the Secretary of War turned to Congress.[71]

After considerable debate and a snarl of amendments, and amendments to amendments, Congress responded in 1919 with a new statute designed to supplement Section 99.[72] Far more limited than the legislation requested by Secretary Baker, the 1919 act arguably did not even cover the very group that gave rise to the question — former Army officers. But attention had been called to the inadequacies of

[69] Day v. Laguna Land & Water Co., 115 Cal. App. 221, 1 P. 2d 448 (2d App. Dist. 1931); Day v. Gera Mills, 133 Misc. 220, 231 N.Y. Supp. 235 (Sup. Ct. 1928). In these cases the defendant relied on the asserted violations of section 99 as a defense to a suit for counsel fees in certain tax claims. The court, while implying that section 99, where applicable, could be set up as a defense in a suit for counsel fees, held that the matters in question in the instant case had not attained the formal status of "pending" claims during plaintiff's government service.

[70] "An officer in the United States Army is not by virtue of that fact alone in the Department of War within the meaning of" section 99. 31 OPS. ATT'Y GEN. 471, 474 (1919). Military officers holding certain Defense posts may, however, be considered part of the Department.

[71] 58 CONG. REC. 1735–36 (1919).

[72] 41 Stat. 131 (1919).

Section 99, and in 1921, 1923, and 1924 congressional committees were again at work on proposals to expand the prohibitions of the section. No legislation ensued from these efforts, however, and not until 1942, under pressure of a new war, did Congress move again in the field of post-employment restraints.

To make it possible during World War II to attract needed professional men into government service, a rider was added to the Renegotiation Act of 1942 exempting from the post-employment restrictions of Section 99 all employees appointed by the Secretaries of War, Navy, and the Treasury and by the Maritime Commission. This exemption provision, however, contained the counterproviso that no such employee should ever prosecute a claim against the United States arising from any matter with which he was directly connected while in office.[73] This was an inconspicuous but important legislative step. What began as an exemption provision actually extended post-employment restrictions beyond a "department" for the first time, made certain restrictions permanent for the first time, and for the first time made the post-employment prohibition turn upon the existence of a direct nexus between the officer and the claim.

In 1944, in an unhappily garbled way, the conflict of interest provisions of the Renegotiation Act were twice amended to produce the direct predecessor to present-day Section 284. Finally, out of the total revision of the federal criminal code adopted in 1948, Section 284 emerged in its present form. The section is a composite of the post–World War I statute passed in 1919 at the instance of Secretary Baker and of the World War II restrictions contained in the Renegotiation Act and the Contract Settlements Act. The language of Section 284 is taken almost entirely from the latter source.[74]

Like Section 99, Section 284 deals with former employees of the government who act as counsel, attorney, or agent for the prosecution of claims against the United States. Also, as in the earlier section,

---

[73] 56 Stat. 982, 985 (1942).

[74] The section reads: "Whoever, having been employed in any agency of the United States, including commissioned officers assigned to duty in such agency, within two years after the time when such employment or service has ceased, prosecutes or acts as counsel, attorney, or agent for prosecuting, any claims against the United States involving any subject matter directly connected with which such person was so employed or performed duty, shall be fined not more than $10,000 or imprisoned not more than one year, or both." 18 U.S.C. § 284 (1958).

the bar imposed is a two-year one. The two statutes differ, however, in three main respects. Section 284 provides a criminal penalty; it covers all agencies of the United States, not only "departments"; and it uses, as the test for claims covered, not the time when the claim became "pending," but the relationship between the employee's duties and the claim — whether it involves a subject matter with which he was directly connected.

A little case law exists under Section 284. The best-known case is the *Bergson* case, brought in 1953 against a former head of the Antitrust Division of the Department of Justice. Within less than two years after leaving office, the official had on behalf of clients applied to the Division for a clearance letter to the effect that if a particular corporate merger were to proceed, the Department would not test its legality nor bring criminal prosecution under the antitrust laws. The former official was indicted under Section 284 on the theory that the application for the clearance letter constituted prosecution of a "claim against the United States." The court rejected this interpretation of the statute, and held the word "claim" in Section 284 to be limited to actions to recover money or property from the United States.[75] The decision produces anomalies. For example, under this view litigation arising out of refusal to pay taxes would not be within the statute, while a suit against the government for the recovery of taxes paid under protest would be covered. Shortly after the *Bergson* decision, the Department of Justice proposed legislation to expand the scope of Section 284 beyond the word "claim," and thus to restrict former government employees from a wider range of activities following the termination of government employment. Congress took no action on the bill.[76]

Two major problems under Section 284 are whether its bar ex-

[75] United States v. Bergson, 119 F. Supp. 459 (D.D.C. 1954).

[76] The Justice Department bill would have made substantial substantive changes in the existing post-employment statutes. The bill prohibited former employees from assisting not only in claims against the government but in various other matters involving the government; it covered advice, as well as outright representation; it barred the former employee if he had recommended, advised, or taken or approved official action with respect to it; and the bar would have been perpetual, rather than for two years. 5 U.S.C. § 99 would have been repealed. See Department of Justice, Press Release on Amendment to 18 U.S.C. § 284, July 14, 1954. The bill was introduced as H.R. 10,000, 83d Cong., 2d Sess. (1954). See 100 CONG. REC. 11496 (1954). It was not reported out of committee.

tends to partners of the former government employee, and how broad an interpretation will be given to the phrase "subject matter directly connected with which" the former employee was "employed or performed duty." There is some likelihood that, as in the case of Section 283 dealing with employees while still in government service, the former employee's partners are barred wherever he is barred by Section 284. If so, this vicarious impact of the statute makes it all the more important to know its scope. There is no case law on these points; but some indication of the way in which the courts might approach the problems, at least where lawyers are concerned, is given by a decision delivered by a federal court in 1955 turning on the lawyers' Canons of Professional Ethics.[77]

The case arose as a by-product of litigation between the United States and an oil company concerning certain alleged overcharges on oil sold by the oil company under the Marshall Plan in Europe at prices greater than legal prices set by the Economic Cooperation Administration. The government was entitled to recover damages if the prices were found illegal. ECA price regulation and administration were carried on entirely at its Washington office; its Paris office was engaged solely in direct operations under the Marshall Plan. The two offices worked independently of each other and had separate functions. Among the lawyers working on the case for the law firm representing the company was a non-partner employee who had been an employee of the Paris office of the ECA. Two years after the termination of the lawyer's employment with the ECA (after the restricted post-employment period set by Section 99 of Title 5 and Section 284 of Title 18) and while the litigation was in progress, he was made a partner of the law firm. Many months later, as the case came to trial, the government moved that the court disqualify the law firm from representing the oil company in the litigation on the ground that one of the firm's partners working on the case had been serving as a lawyer for ECA at the time when the transactions involved in the litigation took place. The government based its motion for disqualification upon the American Bar Association's Canons of Professional Ethics, particularly Canon 36, reading in part: "A lawyer, having once held public office or having been in the public employ, should not after his retirement accept employment in connection with any matter which he has investigated or passed upon while in such office

[77] United States v. Standard Oil Co., 136 F. Supp. 345 (S.D.N.Y. 1955)

or employ." [78] The evidence showed that the lawyer had not in fact had any personal contact with the case while in government service, either in the oil procurement or in setting the price regulations. The question raised by the motion therefore was whether the actions and knowledge of other employees of ECA while the lawyer was an employee would be imputed to him. There was little doubt in the judge's mind that if the lawyer was barred his firm was barred. In an extended opinion, the court concluded that the knowledge of employees of the Washington office would not automatically be imputed to employees of the Paris office, or vice versa, but that within one "office" the knowledge of subordinates would be imputed to higher officials. Whether the Paris and Washington operations worked so closely together as to constitute one office was held to be a question of fact for proof. The motion to disqualify was denied.

Though arising under the lawyers' canons of ethics rather than the federal statutes, this case is worth noting. It well illustrates the kinds of problems encountered by post-employment restrictions, the unexpected complications raised by rules on vicarious responsibility of partners and by fictions of imputed knowledge, and — most important — the kind of government in which conflict of interest restraints must operate today. Fifty years ago the United States government was a small-scale affair, centered in Washington, D.C., and engaged in relatively limited operations. In such a world, it was perhaps reasonable to talk in terms of imputed knowledge as among government employees. Modern government, on the other hand, must operate in a world in which a fire ranger in Alaska and a State Department official in Addis Ababa are both government "employees," and both know as little of each other and each other's work as they know of another "employee" working at the Atomic Energy Commission in Washington, D.C.

This is the real world of modern government. This is the context in which all conflict of interest restraints must be assessed today.

OUTSIDE COMPENSATION
18 U.S.C. § 1914 (1917)

The four statutes passed immediately before and during the Civil War and the two post-employment statutes are oriented pri-

[78] See AMERICAN BAR ASSOCIATION, CANONS OF PROFESSIONAL ETHICS, Canon 36 (1958). The government also relied upon Canons 6 and 37.

marily toward abuses in the prosecution of government claims and
in government contracting. The seventh of the statutes considered
here, Section 1914 of Title 18, is the only conflict of interest statute
that does not share this heritage. Its history and purposes are
unique.

Though Section 1914 dates from the year 1917, it did not arise
out of the war. It appears that the Bureau of Education of the Department of the Interior had entered into "cooperative relations"
with certain private organizations, including the Rockefeller and
Carnegie Foundations, for the purpose of studying and promoting
educational projects, such as Negro education and kindergarten programs. These outside organizations made no direct monetary contribution to the Bureau, but they did pay the real salaries of certain
men who were employed by the Bureau at a dollar a year to perform
Bureau tasks under the direct supervision and control of the Commissioner of Education. Furthermore, a considerable number of
persons throughout the United States who were employed in universities and normal schools or held other educational positions,
such as county school superintendent, were appointed to perform "occasional services" without pay for the Bureau of Education.[79]

At least since Socrates was alleged to have corrupted the
youth of Athens, new educational ideas have been among the more
volatile of social explosives. In 1917 John Dewey and progressive
education were abroad in the land, and in some quarters there was
alarm that the foundations were wielding undue and noxious influence on national educational policy. A real, or ostensible, side
issue in the debate over the influence of the foundation dollar-a-year
men concerned the franking privilege. Senator Chamberlain of Ore-
gon, foremost proponent of legislation in the field, argued: "Some
great educator of this country, who may be ever so highly respected
by our people, writes a thesis on some great educational subject that
may be very dear to the hearts of the American people, and yet he
has no way of getting it before the American people except as he
may be able to pay to get his literature distributed, or insofar as he
may be able to get the press to publish it; and yet one of these pets
of the Bureau of Education, Mr. President, may get his answer to it,

[79] See 54 CONG. REC. 2039, 2045 (1917).

or his own view, before the American people through the franking privilege." [80]

The bill originally introduced by Senator Chamberlain to curb the dollar-a-year employees of the Bureau of Education was restricted in its application to that Bureau and was a rider to an appropriation act. Despite opposition from those who thought some good might derive from cooperative work between government and private agencies, the bill passed the Senate. It failed in the House, apparently on the ground that it was too broad. Yet the bill emerged from conference committee in even more sweeping form and, after two rejections, was finally adopted by both houses. No substantive changes have been made in Section 1914 since its adoption.[81]

The section announces in general that no private source is to pay a government employee for his government work. The technical wording of this statute is particularly crucial, however: read closely, it forbids the employee to receive any "salary in connection with his services as such" from any non-government source; complementarily, it forbids others to make any contribution to, or in any way supplement, the salary of any government employee "for the services performed by him for the government." The section contains an exception for payments received by federal employees from state and local government sources, an exception deemed necessary by representatives of rural areas to preserve the county agent program and other agricultural extension programs. Section 1914 is backed up by criminal penalties.

In the strictest sense, Section 1914 is a conflict of interest statute. The employee does not have to *do* anything improper in his office to violate the statute. His receipt of the outside salary for his government work, coupled with his status as a government employee, is all that is required; his special status makes an unexceptionable act

[80] *Id.* at 2039.

[81] The section reads: "Whoever, being a Government official or employee, receives any salary in connection with his services as such an official or employee from any source other than the Government of the United States, except as may be contributed out of the treasury of any State, county or municipality; or

"Whoever, whether a person, association, or corporation, makes any contribution to, or in any way supplements the salary of, any Government official or employee for the services performed by him for the Government of the United States —

"Shall be fined not more than $1,000 or imprisoned not more than six months, or both." 18 U.S.C. § 1914 (1958).

wrongful — wrongful because of the potential dangers in serving two paymasters.

No cases have been decided under Section 1914, but both the Attorney General and the Comptroller General have frequently been called upon to express opinions upon its meaning. The Comptroller General's posture is interesting. His office becomes involved when an outside private source makes a payment to an employee and a question is raised whether the government may claim the payment for itself as illegal under Section 1914. If the payment was improper in the Comptroller General's view, he may just dock the employee's salary by the amount received. Most often questions of this kind have arisen in the context of travel or accommodation expenses paid to a government employee in connection with, for example, a talk or seminar conducted by him on a topic related to his government job. The Comptroller General has also available to him the argument that outside compensation to an employee of an agency constitutes an unauthorized augmentation of the appropriation of the agency — an abuse his office is charged by Congress to prevent. Thus the Comptroller General from time to time publishes opinions on Section 1914. These opinions generally point out that the Comptroller General is not charged with giving legal opinions, that interpretation of the law is rather within the province of the Attorney General, and that reliance on the Comptroller General's opinions as such cannot be recommended.[82] Nonetheless, an important agency of the government, the General Accounting Office, acts on the basis of the Comptroller General's opinions. Frequently action by the GAO is of greater functional importance to an agency or employee than an abstract legal decision. And the opinion of the Comptroller General on the proper interpretation of Section 1914 has not in fact always corresponded to that voiced by the Attorney General.[83]

As will be seen later, Section 1914 is one of the most comprehensive and troublesome of the conflict of interest statutes. It is interesting, and a touch ironic, to recall its narrow original purpose.

---

[82] See, e.g., 37 DECS. COMP. GEN. 776 (1958).

[83] The Comptroller General has apparently taken a more restrictive position on travel expense reimbursements under section 1914 than has the Attorney General. Compare 36 DECS. COMP. GEN. 155 (1955) and 18 DECS. COMP. GEN. 460 (1938) and 26 DECS. COMP. TREAS. 43 (1919) with 33 OPS. ATT'Y GEN. 273 (1922).

WOCS, WAES, AND SECTION 1914

In general it is against the law to be an employee of the United States government without being paid by the United States.[84] This statement must be distinguished from the rule of Section 1914, just discussed, that if a person works for the United States, it is illegal for another to pay him for that work. The relation, and the distinction, between these two propositions require discussion.

The first rule requires that a United States employee be on the government payroll. Whenever a period of special national emergency arises, or whenever specialized governmental programs cannot be staffed through regular sources, the issue arises whether limited exceptions should be made to permit certain positions to be filled by persons who will serve without compensation. Sometimes such legislative exceptions are made. As has been noted, the persons who are appointed to the positions are given the tagname WOCs from the phrase "without compensation."

The pros and cons of the WOC have been sharply debated since World War I, and the issue is no nearer final resolution than ever.

On one side, all agree that in general government should be staffed by government employees paid by and working primarily for the United States. The government official participating in government action, but in office only temporarily and probably continuing to be paid by an outside source, is subject to incentives and pressures that may influence his official decisions adversely to the interests of the government. Without adopting a theory of history as conspiracy, one can appreciate the risk that some companies or organizations would be ready to use the WOC arrangement as a device for planting agents in government positions for their own ends. The WOC being paid by an outsider may be a conflict of interest incarnate.

Quite apart from arguments based on conflicts of interest, however, the practice of using WOCs can be questioned on grounds of sound personnel administration. The WOC is less subject to agency discipline and, with his outside income, may be a source of irritation to his fellow government workers.

[84] See 33 Stat. 1257 (1906), 31 U.S.C. § 665(b) (1958); 27 Decs. Comp. Gen. 194 (1947). A brief history of this statutory prohibition is contained in Antitrust Subcomm.,

Finally, the rule against the use of WOCs is a necessary safeguard to protect Congress' constitutional power over appropriations and expenditures. The use by an agency of a large and highly paid staff of public relations men whose salaries are paid by an interested outside organization, for example, could constitute a flagrant subversion of congressional control of the purse strings.

The arguments on the other side are equally apparent. WOCs, and the organizations that pay them, if any, are generally acting out of patriotic motives. The WOC often brings to the particular job to which he is appointed special skills which the government desperately needs and which are not available elsewhere. Through the WOC device, the government succeeds in obtaining the services of men who would not have been willing to cut themselves off from their regular jobs and salaries to enter government service on a permanent basis.[85]

Congressional resolution of the WOC problem has been very much what might be anticipated. The general rule is that the United States is able to, and should, pay its own personnel, and that the use of WOCs is forbidden by Congress. This prohibition on the use of WOCs is addressed to the executive branch itself — not to the persons serving as WOCs. Where WOCs are permitted it is only by virtue of special statutory authorization and exception granted by Congress. When Congress make an exception to its general rule it is nearly always because of a national emergency or quasi emergency. As the crisis recedes, Congress has historically cut back or abolished the special WOC authorization.[86] A measure of the nation's current semi-belligerent status is the fact that at the present time some critical defense agencies are permitted to use WOCs.[87]

HOUSE COMM. ON THE JUDICIARY, 84TH CONG., 2D SESS., INTERIM REPORT ON WOC'S AND GOVERNMENT ADVISORY GROUPS 4–7 (Comm. Print 1956).

85 See ANTITRUST SUBCOMM., HOUSE COMM. ON THE JUDICIARY, 84TH CONG., 2D SESS., INTERIM REPORT ON WOC'S AND GOVERNMENT ADVISORY GROUPS 3 (Comm. Print 1956).

86 See the discussion of the background of the WOC program in ANTITRUST SUBCOMM., HOUSE COMM. ON THE JUDICIARY, 84TH CONG., 2D SESS., INTERIM REPORT ON WOC'S AND GOVERNMENT ADVISORY GROUPS 4–7 (Comm. Print 1956). See also the restrictive 1955 amendments to section 7 of the Defense Production Act at 69 Stat. 180, 583 (1955), 50 U.S.C. App. § 2160 (1958).

87 See Hearings Before the Antitrust Subcommittee of the House Committee on the Judiciary on WOC's and Government Advisory Groups, 84th Cong., 1st Sess. 642–44 (1955); ANTITRUST SUBCOMM., HOUSE COMM. ON THE JUDICIARY, 84TH CONG., 2D SESS., INTERIM REPORT ON WOC'S AND GOVERNMENT ADVISORY GROUPS 114–17 (Comm. Print 1956) for figures on the use of WOCs by the Defense Department and other government

The congressional ban on WOCs is thus not rooted solely in conflict of interest considerations. But whenever Congress does authorize the use of WOCs, it finds it collaterally necessary to write some corresponding degree of exemption into the conflict of interest statutes. Section 1914, banning outside compensation, must always be suspended in respect of the WOC to permit him to continue his regular salary from nongovernmental sources; no one expects the WOC to go off all payrolls, public and private. If the WOC will be acting for the government in business transactions with his company, Congress may also give him a limited exemption from Section 434, the statute ordinarily requiring disqualification in situations of conflicting interest. Such a situation could arise, for example, if a company official should work for the government as a temporary WOC expert to set up machinery regulating some activity of the industry in which his own company was engaged. Other conflict of interest rules may be collaterally relaxed by Congress when it authorizes the use of the WOC, but the only statute from which he must always be immunized is Section 1914.

Another category of government employment raises almost the same problems under Section 1914 as the WOC. Part-time consultants to the government, if paid at all, are paid "when actually employed." From this phrase comes, in the argot of Federalese, the term WAE. Strictly speaking, there is less need to exempt WAEs from Section 1914 than WOCs; but where Congress has authorized the use of WAEs, it has often exempted them from Section 1914 to make clear that their regular salaries from their private employers will not be jeopardized by their work for the government as WAEs. As in the case of the WOC, Congress may, but need not, grant the WAE other exemptions from the conflict of interest statutes.

THE STATUTES: A PRELIMINARY EVALUATION

The survey of the seven conflict of interest statutes complete, it is now possible to scan them as a group, to see in an over-all way what they do and what they do not do, what they demand of the

---

agencies. On various dates in 1955, the Department of Defense reported 187 WOCs as employed; the Department of Commerce, 260; the Office of Defense Mobilization, 108; and the Atomic Energy Commission, 33. See *Id.* at 114–15.

employees covered and what they forbid. A preliminary evaluation can also be made at this point of those features of the statutes appearing on their face.

Federal conflict of interest controls are probably associated most in the public mind with compulsory stock divestment, best exemplified by the widely publicized forced sale of Mr. Charles Wilson's General Motors stock. It invariably comes as a surprise, therefore, to find that none of the conflict of interest statutes requires stock divestment in any situation. Section 434 comes closest, in forbidding the employee to act for the government in transactions with business entities in which he is interested, but the section does not require the employee to dispose of the interest; it requires him not to act for the government in the sensitive transaction. It is, of course, possible to imagine the case of an official who would have to disqualify himself so often under Section 434 that he would not be able to carry on his official duties. But even here there is nothing in the statute requiring him to dispose of his holdings.[88] In Mr. Wilson's case the divestment requirement was imposed by the Senate Armed Services Committee as a condition to confirmation.[89]

Five of the seven statutes are aimed at preventing government employees and former employees from assisting outsiders in their dealings with the government, particularly in the prosecution of "claims." In this they directly reflect problems of the nineteenth century in general, and wartime procurement problems in particular. Since these statutes limit representational services, they most affect the conduct of the representational professions and especially the legal profession.

These five overlapping statutes, enacted over a ninety-one-year span to deal with one general problem, crisscross and interweave to form a most peculiar network of substantive regulation.

Section 99 restricts former employees from prosecuting claims for two years, but it applies only to claims that were "pending" while the employee was in service. An employee who is responsible for a particular class of claims and learns about a potential claim

---

88 This statement, of course, refers only to the seven general statutes reviewed in this chapter. It will be recalled that some organic statutes setting up departments or regulatory agencies contain limited restrictions on certain security holdings by officials. See, for example, the restrictions upon various officials and employees set forth in note 3 *supra*.

89 The case is discussed in Chapter V.

while in the employ of government, but waits to file it until the day after he quits, is probably out from under this provision. Section 99 applies only to former employees of and claims before a "department." Thus a former ICC employee could, under this section, work on a railroad claim that he personally worked on while in government service, while a cartographer who formerly worked for the Coast Guard under the Department of the Treasury cannot help a friend by drawing maps to accompany a land claim then pending before the Department of the Interior. Section 99 suffers from the additional peculiarity that it carries no penalty.

Sections 283, 284, and 99 deal with nothing except prosecution of claims. But they are probably limited by the judicial construction under Section 284 that "claim" includes only monetary claims against the government. Thus the former employee, under these provisions, could not on behalf of a client assert a claim for a tax refund in the District Court, but could represent the same client in the same matter if he declines to pay the tax and defends against the government's claim in the Tax Court. What of the former employee who helps defend against a monetary claim brought by the government? No one knows.

Section 216, the hybrid bribery statute, is very narrow, applying only to a "contract" with the United States.

Section 281 is much broader than any of the other statutes in that it applies to any matter in which the United States has a direct or indirect interest. But this section does not apply if the government employee does not accept a fee for his assistance or if the matter is not one "before" an agency or department or other forum of the executive branch.

Sections 281 and 283 overlap, as do Sections 99 and 284, and Sections 216 and 281. Section 216 also overlaps with the general bribery statutes.

For the lawyer called upon to give an opinion interpreting these statutes, they are a nightmare; they spew up one unanswerable question after another. Who is an "officer or employee" under Section 281, for example? The term has been interpreted to include not only full-time regular personnel but part-time and intermittent personnel, whether or not paid by the government.[90] It is usually a sur-

[90] See 40 Ops. Att'y. Gen. 289 (1943) indicating that an expert consultant to the Secretary of War, engaged in "intermittent and temporary" employment, and serving with-

prise to an intermittent adviser to learn that he is legally an "employee" of the government — and not just on the days on which he is actually doing government work. But what of those who have only a passing or sporadic contact with the government? As of January 1, 1959, there were 38,916 uncompensated "employees" of the Selective Service System. Does their voluntarily contributed time subject them to these statutes restricting their activities in dealing with the government? [91] Does the term "officer or employee" include members of the military reserves, the National Guard, or retired officers? [92] Does the term "employee" as used in Section 281 and the related statutes extend as far as or farther than the lawyer's concept of the dividing line between an "employee" and an "independent contractor"? [93] If in a particular situation a satisfactory answer can be found under Section 281, it may not do for the other statutes, for each is slightly different in its statement of who is covered.

To take another recurrent problem under Sections 281, 283, 284, and 99, what does it mean to "assist" in prosecuting a claim? May one appear as a witness to testify in favor of a claim against the government? If not, what can one do if subpoenaed by the claimant? Does one "act as counsel" if he writes a memorandum on a point of law? Again, the answers may vary from statute to statute.

---

out compensation, was covered by the predecessor to 18 U.S.C. § 281. When Congress has desired consultants not to be subject to section 281, it has granted them specific statutory exemption. See the discussion under "Exemptions" *infra*.

[91] In fact members of Selective Service Boards are now exempt from the conflict of interest provisions of 18 U.S.C. §§ 281, 283, 284 (1958) and REV. STAT. § 190 (1875), 5 U.S.C. § 99 (1958), but only because of specific statutory exemption enacted in 1951. 62 Stat. 623 (1951), 50 U.S.C. App. § 463(a) (1958). Are they still subject to 18 U.S.C. § 1914?

[92] Retired military officers are normally to be considered officers or employees of the United States. See Morgenthau v. Barrett, 108 F.2d 481 (D.C. Cir. 1939). Paragraph two of section 281 was enacted after the Barrett case so as to partially exclude retired military officers when not on active duty from the general provisions of section 281. Members of the National Guard of the District of Columbia are likewise granted specific internal exemption from section 281 and from section 283. The problem of the coverage of reservists would likewise be perplexing if it were not for 70A Stat. 632 (1956), 5 U.S.C. § 30r(d) (1958), expressly precluding reservists from being considered officers or employees of the United States. For fuller treatment, see Appendix B *infra*.

[93] One who contracts independently to perform services for another is not considered an "employee." But the line separating these categories may vary depending upon the purpose of the classification. A person contracting to perform services for the government and deemed to be self-employed for tax reasons might, or might not, depending on the facts, be an independent contractor for purposes of conflict of interest regulation. As usual, there is little or no authority, and the lawyer's problem is cor-

Even the apparently simple clauses turn out to be troublesome. Section 284 sets up a ban for the period of "two years after the time when such employment or service has ceased." What employment? Does the two years run from the time the former employee left a particular government job? from the time he left one agency to go to work for another agency? from the time he left government finally? If he is an advisory employee who works only on occasional days when called in for consultation, does the two years start afresh each day he works?

Perhaps the most baffling problems of interpretation arise from the connecting phrases in the statutes — key phrases purporting to define the limits of these criminal offenses. Section 281 forbids the employee to assist the outsider in an executive forum in any "matter in which the United States is . . . directly or indirectly interested . . ." In what matter coming before the executive branch is the United States not directly or indirectly interested? Section 284 forbids the former employee for two years to assist in prosecuting claims involving "any subject matter directly connected with which" he was employed by the government. If a claimant is suing on a defense procurement contract, should the phrase be interpreted to bar a former government employee only if he worked on that contract? if he worked on other contracts for the same kinds of commodities? if he worked on other contracts for another armed service in the Department of Defense? and so forth. How direct a participant must he have been to be barred? Suppose, for example, he was a budget officer, or the design engineer who set the specifications for the contract bidding, one of the men who had nothing to do with the contract itself but who, long in advance, allocated the money for it and decided what would be bought.

Section 434 is unique in that it does not purport to direct anyone in the conduct of his private economic affairs. It is a rule of internal governmental administration, requiring the employee to refrain from acting for the government in certain conflict of interest situations, under threat of criminal penalty. Every employee covered by it should be constantly aware of its existence in order to shape his official conduct. But it does not require any employee to disrupt

---

respondingly increased. See 37 OPS. ATT'Y. GEN. 204 (1933) for an opinion that the predecessor to section 281 does not cover an attorney for a national bank receiver.

his economic affairs when he enters government service or while he is there, and it has no post-employment consequences. An interesting aspect of Section 434 is that it is applicable only to business transactions with business entities. Thus, for example, an officer of a university may, so far as this section is concerned, simultaneously act as a government official with respect to government research grants to his own institution. The section is further limited in that it restricts the employee only when he is acting in the front position as "agent or officer" for the government; behind the scenes participation in a transaction, as by advice or investigation, is apparently not within the language of the section.[94]

There remains Section 1914, the section forbidding outside compensation. If an employee receives no compensation from any outside source while he is in service, he is not affected by the section at all. If he receives outside compensation, but only for services not connected with his government duties, he continues to be unaffected. Thus the government meteorologist may sell real estate on the weekends. What is forbidden is the receipt of "any salary in connection with his services" as a government official. An important point to be noted about Section 1914 is that it does not require any connection whatever between the payor of the outside compensation and either the employee's agency or the government. Not only defense contractors are prevented from supplementing the salary of an employee of the Defense Department; the employee's retired uncle in the Bahamas might also violate the act if he supplemented his nephew's salary "for services performed by him for the Government."

The words "salary in connection with his services" are the source of great difficulty. This is particularly true for the full-time executive appointee who expects to return to his regular job after a couple of years on the Potomac, and for the temporary or intermittent expert or consultant.

In the first place, what is "salary"? The word has been, and probably will be, construed to include almost any kind of a transfer of value to the employee that smacks of compensation. The second clause in Section 1914 is even broader. It is violated by any person who "makes any contribution to, or in any way supplements the

[94] See, however, the discussion in Chapter V, note 80 *infra*.

salary of" the employee.[95] Clearly the appointee's former employer cannot under this section make up the difference between his former salary and his government salary. But can the former employer let the employee use a company apartment or car, take him for a weekend cruise on the company boat, help with his extraordinary moving expenses to Washington? How far must the employee go in cutting off his connections with his former employer? It is a simple matter to stop the monthly paycheck. But what of long range and pre-existing stock options, group medical and life insurance plans, and — probably most important of all — retirement and pension plans? Even if the employee picks up all the payments into any of these group plans, and the employer ceases to participate in making contributions, may the employee under Section 1914 even retain his eligibility as a member of the group and, for instance, continue to accrue retirement credits under the pension plan?

These questions are only an introduction into the uncertainty of the word "salary" in Section 1914. More uncertain still are the words in the critical connecting phrase "in connection with his services" as an official. Clearly an outside source may not, consistently with Section 1914, pay the government official "to" take the government job or "for" his government work. But may a former employer make *any* payment to the employee that will not raise the inference that it was made "in connection with" his government duties? Why else was it made? The effort to answer this question has led to much twisting and turning. It is said that the section is not violated if the employer pays a lump sum "for" past services to the employee when he leaves to go to Washington. Similarly it is agreed that pension or other group plan rights may be lawfully retained by the employee if they are "vested" before the employee leaves his private employer. It can be argued too that payments would be permitted by Section 1914 if made by the employer in consideration of the employee's agreement to return after his government service. There are no rulings.

In fact, any payment may easily be cast in any of these, or many other, forms; the payment itself is the only observable event; and the

___

[95] It is generally assumed that the first sentence is to be read *in pari materia* with the second so as to construe "salary" in the first sentence as meaning, in effect, "salary, or any supplement thereof, or any contribution to such employee."

phrase "in connection with" the official's services is without operational referent. No one knows, or can know, what it will be held to mean in a particular situation.

In the case of the intermittent employee, serving as an expert or consultant without compensation or as a WAE, the difficult problems suggested in the last two paragraphs become impossible. What does Section 1914 require of the government consultant who spends a day a month in Washington on the government's call? Should he have his employer dock him for a day's pay a month? Whose time was he on when he was in Washington? As an executive setting his own schedule, he could have taken that day off to play golf. Does it make any difference that he worked at his regular office all the following Sunday, or that he took no vacation last year? What of *his* stock option, retirement, and insurance plans? How can they be adjusted to take account of one day a month? Questions of this kind can be raised almost without end. They are further complicated by the fact that the adviser may in one week be called in for consultation five days running, then go three months without receiving another call. Every evidence is that in day-to-day administration people choose a sensible interpretation, and Section 1914 is quietly swept under the rug by the intermittent government employee and his agency.

In sheer difficulty of construction, few one-sentence statutes can compete with Section 1914 — and the penalties are criminal.

EXEMPTIONS

A sufficient over-all picture of the conflict of interest statutes has been given to permit an additional complicating element to be introduced — the exemptions to the statutes.

Two of the statutes carry their own exemptive provisions for particular classes of personnel. Sections 281 and 283, relating to assisting outsiders, exclude from their coverage members of the National Guard of the District of Columbia and partially exclude retired officers of the armed forces when not on active duty.[96] The other statutes contain no such general exemptions for these groups. In a helter-

[96] Conflict of interest regulation of retired military personnel is special and complex. See Appendix B.

skelter way, however, Congress has frequently recognized that the rigidity of the general statutes on conflict of interest makes them unworkable as applied to intermittent employees and particular government positions. The United States Code is peppered with spot exceptions and exemptions, total or partial, enacted piecemeal to meet special cases. [97] Inevitably, this process has produced an arbitrary pattern of controls and exemptions, working unequally, for no apparent reason, from position to position and from office to office.

In time of national crisis the conflict of interest statutes have repeatedly been found unworkable and have yielded place to the national need to put the best man in the job. Sometimes the statutes have simply been ignored. On occasion, however, Congress has expressly recognized the need to relax the restraints by exemptive statute. Even so, Congress seldom offers more than partial exemption, and executive regulation then tends to step in and reimpose special restrictions. A few statutory exemptions of this essentially "emergency" character are on the books at the present time.

The exemption statutes vary in response to a host of Congressional attitudes toward the gravity of national crisis, the urgency of particular programs, the availability of appropriately trained personnel, the breadth of the proposed exemption, the employment status of the employee as WOC, expert, or consultant, and the character of the employee's duties, all conditioned by the current political temper and the prevailing climate of opinion toward governmental ethics in general and toward the inherent good or evil of economic man in particular. Two examples will adequately illustrate the character and complexity of these emergency exemptions.

The Defense Production Act of 1950, passed during the Korean War and amended in the semi-peace year of 1955, authorizes the

---

[97] Examples of these *ad hoc* exemption statutes include: 68 Stat. 698 (1954), 16 U.S.C. § 1024 (1958) (granting exemptions from 18 U.S.C. §§ 281, 283, 284, 434 and 5 U.S.C. § 99 to uncompensated advisers on matters relating to the North Pacific Fisheries); 64 Stat. 154 (1950), 42 U.S.C. § 1873(f) (1958) (granting exemptions from 18 U.S.C. §§ 281, 283, 284 and 5 U.S.C. § 99 to advisers under the National Science Foundation Act); 65 Stat. 87 (1951), 50 U.S.C. App. 463(a) (1958) (granting exemptions from 18 U.S.C. §§ 281, 283 and 5 U.S.C. § 99 to members of draft boards); and 71 Stat. 626, 628 (1957), 36 U.S.C. § 747(b) (1958) (granting exemptions from all seven conflict of interest statutes to unpaid members of the Civil War Centennial Commission). *Cf.* the repealer sections of the statute proposed here, Chapter XI, § 38 *infra.*

President, where the situation requires it, to appoint WOCs in agencies concerned with the administration of the Act. WOCs appointed under this authority are not limited to advisory positions as such (though the 1955 amendments came within one Senate vote of imposing this limitation), but "when policy matters are involved," they are "limited to advising appropriate full-time salaried Government officials who are responsible for making policy decisions." [98] These WOCs are exempted from six of the seven conflicts statutes, only Section 216, the semi-bribery statute, remaining in full effect. But the same statute that exempts these WOCs immediately reimposes a whole new set of conflict of interest restraints upon them. Under these special provisions, the net result is approximately that Section 281 is suspended, Section 1914 is necessarily amended to permit outside compensation (but only from the immediately preceding employer of the WOC), the post-employment restrictions are applicable, but only in respect of claims involving matters for which the employee "had any responsibility," and the disqualification provisions of Section 434 are replaced by a reworded equivalent provision. This "exemption" provision then proceeds to add a new requirement in the form of a continuing report of all business entities in which the WOC has an interest, the report to be published in the *Federal Register*.[99]

Experts and consultants appointed as WAEs under the same statute work under somewhat different and less extensive exemptions. They are subject to the same restrictions as WOCs in respect of the claims statutes, but have no exemption at all from Sections 434 or 1914.[100] On the other hand, they are not required to file reports for publication in the *Federal Register*. Regulations issued pursuant to this section of the Defense Production Act may impose additional limitations on these experts and consultants.

The second illustrative exemption provision to be mentioned is contained in Section 704 of the Second Supplemental Appropriations Act of 1951.[101] This section authorizes the Secretary of Defense

[98] The Defense Production Act of 1950, as amended, § 710(b)(3), 69 Stat. 180, 582 (1955), 50 U.S.C. App. § 2160(b)(3) (1958).

[99] The Defense Production Act of 1950, as amended, § 710(b)(6), 69 Stat. 180, 583 (1955), 50 U.S.C. App. § 2160(b)(6) (1958).

[100] See 64 Stat. 819, 820 (1950), 50 U.S.C. App. § 2160(c) (1958), as implemented by Exec. Order No. 10647 § 202, 20 Fed. Reg. 8769 (1955).

[101] See 70A Stat. 118 (1956), 10 U.S.C. § 1583 (1958).

to appoint not more than ten WOCs of "outstanding experience and ability" and authorizes him by regulation to exempt these appointees from all the conflict of interest statutes except, again, the semi-bribery provision in Section 216. With respect to WOCs the Secretary's regulations issued under this provision are identical to the provisions of the Defense Production Act just discussed. But with respect to "experts and consultants" appointed under the 1951 Appropriations Act, the Defense regulations provide for the same partial exemption from Section 1914 as that enjoyed by WOCs.[102] Thus these "experts and consultants" remain subject to Section 434, unlike WOCs appointed under the same act, but have a partial exemption from Section 1914 unlike their counterparts appointed under the Defense Production Act.[103]

Altogether, it is sufficient for the general observer to know that there are some statutory exceptions from the conflict of interest laws, that there are not very many of them, that they seldom exempt entirely, that their provisions are highly technical, that they are erratic in application and content, and that they are intimately linked to the ebb and flow of congressional opinion on the related, but not identical, problem of the proper place of WOCs. To some government appointees these exemptions are of vital concern, to the lawyers asked to track down and construe them, a source of despair.

CONCLUSION

It is difficult to generalize about the individual adjustments made by federal appointees in their personal affairs in response to the con-

---

[102] See Fed. Reg. 2218 (1951), as corrected, 20 Fed. Reg. 2751 (1955). The Second Supplemental Appropriations Act does not confer any special authority on the Secretary of Defense to appoint "experts or consultants." But the regulations issued under the Act distinguish "experts and consultants" from other appointees under the Act, and subject these "experts and consultants" to the provisions of section 434. The regulations thus contain a distinction not referred to in the authorizing statute. There is good reason to believe that the regulations were borrowed wholesale from the regulations issued under the Defense Production Act, which Act does distinguish between WOCs and "experts and consultants."

[103] Another broad exemptive provision grounded in the demands of World War II is contained in section 113 of the Renegotiation Act of 1951, 65 Stat. 22 (1951), as amended, 70 Stat. 729 (1956), 50 U.S.C. App. § 1223 (1958). In general, the provision exempts employees of the Defense, Army, Navy, and Air Force Departments from the provisions of REV. STAT. § 190 (1875), 5 U.S.C. § 99 (1958). See also 40 OPS. ATT'Y. GEN. 289 (1943).

flict of interest statutes because of differences in occupation, personal estate, position involved, time of appointment, and other factors. Most lawyers appear to have only a general awareness of the statutes, and close knowledge of them is rare. It is possible to note, however, that techniques of adjustment have varied widely and that opinions among able counsel on what constitutes compliance defy reconciliation.

With the tacit or even explicit cooperation of the appointing agencies, the statutes have tended to generate an array of legal devices regarded as legitimate means of avoiding the impact of the statutes. A specialist who is unwilling to accept appointment as an employee because of conflict of interest restraints enters instead into a contract with the agency to turn out a work product as an independent contractor — the work product being the report he would have written had he accepted the appointment as a WAE. The holder of stock that might have to be sold upon his appointment transfers it to his wife before accepting the appointment. Or the stock is put into a special trust under which the appointee has no control while he is in office but regains full possession upon his termination of government service. The lawyer resigns from his law firm, but promptly forms another law firm with the same partners, the difference being that all law work relating to the government will, during the time he is in government service, be carried on by the law firm of which he is not a member. (In the more questionable case, the appointee's percentage of interest in the new law firm may be adjusted upwards to offset the loss he sustains through nonparticipation in the original firm's profits attributable to government work.) During the two years of post-employment decontamination under Sections 99 and 284, the former official does not formally join a private concern dealing with the government, but through a variety of independent contracting and accounting arrangements, offices with the concern and draws his income from it.

Interpretations of the outside compensation restrictions of Section 1914 are particularly at variance. To what extent are pre-existing stock options, pension plans, and insurance plans outlawed compensation under the statute? When are the rights under these plans "vested" and when not? In an effort to comply with Section 1914 and simultaneously to maintain the appointee's eligibility under these security plans, subtly differing degrees of quasi resignation or leave of absence are devised. For services carefully designated as past, substantial severance payments may be made, with the payments themselves sometimes spread forward in installments over the period of the appointee's government service. Formal written resignations are executed for the record when the clear expectation of all concerned is that the appointee will in fact return after his stay in Washington.

No one can say with any confidence which of these arrangements, or whether any or all of these arrangements, are legal and permissible under the existing statutes. In the overwhelming majority of instances it appears that, where the statutes are recognized and considered at all, government appointees and their lawyers lean over backwards in an effort to comply. But the crude style of the ancient conflict of interest statutes is an inducement to artifice, and there will always be a minority ready to pursue every advantage. When compliance with the law becomes mainly a matter of form, the law is made to appear ludicrous, legal administration is undermined, the underlying policy of the law may be subverted, and the most conscientious bear the heaviest burden. And it is usually a sign that the law is out of touch with reality.

IV

Regulations
and Administration

Statutes are words on paper. They do not enforce themselves, and they do not automatically penetrate the minds of those whose conduct they are intended to affect. Statutes are as effective as their administration. In this chapter, therefore, attention is turned to the ways in which the executive branch has supplemented the conflict of interest statutes by regulation, the techniques it has devised to administer and enforce them, and the results that have been achieved through administrative action.

Particular importance must be attached to this topic in the field of conflict of interest. The patchy quality of the statutes makes fill-in regulation the more necessary. And the infrequency of prosecution under the statutes has resulted in virtually unbroken judicial silence on questions of interpretation.[1] As a consequence, administrative regulations and opinions on conflict of interest matters are apt to be given greater than usual weight.

The easiest way to conduct a review of administration is to start at the top with a look at the Presidency, follow with a survey of the general or over-all agencies concerned with the conflict of interest issue, and conclude with a consideration of administration at the department and agency level. The administrative pattern that emerges is highly uneven, showing little cohesion and great variance

[1] Between July 1, 1942, and June 30, 1952, the Department of Justice brought only eleven prosecutions of matters involving possible violations of the conflict of interest laws, and most of these dealt with alleged violations of the bribery statutes. See *Hearings Before the Special Subcommittee to Investigate the Department of Justice of the House Committee on the Judiciary*, 82d Cong., 2d Sess., ser. 20, pt. 2, at 982 (1952).

from agency to agency in the seriousness and detail with which the problem is treated.

GENERAL AGENCIES

THE PRESIDENCY

No central office in the executive branch has responsibility for controlling or coordinating the administration of ethical conduct among government employees. In an ultimate sense it is the President who bears the responsibility for establishing and maintaining suitable standards of employment in the federal agencies, but, for a variety of reasons, no President has yet done much to build up an institutional structure for this purpose.[2] A recurring debate in the field of personnel administration in recent years has concerned the organization of presidential responsibility for federal personnel policies.[3] Presidents beginning with Franklin D. Roosevelt have assigned some measure of responsibility for personnel policy to a White House assistant.[4] Active in recruiting political executives, these assistants have played little part in the development of policy, and their office has not developed into a significant bureaucratic force.

THE CIVIL SERVICE COMMISSION

The Civil Service Commission has general authority to promulgate rules governing the conduct of civil service employees.[5] Despite

2 See THE PRESIDENT'S COMMITTEE ON ADMINISTRATIVE MANAGEMENT, ADMINISTRATIVE MANAGEMENT IN THE GOVERNMENT OF THE UNITED STATES (1937); VAN RIPER, HISTORY OF THE UNITED STATES CIVIL SERVICE chs. 13–16 (1958).

3 See, e.g., COMMISSION ON ORGANIZATION OF THE EXECUTIVE BRANCH OF THE GOVERNMENT (Second Hoover Commission), REPORT TO CONGRESS ON PERSONNEL AND CIVIL SERVICE (1955); COMMISSION ON ORGANIZATION OF THE EXECUTIVE BRANCH OF THE GOVERNMENT (First Hoover Commission), REPORT TO THE CONGRESS ON PERSONNEL MANAGEMENT (1949); Reeves & David, Personnel Management in the Federal Service, in STUDIES ON ADMINISTRATIVE MANAGEMENT IN THE GOVERNMENT OF THE UNITED STATES (1937); SENATE COMM. ON POST OFFICE AND CIVIL SERVICE, 85TH CONG., 1ST SESS., ADMINISTRATION OF THE CIVIL SERVICE SYSTEM (Comm. Print 1957).

4 Under President Eisenhower, the position has carried the title of Special Assistant to the President for Personnel Management.

5 Under REV. STAT. § 1753 (1875), 5 U.S.C. § 631 (1958) derived from an act of 1871, and the Civil Service Act of 1883, the President is authorized to issue rules and orders relating to federal personnel policies. By act of October 31, 1951, 65 Stat. 712 (1951), 3 U.S.C. § 301 (1958), the President may delegate many of his functions to other officials. Under Executive Order 10530, promulgated on May 11, 1954, personnel authority was delegated to the Civil Service Commission. However, it is important to note that this power is incomplete in that it applies to civil service personnel only

this authority, however, the Commission has effectively resisted pressures to deal directly with problems of conflict of interest. The Commission's position has been that only the Department of Justice can deal with conflict of interest matters, because it has exclusive jurisdiction over criminal offenses. The Commission appears to have believed, quite rightly, that the major conflict of interest problems concern presidential appointees and positions excepted by statute or executive order from the classified service, and therefore that they lie outside the Commission's organic jurisdiction. In any event, the Commission has issued no regulations supplementing or enforcing the conflict of interest statutes as applied to any employees other than those working for the Commission itself.[6] It has not been a significant centripetal or unifying force in the field of administration of conflict of interest restraints.

THE ATTORNEY GENERAL

The Attorney General has been far more active. But his relationship to the conflict of interest problem is unique and peculiarly a product of his position as chief federal legal officer. His contacts with the administration of the statutes are several.

The Department of Justice is charged with responsibility for

---

and does not relate to employees under any of the other personnel systems of the government, including political appointees. The antique conflict of interest statutes themselves, hardly contemplating the twentieth-century administrative process, are not drawn to set general standards for regulatory implementation.

6 Chapter C–2 of the Commission's Federal Personnel Manual, entitled "Conduct of Officers and Employees," sets forth some general rules of conduct for federal employees, but they deal only fleetingly with matters even peripheral to conflict of interest. An example is the rule against participating in stock and bond speculations. "No officer or employee shall participate directly or indirectly in any transaction concerning the purchase or sale of corporate stocks or bonds or of commodities for speculative purposes, as distinguished from bona fide investment purposes." Even this rule was not of the Commission's making but is drawn directly from a circular letter of April 22, 1937, sent out over President Roosevelt's signature. See Letter From President Franklin D. Roosevelt to the United States Civil Service Commission, April 22, 1937, cited in United States Civil Service Commission, Federal Personnel Manual, p. C–2–26 (1949).

Under the Defense Production Act, the Commission performs one chore tangential to the conflict of interest area. It "inspects" the appointment of WOCs in twelve agencies authorized by that act to use such personnel. This inspection, however, is limited to an inquiry into their number and location in the executive establishment, and the Commission undertakes no informational or policing function in the matter of conflicting interests of the WOCs. See Chapter III, notes 98 & 99 *supra* and accompanying text.

prosecution of criminal violations of the conflict of interest statutes. The Attorney General is also required by law to give opinions on the interpretation of statutes and other legal provisions at the request of the President. Opinions of the Attorney General are advisory only, but the relative scarcity of judicial interpretation of the conflict of interest statutes gives special significance to the Attorney General's opinions in this field. Since 1842 the Attorney General has published about thirty opinions bearing on conflict of interest, most of them devoted to construction of narrow phrases or individual words.[7] Occasionally, however, these opinions assume a rule-making character as they reach beyond the statutes. For example, in 1942, Attorney General Biddle said in a formal published opinion:

Apart from statute, there are certain principles of fair dealing which have the force of law and which are applicable to all officers of the Government. A public office is a public trust. No public officer can lawfully engage in business activities which are incompatible with the duties of his office. He cannot in his private or official character enter into engagements in which he has, or can have, a conflicting personal interest. He cannot allow public duties to be neglected by reason of attention to his private affairs. . . . Such conflicts of interest are not tolerated in the case of any private fiduciary, and they are doubly proscribed for a public trustee.[8]

The Department of Justice has several other functions relating to conflict of interest. One of these relates to the important process of selecting nominees for top political posts — and getting them cleared through the Senate's confirmation committee. Administrative procedures for this purpose are apparently becoming regularized and more effective. When an appointee is about to be, or has been, named to an appointive office requiring confirmation, the President's staff, frequently working together with the appointee's lawyer and the legal staff of the agency to which he is to be appointed, reviews the background and private interests of the appointee. Questions likely to be raised during confirmation hearings are analyzed, and

[7] For example, under 18 U.S.C. § 283 (1958) and its predecessors, "officer" or "person holding any place of trust or profit" has been interpreted to cover (a) officials of the War Department and officers of the former Bureau of Military Affairs, 16 OPS. ATT'Y GEN. 478 (1880); (b) counsel to the United States delegates to the Pan-American Conference, 23 OPS. ATT'Y GEN. 533 (1901); (c) a temporary, expert consultant to the Secretary of War, serving without compensation, 40 OPS. ATT'Y GEN. 289 (1943); and (d) retired officers of the Regular Army, 40 OPS. ATT'Y GEN. 533 (1947).

[8] 40 OPS. ATT'Y GEN. 187, 190 (1942).

among these are conflict of interest questions. At this point the Department of Justice may be brought in. Generally the Department of Justice has maintained that it could not undertake to give legal advice to a presidential nominee respecting his compliance with the conflict of interest laws since it might at some later date be called upon to prosecute him for violation of one of the criminal statutes. On occasion, however, the Department appears to have modified its position.[9] At the request of the White House staff, a Justice Department attorney may confer with and advise the prospective nominee. Occasionally the Department attorney has undertaken the politically sensitive task of conferring with leading members of the confirming Senate committee or its staff to work out an adjustment satisfactory to the confirming committee. These adjustments involve not so much the requirements of law as the further requirements set by the committee. In this extracurricular way the Attorney General has become a participant in the gradual formation of conflict of interest standards for executive appointees.

In 1957 the Justice Department established an Office of Administrative Procedure to coordinate adjudicatory procedures among agencies.[10] One function of this office is to serve as a clearing house and adviser on codes of conduct for federal employees and officials.

Under the Defense Production Act the Attorney General reviews the arrangements made by various agencies to appoint and use public advisory committees made up of private persons who are not otherwise "government employees." The purpose of this review, conducted by the Antitrust Division, is to prevent such advisory committees from fixing prices or otherwise engaging in anticompetitive practices. Standards of evaluation are general and even ambiguous, but the aim is to prevent violations of the conflict of interest statutes as well as the antitrust laws. While the Defense Production Act was intended to apply mainly to industry advisory committees concerned with economic mobilization, it has been applied broadly to committees engaged in other activities as well. Congressional concern with the problem of the proper use of public advisory committees, such as the Business Advisory Committee in the Department of Com-

---

9 See, *e.g.*, the confirmation proceedings of Mr. McCone of the Atomic Energy Commission, discussed in Chapter V *infra*.

10 See UNITED STATES GOVERNMENT ORGANIZATION MANUAL 1959–60, 207 (1959).

merce, has recently inspired the Attorney General to press for a general presidential order setting mandatory standards for the use of such committees by executive agencies.[11] Other agencies have opposed this plan, arguing for the need of flexibility.[12]

From time to time the Department of Justice has studied conflict of interest problems with a view toward the preparation of improved legislation. But its activities in this regard have been exercised fitfully. Since 1953 it has turned out no proposals for conflict of interest legislation other than its request to Congress, following the *Bergson* decision, to expand Section 284. On August 17, 1955, the Budget Director proposed that the Attorney General prepare a general consolidation and revision of the conflict of interest statutes. A report of the Attorney General in 1956 indicated that the topic was under review, but as of the present writing, no public report of the results of that review has been made. On the other hand, the Department of Justice has, together with the Bureau of the Budget, successfully stood against efforts by other agencies to obtain exemptions from the conflict of interest statutes for certain of their employees.[13]

THE BUREAU OF THE BUDGET; THE CABINET SECRETARIAT

The Bureau of the Budget has played some role in the administration of restraints on conflicts of interest. As the major presidential agency concerned with the organization and operating effectiveness of the executive branch, it tends to be well informed on emerging problems in federal agencies, and has informally become something of a center of information on matters of conflict of interest and ethics. In exercising its function of legislative clearance, the Bureau has attempted to guard against special pleading by agencies pressing for statutory exemptions from the conflicts laws. And in its review of administrative proposals made by the Hoover Commission and other groups, the Bureau has been relatively active in its emphasis on the problem of conflict of interest. In June 1954 the Director of the Budget issued instructions to the heads of all agencies to review their

[11] See CABINET PAPER, CP–58–82, May 19, 1958. A modified draft was submitted on May 31, 1958.

[12] See, *e.g.*, Department of Health, Education and Welfare, Staff Paper, *Department of Health, Education and Welfare Advisory Committees*, August 14, 1958.

[13] See Letter From William P. Rogers, Deputy Attorney General, to Joseph M. Dodge, Director of the Budget, March 10, 1954.

inspection programs for detecting and preventing employee misconduct.[14] Apparently there has been little systematic progress under
this instruction, but some action was stimulated in some agencies.[15]
In the summer of 1955, the Budget Bureau staff prepared papers
urging the Director to propose to the Cabinet a government study of
the conflicts problem.[16]

The other executive unit occasionally involved in matters related
to conflict of interest is the small permanent staff attached to the
Cabinet — the Cabinet secretariat. From time to time it has prepared
study papers in the area. Under congressional pressure during 1958–
59, it assembled detailed information on the use of public advisory
committees, which had been severely criticized by House committees
for alleged excessive influence. Based in part on these data, and
through the combined work of several agencies, there emerged under
date of February 2, 1959, a compromise but unsigned and unidenti-
fied "guide" respecting the use and procedures of such committees,
which met some of the congressional objections to them.[17] The Cabinet secretariat has not, however, assumed any continuing responsibility in the area of conflict of interest.

Survey of the administrative role of the Presidency and of the
agencies of general jurisdiction in conflict of interest matters yields
two conclusions. Regardless of the administration in office, the Presidency has not provided central leadership for the executive branch
as a whole in the administration of conflict of interest restraints. Nor
has the Civil Service Commission, the Attorney General, the President's Assistant for Personnel Management, the Budget Bureau, or
the Cabinet secretariat filled the gap, though each of these in minor
respects brushes against the administrative problem. Administration
of conflict of interest restraints can be observed only on a fragmented
basis — department by department, agency by agency.

14 Memorandum, From the Director of the Budget to the Heads of Executive Departments and Establishments, *Review of Agency Inspection Programs,* June 14, 1954.

15 STAFF OF SUBCOMM. NO. 5, HOUSE COMM. ON THE JUDICIARY, 85TH CONG., 2D SESS.,
REPORT ON FEDERAL CONFLICT OF INTEREST LEGISLATION pts. III, IV & V, at 32 (Comm.
Print 1958).

16 See especially CABINET PAPER NO. 30, *Conflict of Interest Statutes,* 1955.

17 See *Standards and Procedures for the Utilization of Public Advisory Committees
by Government Departments and Agencies,* Feb. 2, 1959.

AGENCY REGULATION

The individual operating agencies have been appreciably more active in the administration of conflict of interest restraints than the presidential establishment or the agencies of general personnel jurisdiction; but the record is very uneven. A few agencies have done little or nothing in the field; a large majority have done something by way of issuing regulations but have been unenergetic in their administration; a small number of agencies have developed more refined and imaginative regulations and have enforced them with some degree of vigor.

All executive departments have in one degree or another attempted to define the obligations of their employees in matters of conflicting personal interest. Of the independent (non–Cabinet department) agencies, three relatively small ones appear to have no regulations on conflict of interest,[18] and the Selective Service System has virtually none. The National Labor Relations Board and the Tariff Commission regulate the conduct of former employees but not of those currently employed. At the opposite extreme stands the Housing and Home Finance Agency, whose detailed regulations and vigorous enforcement program were developed in response to past disclosures of improper conduct by FHA employees. The category of more active agencies also includes a few administering novel and specialized programs, such as the Atomic Energy Commission and the Small Business Administration.

In a category of its own is the Department of Defense. This Department and its subsidiary armed services have shown an awareness of the special risks inherent in the administration of multibillion dollar procurement programs.[19] In part this sensitivity takes the form of specific restraints on conflicts of interest and other rules for ethical conduct; in part it is apparent in the Department's elaborate structure of internal administrative checks, reviews, audits, and other

[18] The Indian Claims Commission, the National Mediation Board, and the Operations Coordinating Board.

[19] See, for example, Air Force Regulation 30–30 (1953) for the extensive Air Force conflict of interest regulations singled out for praise by the Preparedness Subcommittee of the Senate Armed Services Committee, in its letter of submittal accompanying its Twelfth Report issued May 20, 1957, at iii. See Chapter V, note 58 *infra.*

controls in those contracting operations not protected by competitive bidding. Many persons familiar with the operations of the Department believe that actual risks of abuse in its procurement are today very small for the reason that all substantial contract commitments are the product of the joint decision of many officials cross-checking each other at many levels of responsibility.

The regulations of some of the agencies are little more than restatements, sometimes verbatim, of the conflict of interest statutes. Commonly the regulations also include a hortatory declaration of the high aims of government service and the consequent obligations of the government employee. For instance, in its regulation forbidding employees to engage in outside activities "which may create, or tend to create, a conflict of interest, or interfere with objective and impartial performance" of official duties, the Public Housing Administration adds: "The nature of the PHA's statutory responsibilities makes it imperative that every PHA employee be completely above suspicion in the performance of his official duties. While it is not possible to anticipate all instances in which a conflict may be involved, certain situations clearly fall within the broad terms of the policy and statutory limitations stated in this release. Any doubtful cases should be resolved against participation in the outside activity. To maintain the highest degree of public confidence in Governmental administration is the every-day responsibility of all who share it."[20]

Another group of regulatory provisions may be identified as special provisions adopted in response to the particular functions and programs of the issuing agencies. For example, special areas of "quarantine" are commonly declared by agencies whose functions are closely connected with a specific business or other activity. For employees of the Federal Communications Commission, the radio, television, and wire communications industries are "quarantine" areas; similarly, employees of the Civil Aeronautics Board are prohibited from participating in or having any connection with the civil aviation industry.[21] Regulations indicating a "quarantine" area oc-

[20] See Public Housing Administration, Administrative Manual, Personnel, especially § 82–9–2 (1953).

[21] See Chapter III, note 3 *supra*. See also Civil Aeronautics Board Manual, Administrative Memorandum No. 31, *Pecuniary Interests in Civil Aeronautics Enterprises* (1956).

cur most often in categories of prohibitions on outside activities, financial interests, and restrictions on former employees.

Many agencies, however, deal in one way or another with such a broad segment of the American economy or society that no particular area can be isolated and marked out for special treatment. In agencies like the Federal Trade Commission, whose work cuts across all of American industry, the task of defining regulations for heading off conflicts of interest is extremely difficult. This factor is one source of the conflict of interest problems of the Department of Defense; the Department buys some of almost everything and has contact with virtually the entire economy. Similar difficulties arise for agencies whose functions, although confined to a certain industrial or economic area, embrace a broad range of private economic activity. Thus, while it is feasible for the CAB to keep its employees out of the private airline business, it is not practical for HHFA to keep its employees completely out of real estate transactions.

Some further illustrations of special provisions may be helpful. In the Export-Import Bank, a small agency with a highly specialized clientele, employees may not recommend the services of any attorney, engineer, economist, or other consultant or adviser to any person or firm in connection with matters that have been, or can be expected to be, brought before the agency. Employees of the Tennessee Valley Authority are prohibited from purchasing surplus property from the TVA by direct negotiation, or purchasing real or personal property sold by the agency at public auction when the employees intend to resell or speculate with such property or when they are able to obtain information about the property not available to the general public. After many years of a contrary rule, the Department of Justice in 1953 forbade all Department and United States attorneys to do any law practice whatever outside their government work. The Small Business Administration, which makes loans to business firms, prohibits its clients from employing, tendering any office or employment to, or retaining for professional services any employee of SBA who served in a position in which he exercised discretion with respect to granting assistance to small business.[22]

[22] The relevant regulatory material appears in the following references: Export-Import Bank of Washington, Staff Memorandum No. 46, *Eximbank Policy Concerning Employee Standards of Conduct*, ¶ 8 (1954); Tennessee Valley Authority, Interdivisional

These regulations illustrate the adaptability and flexibility of administrative, as opposed to legislative, handling of problems of employee conduct. Agencies whose functions center upon a single industry or type of economic activity can restrict with special rigor the outside activities of their employees relating to the industry or economic activity affected by agency programs. Agencies that are particularly exposed to ethical problems, such as those engaged in economic regulation or distribution of funds or franchises, have the opportunity to extend or tighten their rules on employee behavior. Some of the differences among agency regulations on conflict of interest are healthy indications of adaptation to differing needs.

RECURRENT REGULATIONS

Beyond these individualized spot rules, the administrative regulations of most agencies exhibit a marked similarity in the kinds of employee conduct with which they are concerned. This standardization is remarkable, given the erratic character of the underlying conflict of interest statutes and the absence of any administrative coordinating force in the executive branch.

Five areas of employee conduct are the recurrent topic of the agency regulations. They are: acceptance of gratuities; outside employment; financial interests; use and disclosure of government information; and dealings with the agency by former employees. Thus — in both content and scope — agency regulations differ markedly from the conflict of interest statutes. In the following paragraphs are some representative regulations drawn from each of these five categories, illustrating some of the different ways in which various agencies have dealt with common problems.[23]

Gratuities

Acceptance by an official of a payment in return for an official act is bribery. Mere acceptance of gratuities by an official falls short

---

Instructions, *Policies and Regulations Affecting Employee Conduct* 2 (1955); Department of Justice, Order No. 46–54 (1954); Small Business Administration, Manual No. 100, § 903.014(f) (1956); and Interstate Commerce Commission, *General Rules of Practice Before the Commission*, Canon 4 of its Canons of Ethics at 27 (1956).

23 An excellent compilation of regulatory material may be found in STAFF OF SUBCOMM. NO. 5, HOUSE COMM. ON THE JUDICIARY, 85TH CONG., 2D SESS., REPORT ON FEDERAL CONFLICT OF INTEREST LEGISLATION, pt. IV (Comm. Print 1958).

of the bribery offense, but is uniformly agreed to be poor practice and a sure road to a position of dangerously conflicting interests. The problem is how to design a sensible restriction on gifts that separates the bad ones that are close to bribes from the unobjectionable ones such as tokens of filial affection. Clearly the distinction lies somewhere in the kind and degree of relationship between the donor and the work of the official and his agency. Different agencies in the executive branch have struggled to find satisfactory ways of expressing this relationship. The General Services Administration forbids its employees to accept any gift or favor from any person or entity "which has done, is doing, or proposes to do business with this Administration." [24] The Atomic Energy Commission prohibits the acceptance of any personal advantage from anyone under circumstances that might reasonably be interpreted to influence the recipient in his official duties.[25] The AEC also forbids its employees to accept "gifts, personal loans, advances, or other financial accommodations, not readily available on the same terms to the general public," from AEC contractors or licensees, actual or prospective.[26] There is no specific rule in the Department of Defense on acceptance of gratuities, but the regulations of the service departments bar gratuities from any person or firm doing business with the department concerned.[27]

Outside employment

So long as a government employee does his work and keeps hours, most agencies have no objection to his working outside. Some kinds of outside employment, however, are incompatible with some kinds of government positions: take the case of a civil service examiner who runs a night cram school for civil service examinations. Regulations often proscribe outside employment that might prove embarrassing to the agency. Different bureaus within the Department of the Interior have tried a number of variations. In the National Park

[24] General Services Administration, GS 2–3, § 902.07, "Standards of Conduct — Gratuities" (1957).

[25] Atomic Energy Commission, AEC Manual, ch. 4124, "Conduct of Employees," § 033 (1956).

[26] Ibid.

[27] Army Regulation 600–10, § 8-b (1953); Navy Regulations, art. 1257 (1948); Air Force Regulation No. 30–30, § 8 (1953).

Service an employee is permitted to engage in part-time employment outside the government provided he does not impair his efficiency in performing his regular governmental duties, or utilize information obtained through his official position, or embarrass the Department.[28] The Fish and Wildlife Service will in addition deny an employee permission to undertake outside employment if the activity might be construed to be an official act of the Service or the Department, if it is performed during official duty hours, or if it involves services closely related to official duties.[29] The Solicitor's Office in the Interior Department requires prior written approval of the Solicitor before a departmental attorney may perform compensated legal work for others outside the government.[30]

Personal financial interests

Perhaps the simplest conflict of interest situation is that created by the employee's personal property holdings. Before Senate confirming committees the issue is most often raised where some of the appointee's property is in the form of stock, though the problem is the same regardless of the form of the holding. Government employees are not second-class citizens, and should be left as free as possible to lead their private economic lives. As in the case of gratuities, the problem is how to distinguish acceptable from objectionable outside economic interests. In their regulations, the agencies have tried several different approaches. The United States Information Agency forbids an employee to acquire a financial interest that "may result in a conflict between the private interests of the employee and his official duty, or tends to bias his judgment."[31] The Export-Import Bank rules out of bounds any investment by an employee "in a company having before the Bank a loan application which is likely to be acted upon favorably."[32] The Interstate Commerce Commission forbids the holding of any securities or the existence of any other pecuniary interest in any carrier or other agency

---

28 National Park Service, Employee Handbook 43 (1955).

29 Fish and Wildlife Service, Memorandum for Regional Directors and Project Leaders § 1538, Jan. 17, 1957.

30 Department of Interior, Order No. 2259 (1946).

31 United States Information Agency, Manual of Organization & Administration, pt. V-A, § 553(a)4 (1955).

32 Export-Import Bank of Washington, Staff Memorandum No. 46, *Eximbank Policy Concerning Employee Standards of Conduct,* ¶ 4 (1954).

subject to regulation under the provisions of the Interstate Commerce Act.[33]

Inside information

Control of government employees' use of government information has troublesome overtones, suggesting problems of national security, bureaucratic suppression of information damaging to the bureaucracy, and freedom of speech. Yet for centuries the common law has been brutally strict with the unfaithful agent who uses inside information to get a jump on the market or to run up the price of something his employer will buy. The arguments for such rules in a governmental context are even stronger. Regulations against the misuse of inside information are less common than restraints on the other forms of conduct discussed here, but they tend to appear in specialized agencies.

Perhaps the most detailed rules on the unauthorized use of information are those of the Federal Power Commission. The FPC does not expressly prohibit the use of confidential information for private gain, but it does restrict in detail the manner of public release of information about matters pending before the Commission. Even conferences of FPC employees with parties to proceedings before the Commission are restricted.[34] In the Securities and Exchange Commission, employees are forbidden to divulge confidential information to unauthorized persons or to release such information prematurely. In addition they are forbidden to engage in any outside activities that accrue from or are based upon confidential information.[35] Carefully devised rules and practice attempt to eliminate any chance of leaks of agricultural statistics from the Department of Agriculture.[36]

Post-employment dealings

The last of the five main areas of employee conduct covered by

[33] Interstate Commerce Commission, Managing Director's Memorandum No. 69, *ICC Inspection Program and Standards of Employee Conduct,* ¶ 10 (1954).

[34] See Federal Power Commission, Administrative Orders Nos. 7A (1953), 14 (1947), 14A (1955), and 56 (1956).

[35] Securities and Exchange Commission, *Regulation Regarding Conduct of Members and Employees and Former Members and Employees of the Commission,* rule 1 (a), (d) (1956).

[36] See 22 Fed. Reg. 10479 (1957).

regulation is that of post-employment relations with the agency. The regulations tend to be more strict than the conflict of interest statutes they overlap.

Section 284 of Title 18 forbids a former employee, for two years after leaving government service, to represent a client in prosecuting a claim against the United States involving any subject matter directly connected with which the former employee was employed or performed duty. The noncriminal post-employment statute, Section 99 of Title 5, similarly imposes a two year limit. But several agencies, including the Department of the Treasury, have imposed an additional and permanent bar preventing a former employee from ever appearing on behalf of a client to prosecute a claim against the United States if he gave personal consideration to the matter as a government employee or if he gained personal knowledge of it while in government service.[37] The Department of the Treasury also adds to the bar of the statutory post-employment restrictions respecting "claims" by forbidding the former employee to act as attorney or agent, within two years after the termination of employment, in any "matter" pending in the Department during the period of his employment, unless he receives the written consent of the Department. All former Treasury employees who wish to handle a case before the Internal Revenue Service must secure the permission of the Director of Practice of the Service. Under the Department's rule, a lawyer will never be able to handle a case if he was involved in it in any way while serving in the Department. Determinations in these cases are not reviewable except when a complaint is filed by the former employee, a rare occurrence.[38]

Another example is offered by the Securities and Exchange Commission. If, within two years after the end of his service, a former employee of the SEC is employed to represent any person in any matter in which he will appear before the Commission, he must file with the Commission a statement of the nature of his employment within ten days of the time that it becomes apparent that he will have to appear before the Commission. If the former employee worked on any investigation or formal proceeding involving such

[37] STAFF OF SUBCOMM. NO. 5, HOUSE COMM. ON THE JUDICIARY, 85TH CONG., 2D SESS., REPORT ON FEDERAL CONFLICT OF INTEREST LEGISLATION pts. III, IV & V, at 58–60 (1958) found fifteen agencies with such a lifetime ban.

[38] See 31 C.F.R. § 10.3 (1951).

matter during the period of his SEC service, he will not be permitted to appear before the Commission.[39]

One comes away from a review of the conflict of interest regulations of the administrative agencies with three main impressions. First, they are uneven, reflecting the lack of any consistent administrative drive from on top. Second, they vary in their particular provisions where special risks of the agency create special needs. Third, they are nevertheless remarkably uniform in their over-all conception of the kinds of employee behavior that are likely to be dangerous. When compared with the conflict of interest statutes, the substantive regulations of many agencies show forth as relatively integrated, more modern, better drafted, and, most important, as relevant expressions of public policy.

ADMINISTRATION AND ENFORCEMENT

As in the case of statutes, the effectiveness of regulations lies more in their enforcement than in their writing. The agencies reveal considerable uniformity in their allocation of responsibility for enforcement. Techniques and administrative practices of enforcement vary greatly, however.

ORGANIZATION

Small agencies, such as the Bureau of the Budget and the independent regulatory commissions, vest responsibility for administering the regulations in some high official, such as the assistant director of the Bureau of the Budget or the managing director in the Interstate Commerce Commission. This official, sometimes with staff assistance, doubles as inspection officer to investigate alleged violations. Regulations are promulgated for the agency as a whole.

In larger agencies, administration tends to be decentralized. Rule-making authority in the largest agencies is often delegated and the general regulations of the agency are supplemented by detailed regulations of its bureaus and divisions. The larger agencies are apt to have better worked out procedures and safeguards.

[39] See Securities and Exchange Commission, *Regulation Regarding Conduct of Members and Employees and Former Members and Employees of the Commission*, rule 6 (1956).

The Housing and Home Finance Agency has taken the unusual step of creating an effective and well staffed Compliance Division, which investigates allegations of improper employee conduct and cooperates with the Director of Personnel in enforcing ethics regulations. HHFA has also established a top-ranking Outside Activities Committee, which renders advisory opinions in difficult cases calling for interpretation of the agency's restrictions on outside activities.[40] The Committee also reviews from time to time the effectiveness of agency regulations and recommends changes and new policies.

In recent years the Department of Commerce has been particularly energetic in organizing itself to combat the risk of conflicts of interest inherent in many of its operations. It seeks to indoctrinate its employees on the subject at the beginning of their employment and at periodic intervals during their period of service, and it makes advice available on personal problems relating to conflicts of interest. An agency inspection staff, attached to the office of the Assistant Secretary for Administration, is continuously active in this area. This staff helps employees of the Department resolve questions of compliance with the Department's regulations. It also performs the unusual and valuable function of giving advance advice on whether employees' activities or interests conflict with the performance of official duties.

The organization of the Department of Defense is unique, as would be expected. Several different legal offices within the Department play important roles in the issuance and administration of conflict of interest regulations. The General Counsel's staff in the Office of the Secretary of Defense has been primarily concerned with the problem of permissible outside financial interests of presidential appointees to Defense posts. This staff has developed a good deal of experience in dealing with the conflict of interest standards set by the Senate Armed Services Committee. Within each of the three military departments, two separate legal offices, the civilian Office of the General Counsel and the military Office of the Judge Advocate General, have a part in interpreting and drafting regulations. The Judge Advocate Generals of the military departments publish opin-

40 The Committee is made up of the General Counsel, the Assistant Administrator (Administration), the Community Facilities Commissioner, the Urban Renewal Commissioner, and the Assistant Administrator (Congressional Liaison and Public Affairs).

ions regularly, and a substantial number of JAG opinions on conflict of interest matters are on the books. Some of these concern the seven basic conflict of interest statutes. Many of them, however, deal with special statutes and regulations affecting military personnel only. Within the military departments, these formal published legal opinions have great weight. It should be noted that there is a third layer of legal counsel and other officers within the technical branches and services of the Department of Defense. Conflict of interest problems at the operating level — may contracting officer X deal with retired General Y who just walked in the door representing Company Z? — are undoubtedly handled in greater quantity here than anywhere else, but through a swift and unreported process of uncapturable practice and rule of thumb.

Thus some agencies have consciously adjusted their internal organization to cope with the administration of conflict of interest restraints. But such agencies are unusual.

ADMINISTRATIVE TECHNIQUES

Orientation

At a minimum, it would seem that the agencies have an obligation to inform their employees of the rules of conduct they are expected to follow. Yet, in discussing instances of wrongdoing and irregularities in the federal government, one student of government administration noted in 1952: "I know of no governmental in-service training programs that discuss the environment in which government operates or the points of ethics involved in standards of good government practice . . . New government officials are presumed to know the rules, and there is a surprising lack of indoctrination on proper conduct. There are surprisingly few departmental conferences to develop or to teach desirable standards of conduct. Here there is room both for research and for invention. We need new methods to overcome these unrealistic assumptions." [41]

Some progress has been made since 1952. In August 1957 President Eisenhower approved a proposal to establish an orientation program for newly appointed political executives. And some central direction from the White House has been provided to stimulate and

41 Emmerich, *A Scandal in Utopia,* 12 PUB. ADMIN. REV. 1, 7 (1952).

police orientation programs developed by the agencies.[42] Many agencies have also prepared attractive booklets outlining the standards of behavior to which federal employees will be held.[43] But while these pamphlets provide some of the raw materials of an indoctrination program, they do not themselves serve as a program, and much remains to be done in this field.

Certification

An administrative device used by some agencies is the requirement that employees certify in writing that they have read and understood the regulations governing employee conduct, including those relating to conflict of interest. The Department of Commerce requests each new employee to read the departmental regulations on conflict of interest and to certify either that he has no private business activity that could reasonably be considered to involve a question of propriety under departmental orders, or that he has some private interest which may possibly involve a question of propriety. In the latter case, he must describe the interest and request a departmental ruling on its propriety.[44] In connection with the preparation of crop and livestock estimates, the Agricultural Marketing Service requires each employee to certify that he has read the statutes and regulations applicable to the preparation of such estimates and the protection of their confidentiality.[45] The Atomic Energy Commission brings to the attention of its many consultants at the time of their appointment the Commission's rules of conduct, including those dealing with conflict of interest. In employing consultants, the AEC uses a Personal Service Contract in which the con-

[42] See Miles, *The Orientation of Presidential Appointees,* 18 Pub. Admin. Rev. 1–6, 106–12 (1958). See also Bernstein, The Job of the Federal Executive 176–99 (1958).

[43] For example, the Department of Justice gives each new employee a copy of a cartoon-illustrated pamphlet, *You and Your Job.* The Patent Office in the Department of Commerce distributes to all employees a pamphlet, *Your Job in the United States Department of Commerce,* chapter VII of which discusses "Your Obligations as a Public Employee." The Treasury Department has prepared a booklet, *Information for Treasury Employees,* which includes a discussion of standards of conduct; and some bureaus in the Department have prepared more detailed materials for indoctrination purposes. The Air Force has issued a pamphlet, *Do's and Don'ts for All Air Force Personnel Associated with Procurement.* The Atomic Energy Commission goes further than most agencies by imposing responsibility upon its executives to supply copies of regulations on conflicts of interest to contractors under their jurisdiction.

[44] See Department of Commerce, Department Order No. 77, as amended (1955).

[45] See Department of Agriculture, Agricultural Marketing Service, Agricultural Estimates Division, Form CEF–75 (1958).

sultant states that he "is familiar with and agrees to conform to the provisions of Commission policy regarding conflict of interests"; insofar as he knows, "there does not exist any actual or potential conflict between his private interests (including corporate stockholdings) and his services for the Commission"; and he "will, in the event of a change in either his private interests or services for the Commission raise with the Commission any question regarding possible conflict of interests which may arise as a result of such change." [46] There are other instances of the use of this certification mechanism, but it remains limited to a minority of agencies.

Disqualification

Agency regulations commonly echo and supplement Section 434 in requiring employees to disqualify themselves from acting on matters in which they have a pecuniary interest.[47] Necessarily, however, in the absence of elaborate disclosure requirements, initiative here must rest in the hands of the employee, and few agencies have done anything to provide administrative procedures for such disqualification.

Better worked out than most are the provisions of the Department of Defense, the AEC, and the SEC. In the Department of Defense each officer and employee is charged with responsibility to inform his superior or department head whenever he feels he should be disqualified from taking action in a particular case. He is then relieved of his duty and the matter is assigned to someone else of equal or higher rank. Responsibility is also imposed upon supervisors to avoid assigning to individuals matters that may create a real or apparent conflict of interest.[48] The AEC regulations specify

---

[46] See Atomic Energy Commission, AEC Manual, ch. 4139, "Employment of Consultants and Designees," especially app. 4139–071–A & B (1956).

[47] For example, the regulations of the Federal Trade Commission provide that an employee shall notify his immediate superior in writing whenever the circumstances are such that his official duties affect or may affect any private person or organization (i) by whom he has been employed or in whom he has had any economic interest within the preceding two years, (ii) in whom he currently has any economic interest, (iii) with whom he has a close family relationship, or (iv) with whom he has arranged or is negotiating for future employment or business relations. Federal Trade Commission, Personnel Bulletin No. 12, *Conflict of Interest* (1957), complementing Personnel Bulletin No. 7, *Conduct of Employees and Disciplinary Action* (1955).

[48] See Letter From Charles E. Wilson to the Secretaries of the Military Departments, etc., on the "Conduct of Personnel Assigned to Procurement and Related Activities," Jan. 28, 1953.

certain disqualification procedures for any case in which an employee believes that he should be disqualified because of personal, family, financial, or other considerations. The supervisor has primary responsibility for making the decision on disqualification. Where continued need to invoke the disqualification can be anticipated, consideration is given to the transfer of the employee to another position.[49] Each employee of the Securities and Exchange Commission is expressly required under the regulations to inform his supervisor if he is assigned to a matter involving a company in which he owns securities or has any personal interest, with which he has been associated in the past, or with which he is negotiating for future employment.

Reviewing outside employment

Only a few agencies have established administrative machinery to enforce regulations restricting employment of their employees outside of the government. Employees of the Civil Service Commission are required by Commission regulations to request in writing, and secure, the approval of a designated official before accepting appointment as a faculty member for after-hours teaching. An employee who engages in any type of outside paid employment on a more or less regular basis is required to report the details of such employment in writing to his supervisor. In the Housing and Home Finance Agency, new employees are required to execute a form on which they list all employment of whatever nature, whether or not for gain. Responsibility is placed on supervisors to deal appropriately with possible conflicts of interest disclosed by this procedure. As noted earlier, HHFA's standing Outside Activities Committee is exceptional.

Reporting

Energetic enforcement of agency regulations against holding incompatible outside economic interests would call for regular reporting requirements. Only a handful of agencies, primarily the Housing and Home Finance Agency and the Securities and Exchange

---

[49] See Atomic Energy Commission, AEC Manual, ch. 4124, "Conduct of Employees" § 032 (1956).

Commission, attempt any such reporting scheme. In HHFA new employees of the central office in the Office of the Administrator must complete a form listing interests and activities, business and personal, that may be reasonably construed "as being in conflict with official duties or any interests of the . . . Agency." This form is then required to be maintained on a current basis. Supervisors are expected to report to the Director of the Compliance Division all information of possible conflicts of interest. In the Federal Power Commission, each new employee files with the Commission a list of the securities he owns. Thereafter, whenever he acquires any securities that come within the prohibitions against acquisition of securities, the employee must report the acquisition to the Commission within thirty days. By all odds the SEC goes farthest in its disclosure requirements. Its commissioners and employees are required to report every transaction in any security or commodity within five days of the transaction. Similarly, changes in holdings resulting from inheritance, stock splits, or other happenings must be reported to the Director of Personnel. A new member or employee must also report to the Commission his securities and those of his spouse and of estates of which he is a fiduciary or beneficiary. He must also report the status of his accounts with securities firms, and of relatives who are associated with securities firms, investment companies, investment advisers, or public utilities.

Disciplinary proceedings and sanctions

When allegations of improper conduct under conflict of interest or other ethical rules are made against an employee, most agencies proceed against the employee as in any other disciplinary proceeding. In only a few agencies, such as HHFA and the Department of Commerce, is there a special committee or panel specially conversant with the regular run of similar problems that arise within the agency. A few agencies, such as the United States Information Agency and the Department of the Interior, distinguish between minor and more serious offenses and provide for formal hearings in the latter cases.[50]

[50] See United States Information Agency, Manual of Organization & Administration, pt. V-A, § 565 (1958); Bureau of Reclamation, Personnel Manual, pt. 2, ch. 2.1, § .8 (1952).

All regulations, however, provide for administrative sanctions. The administrative process enjoys a great advantage over the criminal approach in the wide and flexible range of possible sanctions. Violations of the agency's regulations may, depending upon their seriousness, be penalized by oral or written warning, reprimand, suspension, demotion, or outright dismissal. When the evidence suggests the violation of one of the criminal statutes, the matter is referred to the Department of Justice.

Most agencies do not specify the penalties for infractions of the regulations. An exception is the Federal Trade Commission, which has published tables of penalties for certain offenses, depending on the circumstances and the previous record of the offender. A note appended to the tables reserves flexibility of administrative judgment, however.[51] Another exception is the Bureau of Reclamation in the Department of the Interior. The Department follows the general practice of omitting penalties, but this Bureau has established a table of penalties for certain prohibited practices, some of which relate to conflicts of interest. For instance, "engaging in work for parties dealt with in official capacity" is punishable by ten to thirty days' suspension or removal from office, depending on the circumstances.[52]

To judge by the concern shown by agency regulations, the problem of conflict of interest is as wide as the executive branch. Despite the absence of central leadership and coordination, these regulations are in substantial agreement upon the areas of risk, and the misconduct the regulations center upon is hardly mentioned in the conflict of interest statutes. A few agencies make substantial, well conceived efforts to administer their rules on conflicts of interest, but the majority of agencies, their regulations once written, have left the burden of compliance up to the individual employee.

What a few agencies have done, all could do. The record of the agencies is sufficient to show that, with leadership, the administrative process is far better adapted to deal with the conflict of interest problem than is the criminal law.

---

51 "The tables above serve as guidelines. In general they will be followed but circumstances may require greater or lesser penalties for certain offenses." Federal Trade Commission, Personnel Bulletin No. 7, *Conduct of Employees and Disciplinary Action* 7 (1955).

52 Bureau of Reclamation, Personnel Manual, pt. 2, ch. 2.1, § .8 (D) (1952).

V

The Role
of Congress

The most obvious thing Congress does in the federal government is to legislate. But Congress' role does not end — it barely begins — with the statutes it passes. The floor and the committee reports of Congress are a great sounding board transmitting a steady stream of opinions, all bearing the potential of mustering a majority. Executive officials of agency, bureau, and department monitor the congressional frequency day and night for hints of what Congress might want tomorrow, might think today. When Congress has suggested its displeasure with standards of ethical conduct in the executive branch, action has usually followed. In their impact upon the field of conflicts of interest within the executive branch, Congress' nonlegislative expressions have ranked in importance with its statutory acts.

In addition to enactment of legislation, congressional activities bearing on conflict of interest standards may be grouped into three categories: Senate confirmation; investigation of broad problems or issues; and investigation of individuals or particular transactions.

SENATORIAL CONFIRMATION

The President is empowered by the Constitution to appoint high-ranking executive officials "by and with the Advice and Consent of the Senate." [1] The Senate confirmation process has produced some of

1 U.S. CONST. art. II, § 2.

the more spectacular participation of Congress in the field of executive conflicts of interest. In fact, it is probable that in the public mind, conflict of interest regulation is mainly identified with the restrictions imposed on appointees by Senate confirming committees. Highly individual in content, occurring at random intervals over time, played by an ever-changing cast, and strongly influenced by the political currents of the day, the confirmation hearings do not lend themselves to generalization. Something of a feel for the Senate committees' institutional role in this field can, however, be gained from a review of some of the more important and better known individual instances in which a confirming Senate committee has pressed its inquiry into the subject of the appointees' supposed conflict of interest situations.

Though the best known case is that of Mr. Charles E. Wilson, first place by seniority might go to Mr. Charles Warren, nominated by President Coolidge to be Attorney General in 1925. Mr. Wilson was, after agreeing to dispose of his stock, confirmed as Secretary of Defense; Mr. Warren was rejected by the Senate by one vote, still holding the interest that was the source of the trouble.[2]

During the Truman Administrations from 1945 to 1953, only one instance has been found in which the Senate dealt directly with a clear-cut issue of conflict of interest in a confirmation proceeding. The issue at the hearing was whether Carl A. Ilgenfritz, nominated chairman of the Munitions Board in 1949, would be permitted to continue to receive his salary as an executive of the United States Steel Corporation. The Senate declined to free him from the prohibitions of Section 1914, and by a vote of 28 to 40 refused to confirm him.[3]

[2] Mr. Warren had been president and director of two companies under antitrust indictment by the Federal Trade Commission. Upon his appointment as Attorney General he resigned from one of the companies, but was apparently still serving as president and director of the other. The company had also recently requested advance clearance from the Department of Justice to permit certain mergers, which requests had been denied; as Attorney General Mr. Warren would be in a position to grant the merger applications. The Senate divided evenly on the vote to confirm, and, Vice President Dawes not being present at the time, the motion to confirm failed. On a motion to reconsider, the only Democratic Senator who had voted to confirm changed his vote, and that motion was defeated 41 to 39. President Coolidge was reported to be very angry, and proposed to go ahead with a recess appointment for Mr. Warren, but it was declined. See N.Y. Times, Feb. 10, 1925, p. 3, col. 3; N.Y. Times, Feb. 11, 1925, p. 3, col. 1; N.Y. Times, Mar. 11, 1925, p. 1, col. 5.

[3] 95 CONG. REC. 12942–54, 12957–61 (1949).

SENATE ARMED SERVICES COMMITTEE

In its modern form the story of conflicts of interest and Senate confirmation is almost entirely a story of the Senate Armed Services Committee. Only this committee has maintained a sustained line of inquiry into possible conflicts of interest of presidential nominees for high office. The Committee has been primarily concerned with the elimination of nominees' interests in firms doing business with the military departments, and has focused sharply on the procurement functions of the Department of Defense. Nearly all doubts on the need for stock divestment and for severance of business relationships by nominees have been resolved by the Committee in favor of strictness. Concerned with actual conflicts of interest, the Committee has repeatedly revealed its sensitivity as well to the appearance of impropriety; "Caesar's wife" appears again and again in the hearings. The Committee decides, proceeding by proceeding, what adjustment the nominee must make in his private finances to earn the Committee's recommendation for confirmation. In practice, the Committee functions as a board of adjustment, using *ad hoc* criteria. The statutes on conflict of interest and the standards articulated in them are almost never mentioned.

If President Eisenhower's first nominee to a Defense post had not been president of a company that was one of the largest corporations in America and one of the largest Defense contractors, the subsequent record of the Armed Services Committee in the area of conflict of interest might have been quite different. When Charles E. Wilson of General Motors Corporation appeared before the Committee on January 15, 1953, he apparently assumed that the proceeding would be a routine affair. Reporting that he owned 39,470 shares of General Motors stock, was a beneficiary of the GM bonus plan, and a recipient of pension and insurance benefits, Wilson indicated to the Committee his intention to retain this stock.[4] The nominee proposed to avoid any problem of conflicting interests by disqualifying himself in transactions dealing with General Motors, and seemed in general not to think the problem serious.

[4] *Hearings Before the Senate Committee on Armed Services on Nominees Designate: Charles E. Wilson, Roger M. Kyes, Robert T. Stevens, Robert B. Anderson, Harold E. Talbott, etc.,* 83d Cong., 1st Sess. 6–19 (1953).

Senator Hendrickson: Well now, I am interested to know whether if a situation did arise where you had to make a decision which was extremely adverse to the interests of your stock and General Motors Corp. or any of these other companies, or extremely adverse to the company, in the interests of the United States Government, could you make that decision? *Mr. Wilson:* Yes sir; I could. I cannot conceive of one because for years I thought what was good for our country was good for General Motors, and vice versa. The difference did not exist.[5]

The Committee did not try to measure the value of Wilson's stock as compared to his total estate or to the total value of GM stock outstanding. As the Committee saw it, the issue was whether owner-ship of *any* GM stock created an unacceptable appearance of con-flicting interests. Wilson sensed the point later in the proceeding: "The thing that perhaps I overlooked myself was that not only did I have to operate honestly and fairly without prejudice, but all the people should also think that that was the way I was operating and that part of it I did not quite appraise." [6] But he tended to person-alize the questioning throughout the hearing.

Mr. Wilson: I know what you are talking about, but I really feel that you are giving me quite a pushing around. *Senator Russell:* I am sorry you feel that way, Mr. Wilson. I am not trying to push you around, but I have my responsibility, too. *Mr. Wilson:* I understand that. But I am just human, and I am making a great sacrifice to come down here.[7]

The Committee finally agreed to recommend Mr. Wilson's confirma-tion, but only on the stringent condition that he sell all of his General Motors stock.

Roger M. Kyes, the new administration's nominee-designate for Deputy Secretary of Defense, appeared next before the Committee. By then conflicts of interest were headline news. Kyes was also an executive of General Motors Corporation. Like Wilson, he owned common stock in GM and was a beneficiary of the GM bonus plan. Wilson was retiring from GM; Kyes was resigning but might return later.

Senator Johnson: Have you any plans or any arrangements or agreement to return to General Motors following your Government service?

5 *Id.* at 26.   6 *Id.* at 110.
7 *Id.* at 143. Compare the later statement of Senator Symington quoted *infra* on page 109.

Mr. Kyes: General Motors has told me, because of my record, they would be very happy to have me come back at any time. I enjoyed my association with General Motors, but there is absolutely no commitment on the part of either party with respect to the future.[8]

Senator Stennis wanted to know what Kyes intended to do after he left the Government.

Mr. Kyes: Well, I imagine after I am through with my tour, I would go back to industry, because that is all I know, as you can see from my record.

While there are absolutely no commitments at all, it would be a rather normal thing for me to go back if things had not changed. I might add another thing, and that is that a man has been picked to take my place, and that slot is closed. You know how life is in a corporation; they say absence makes the heart grow fonder, but that is not so in business. . . .[9]

The Committee's interest in the probability of Kyes' returning to his former employer suggests doubt in its mind whether divestment of stock is in itself adequate protection against conflicting interests.

In his second appearance before the Committee, Kyes declared:

. . . I, therefore, advise this committee that, if confirmed, I will sell all of my General Motors stock, with the exception of that portion which I may give to charity, and, in addition to this, I will dispose of my stock in Aeroquip Corporation, Monsanto Chemical, Abbott Laboratories, General Mills, International Business Machines, Gulf Oil, Minnesota Mining & Manufacturing, and Cities Service without retaining any beneficial or reversionary interest. I believe that these are my only holdings which could possibly be related to any transactions that might take place with the Department of Defense. You will note that I plan to retain my holdings in the National City Bank of New York, and the Fidelity Phoenix Fire Insurance Co., because I cannot possibly conceive of these involving any conflict of interest in connection with my position with the Department of Defense.[10]

Kyes' nomination was confirmed. But perhaps Senator Hunt of the Armed Services Committee reflected the view of more than one on the Committee. In an exchange of views with Mr. Wilson, the senator had indicated his opposition to the policy of requiring divest-

8 *Id.* at 49.   9 *Id.* at 51–52.
10 *Hearings Before the Senate Committee on Armed Services on Nominations of Roger M. Kyes, Robert T. Stevens, Robert B. Anderson and Harold E. Talbott,* 83d Cong., 1st Sess. 2 (1953).

ment: "Mr. Wilson, let me say this, I am not one who has been in harmony with this procedure that we have been following, to make any man who comes into the Government surrender all his stock, disassociate himself entirely from his company, and receive no remuneration whatsoever for past services. I have never been one who has gone along with that theory, and it has kept us from getting many good men." [11] But Senator Hunt was nevertheless troubled by these nominations. In the Kyes hearing he said:

> Mr. Chairman, I haven't any questions. I intend to vote with the committee with reference to Mr. Kyes' nomination.
> He is in exactly the same position, I see no differences at all between his situation and Mr. Wilson's, but I do have, Mr. Chairman, some hesitancy in giving my full approval to both the president and the vice-president of the largest corporation that we do business with moving in on one establishment of Government, the Defense establishment.
> Now, these men are absolutely honest. I think they will bend backward to see that General Motors doesn't get favors, but it just doesn't seem to me good public relations or good policy, and that is all I have to say, Mr. Chairman.[12]

The nomination of Robert T. Stevens to be Secretary of the Army presented the problem of conflicting interests in a somewhat different context. While Stevens had a diversified portfolio of stockholdings, his principal interest lay in J. P. Stevens and Company, a family-controlled company in which he owned 42,000 shares and a trust in which he participated owned over 200,000 shares. In one of the rare instances where the Committee has considered the conflict of interest statutes, it discussed in passing whether an official whose only contact with a company is through the receipt of dividends may be said to be "directly or indirectly interested in the pecuniary profits" of the company under Section 434. It will be recalled that under that section a government official may not transact business for the government with a business entity in which he is so interested.[13] Counsel for the Committee was unable to find any control-

11 *Hearings Before the Senate Committee on Armed Services on Nominees Designate: Charles E. Wilson, Roger M. Kyes, Robert T. Stevens, Robert B. Anderson, Harold E. Talbott, etc.,* 83d Cong., 1st Sess. 25 (1953).

12 *Hearings Before the Senate Committee on Armed Services on Nominations of Roger M. Kyes, Robert T. Stevens, Robert B. Anderson, and Harold E. Talbott,* 83d Cong., 1st Sess. 3 (1953).

13 See the discussion of section 434 in Chapter III *supra.*

ling opinions on the matter.[14] Textile sales to the government made up 29.8 per cent of the business of J. P. Stevens and Company in 1952.[15] Stevens argued that retention of his interest in the company raised no issue of conflicting interests because the procedures of textile procurement precluded the Secretary of the Army from intervening in contract negotiations. Moreover, he felt he could disqualify himself from participating in any matter involving the company. Stevens also pointed out that the company got almost all its government business through competitive bidding that left no room for the exercise of influence.

The Stevens hearing dramatically raised the problem of the impact of the Committee's divestment policy on family-held businesses. Stevens argued:

In telling you about the Stevens Co., and raising the question of my retention of stock therein, I do so not in my own interest but because I believe such an important principle and precedent is involved in the question. This principle or precedent is in my judgment something that will vitally affect in the future the welfare of the United States. The fabric of our free enterprise system is built upon those thousands of small or intermediate-size successful businesses which are the result of the efforts of individual men. In many cases these businesses are owned in whole or in part by the man who has founded or built them up. In most cases there is no market for their stock. It is my humble but considered opinion that in calling able men to serve their Government the requirement of me that I dispose of my Stevens stock would have a long and

14 "*Mr. Herberg* (Committee counsel): It seems to me there are two possible tests that could be applied in determining whether the requisite pecuniary interest is present. On the one hand, you could make the quantum of outstanding stock the measure, and judge the individual's holdings in relation to that. On the other hand, you could apply a personal test, in other words — does the amount of stock held by the individual in a particular corporation, taking into account his net worth, suggest that it would seriously influence him in the light of all his personal circumstances? Which of these two tests would be applied? If indeed, a court would admit that a quantitative measure should be applied, I frankly do not know if I were obliged to make a curbstone guess, I would think that if the court were to permit the quantitative test to be applied, it probably would use the personal test as being more nearly indicative of the probable impact on the individual of an adverse situation with respect to the corporation." *Hearings Before the Senate Committee on Armed Services on Nominees Designate: Charles E. Wilson, Roger M. Kyes, Robert T. Stevens, Robert B. Anderson, Harold E. Talbott, etc.*, 83d Cong., 1st Sess. 80 (1953). There is no authority for either of the "tests" suggested by the Committee's counsel, and the language of section 434 itself would cover any pecuniary interest.

15 *Hearings Before the Senate Committee on Armed Services on Nominations of Roger M. Kyes, Robert T. Stevens, Robert B. Anderson and Harold E. Talbott*, 83d Cong., 1st Sess. 10 (1953).

serious adverse effect on the willingness of those successful business
executives to serve . . .[16]

As I stated in my testimony of January 16, the problem is fundamentally one of basic integrity, an integrity which cannot be achieved
through the simple expediency of the sale of stock.

In closing my presentation, I would like once again to stress as force-
fully as I know how that it is the precedent and the principle as it may
affect the able, small, and medium-sized businessmen with whom I am
concerned. The issue is far greater than any one individual.[17]

But several senators continued to reveal serious and even anxious
concern about the problem of conflicting economic interests. For
example:

Senator Smith: I personally feel that if you divest yourself of your stock
you still can't help being interested in the company that you have come
up with through the years, but as a member of the committee I also
must remember that there is a law that we must think about.[18]
Senator Case (of South Dakota): Mr. Stevens, you have very clearly expressed the principle which you think is important here, and that is that
small-business men, or relatively small-business men or independent
businessmen or men who have been associated with a business which
represents a considerable effort on their part or their family, shall not
feel that they are barred from holding a position with the Government. . . . It should be obvious, however, that there is nothing in this
situation as it has been disclosed that would prevent you or anyone in
similar circumstances from serving in some other capacity, for example,
Secretary of State or Secretary of the Interior, so that even if the principle
which has disturbed the committee should be upheld in your instance,
it wouldn't bar you from serving the Government in some other capacity.[19]

Senator Case continued:

Your colleagues would hesitate to call offside on you or on anything
which might be interpreted as a matter of your interest, just the same as

16 *Id.* at 11.
17 *Id.* at 16.
18 *Id.* at 27–28. No general conflict of interest statute requires divestment. The
senator may have had in mind a combination of statutory prohibitions upon the
delegation of certain duties together with the personal disqualification requirement
of section 434. Taken together they might render both Mr. Stevens and the members
of his staff impotent to act in some matters. The question of these statutory restrictions upon delegation of authority had arisen at the hearing. *Id.* at 22–23.
19 *Id.* at 29.

the Senate hesitates to take action when a fellow Member of the Senate
is involved, the same as with a member of a football team. So the real
answer to the problem seems to me to be a complete divorcement of
interest, either by separating the business from the Department, as Senator Stennis suggested, or by taking the decision that is involved completely
out of the Defense Department so far as the determination of a profit is
concerned.[20]

Mr. Stevens' arguments went for nothing. After its deliberations,
the Committee voted to report favorably the nomination of Mr.
Stevens to be Secretary of the Army, but only upon the understanding that he would dispose of all his stock in J. P. Stevens and Company, and in the meantime would disqualify himself with respect
to any business transactions between the Department of Defense and
the company.[21]

Harold E. Talbott, nominee-designate to be Secretary of the Air
Force, presented a still different problem to the Committee. He
owned stock in several corporations that held contracts with the
Department of Defense, and he was also a partner in an engineering
firm that specialized in making studies of clerical efficiency and
controls. Talbott agreed to sell his stockholdings, but he proposed
to retain a partial interest in the partnership in a modified form:

Mr. Talbott: Now, in setting myself up as a special partner, our lawyers
drew up an agreement with the other partner — there were only two
partners, Mulligan and myself — that no work was to be done while I
am in Washington, that had to do with defense work essentially. They
may be doing some work for Ford, for example, but that is not essentially
a war contract. But where it is possible, they will stay away from any
of the aircraft companies.[22]

Talbott was confirmed under this arrangement.[23]

The special partnership agreement satisfied the Committee primarily because the work of partnership did not fall directly in the
category of defense procurement. Similarly, Wilson had been allowed to retain his interests in a Texas company that had no dealings
with the defense agencies. Members of the Committee indicated that
Stevens could also have avoided selling his Stevens Company stock

20 *Id.* at 32.   21 *Id.* at 53.

22 *Hearings Before the Senate Committee on Armed Services on Nominees Designate:
Charles E. Wilson, Roger M. Kyes, Robert T. Stevens, Robert B. Anderson, Harold E.
Talbott, etc.,* 83d Cong., 1st Sess. 92 (1953).

23 But see the discussion on page 125 *infra.*

if he had been willing to terminate the defense contracts held by the company.

Procurement in general has preoccupied the attention of the Armed Services Committee, but the Committee has imposed a special taboo on oil. Perhaps the ghost of Teapot Dome is responsible. Whatever the cause, even a minor holding in an oil company is certain to subject a nominee to searching scrutiny by the Committee. The case of Dudley C. Sharp is illustrative.

Sharp was nominated to be an Assistant Secretary of the Air Force in 1955. He was a shareholder in several companies, one of which was Texas Fund, Inc., an investment company whose portfolio included electric utilities, natural gas pipelines, banks, insurance companies, and chemical, oil, and gas companies, no single company's securities comprising more than 4 per cent of the total value of the Fund and the chemical, oil, and gas securities constituting only about 26 per cent of the total.[24] Sharp's personal holding in the investment company amounted to one-fourth of one per cent of the outstanding stock. He was, however, a member of the fifteen-man board that controlled the investments of the Fund.

Sharp agreed to sell his stockholdings in corporations doing business with the defense establishment. He argued, however, that he should be permitted to retain his holdings in the Texas Fund on the grounds that he had no power in his personal capacity to control the Fund's investment policy, that earnings coming to him through the Fund and traceable to government business were extremely small, and that procurement procedures in the Air Force made it impossible for him to exercise influence in the award of contracts:

I might add here that the largest single holdings in the Texas Fund are in the Texas Co., which is an investment of approximately $800,000, actually $794,000 at the time of this statement.

If I could in any way influence the sale or the purchase of petroleum products from the Texas Company in a way — if we would happen to do all the business of the Air Force with the Texas Co., this could conceivably increase the value of this Texas Co. holding by a modest amount perhaps, let us say, 25 per cent. That would be $200,000.

24 *Hearings Before the Senate Committee on Armed Services on the Nomination of Dudley C. Sharp to be an Assistant Secretary of the Air Force,* 84th Cong., 1st Sess. 4–16 (1955).

My one-quarter of one one-hundredths of $200,000 would amount to $500. That is the maximum that could be the — influence that I could have on any one security in the holdings.[25]

There is a very remote possibility that there would be a conflict between my new position and the interests of any oil company in view of the fact that all oil purchases for the Air Force are made through the Joint Purchasing Commission, Army, Navy, Air Force.

Of course, the Air Force has one representative out of 3 on that committee. It is my understanding that all purchases are made on a competitive bid basis . . .[26]

But the specter of Teapot Dome was more persuasive than Mr. Sharp's logic. Where oil was involved, the Committee refused to admit of any adjustment short of total divestment, and Sharp's nomination was approved only after he agreed to dispose of his interest in the mutual fund.[27]

It has been frequently charged that the Armed Services Committee has acted capriciously *ad hoc* and *ad hominem*. Two confirmation hearings involving stock of Procter and Gamble Company offer a rare opportunity for close comparison of cases. In 1955, Reuben B. Robertson, Jr., nominee-designate for Deputy Secretary of Defense, was required to dispose of 340 shares (0.005 per cent of the outstanding shares) of Procter and Gamble because it was a defense contractor.[28] Two years later, in 1957, when Neil McElroy,

[25] *Id.* at 9.

[26] *Id.* at 13.

[27] *Sharp:* "I will be glad to do it. It was quite a hard decision for me to make, because I did not want to give it up; it is difficult to give it up. As a proof of my sincerity, I am willing to do it. I know that I have to prove to the members of this committee somehow that I am really sincere in what I say, when I say that there will be no conflicts of interest between my personal interests and the interests of the Government. And if there are any conflicts of interest, that they will always be resolved in favor of the Air Force. I make that statement unequivocally, if I am placed in this position." *Id.* at 20, 24.

An apparent exception to the Committee's usual rigidity on oil holdings was the case of Paul D. Foote, an executive of Gulf Oil Company, appointed in August 1957 as Assistant Secretary of Defense for Research and Engineering. Mr. Foote's career had been with the company, most of his estate was committed to it, and he was not willing to sell his holdings. The Defense Department position involved is one of the most important ones and probably the hardest post in the Department to fill. After a seven months' impasse, the Committee finally confirmed Mr. Foote, having required him to sell some stock in two meat packing companies. *Hearings Before the Senate Committee on Armed Services on Nominations of Paul D. Foote and Richard Jackson,* 85th Cong., 1st Sess. 1–9 (1957).

[28] *Hearings Before the Senate Committee on Armed Services on the Nomination of Reuben Buck Robertson, Jr., to be Deputy Secretary of Defense,* 84th Cong., 1st Sess.

president of Procter and Gamble, appeared before the Committee on his nomination to be Secretary of Defense, the Committee allowed him to retain far more extensive holdings in the same company.[29]

Reasons for the differential treatment can only be speculative. Given the apparent difficulty of the Administration in filling top posts in the military departments, the Committee may have begun to be shaken by the view that recruitment of needed executives had been obstructed by the Committee's divestment policy.[30] The Committee may also have been influenced by an informal opinion submitted to McElroy by the Office of the Attorney General stating that since procurement for troop subsistence had been centralized in the office of the Secretary of the Army, the Secretary of Defense could legally disqualify himself from participating in any action involving Procter and Gamble and thus avoid "transacting business" with it.[31] Perhaps by 1957 the Committee was seeking some avenue of dignified retreat from the rigid position it had taken on divestment of stock ownership beginning with the nomination of Charles E. Wilson. Soap may have appeared less politically sensitive than either tanks or oil, and the McElroy nomination may have seemed to offer a suitable occasion for a *détente*.

The Senate Armed Services Committee has pursued its general policy of compulsory stock divestment in many confirmation hearings.[32] The instances just reviewed, however, illustrate the character of all the proceedings, and permit a few generalizations.

5–6 (1955). For the same reason he was also forced to sell his holding of 75 shares of B. F. Goodrich Company, eight ten-thousandths of the outstanding shares of that company. *Ibid.*

29 See *Hearings Before the Senate Committee on Armed Services on the Nomination of Neil Hosler McElroy to be Secretary of Defense*, 85th Cong., 1st Sess. (1957).

30 *Fortune* magazine noted on the McElroy nomination: "[I]t is an open secret that several other prominent businessmen had been approached before McElroy was finally prevailed upon to accept the Defense job. It is a reasonable presumption that one reason the other business leaders refused to be nominated was the conflict of interest bogey." *Conflict of Whose Interest*, Fortune, Sept. 1957, p. 120. See also Chapter VII *infra*.

31 *Hearings Before the Senate Committee on Armed Services on the Nomination of Neil Hosler McElroy to be Secretary of Defense*, 85th Cong., 1st Sess. 12–14 (1957).

32 Since 1953 the Senate Armed Services Committee has regularly raised the conflict of interest issue in confirmation proceedings. The most important hearings on the point are: *Hearings Before the Senate Committee on Armed Services*, 83d Cong., 1st Sess. (1953) (nominations of Charles E. Wilson, Roger M. Kyes, Robert T. Stevens, Robert B. Anderson, and Harold E. Talbott); *Hearings Before the Senate Committee*

The economic interest that has consistently drawn the Committee's attention has been stock. Other kinds of property and economic interest are seldom mentioned in the hearings.

The governmental activity with which the Committee has been primarily concerned has been procurement contracts. Other kinds of government action affecting private parties are seldom discussed.

It is difficult to identify any consistent standards of judgment used by the Committee, and the Committee members have expressed their own concern at this lack. The statutes on conflict of interest are only occasionally referred to; the senators have viewed their problem as extending far beyond the statutory prohibitions. It is unlikely that the Committee would have proceeded differently if no statutes were on the books.

Insofar as may be judged from the available facts, it is hard to predict, in any given confirmation hearing, whether the Committee will be relatively strict or comparatively lenient in its attitude on conflicts of interest. How closely must a company's business be related to defense, for example? Oil stocks are trouble, almost certainly; yet in one instance meat company stocks looked dangerous to the Committee as well.[33] And the Committee seems equally concerned, no matter how small the holding may be — whether relative to the owner's net worth, relative to other shareholders, or relative to the company's total business with the Defense Department. On the other hand, even large holdings in companies doing an extensive business with other departments or agencies seem to go unquestioned. Holdings by other family members of the appointee have never been pursued.[34]

on Armed Services on the Nomination of Dudley C. Sharp to be an Assistant Secretary of the Air Force, 84th Cong., 1st Sess. (1955); Hearings Before the Senate Committee on Armed Services on the Nomination of Reuben Buck Robertson, Jr., to be Deputy Secretary of Defense, 84th Cong., 1st Sess. (1955); Hearings Before the Senate Committee on Armed Services on the Nomination of Neil Hosler McElroy to be Secretary of Defense, 85th Cong., 1st Sess. (1957); Hearings Before the Senate Committee on Armed Services on the Nominations of Paul D. Foote and Richard Jackson, 85th Cong., 1st Sess. (1957); Hearings Before the Senate Committee on Armed Services on Nominations of Fred A. Bantz, Robert Dechert, William Howard Francis, Jr., etc., 85th Cong., 1st Sess. (1957).

33 See note 27 supra.

34 See the discussion on page 127 infra of the case of Robert. T. Ross, an instance in which the holdings of the immediate family of a government official were considered important, though not in a confirmation proceeding.

Many factors appear to enter into the Committee's judgment. Who is the nominee and how does he conduct himself? How pressed is the Committee for time? Does the nominee have individual support from a Committee member? Is public concern with the question of ethics running high? How much push has come from the White House and the Attorney General? Is the job specialized and hard to fill? Partisanship seems never to have entered significantly into the Committee's deliberations or judgments on these conflict of interest questions. Whatever may be thought about the Committee's policy in this field, and its application of that policy, it has proceeded on grounds other than party advantage.

The hearings clearly show that the Committee's preeminent concern is the appearance of impropriety. The Wilson case is illustrative. No senator argued that Mr. Wilson's behavior in office would be different after selling his General Motors holdings from what it would have been if he had kept them. Indeed, one of the senators reportedly stated that if he thought Mr. Wilson was the kind of person whose conduct *would* be affected by whether he retained or sold the shares, he would vote against his confirmation no matter what the appointee offered to sell.[35] In some measure the required stock divestment partakes of a ritual public cleansing, an act of forced ablution dedicating the actor to a public role after a private past. If Mr. Wilson had not disposed of his General Motors stock, opinion of the public and of competitors would have made it embarrassing for the Defense Department to deal with General Motors so long as Mr. Wilson was Secretary of Defense. So viewed, the objective consequence of the divestment rule is to permit, not forbid, Mr. Wilson to act for the United States in its dealings with his former company.

It is not difficult to paint the Senate Armed Service Committee's policy on stock divestment as inconsistent, and ineffective to achieve any real protective purpose. On the other hand, the Committee members have not been happy about the course they have embarked upon. In seeking to protect the integrity of the defense establishment, they have taken what they thought to be the only proper route open to them. The experience of past wars, especially in procurement

---

[35] Another expressed example of this concern for appearances is the statement of Senator Anderson made during the nomination hearings of John A. McCone. See *Hearings Before the Joint Committee on Atomic Energy on the Nomination of John A. McCone,* 85th Cong., 2d Sess. 5 (1958).

practices, counsels extreme caution against unethical practices in the prosecution of the present Cold War. While the Committee accepts the proposition that a President does not appoint knaves or fools to high posts, it has also hoped to protect itself, if things go wrong in the future, against any charge of complicity by carelessness. The Committee cannot go so far as to disapprove all nominees who have had past private interests involving defense contracting; to do so would disqualify almost all persons with experience relevant to the work of the defense establishment. In fact, divestment of present shareholdings is just about the only adjustment within the power of the Committee to enforce. Compulsory stock divestment is a cleaver, not a scalpel, but in the Committee's view it is better than nothing.

Do the Committee members believe that their conflict of interest policy has hampered the Chief Executive in filling executive posts in the defense establishment? Some of the Committee's members apparently suffer periodic twinges of concern on the point. At the same time, it is clear that the Committee has not been much impressed by pleas of personal sacrifice by nominees. As Senator Symington expressed it during the Sharp hearings in 1955:

I am personally getting a little fed up with all the talk about the great sacrifices being made by businessmen who come into government.

In this room, and around this table, if I may respectfully say so, are people like the chairman who many years ago . . . decided they wanted to be public servants. There are many people in this room, in uniform, this morning who, in effect did the same thing. The reason why these businessmen and bankers have been able to make these fortunes and have this money is because of the nature of the Government of this country, a Government which makes it possible for them to do so. There are other people who decide they prefer public service or scientific research, or go into professions or the ministry, and they are not interested in piling up money in industry.

I am a complete believer in the system of free enterprise and the profit motive but I must say that, based on the activities of this committee, all of which have been sound attempts to delineate between the obligations of a businessman and his obligation to his Government, I am beginning to get tired of listening about these great sacrifices made by people who have the opportunity to serve this Government.[36]

36 *Hearings Before the Senate Committee on Armed Services on the Nomination of Dudley C. Sharp to be an Assistant Secretary of the Air Force*, 84th Cong., 1st Sess. 14 (1955).

In the last years of the 1950's the Armed Services Committee appeared to be looking for a way to retreat somewhat from the Draconian precedent set by the Wilson hearings in 1953. Whether it actually retreats may depend in part on the development of feasible new alternative protections against the risks of conflict of interest.

OTHER SENATE COMMITTEES

In comparison to the Armed Services Committee, other Senate committees have expressed only a passing concern for the outside financial interests of presidential nominees. A few examples drawn from confirmation hearings of other committees will serve as illustrations.

Senate Finance Committee

On January 19, 1953, only four days after Mr. Wilson's first appearance before a congressional committee, the Senate Finance Committee considered the nomination of George M. Humphrey as Secretary of the Treasury.[37] Humphrey was a member and former chairman of the Business Advisory Council of the Department of Commerce. He reported that he had resigned all offices and directorships in various companies, but he was on leave without pay as an employee of the Industrial Rayon Corporation, which permitted him to retain group insurance, and of the M. A. Hanna Company, which continued his retirement rights.[38] He testified that he would receive no salary or bonus in addition to his government pay. His securities holdings consisted entirely of common stocks of four companies of whose managements he was a dominant member, including the M. A. Hanna Company, which owned substantial stock in several major corporations.

Humphrey told the Committee that he would insulate himself from any activity involving these companies: "I shall, of course, advise my immediate assistants to see to it that I have no participation in the decision of any case or transaction involving any of the companies in which, through stock ownership, I am directly or in-

[37] See *Hearings Before the Senate Committee on Finance on Nominations of George M. Humphrey, Secretary of the Treasury–Designate; Oveta Culp Hobby, Federal Security Administrator–Designate,* 83d Cong., 1st Sess. (1953).

[38] Compare the discussion in Chapter III *supra* respecting the scope of section 1914 of title 18.

directly interested." [39] The Committee was skeptical. Senator Kerr noted that personal disqualification did not eliminate his responsibility for the acts of his subordinates. Senator Johnson, who had also participated in the Wilson hearing, declared: "Mr. Humphrey, you have stated that should any occasion arise where a decision had to be made as between some of these companies with which you had a former connection and the Treasury, that you would delegate that function to your aides. These aides are, of course, beholden to you and work for you and naturally would be prejudiced." [40] In the end, however, the Committee permitted Humphrey to retain his stock. One factor, no doubt, was that the Secretary of the Treasury has almost nothing to do with the assumed danger area, procurement. Further, divestment did not seem a practical precondition to the post of Secretary of the Treasury. As Humphrey said:

. . . suppose I sold everything I had. . . . It would be a tremendous hardship and whether it could be done or not is a problem, but suppose you did. How would you account for what you received for it? Would you leave it in cash in the bank? If so, would you then be under the compulsion of perhaps favoring in some way that bank because, of course, the Secretary deals with that bank in one way or another. Would you put it in Government bonds? If so, there is nothing that the Secretary of the Treasury could so influence by his conduct as Government bonds.

I can as Secretary . . . have more influence on the price of Government bonds and the value of them, a whole lot, than I can on the value of M. A. Hanna common stock when I am no longer an officer, representative, or connected with the firm.

Now you get yourselves into a situation where, if you do not be practical about this thing that you can so draw the laws that you just cannot have a Secretary of the Treasury unless he is a man who has nothing.[41]

Mrs. Oveta Culp Hobby followed Humphrey to the stand. Her nomination as Federal Security Administrator was warmly endorsed by the two Texas Senators, Lyndon Johnson and Price Daniel. Mrs. Hobby reported that she had resigned from all boards of directors and other offices which she had previously held. She filed a list of

---

39 See *Hearings, supra* note 37, at 3.
40 *Id.* at 6.
41 *Id.* at 9. It is interesting that Mr. Humphrey's hypothetical example is one squarely met by 5 U.S.C. § 243, forbidding the Secretary of the Treasury to own Government securities. See Chapter III, note 3 *supra*.

holdings with the Committee, and reported that she could visualize no conflict between her business interests in oil, real estate, hotels, banks, paper mills, and a Houston newspaper firm and the government position to which she had been appointed. The hearing was gay and pleasant, and the Committee indicated unofficially its approval of her nomination.[42]

In subsequent hearings the Finance Committee has only occasionally asked nominees a few questions about their financial interests.[43]

Joint Atomic Energy Committee

One hearing before the Joint Committee on Atomic Energy merits mention. On June 6, 1958, President Eisenhower nominated John A. McCone to be a member of the Atomic Energy Commission. Membership on the AEC was a highly sensitive post from the standpoint of conflicts of interest, because of the web of contractual relationships of the AEC with hundreds of business enterprises, educational institutions, and other firms. In hearings before the Senate Section of the Joint Committee on Atomic Energy, McCone was requested to submit a statement of his financial holdings, business activities, and other affiliations and those of his wife. He stated to the Committee that in accordance with the Atomic Energy Act he would not, during his term of office, engage in any outside business, occupa-

---

[42] See *Hearings Before the Senate Committee on Finance on Nominations of George M. Humphrey, Secretary of the Treasury–Designate; Oveta Culp Hobby, Federal Security Administrator–Designate,* 83d Cong., 1st Sess. (1953).

[43] For example, one week after the appearance of Mr. Humphrey and Mrs. Hobby, the Committee heard testimony from several nominees to positions in the Treasury Department. See generally *Hearings Before the Senate Committee on Finance on the Nominations of Ivy Baker Priest, Marion B. Folsom, H. Chapman Rose, Albert P. Tuttle, and T. Coleman Andrews,* 83d Cong., 1st Sess. (1953). In a three-minute hearing, Mrs. Ivy Baker Priest, Treasurer of the United States–designate, reported that she had no conflicting financial interests. Marion B. Folsom, Under Secretary of the Treasury–designate, in a ten-minute appearance reported that he had resigned from the Federal Reserve Bank of New York, retained his vested pension rights with Eastman Kodak Company, held shares in Kodak and other companies, and would receive a "wage dividend" from Eastman Kodak for past services. H. Chapman Rose, who was nominated to be an Assistant Secretary of the Treasury, stated that he had resigned from his law firm and from all directorships, would dispose voluntarily of minor investments in oil leases, and believed that no conflict existed between his personal interests and his government post. Albert P. Tuttle, nominated to be General Counsel of the Department, reported his resignation from his law firm and the sale of all of his stockholdings except in one small textile mill. T. Coleman Andrews, designated to be Commissioner of Internal Revenue, indicated in a somewhat longer hearing of thirty minutes that, if confirmed, he would resign from all business firms with which he was connected. All were promptly confirmed.

tion, or profession.[44] He arranged to dispose of minority holdings in two small companies because control of the companies was in the hands of a family that also controlled Bechtel Corporation, an AEC contractor. He proposed to dispose of his partnership interests and to resign as a director and officer of all profit-making, educational, and nonprofit organizations holding AEC contracts. He offered to dispose of his shares in Dow Chemical Company and Tennessee Gas Transmission Company, both important AEC contractors. He also owned stock in several smaller personally owned companies unrelated to atomic energy. The latter stock he put in an irrevocable trust with a bank as trustee for a period of seven years or for his term of office, whichever proved shorter. The trust agreement, a copy of which he filed with the Committee, provided that he would remove himself from the control of these corporations, either directly or indirectly, that the trustees were empowered to vote the stock, that he would be free from all management responsibilities, and that the companies involved were prevented from entering into contracts with the AEC or acquiring any stock in companies holding AEC contracts.[45] Anticipating the line of questioning the Committee was likely to follow, McCone sought and got a legal opinion supporting this arrangement from the Assistant Attorney General in charge of the Office of Legal Counsel in the Department of Justice. This opinion was produced at the hearing for the consideration of the Committee.[46] The Committee went along with the adjustments outlined by McCone, and McCone was confirmed.

The McCone instance is interesting. It may illustrate that careful pre-hearing staff work, a well worked out adjustment plan, and legal assistance from within the executive branch can together make a substantial impression on the confirming committee and in the long run lead to the stabilization of standards in this now unordered field.

Senate Commerce Committee

The Senate Commerce Committee conducts confirmation hearings for nominees to five regulatory commissions: The Civil Aeronautics Board, the Federal Communications Commission, the

---

[44] See 68 Stat. 924 (1954), 42 U.S.C. § 2032(b) (Supp. IV, 1957).

[45] *Hearings Before the Joint Committee on Atomic Energy on the Nomination of John A. McCone*, 85th Cong., 2d Sess. 4 (1958).

[46] The concluding paragraph of the legal opinion is printed in the McCone hearings. *Id.* at 6.

Federal Power Commission, the Federal Trade Commission, and the Interstate Commerce Commission. In the six years from 1953 through 1958, the Committee conducted forty-eight hearings on commissioners-designate. In only one of these hearings was a substantial issue of conflicting interests raised.[47] In fifteen hearings, one or two minor or passing questions relating to conflicts of interest were asked.[48] In thirty-two hearings, not a single query was raised on the point. When questions related to conflicts of interest arose, they were normally incidental to a general discussion of the capacity of the nominee to serve as commissioner without bias or prejudice. About two-thirds of all nominees to posts on the regulatory commissions are lawyers. The Committee tends to be satisfied if the

[47] And that case offers a perfect example of the way in which personal economic conflict of interest issues shade off into differences in policy viewpoints, as was discussed in Chapter II. John B. Hussey was nominated by President Eisenhower in 1958 to be a member of the Federal Power Commission. Hussey, a Democrat and Commissioner of Conservation of the State of Louisiana, had been permitted to practice law while serving as State Commissioner. In 1955, upon the proposal of certain oil firms, Hussey had intervened in the name of the State of Louisiana in three rate cases involving the oil firms. The purpose of his intervention was to testify that Louisiana did not consider the gas-producing industry to be a utility or public service industry. The state was not a party to the proceedings, and Hussey's expenses were paid by the oil firms, but he did not receive a legal fee. In the confirmation hearing Hussey was pursued on the point of his dual public-private role, and he agreed to resign from his law firm if confirmed. But though the main line of questioning was couched in conflict of interest terms, the concern on the part of some senators seemed to be that Hussey might be committed to one side of the controversy over pricing methods in natural gas and over the proper jurisdiction of the FPC in regulating the natural gas industry. See *Hearings Before the Senate Committee on Interstate and Foreign Commerce on Miscellaneous Nominations,* 85th Cong., 1st & 2d Sess. 193–211 (1958). Hussey was ultimately confirmed.

[48] An example is provided by the hearing on the nomination of John S. Cross to be Commissioner of the Federal Communications Commission to succeed Richard A. Mack, who resigned under fire of charges of unethical behavior. Cross was a federal civil servant from 1932 to 1958, except during the period of World War II. He testified that neither he nor his family had any pecuniary interests related to the communications industry, and that he had never represented private organizations before any commission or agency. In reply to senatorial questions, he asserted that a man in public life should not accept favors; he agreed that a public official "must appear to be right as well as be right," and that a commissioner should not have his expenses paid by private hosts when he also accepts expense money from the government. Thus, though the general subject of ethics was raised, no effort was made to pursue a line of questioning about the individual's private economic interests. See *Hearings Before the Senate Committee on Interstate and Foreign Commerce on Miscellaneous Nominations,* 85th Cong., 1st & 2d Sess. 245–86 (1958).

The atmosphere of the Committee's hearing on the nomination of Richard A. Mack to the FCC was friendly and gave no hint of the trouble to come. See *Hearings Before the Senate Committee on Interstate and Foreign Commerce on Sundry Nominations,* 84th Cong., 2d Sess. 73–78 (1956).

lawyer-nominee severs his relations with his former law firm, and questions of stockholdings and severance from business entities are not apt to arise.

Senate Labor Committee

In six hearings conducted by the Senate Labor Committee on nominations to the National Labor Relations Board from 1953 through 1958, the issue of conflicting interests was raised in only one case. The matter arose in highly partisan circumstances. Albert C. Beeson, an executive of Food Machinery and Chemical Corporation, was nominated to the NLRB in 1953.[49] The hearing was acrimonious and partisan. Underlying the element of partisanship was the fact that the Board was evenly divided in party designation, with two Republicans, two Democrats, and one vacancy. Beeson's confirmation would give the Republicans a majority. Beeson had been granted a leave of absence by his company. This permitted him to retain pension rights he would have lost if he had resigned. Senator Kennedy suggested that retention of the pension rights in his company while serving on the NLRB would create an impermissible conflict of interest. The recorded opposition to Beeson centered on this alleged incompatibility and on charges of contradictory testimony, but the main ground for Democratic opposition appeared to be his assumed views on labor issues. In the end he was confirmed.

The over-all record of the Senate in confirmation proceedings may be summarized more clearly than its details.

Only the Armed Services Committee regularly inquires into the outside financial interests of presidential nominees. This committee proceeds case by case on an *ad hoc* basis, but in general has been very strict in its stock divestment requirement. Contract procurement in the defense program is considered especially sensitive to risk, and this concern largely accounts for the special attention given by the Armed Services Committee to conflict of interest questions. The strict divestment policy of the Armed Services Committee has been a thorn in the President's side in making appointments to the Department of

---

[49] *Hearings Before the Senate Committee on Labor and Public Welfare on the Nomination of Albert C. Beeson to be a Member of the National Labor Relations Board,* 83d Cong., 2d Sess. (1954).

Defense.[50] It has begun to appear that accumulated experience, as well as preparation and legal staffing by the executive branch in advance of the hearings, may be having a stabilizing effect, and that the Committee itself may be moving away from its most extreme position on divestment.

On rare occasions, three or four other committees in the Senate have looked into possible conflicting interests of nominees appearing before them. While the Armed Services Committee has performed its function of giving advice and consent with an apparent minimum of partisanship, the few instances where conflicts issues have arisen before other confirming committees appear to have entailed partisan considerations or differences of opinion on issues of public policy.

The statutes on conflict of interest have received little mention in confirmation hearings. The confirmation hearings repeatedly emphasize the significance of appearances and the need for maintaining public confidence.

INVESTIGATIONS OF GENERAL ISSUES

The Senate's confirmation practices have little operational effect on the day-to-day working of the executive branch. The hearing process is a one-time individual gantlet run by a top executive; it has no sustained significance to the institutional life of his agency. What Congress does through its continuing investigation committees is of a different order. Investigations, inquiries, and resolutions reaching back many years often result in legislation. But the investigatory process has its own independent effects on history — whether or not legislation ultimately materializes from it.

Congress has devoted much time in recent years to the problem of ethics in the executive branch. Much of this attention has taken the form of general investigations. Concern for good government, fundamental institutional competition between Congress and the executive, the political appeal in smiting the Devil hip and thigh, and the normal instincts of the non-Administration party in Congress to take pot shots at the Administration's officials — these and other factors make it easy to account for the zest with which members of Congress plunge into surveys of the public morality of the executive

50 See Chapter VII, notes 6 & 7 *infra* and accompanying text.

branch. Congressional investigations and hearings have seldom dealt exclusively with the conflict of interest problem; as a rule they are broader in scope, with the conflict of interest issue subsumed as one of many issues, or touched upon only peripherally.

Between 1948 and 1953, Congress was active in studying instances of alleged improprieties in various agencies.[51] In these inquiries conflicts of interest generally played only a secondary role. In the studies of alleged speculation in commodity markets in agricultural produce, the committees did deal with purported misuse by officials of confidential information for personal, private gain. Activities of an "influence ring" reaching into White House offices were uncovered by Senator Fulbright and his associates. But no prosecutions under the conflict of interest statutes resulted. Similarly the work of the House Ways and Means Committee in 1951–52 led to discovery of instances of corruption in the Treasury Department and the Internal Revenue Bureau, but the consequent prosecutions were grounded on other criminal statutes, not the conflict of interest statutes.[52]

The investigation of the Department of Justice treated conflict of interest matters briefly. A legal consultant to the Office of the Assistant Attorney General was interrogated about the Department's enforcement of the conflict of interest statutes, and a troublesome case was smoked out involving fee-splitting between a Justice De-

[51] Speculation in commodity markets was investigated by both the Senate Committee on Agriculture and Forestry and the Senate Appropriations Committee in 1948 and also by a House Select Committee to Investigate Commodity Transactions in 1949. Maladministration in the Reconstruction Finance Corporation was studied extensively from 1949 to 1951 by the Senate Committee on Banking and Currency. A further study of the storage and processing activities of the Commodity Credit Corporation in the Department of Agriculture was completed by the Senate Committee on Agriculture and Forestry in 1952. Scandals in the Bureau of Internal Revenue were investigated by the House Ways and Means Committee in 1952. A subcommittee of the House Committee on the Judiciary launched an inquiry into the administration of the Department of Justice in 1952 but did not submit its report until 1953. The last investigation of an agency's activity during the Truman Administrations was the inquiry by the Senate Banking and Currency Committee in 1954 into the management of the Federal Housing Administration.

[52] See *Hearings Before the Subcommittee on Administration of the Internal Revenue Laws of the House Committee on Ways and Means Concerning an Internal Revenue Investigation,* 82d Cong., 1st & 2d Sess. (1951–52). The findings, recommendations, and results are contained in H.R. REP. No. 2518, 82d Cong., 2d Sess. (1952). In 1952 the President also submitted proposals to strengthen the administrative organization of the Bureau of Internal Revenue to assure honest and impartial administration. See *Hearings Before the House Committee on Expenditures in the Executive Departments on Reorganization Plan No. 1 of 1952,* 82d Cong., 2d Sess. (1952).

partment attorney and a former departmental employee.[53] In its examination of the program of the Federal Housing Administration, the Senate Banking and Currency Committee concluded that one of the more significant factors accounting for unrealistic estimates and appraisals by FHA employees was their conflicting private interests.[54]

In long-range significance the work done in 1951 by the subcommittee of the Senate Committee on Labor and Public Welfare, under the chairmanship of Senator Douglas of Illinois, ranks high. The work of the Douglas Committee in the general field of governmental ethics, including conflict of interest, was the first such broad review in a quarter-century.[55] The final report told the nation that the government had a problem of general ethics on its hands, not a matter of snaring a few moral delinquents but rather one of identifying and remedying major patterns of practice throughout the modern federal establishment. As a result of the disclosures of instances of unethical practices in the waning days of the Truman regime, the Douglas Committee hearings and report, and the high political temperature of the issue of ethics in the 1952 election, there was extensive redrafting and tightening of agency regulations and practices in the years following. Even without new legislation and by their mere existence, the congressional investigating committees achieved some of their objectives.

In the late 1950's, a congressional investigation was finally trained

53 *Hearings Before the Special Subcommittee of the House Committee on the Judiciary Concerning an Investigation of the Department of Justice*, 82d Cong., 2d Sess. 966–90 (1952). In 1953, under the chairmanship of Congressman Keating of New York, the Special Subcommittee to Investigate the Department of Justice conducted extensive hearings and investigated several hundred complaints of improper conduct in the Department, including those against T. Lamar Caudle, a former Assistant Attorney General in charge of the Tax Division, who was later indicted and convicted. See *Hearings Before the Special Subcommittee of the House Committee on the Judiciary Concerning an Investigation of the Department of Justice*, 83d Cong., 1st Sess. 659–82, 691–705, 707–41, 1419–71, 1970–2018 (1953), and N.Y. Times, June 15, 1956, p. 1, col. 6.

54 It was disclosed, for example, that a former FHA state director had retained his partnership in a firm that had 64 FHA rental housing projects processed through the state FHA office under his direction. Other instances were cited in which lower-rank employees were hired by builders to work on plans to be submitted for approval to the FHA. In some cases, FHA employees had approved, in their official capacity, plans which they had drafted or helped to prepare for builders. See S. Rep. No. 1, 84th Cong., 1st Sess. 18–29 (1955).

55 Subcomm., Senate Comm. on Labor and Public Welfare, 82d Cong., 1st Sess., Report on Ethical Standards in Government (Comm. Print 1951).

directly upon the separate problem of conflict of interest. The Antitrust Subcommittee of the House Committee on the Judiciary — under the chairmanship of Representative Emanuel Celler of New York — began its work in pursuit of a relatively narrow question: whether violations of the conflict of interest statutes is apt to lead to violations of the antitrust laws. This approach first led the subcommittee to an exploration of the government's use of experts and consultants. As the investigation proceeded, however, the Celler Committee expanded its attention to the whole related field of conflict of interest. The subcommittee's staff report, published in December of 1958, is a lengthy work based on a careful review of the conflict of interest statutes, regulations, and practices.[56] It is not now possible to predict what effects this serious study may have. Indications are that the inquiries preceding the Celler report and the report itself have awakened some agencies to the need for revision of their own practices in this field. Further hearings by the Celler subcommittee opened in February 1960.

Apart from its recurrent interest in the general level of ethical conduct in the executive branch, illustrated by the activities of the Douglas and Celler Committees, Congress has in recent years pursued several specific issues relating to conflict of interest. Four such topics have been covered in varying degrees by different congressional committees.

One was an inquiry into the regulation of outside employment of government employees. In its hearings in 1958 on this subject the Senate Committee on Government Operations hoped to develop a basis for legislation prohibiting government employees from engaging in nongovernment work closely related to their official duties without the prior approval of their administrative superiors.[57]

The second topic was the special problem of the relationships

---

56 See STAFF OF SUBCOMM. NO. 5, HOUSE COMM. ON THE JUDICIARY, 85TH CONG., 2D SESS., REPORT ON FEDERAL CONFLICT OF INTEREST LEGISLATION (Comm. Print 1958).

57 As a result of complaints received by the Senate Committee on Government Operations in 1956, the General Accounting Office was requested to investigate the practice of certain federal employees who engaged in map-making work for private concerns. After the General Accounting Office reported to the Committee in 1957, Senator Aiken sponsored a measure to prohibit government employees from engaging in any outside employment "which (1) is so related to their official duties . . . or to the functions of the respective agencies in which they are employed, that a reasonable question of propriety might be raised, or (2) may tend to impair their mental or

between military officers and government contractors. There was
nothing novel in congressional anxiety about the handling of procurement contracts related to defense, but neither the relations between procurement officials and contractors, nor the employment of
former personnel of the Defense Department by defense contractors,
had been explored by a congressional committee until 1957.[58] A
second set of hearings on retired officers dealing with defense departments on procurement matters was held in the summer of 1959
by the Subcommittee on Special Investigations of the House Armed
Services Committee, and in a report released in January of 1960,
this subcommittee proposed several amendments to the statutes
applicable to retired officers.[59]

Third, since 1957, hearings and debate have been more or less
continuous on the problem of ex parte communications with quasi-
judicial agencies. Many bills have been introduced designed to pre-

---

physical capacity to render proper and efficient service." For a full account, see *Hearings
Before the Senate Committee on Government Operations on S. 2259*, 85th Cong., 2d
Sess. (1958). Various agencies opposed the bill on the ground that they already possessed
ample authority to deal with abuses of outside employment. The Bureau of the
Budget, for example, noted that "the internal administrative regulations of the
agencies are designed to cover the situations . . . . in a more thorough and restrictive
manner than would be possible under a general statute." *Id.* at 9. The objective of the
bill was not to prohibit all employment after hours, but to require prior approval.

58 In 1957, in its Twelfth Report, the Preparedness Investigating Subcommittee of
the Senate Armed Services Committee studied the role of military officers in defense
procurement. Chairman Johnson stated: "The question is pointed up because, from
the military as from other Government departments and agencies, there is a steady
flow of personnel, civilian and military, into jobs in private industry with firms engaged
in defense work. The subcommittee draws no adverse inferences from this fact alone,
and it is not our intention to single out either the civilian or military personnel leaving
the service as special objects of our remarks. At the same time, the subcommittee con-
cedes that efficacious administrative safeguards in aid of pertinent legislation are
essential ingredients of any program entirely dedicated to the public interest in
economical and efficient procurement." The report provided a detailed analysis of
pertinent legislation and administrative regulations in the armed services. The regulations of the Air Force governing conflicts of interest were described as satisfactory, those
of the Army as limited in effectiveness, and those of the Navy as almost wholly inadequate. Emphasis was placed upon the lack of uniformity among the services in the
interpretation of the statutes. The subcommittee recommended that the Secretary of
Defense issue regulations applicable uniformly to all services. PREPAREDNESS INVESTIGAT-
ING SUBCOMM., SENATE COMM. ON ARMED SERVICES, 85TH CONG., 1ST SESS., TWELFTH RE-
PORT, CONFLICT OF INTEREST IN THE ARMED SERVICES iii and *passim* (Comm. Print 1957).

59 See SUBCOMM. FOR SPECIAL INVESTIGATIONS, HOUSE COMM. ON ARMED SERVICES,
86TH CONG., 1ST SESS., REPORT ON EMPLOYMENT OF RETIRED COMMISSIONED OFFICERS BY
DEFENSE DEPARTMENT CONTRACTORS (Comm. Print 1960). See discussion Chapter X *infra*,
under "Military procurement and employment of retired officers," and Appendix B.

vent secret, behind-the-scenes pressures on regulatory agencies like the Federal Communications Commission.[60]

The fourth topic of investigation relating to conflict of interest problems was the employment of experts and consultants without compensation in federal agencies. This was a dominant issue during 1955 and 1956 and the topic with which the Celler subcommittee began. The Democratic majority in the subcommittee's 1955 Report saw in the Business Advisory Council of the Department of Commerce the exploitation of government by a private group for private advantage; the Republican minority found satisfaction in the "free exchange of ideas between Government executives and their advisers from the public at large" and the maintenance of "the citizens' right to confer with their Government." [61] In a 1956 report, the Celler subcommittee was concerned particularly with the employment of persons serving without compensation (WOCs) in the Business and Defense Services Administration of the Department of Commerce. Here the Democrats concluded that "the objective really being served in the appointment of many WOC's in . . . [the Business and Defense Services Administration is] the placing of company or industry representatives in the agency." [62] The Republican minority challenged this conclusion:

A theme that runs through the report is the implication that it is not entirely proper for the Department of Commerce, and in turn BDSA, to serve as a conduit and sounding board for the views of the business community. The logic of this complaint with respect to the agency of Government charged with fostering and promoting this country's trade and commerce is indeed difficult to comprehend. What is more natural than the utilization by such an agency of business advisory groups and without-compensation personnel, particularly when authorized by express congressional enactment? It seems plain that the disclosure by the sub-

[60] See *Hearings Before a Subcommittee of the Senate Committee on the Judiciary on a Proposal to Prohibit Communications on Matters for Adjudication,* 85th Cong., 2d Sess. (1958). See also H.R. REP. No. 2711, 85th Cong., 2d Sess. (1958). Major portions of the House report were devoted to individual cases of alleged improprieties involving regulatory commissions, some of which are discussed in this chapter *infra.* But the subcommittee was particularly concerned about improper ex parte pressures in adjudicatory and rule-making proceedings.

[61] ANTITRUST SUBCOMM., HOUSE COMM. ON THE JUDICIARY, 84TH CONG., 1ST SESS., INTERIM REPORT ON THE BUSINESS ADVISORY COUNCIL FOR THE DEPARTMENT OF COMMERCE 34, 35 (Comm. Print 1955).

[62] ANTITRUST SUBCOMM., HOUSE COMM. ON THE JUDICIARY, 84TH CONG., 2D SESS., INTERIM REPORT ON WOC's AND GOVERNMENT ADVISORY GROUPS 34 (Comm. Print 1956).

committee's investigation of a few deviations from what the report considers to be the norm is being resorted to for the purpose of making an oblique attack on American business and industry.[63]

In the course of and as a part of the general foment of congressional interest in executive ethics, the last few sessions of Congress have seen a stream of proposed bills on different aspects of the topic. The footnote collects, by way of illustration, related bills and resolutions introduced in 1958 in the 85th Congress, second session.[64] Most of these bills and resolutions were referred to committee and disappeared; hearings were held on some; some were almost unrecognizably amended and consolidated into others. Out of the welter of proposals, nothing had yet emerged as legislation by the spring of 1960, but the two houses of Congress did pass in 1958 a joint resolution in favor of integrity in the government service.[65] This joint

[63] *Id.* at 109.

[64] These bills and resolutions include: S. 4223 (disclosure of interests bill); S. 4078 (code of ethics bill); S. 3979 (bill to include members of Congress under various conflicts sections); S. 3306 (ex parte contacts and gifts bill); S.J. Res. 186 (bill to establish a Commission on Ethics); H.R. 13216 (code of ethics bill); H.R. 13036 (ex parte contacts bill); H.R. 13035 (ex parte contacts bill); H.R. 12547 (bill aimed at a comprehensive revision of the conflict of interest statutes); and H.R. Con. Res. 175 (code of ethics bill).

[65] H.R. Con. Res. 175, 85th Cong., 2d Sess. (1958). The resolution reads:

"*Resolved by the House of Representatives (the Senate concurring),* That it is the sense of the Congress that the following Code of Ethics should be adhered to by all Government employees, including officeholders:

CODE OF ETHICS FOR GOVERNMENT SERVICE

Any person in Government service should:

1. Put loyalty to the highest moral principles and to country above loyalty to persons, party, or Government department.

2. Uphold the Constitution, laws, and legal regulations of the United States and of all governments therein and never be a party to their evasion.

3. Give a full day's labor for a full day's pay; giving to the performance of his duties his earnest effort and best thought.

4. Seek to find and employ more efficient and economical ways of getting tasks accomplished.

5. Never discriminate unfairly by the dispensing of special favors or privileges to anyone, whether for remuneration or not; and never accept, for himself or his family, favors or benefits under circumstances which might be construed by reasonable persons as influencing the performance of his governmental duties.

6. Make no private promises of any kind binding upon the duties of office, since a Government employee has no private word which can be binding on public duty.

7. Engage in no business with the Government, either directly or indirectly, which is inconsistent with the conscientious performance of his governmental duties.

8. Never use any information coming to him confidentially in the performance of governmental duties as a means for making private profit.

9. Expose corruption wherever discovered.

10. Uphold these principles, ever conscious that public office is a public trust."

resolution is a new decalogue for the government employee. Hortatory in tone and sweeping in content, it does not seriously purport to offer any administrative machinery for improving the conduct of federal employees.

To judge from the amount of congressional activity observable in the 1950's, the slow yeasting process of legislation in the field of governmental ethics appears to be in course. Interest is high. The number of committees working in the area is large; the amount of political capital committed to the topic is substantial; and obligingly from time to time some executive official gets caught off base and ethics are back in the headlines. New legislation in the field may not be far off. A number of agencies, hoping perhaps to anticipate restrictive congressional action and thereby head it off, are involved in a reworking of their own procedures and regulations.[66] Whether or not new legislation crystallizes, the main current of general congressional investigation has been a significant force.

INVESTIGATIONS OF INDIVIDUALS AND PARTICULAR TRANSACTIONS

Only the Senate has the legal power of confirmation. But each House has what might be called a limited political power of deconfirmation — the capacity in some circumstances to force executive resignations. A major role of Congress in conflict of interest matters is in this deconfirmation process, where Congress acts as investigator, grand jury, and publicizer in individual cases of officials and employees charged with misconduct. The investigatory process aimed at a particular individual is usually easy to differentiate from a general legislative investigation of a topic — but not always. What begins as a probe into the deviations of one man sometimes develops into a broader inquiry into the circumstances that permit or perhaps encourage men to deviate. The investigation of an FCC Commissioner, for example, developed into a full scale consideration of the problem of ex parte communication with regulatory commissions.

As investigator, Congress is apt to perform in highly partisan

---

[66] For example, in 1959 the Federal Power Commission was considering adopting new regulations on ethics and conflict of interest. See N.Y. Herald Tribune, July 6, 1959, p. 11, col. 5. See also the efforts of the Attorney General to develop a basis for government-wide rules on advisory committees, Chapter IV *supra*.

fashion. Partisanship has not destroyed its effectiveness, however. Indeed, through the process of forced executive resignations, Congress has by and large been more successful in articulating standards of employee conduct than it has in its other functions relating to conflict of interest. Some examples of this process at work during the last two administrations will illustrate.

During the last four years of the Truman administration, congressional investigations charged several executives and others connected with the government with unethical conduct.[67] Most of these cases did not fall within the category of conflicts of interest, but two instances may be so viewed. In the course of inquiries by the Fulbright Committee in 1950–51, Donald S. Dawson, personnel adviser to President Truman, was charged with improperly using his White House influence to persuade the RFC to grant certain loans.[68] Before Senator Hoey's Investigations subcommittee, Harry A. Vaughan, a Major General and President Truman's military aide, was charged with abusing his White House position in various ways ranging from accepting gifts from favor seekers to allowing a friend to use his office to carry on personal and illicit business activities.[69] While neither man resigned, these investigations by congressional committees helped to focus public attention on the issue of the ethics of government officials, and had significant political repercussions.

[67] Some of the instances involved issues approaching bribery. Some were cases of "influence peddlers," including both high officials and private people with government connections, called "five percenters" because of their fee charged for assistance in obtaining government contracts. Some were of a special nature, such as the case of an alleged influence peddler who was convicted for perjury before a congressional committee. See S. REP. No. 76, 82d Cong., 1st Sess. (1951); *Hearings Before the Senate Committee on Banking and Currency Concerning a Study of the Reconstruction Finance Corporation*, 81st Cong., 2d Sess. pt. 3 (1950); *Hearings Before the Senate Committee on Banking and Currency Concerning an Investigation of the Loan Policy of the Reconstruction Finance Corporation*, 81st Cong., 1st Sess. (1949). See also *Hearings Before the Special Subcommittee of the House Committee on the Judiciary Concerning an Investigation of the Department of Justice*, 82d Cong., 2d Sess. (1952) and 83d Cong., 1st Sess. (1953).

[68] See *Hearings Before a Subcommittee of the Senate Committee on Banking and Currency Concerning a Study of the Reconstruction Finance Corporation*, 81st Cong., 2d Sess. (1950). The findings are summarized in S. REP. No. 76, 82d Cong., 1st Sess. (1951).

[69] See *Hearings Before the Investigations Subcommittee of the Senate Committee on Expenditures in the Executive Department on Influence in Government Procurement*, 81st Cong., 1st Sess. (1949). The findings are summarized in S. REP. No. 1232, 81st Cong., 2d Sess. (1950).

More of the ethical questions that have arisen since the change of administration in 1953 have been conflict of interest questions and problems of public appearances. The seven instances reviewed here are illustrative of the kinds of issues that have arisen.[70] To be noted especially in these instances is the continual reaching out by the congressional committees for standards of judgment and behavior more demanding than anything appearing in the conflict of interest statutes or the regulations. The assumption seems almost to be that there is a stringent body of principles governing employee conduct that, though unwritten, has virtually the force of law — that executive officials are charged with knowledge of these principles, and violate them at the risk of public disgrace.

In the Senate, the prosecuting function has been carried out by the Permanent Subcommittee on Investigations of the Committee on Government Operations. Before this subcommittee in 1955 came the case of Harold E. Talbott, Secretary of the Air Force.[71] The hearings disclosed that Talbott had apparently recommended the services of a firm in which he was a partner to certain companies doing business with the military departments, including the Air Force.[72] Talbott had not violated any of the conflict of interest statutes; the issue was whether he had used his public office to help direct business toward his own firm. Talbott submitted his resignation. The subcommittee concluded that the case had been resolved satisfactorily, and the investigation was terminated.

The same subcommittee considered the case of Hugh W. Cross, Chairman of the Interstate Commerce Commission.[73] The Cross case

[70] Three relevant committee investigations since 1953 are not discussed here since they throw no novel light on the general conflict of interest problem. See *Hearings Before the Antitrust Subcommittee of the House Committee on the Judiciary on the Conduct in Office of Robert Tieken*, 85th Cong., 2d Sess. (1958); ANTITRUST SUBCOMM., HOUSE COMM. ON THE JUDICIARY, 85TH CONG., 2D SESS., REPORT ON CONDUCT IN OFFICE OF ROBERT TIEKEN (Comm. Print 1958); S. REP. No. 1, 84th Cong., 1st Sess. (1955) (Clyde M. Powell); and JOINT COMM. ON DEFENSE PRODUCTION, 84TH CONG., 1ST SESS., DEFENSE PRODUCTION ACT PROGRESS REPORT NO. 33, TO HEAR EDMUND T. MANSURE, ADMINISTRATOR, GENERAL SERVICES ADMINISTRATION (Comm. Print 1955).

[71] *Hearings Before the Permanent Subcommittee on Investigations of the Senate Committee on Government Operations Concerning Harold E. Talbott — Secretary of the Air Force*, 84th Cong., 1st Sess. (1955).

[72] The partnership was the partnership referred to in Talbott's confirmation hearings. See note 22 *supra* and accompanying text.

[73] *Hearings Before the Permanent Subcommittee on Investigations of the Senate Committee on Government Operations Concerning Hugh W. Cross, Chairman of the Interstate Commerce Commission*, 84th Cong., 2d Sess. (1955).

was similar to the Talbott case in that the issue was again the alleged use of the prestige and influence of public office to gain personal advantage in private life. The particular charge was that Cross had sought to have certain railroads give a contract to a company with which he apparently desired to assume a position upon leaving government employ. Again, such conduct would not have been illegal under the statutes, but in the midst of the publicity raised by the subcommittee's investigation, the President accepted Cross's resignation.

The Antitrust Subcommittee of the House Judiciary Committee in 1955 investigated the activities of Peter A. Strobel, Public Buildings Commissioner.[74] Strobel had been a partner in a firm of consulting engineers, and under a modified arrangement, he retained his partnership interest on entering government service. In a highly partisan hearing, it was charged that as a government official he had continued his activity in the partnership and had solicited business for it. Three Democrats on the subcommittee concluded that Strobel's position was "fundamentally inconsistent and untenable." [75] The three Republicans on the subcommittee found no evidence of "any conduct that was unethical or in violation of any conflict of interest statutes," though they agreed that Strobel's retention of a substantial interest in his firm placed him in a "fundamentally inconsistent and untenable position." [76] A fourth Democrat who was resigning from the House filed a letter with the subcommittee between the time of the hearings and the time the subcommittee met to consider them. He found any implication of wrongdoing by Strobel "completely unjustified." [77] In the meantime, before the subcommittee report was out, Strobel resigned.[78]

---

[74] *Hearings Before the Antitrust Subcommittee of the House Committee on the Judiciary Concerning Activities of Peter A. Strobel*, 84th Cong., 1st Sess., ser. 14 (1955); ANTITRUST SUBCOMM., HOUSE COMM. ON THE JUDICIARY, 84TH CONG., 1ST SESS., REPORT ON THE ACTIVITIES OF PETER A. STROBEL (Comm. Print 1956).

[75] *Id.* at 15.　　　　[76] *Id.* at 26.　　　　[77] *Id.* at 36.

[78] *Id.* at 14.

Congressman Keating feared that a rule requiring government officials to sever all outside business and financial connections would seriously deter recruitment of competent executives. He may also have been concerned about applying to the executive branch a rule that congressmen could not live with. He said: "It raises a much bigger question, whether anyone coming into Government employ should give up completely all outside business connections and interests, dispose of his holdings and get out. That can be done sometimes with regard to a person who has only stock holdings in a company, when it cannot be done by a person situated like you are, being the sparkplug

In the case of Robert T. Ross, Assistant Secretary of Defense, the House Committee on Government Operations brought a new emphasis to the congressional thesis that appearances count as part of actuality.[79] Investigators for the Committee discovered that while Ross was in office a clothing firm run by his wife, and another headed by his brother-in-law, had received contracts from the Department of Defense. There was no evidence that Ross had influenced or sought to influence the award of these contracts or had violated any statutes on conflict of interest, or that he had personally profited from the contracts. Nonetheless, in the Committee's mind, the business activities of close members of his family raised the issue of impropriety, and, under pressure of adverse publicity raised by the Committee, Ross resigned.

The well-known controversy over the Dixon-Yates power contract ultimately came to a head in an issue of personal conflict of interest. In 1954 the Atomic Energy Commission entered into a contract with the Dixon-Yates group under which a private power company was to provide additional electric power to the Tennessee Valley region. The uproar that followed arose initially out of the continuing struggle between the advocates of public and private power. But after months of hearings before a Senate subcommittee, attention became centered upon the role played by Adolphe Wenzell, an expert consultant to the Bureau of the Budget, during the period of preliminary negotiations on the Dixon-Yates contract. Wenzell was an officer of First Boston Corporation, an investment banking firm. There was "a substantial possibility that . . . First Boston . . . might

---

of a business which you hope some time to return to. Perhaps that is what we must come to in Government in order to divorce Government people entirely from any possible temptation to further their own outside interests as against the interests of the Government. If we do come to that, of course, it is going to result in some deterioration in the caliber of the people working for the Government. . . . If we are going to do that, obviously the same rule should apply to Members of Congress because the situation is just the same. We are servants of the Government. There are relatively few Members of Congress who have given up all their law practices, all their cotton, tobacco, and peanut farms, and all their stock in any companies in order to serve as Members of Congress. Perhaps that is what we must come to, because certainly the purity and singleness of interest of anyone serving the Government, whether it be in the executive branch or the legislative branch, must be beyond any question." See *Hearings Before the Antitrust Subcommittee of the House Committee on the Judiciary Concerning Activities of Peter A. Strobel,* 84th Cong., 1st Sess., ser. 14, 65 (1955).

[79] H.R. REP. No. 1168, 85th Cong., 1st Sess. (1957).

be employed by the company which got the contract." Wenzell's position was fully disclosed and known to the government officials engaged in the negotiations. A Staff Report of the Senate subcommittee took the view that Wenzell's conduct had violated Section 434. After the city of Memphis announced its decision to build its own power plant, the government in 1955 ordered the cancellation of the Dixon-Yates contract. When the private contractor sued the United States for damages, the government claimed as one defense the invalidity of the Dixon-Yates contract by reason of the alleged violation of the conflict of interest statute. The Court of Claims rejected the argument, holding that the possibility that First Boston might profit as a financial agent if the proposal ripened into a contract was too remote to give Wenzell a present interest in the contract in violation of Section 434. At the present writing, the government's application to the Supreme Court for certiorari is pending, with the issue on review limited to the question of the interpretation of Section 434.[80]

The most publicized and dramatic instance to arise in recent years was that of Sherman Adams, Assistant to the President from 1953 to 1958. Adams was generally regarded as the President's chief aide and the instrument of much Presidential power. In the summer of 1958 it developed in hearings before a House investigating subcommittee that Adams had received gifts from a manufacturer who had matters pending in federal agencies and who had been a friend since Adams' days as Governor of New Hampshire. Adams admitted that he had communicated with agency officials on matters involving the manufacturer, but he denied any chain of cause and effect between the gifts and the calls. He agreed that he had not acted as prudently as he should.[81] Criticism of Adams was intense, in part because Democrats remembered his earlier vigorous attack

---

80 See *Hearings Before a Subcommittee of the Senate Committee on the Judiciary on Investigation Concerning the Charges of Monopolistic Influences in the Power Industry*, 83d Cong., 2d Sess. (1954); *Hearings Before a Subcommittee on Antitrust and Monopoly of the Senate Committee on the Judiciary*, 84th Cong., 1st Sess. (1955); STAFF OF SUBCOMM. ON ANTITRUST AND MONOPOLY, SENATE COMM. ON THE JUDICIARY, 84TH CONG., 1ST SESS., REPORT ON INVESTIGATION CONCERNING THE CHARGES OF MONOPOLISTIC INFLUENCES IN THE POWER INDUSTRY (Comm. Print 1956); Mississippi Valley Generating Co. v. United States, 175 F. Supp. 505 (Ct. Cl. 1959) (text quotation at 514).

81 A transcript of Adams' testimony before the Committee appears in the N.Y. Times, June 18, 1958, p. 16, col. 1. See also N.Y. Times, June 18, 1958, p. 1, col. 8. See also H.R. REP. No. 2711, 85th Cong., 2d Sess. 46–50, 73–76 (1959).

upon the ethical standards of the Truman Administration.[82] President Eisenhower stood by his assistant through the summer, but in September Adams resigned.

Only slightly less dramatic, and probably of more permanent impact, was the case of Commissioner Richard A. Mack of the Federal Communications Commission. The Mack case had a quiet beginning in a little-noticed resolution approved by the House of Representatives on February 5, 1957, calling upon the House Committee on Interstate and Foreign Commerce to conduct a study of the independent regulatory agencies. The Commerce Committee established a new Special Subcommittee on Legislative Oversight for the purpose. Early in its deliberations the subcommittee undertook an inquiry into the circumstances under which a franchise for a Miami television channel had been granted after years of hearings.[83] Evidence was uncovered indicating that Commissioner Mack had received loans and other favors from the attorney for the successful applicant.[84] Mack had voted for the attorney's client. Mack's resignation was accepted by the White House, and five months later he and the attorney were indicted on charges of conspiring to defraud the United States.[85] The continuing inquiry by the Special Subcommittee disclosed practices of FCC commissioners and staff casting doubt on the procedures used to allocate radio and television channels.

Unlike most of the publicized episodes of alleged misconduct, the Mack case raised issues that went not only to the personal morality of the official involved but to the workings of the entire administrative process. Raising in combined form problems of ex parte communications, influence peddling, and conflict of interest, the case also pointed up the weakness of legal protections and procedures against improper conduct at the level of the agency com-

[82] For example, see Adams' speech to the American Paper and Pulp Association Convention in 1954, N.Y. Times, Feb. 19, 1954, p. 1, col. 4.

[83] See SCHWARTZ, THE PROFESSOR AND THE COMMISSIONS (1959). See also N.Y. Times, Feb. 12, 1958, p. 1, col. 5; N.Y. Times, Feb. 13, 1958, p. 1, col. 6; N.Y. Times, Feb. 13, 1958, p. 28, col. 5.

[84] See Hearings Before the Subcommittee on Legislative Oversight of the House Committee on Interstate and Foreign Commerce Concerning an Investigation of Regulatory Commissions and Agencies, 85th Cong., 2d Sess. 392, 1261, 1475 (1958). See SCHWARTZ, op. cit. supra note 83, at 194–203.

[85] N.Y. Times, Feb. 14, 1958, p. 1, col. 8.

missioner and the vagueness of the standards set for administrative
judgment. The Mack investigation was a major catalyst to congressional interest in the operation of regulatory agencies as a whole.
The conflict of interest statutes passed in the mid-nineteenth century
are in large measure attributed by historians to the Gardiner and
Hall carbine affairs.[86] If Congress within the next few years enacts
new legislation in the field of ethical practices, future historians are
likely to assign a similar place to the Mack incident.

In statutes enacted over the last hundred years, Congress has
made its weight felt in the field of conflict of interest in the executive
branch. It is likely, however, that Congress has had a greater effect
on the operating conduct of the executive branch when acting in its
other roles of confirmer of appointments, investigator of problem
areas, and prosecutor at the bar of public opinion. Congress has
often taken the initiative in inquiring into the ethical conduct of
federal executive employees, in articulating proper standards, in
devising protective proposals, in rooting out evildoers, and in generally displaying sensitivity to the problem. The dominant motivating
force has often been pure partisanship or Congress-versus-President
feuding; but whatever the motivation, Congress has sometimes been
an effective policeman, and has served as a goad to the executive
branch to take remedial measures on its own.

86 See Chapter III *supra.*

VI

A Modern Setting
for Judgment

Without a modern setting for judgment it is not possible to evaluate the present pattern of conflict of interest restraints or to devise a better one. One reason for the inadequacy of the present statutes is that the problems to which they were directed have changed shape as the American society and government have changed shape. No revision of the system of restraints will be an enduring improvement unless it is properly adapted to a group of major social forces that directly affect conflict of interest problems today. A review of these forces is the subject of this chapter.

GROWTH OF GOVERNMENT AND THE MIXED ECONOMY

As was noted in Chapter I, first importance must be given to sheer growth in the federal government. Increase in size of the federal establishment has necessarily brought with it demands for executives and for general personnel on a scale and at a level of competence never before known in this country. The same increase has induced a dramatic shift in the scale on which conflicts of interest arise among federal employees.

As government has grown in size, it has undertaken many new functions formerly private, and has become a more or less overt force in many more. Without moving to socialism, the American economy has long since abandoned nineteenth-century laissez faire in favor of a pragmatic and unideological blend of private and public enterprise. Direct governmental production, as in TVA, remains relatively rare. Direct regulation of industry and control of franchises, while more common, are limited in general to recognized utilities, and have spread only as old utilities have grown or new ones have appeared. These, however, are but the beginnings of the federal government's participation in the national economy. Taking in over twenty per cent of the national income in taxes (including social security contributions), spending one fifth of the national income, controlling (within limits) the money supply and interest rates, regulating foreign trade, setting the laws on patents, bankruptcy, and labor-management relations, and redistributing purchasing power through veterans' payments, social security, and, indirectly, unemployment compensation, the federal government today is the most important single force in the general economy.

The impact of its individual programs, particularly those of a promotional nature, is even more direct. Housing, road building, oil exploration and imports, shipping, farm production, communications, small business financing, atomic energy, medical and other scientific research, slum clearance, export trade, and the sprawling promotional concerns of the Department of the Interior make up only a partial list.[1] These are the programs most apt to be carried out in a complex semigovernmental, semiprivate way through contracts, subsidies, guaranties, financing, grants, staff assistance, tax benefits, technical advice, and a thousand other devices for pooling resources and providing incentive through stick and carrot. To these must be added a rising defense budget, currently exceeding $40 billion a year, one-third to one-half of which goes directly for procurement. Government and the private segment of the economy have become merged beyond separation.

The importance of the new mixed economy to modern conflict of interest problems cannot be overemphasized. In the first place, it has infinitely multiplied the contacts between citizens and the government, between private economic interests and the government. When the conflict of interest statutes of the last century were passed, it could be justifiably assumed that the most significant

1 For a broad collection of materials illustrating the unique economic order of the United States, see FAINSOD, GORDON & PALAMOUNTAIN, GOVERNMENT AND THE AMERICAN ECONOMY (3d ed. 1959). See also WILCOX, PUBLIC POLICIES TOWARD BUSINESS (1955).

economic contacts between citizens and government would be those
involving the citizens' "claims" against the government — demands
for money or property. Some few citizens would also have "contracts"
with the government. But today in the economic life of all Americans, Uncle Sam is ubiquitous. The citizen's total number of direct
and indirect economic contacts with his government is countless,
and conversely, virtually any governmental decision on almost any
issue will have critical repercussions upon the economic fortunes
of individuals, industries, or geographic areas. In these circumstances,
legislation myopically focused on "claims" and "contracts" is obsolete.

Second, a widening of the range of governmental activities puts
an increasing premium on adequate staffing of government operations and on the flow of information between government and the
private sector. Commensurately with the growth of complex responsibilities, specialists and top executives must be enlisted into government service.

Third, the merger of private and public carries significant implications for the whole underlying concept of conflict of interest
among government employees. To talk at all of a conflict of interest
presupposes a separateness of interests, a dichotomy between what
is a private interest and what is a governmental one. In a simpler
world conforming to the Jeffersonian idyll, government would be
small and closely restricted in its activities, and the line between
private and public would be clear to all. In such a world, a conflict
of interest would not be hard to define. But as the line between private and public blurs into a broad gray band, the possibility of joint
or overlapping interests increases, the whole premise of conflicts regulation begins to be undermined, the problems become more subtle,
and regulation grows more difficult. This point will arise again in
later discussion.

Although the interpenetration of public and private has been in
process for a long time, the Cold War has accelerated its rate and
intensified its effects. The high state of international tension since
the end of World War II is not in itself an independent source of
conflict of interest problems; rather it serves as a catalyst to other
pressures. It largely accounts for the magnitude of defense expenditures and scientific programs, and these in turn contribute heavily

to the impact of governmental activities upon the economy as a whole. And in a war, cold or hot, the task of filling the government's personnel needs becomes a matter not merely of convenience but of survival.

THE FEDERAL PERSONNEL SYSTEM

A system of conflict of interest restraints for the twentieth century must be geared to the personnel system of this century. The federal government has altered as radically in its methods of staffing over the past hundred years as it has in size and function.

THE CIVIL SERVICE

While every high school student recognizes the spoils system as a synonym for Andrew Jackson, professional scholars of the history of public administration tell us that political leaders in the states and cities had been using public offices for partisan purposes since 1800. The spoils system in effect paid for party organization at the state and local level before its ideological introduction into the federal government by President Jackson.[2] Even the slogan "To the victor belong the spoils" came not from Old Hickory but from Senator Marcy of New York.[3] But if the origin of the spoils system cannot be traced to Jackson, its spread in the federal government and the formulation of a theory of spoils may be attributed to him.[4] Coming

---

[2] "In many minds, the spoils system is equated with Andrew Jackson. . . . Jackson did not even come close to overturning the federal civil service during his eight years in office after 1829. He made few more removals, percentage-wise, than had Jefferson nearly thirty years before." VAN RIPER, HISTORY OF THE UNITED STATES CIVIL SERVICE 30 (1958).

[3] REGISTER OF DEBATES, 22d Cong., 1st Sess. 1325 (Jan. 24, 1832).

[4] Jackson's statement at his first inaugural is worth quoting: "There are, perhaps, few men who can for any great length of time enjoy office and power without being more or less under the influence of feelings unfavorable to the faithful discharge of their public duties. Their integrity may be proof against improper considerations immediately addressed to themselves, but they are apt to acquire a habit of looking with indifference upon the public interests and of tolerating conduct from which an unpracticed man would revolt. Office is considered as a species of property, and government rather as a means of promoting individual interests than as an instrument created solely for the service of the people. Corruption in some and in others a perversion of correct feelings and principles divert government from its legitimate ends and make it an engine for the support of the few at the expense of the many." 2 RICHARDSON, MESSAGES AND PAPERS OF THE PRESIDENTS 448–49 (1897). See also VAN RIPER, op. cit. supra note 2, at 36–37.

into office at the end of a long period of opposition rule, Jackson was basically of the view that "more is lost by the long continuance of men in office than is generally gained by their experience." [5] Between 1829 and the end of the Civil War, the period of enactment of the main body of the conflict of interest statutes, the spoils system was dominant in the federal service.[6] After the passage of the Pendleton Act in 1883, the selection and retention of civil servants on the basis of merit spread quickly, and the spoils principle declined.

The mass of low-ranking political appointees was the main group at which the conflict of interest statutes were aimed one hundred years ago. Today this group has almost ceased to exist. Currently, over ninety per cent of the government's 2.4 million civilian employees are under civil service or some other merit system. Career civil service executives carrying high responsibility for the conduct of governmental programs include 400 to 500 officials serving as deputy and assistant heads of agencies, executive assistants, bureau and staff office chiefs, and assistant bureau chiefs. If division chiefs, regional and district office directors, and senior aides and assistants are included, the number of career executives probably comes to 4,000 and over.

The civil servant is commonly thought of as a government career man, and this is substantially true, for the great majority are recruited at junior levels and the top civil service positions are usually held by persons of considerable tenure in government service. But it is important that the career factor not be exaggerated. Recent experience indicates that 20 to 25 per cent of federal civil service employees leave the government each year, and about half of these, or 11 to 12 per cent of all civil service employees, voluntarily quit

[5] *Ibid.*

[6] "Despite the rising tide of spoils, there constantly remained a stratum of the civil service which helped to maintain continuity and competence in administration. Even the most partisan of executives could comprehend the need to maintain a basic level of administrative efficiency by retaining a few key officials. Hence the comptroller, auditors, and chief clerks of the departmental service in Washington frequently kept their positions through several administrations. So did a portion of the minor clerks, a number of the small group of scientific and technical personnel, and the officer corps of the army and navy. In the field agencies politics reigned, though not always to the exclusion of integrity and competence. . . . In a sense the federal service was manned and managed through two personnel systems, though at this time that governed by the principle of spoils was by far the most dominant. Ever since the time of Jackson the proper relationship between these two systems has been a matter of considerable concern and argument." VAN RIPER, *op. cit. supra* note 2, at 51.

their government jobs.[7] The problem of retaining civil servants in the federal service is a very real one, and a subject of continuing study.[8] Some civil servants who leave to take private employment originally intended to work in government for only a few years before moving on to a job in private life. Others find that their government experience opens up opportunities in private employment that are hard to resist. In either case, the government fills an important role in society today in providing training for positions outside government. Correspondingly the value of government experience as preparation for a nongovernment career remains a significant factor in recruitment for civil service positions. Thus, even in the relatively stable area of the civil service, the flow of individuals from government service to private employment, and vice versa, is a significant characteristic of federal employment and a contributory force in American society as a whole.

POLITICAL EXECUTIVES

The combination of a civil service merit system and a revolving layer of political appointees loyal to the party in power in the executive branch is an indigenous characteristic of the federal personnel system. Executives who are appointed outside of the civil service to important policy-making positions number about 1,100. The 1,100 appointed executives, referred to here as "political executives," include about 250 heads of agencies and their deputies, about 250 non–civil service bureau chiefs, and about 600 subordinate executives ranging from assistant agency heads to political assistants. These political executives serve for relatively short periods of time, and do not expect to make government service a career.[9]

The traditional major sources of manpower for top political posts

[7] UNITED STATES CIVIL SERVICE COMMISSION, 1958 ANNUAL REPORT 86 (1959); 1957 ANNUAL REPORT 16, 127, 128 (1958).

[8] See note 16 *infra*.

[9] The average tenure of Cabinet members during the Roosevelt and Truman administrations was about four years, including the long periods of service by Harold Ickes, Frances Perkins, and Henry Morgenthau. During the same period, the average tenure of undersecretaries was less than two years; of assistant secretaries, about two and one-half years. For other political aides below the sub-Cabinet level, periods of service of two to three years have been typical. See COMMISSION ON ORGANIZATION OF THE EXECUTIVE BRANCH OF THE GOVERNMENT (Second Hoover Commission), TASK FORCE REPORT ON PERSONNEL AND CIVIL SERVICE 212–24 (1955). Regulatory commissioners have averaged about four years during this period. See Bernstein, "Federal Regulatory Commissioners," unpublished report written for the Brookings Institution (1960).

have been business, the law, the universities, and government, with the relative weight among them differing from administration to administration. Increasingly appointments are being made from among top career executives already in government service and from the military.[10] On the whole the political parties have not been major sources of supply of political executives.[11]

Though these political executives to some extent share their discretion in policy matters with the men around the President, and with the career executives, they remain the vital source of administrative leadership. If weak, though they may not cause catastrophe, they will surely bring on governmental anemia. Furthermore, in a fundamental sense these executive appointees in American political life have a function that career civil servants cannot perform. As the Second Hoover Commission's Task Force on Personnel emphasized: "In the National Government, it is the function of political executives to represent within the administration the policy purposes of the President, to bring the general public's point of view to bear upon administrative decisions, to provide leadership in developing national policy, to exercise statutory powers vested in them as public officials, and to act for the Chief Executive in seeing that all of the laws are faithfully executed; in short, to take the responsibility for governing." [12]

Recruitment

These top political positions have many attractions. The excitement of a new and responsible job, the likelihood of making new

[10] Curiously there have been almost no studies on the sources of supply and career ladders of federal executives. Among the very few works are MACMAHON & MILLETT, FEDERAL ADMINISTRATORS (1939), and HERRING, FEDERAL COMMISSIONERS (1936). The Brookings Institution was in the spring of 1960 engaged in a wide-ranging study directly focusing on these matters.

[11] The gap between the presidential wing of a party, with its orientation toward national and international issues, and the state-local wing of the party, which usually controls the party national committee, may raise problems for the President who looks to his party for executives. For discussion of the declining significance of the party in this and other areas, see DAVID & POLLOCK, EXECUTIVES FOR GOVERNMENT 149–70 (1957); Mansfield, *Political Parties, Patronage, and the Federal Government Service,* in THE AMERICAN ASSEMBLY, THE FEDERAL GOVERNMENT SERVICE: ITS CHARACTER, PRESTIGE, AND PROBLEMS 81–112 (1954).

[12] COMMISSION ON ORGANIZATION OF THE EXECUTIVE BRANCH OF THE GOVERNMENT (Second Hoover Commission), TASK FORCE REPORT ON PERSONNEL AND CIVIL SERVICE 1 (1955).

contacts and acquiring new experience, the desire to perform one's civic duty, local political inducements, interest in a particular governmental program — these and many other factors tend to make the positions desirable and sought after. Yet recruitment of top executives for the federal establishment has constituted a major problem for recent administrations.[13] An informative study reports that "every recent administration has experienced difficulty in filling its political executive positions on a satisfactory basis and in keeping them filled on such a basis." [14] Even in non–civil service positions below the level of assistant secretary or bureau chief, such as policy-determining or confidential positions placed in Schedule C, "from 20 to 25 per cent of the jobs have generally been vacant." [15]

During the 1930's and 1940's the overriding issue of federal personnel management was considered to be the improvement of personnel organization affecting civil service employees.[16] During the 1940's, however, concern over the recruitment and retention of qualified political executives gradually developed, and executive recruiting difficulties in the Korean war period (1950–1952) intensified awareness of this problem.[17]

While the staffing problem at executive levels is most severe when a different party takes over the White House, the problem is never absent during a presidential term. "There is rarely a time

13 Recent studies of the federal executive recruitment problem include: BERNSTEIN, THE JOB OF THE FEDERAL EXECUTIVE (1958); CORSON, EXECUTIVES FOR THE FEDERAL SERVICE: A PROGRAM FOR ACTION IN TIME OF CRISIS (1952); DAVID & POLLOCK, EXECUTIVES FOR GOVERNMENT (1957); HARVARD BUSINESS SCHOOL CLUB OF WASHINGTON, D.C., BUSINESSMEN IN GOVERNMENT, AN APPRAISAL OF EXPERIENCE (1958); and Robinson, *New Price Tags For Government Managers,* Harv. Bus. Rev., Sept.–Oct. 1958, p. 81.

14 DAVID & POLLOCK, EXECUTIVES FOR GOVERNMENT 10 (1957). See particularly Chapter 2, "The Supply of Qualified Political Executives."

15 SENATE COMM. ON POST OFFICE AND CIVIL SERVICE, 85TH CONG., 1ST SESS., ADMINISTRATION OF THE CIVIL SERVICE SYSTEM 36 (Comm. Print 1957).

16 A leading study of the period was the report of the committee appointed by President Roosevelt under the chairmanship of Justice Stanley F. Reed. H.R. DOC. No. 118, 77th Cong., 1st Sess. (1941), *Report of President's Committee on Civil Service Improvement.* Some academic writings on the problem of political executive recruitment appeared in the 1930's. See MACMAHON & MILLETT, FEDERAL ADMINISTRATORS (1939); HERRING, FEDERAL COMMISSIONERS (1936).

17 For analyses based largely on the experience of the Korean war period, see CORSON, EXECUTIVES FOR THE FEDERAL SERVICE: A PROGRAM FOR ACTION IN TIME OF CRISIS (1952); NATIONAL CIVIL SERVICE LEAGUE, THE NATIONAL CIVIL SERVICE LEAGUE'S SURVEY OF BUSINESS EXECUTIVES WHO HAVE HELD HIGH-LEVEL GOVERNMENT ADMINISTRATIVE POSTS, mimeo. (1952); and David, *The Development and Recruitment of Administrative Leadership in National and International Programs,* in WALKER, ed., AMERICA'S MANPOWER CRISIS 137 (1952).

when one or more Cabinet members are not preparing for an early departure, with consequential changes in the leadership structure immediately below them; and sub-Cabinet members leave even more frequently. . . ." [18] During its first few months, a new administration probably can recruit many of its executives from among its enthusiastic political supporters, though it also has political obligations to meet, congressional support to mobilize, and partisan conflicts to resolve. As it ages, the character of its recruitment problems changes. In middle life, "the administration becomes more experienced in spelling out its political and administrative requirements, more concerned with qualifications directly related to performance on the job, less concerned with rewarding partisan supporters of the past but perhaps increasingly aware of the necessity for political alliances looking to the future." [19] As the end of the presidential term approaches, "sources of qualified political executives outside the government tend to dry up. . . ." [20]

The special circumstances of the election victory of the Republican Party in 1952 complicated the contemporary recruitment of executives. [21] The Eisenhower victory brought to an end two decades of Democratic administrations, and hundreds of political executive positions were vacated and new appointments made over a short period of time. Throughout its two terms the Eisenhower administration has been presented with an unending problem of finding replacements, most acutely felt in the Defense Department. Not uncommonly a score or more persons have been offered executive posts before a willing candidate has been found. In the critical area of scientific research and development, top positions have on occasion remained vacant for several months. To illustrate, in March 1957 about twenty per cent of the sub-Cabinet positions in the executive departments were recorded as vacant, and in the Department of Defense and the three military departments, the proportion of vacancies in sub-Cabinet positions was nearly one-third.[22]

The shortage of qualified political executives has been intensified

[18] DAVID & POLLOCK, EXECUTIVES FOR GOVERNMENT 13 (1957).
[19] Ibid.
[20] Ibid. See also Perkins, Staffing Democracy's Top Side, 17 PUB. ADMIN. REV. 1–9 (1957).
[21] Somers, The Federal Bureaucracy and the Change of Administration, 48 AM. POL. SCI. REV. 131–51 (1954).
[22] DAVID & POLLOCK, EXECUTIVES FOR GOVERNMENT 10 n.5 (1957).

by conditions of sustained growth and full employment in the economy since World War II. An abundance of opportunities in business, universities, foundations, and other institutions has led to a general shortage of available executives. Many other factors have added to the government's recruiting difficulties, one of the most important being inadequate compensation. Under present pay scales the government cannot possibly compete for executives with private industry or even with universities and foundations. For the kind of person who is appointed to a political executive position, the government salary scale is well below that of the market-place.[23] Further, the appointee usually incurs the major expense of maintaining a Washington residence in addition to the financial commitments of his home base. Altogether the government must usually proceed on the assumption that if a man will accept a governmental position at all, he is likely to be prepared to do so at some financial sacrifice. And the level of sacrifice has probably been rising.

Even more powerful a deterrent to acceptance of government appointment is the risk the executive takes of forfeiting a favorable position with his private employer. Studies in 1950 indicated that about three out of ten top executives in a representative group of companies had had their entire business experience within their company, and that the proportion was rising.[24] A commentator made the point strikingly in 1954: "For the young man whose fame and fortune lie ahead, and for the older man whose fame and fortune are already established, even a four-year tour in Washington might be attractive. But for the business executive in the prime of his career, an extended non-emergency tour in Washington is a contradiction in his apparent personal aims. His dispensability to his corporation and his corporation's indispensability to him are bound to remain the crux of his problem."[25]

23 For a publicized illustration see Chapter VIII, note 16 *infra*. See also Robinson, *supra* note 13.

24 See NEWCOMER, THE BIG BUSINESS EXECUTIVE: THE FACTORS THAT MADE HIM, 1900–1950, 96–98 (1955). "Society itself may be more mobile but the fellow on the make somewhere below the top of the executive ladder cannot move around much except within his own company or industry. It is the rigidity at the top that worries me. More and more, the way a fellow holds on to the opportunity to compete for an executive position is by staying in that corporation where he already has an established position." Quoted in BERNSTEIN, THE JOB OF THE FEDERAL EXECUTIVE 154 (1958).

25 McDonald, *The Businessman in Government,* Fortune, July 1954, p. 58, 158.

A major obstacle to entering government service is the appointee's probable loss of benefits under group welfare and security plans. Contemporary social writing takes as a favorite subject the "organization man," one who works for a large organization and is acutely concerned about security.[26] Whether or not the stereotype is a valid picture of anyone, there is no doubt that group insurance plans, stock options, pension plans, and other welfare plans have become common features of contemporary America. It is no longer even safe to refer to these plans as "fringe" benefits; they can play the most important part in an employee's total compensation. Since the executive cannot take his security plan with him, he inclines to stay where he is.[27]

Group security and welfare plans are often discussed as a product of corporate enterprise, but the phenomenon is more widespread; increasing commitment of the individual to the hierarchical structure of large organizations is a feature of modern American society generally. The lawyer in the large departmentalized firm, the labor leader whose whole power and position are organizational, the administrator or professor at the university, the labor union member under a seniority rule, the scientist in the established research laboratory, the accountant partner in a national chain of accounting partnerships — all tend to be institution-bound. There is every reason to believe that the movement in the direction of group institutionalization will continue. Before long every major occupation will probably have succeeded in obtaining for itself some kind of security system — professional men, individual proprietors, and farmers as well as union members and corporate executives. Whether this movement toward group commitment and security is a glorious social advance or a monstrous atavism, or neither, is happily not at issue here. It is clearly happening, and it will provide one of the dominant features of the economic landscape within which a modern set of restraints on conflict of interest in government must operate.

Recruitment for top government office is difficult for many reasons. Factors such as exposure to political harassment and newspaper publicity, ideological disaffinity to "government," distaste for

26 See RIESMAN, THE LONELY CROWD (1950); WHYTE, THE ORGANIZATION MAN (1956).
27 James L. McCamy, in DAVID & POLLOCK, EXECUTIVES FOR GOVERNMENT 27 n.18 (1957), likens this executive to "a kind of elegant indentured servant."

the generally more regulated environment and low prestige of government office, may all tend to lead a given individual to refuse appointment.[28] And personal considerations such as a wife's veto, a desire not to upset children's school arrangements, and the nuisance of a temporary move into a strange community may all argue against the move to Washington. But the most compelling single reason is that the economic future and security of potential appointees are usually anchored to some institution or organization, and the cost of forfeiting these prospects and leaving the promotion escalator is too great. Government can provide, at the career and civil service levels, occupational advancement and security; but there is little that it can offer transient political executives except the opportunity for stimulating service. That is often not enough.

The traditions and institutions of ancient Rome and of England made it possible for them to enlist into the service of the government many of the ablest men of the time; the Soviet Union can today mobilize its full manpower resources to the uses of the state. The United States has been thrust into a position of world leadership encumbered with the staffing system, traditions, and attitudes toward public service of the nineteenth-century laissez faire government of a second class power.

In office

The political appointee in high office finds himself in a strange, uncertain position. It is difficult for him to form a clear image of what he is and how he should act as a government official. Other officials — the civil servant, the military man, the judge — have a clear-cut conception of their role in relation to government and to the outside world, an essentially monastic and separated role. They are the government's men, and they know whose men they are. But

---

[28] According to an experienced government executive: "One of the amazing things about service in Washington is that you can leave town and within hours be with a group of former associates who couldn't care less about government. Not only are they ignorant of your problems, but they don't really get emotionally involved in any way. To them it is a popular sport to criticize government. . . . What concerns me the most is the lack of concern, almost the unwillingness to debate questions related to the purposes of government. When a fellow is asked to accept a political appointment in Washington, he may wonder whether it is a good thing for him to associate himself with a government that many of his associates regard as a great spending machine that is eating away the vitals of our liberties." Quoted in BERNSTEIN, *op. cit. supra* note 24, at 154–55.

for the temporarily appointed executive, while there is a strong tendency to identify himself with the Chief Executive, other forces are necessarily also at work. The appointed executive is there on a temporary basis and he knows it. In all but the case of the very top business executive or the occasional person with an independent income, the appointee faces the necessity of keeping a weather eye out for tomorrow's departure that might literally come tomorrow. Appointed to do a spot job, perhaps affiliated strongly with one of the political parties, he has not made a deep emotional commitment to the government as an over-all institution. Such a sense of commitment may come in time, but the usual political executive planning to stay two or at most three years cannot consider himself a "government man" with the secure and simple assurance of the military officer or the judge. He is a government-leased man, and the outside world has the reversionary interest.

Whether the federal government should rely so heavily for its leadership on amateur transient executives is a debatable, and frequently debated, question. Proponents of a corps of senior civil service executives, resembling the British system, argue that modern government calls for expertise and that the average American political executive goes home at just about the time he learns how to do his government job. Advocates of the present system point to the value of the fresh ideas and information brought by the outsider, the dangers of ossification in a permanent bureaucracy, and the importance of providing the President with a team of executives sympathetic to his policies. Perhaps the issue is primarily one of degree. In any case, whatever the balance between civil service and political appointment, a significant number of the most influential officials will be in government posts only temporarily. This is an important fact in the consideration of conflict of interest problems in the executive branch.

To act in the face of a conflicting interest is not heinous, it is merely potentially dangerous; it may be a kind of thing that "just isn't done." In many situations, successful administration of conflict of interest restraints in government must depend on someone's sensitivity to whether questioned practices are ethically wrong, potentially dangerous, or apt to cause unfavorable comment. When the heads of government departments and agencies — the policy and standard setters — have been recently active in the private sector of the economy, the answers given to such questions in government will tend to be conditioned by the attitudes of the private sector. Frequently when it is suggested that in government a practice "just isn't done," it will be found that in much of American society it is done.

It is widely believed, and probably true, that the general moral standards of the private economy have improved in the last fifty or one hundred years in this country. The cynical purchase of legislators, shoulder-shrugging resignation to bribery as a fact of life, and similar flagrant offenses are undoubtedly less common than they once were. At the same time instances of misconduct such as inflated expense accounts, cheating on examinations, deceptive advertising, business negotiation by entertainment, gifts to customers and purchasers and clients, rigged athletic and quiz shows, reliance on personal contacts and influence, payoffs and kickbacks, are not exceptional in the general private economic life of the United States today. When it comes to more subtle problems such as the danger of playing potentially conflicting roles, most people in private life are hardly aware of the issue at all.

The lawyer, because of a professional history and the accidents of the adversary litigation system, has learned in the conduct of his professional life to avoid situations in which he is representing both sides.[29] In a similar way, the newer professions of accountancy and management and technical consulting have found that to the extent that they aspire to professional status they must not become entangled in positions of conflicting interests.[30] A few practices in the

[29] See the Canons of Professional Ethics cited in United States v. Standard Oil Co., 136 F. Supp. 345, 353 (S.D.N.Y. 1955).

[30] See CAREY, PROFESSIONAL ETHICS OF CERTIFIED PUBLIC ACCOUNTANTS (1956), which sets forth at pp. 213–16 the Rules of Professional Conduct of the American Institute of Accountants (revised 1950). Rule 4 provides that "A member shall not engage in any business or occupation conjointly with that of a public accountant, which is incompatible or inconsistent therewith" (p. 214). Rule 13 states: "A member shall not express his opinion on financial statements of any enterprise financed in whole or in part by public distribution of securities, if he owns or is committed to acquire a financial interest in the enterprise which is substantial either in relation to its capital or to his own personal fortune, or if a member of his immediate family owns or is committed to acquire a substantial interest in the enterprise. A member shall not express his opinion on financial statements which are used as a basis of credit if he owns or is committed to acquire a financial interest in the enterprise which is substantial either in relation to its capital or to his own personal fortune or if a member of his immediate family owns or is committed to acquire a substantial interest in the enterprise, unless in his report he discloses such interest" (pp. 215–16). Carey further discusses conflicts of interest of accountants at pp. 46–48.

commercial world are expressly forbidden by law because of the risk of conflicting interests: a trustee may not deal with his trust, for example, nor may a commercial bank engage in investment banking.[31] But in most areas of economic life, there is little or no awareness of the conflict of interest problem. Multiple directorships and cross-officerships among corporations or other organizations whose activities may conflict in interest are commonplace. Some businesses are built squarely on economic activities that are by their nature pregnant with the possibility of conflicts of interest. The finder and the real estate agent are ready examples.

No obloquy is here implied. These activities are economically valuable, perhaps necessary in substantially their present form, and the law and society generally accept their legitimacy. The point is merely that much of what is accepted practice in the private world of economics is exactly what is condemned by conflict of interest restraints in federal employment. With government executives moving in and out of the two environments, this difference between them must be borne in mind in evaluating any system of conflict of interest restraints.

TEMPORARY AND INTERMITTENT EMPLOYEES

A major change in the staffing of the federal government in the last generation has been the increasing use of experts, consultants, and other temporary and intermittent employees. In the sense used here, a consultant or expert has a formal relationship to the government and is under the law a government employee.[32] An official's casual or occasional solicitation of the views of a friend at a party or on a park bench does not make the latter a consultant; the consultant or expert holds a temporary appointment, is on an agency's roster, and has a file in the agency's personnel office.

[31] See 2 SCOTT, TRUSTS §§ 170–170.25 (2d ed. 1956); 49 Stat. 707 (1935), 12 U.S.C. § 378 (1958).

[32] Authority for agencies to employ experts and consultants for compensated service outside the civil-service and classification laws is available in section 15 of the Administrative Expenses Act of August 2, 1946, 60 Stat. 806, 810 (1946), 5 U.S.C. § 55a (1958), and in Civil Service Regs., 5 C.F.R. § 6.101(n), a provision covering positions (other than those of a confidential or policy-determining character) for which it is not practicable to examine. Under section 15 of the Administrative Expenses Act, however, appointment of individuals to render compensated service as experts or consultants (WAEs) requires authorization "in an appropriation or other Act." In most agencies, specific authority to employ experts and consultants (WAEs) is furnished in the appropriation applicable to it.

The distinction between an expert and consultant is not always clear. In general, however, consultants are used in an advisory, non-operative capacity only. An expert may have temporary operational responsibility for a particular project in his area of specialization. The consultant, more often than not, is part-time or intermittent in his services. An expert, though temporary as compared to a regular government employee, may often work full-time on a particular assignment for several weeks or months.

Often a group of consultants will be appointed to constitute an advisory committee. The number of these advisory committees has increased so rapidly that no one appears to know how many there really are, although estimates place the number between 1,500 and 2,000.[33] Many of these committees and consultants advise on technical or scientific matters; others assist on matters of policy at all levels.

Often Congress has by statute defined the purpose, composition, and conduct of advisory committees. In addition, many agencies have found it necessary or desirable to establish advisory committees in an astonishing variety of substantive areas. For example, the Public Health Service alone had sixty advisory committees in operation in 1958, not including some fifty study groups who work with the National Institutes of Health. Examples of the former include the National Advisory Cancer Council, the National Advisory Heart Council, and the Federal Hospital Council. The Department of Commerce also has established several score committees active in various bureaus and divisions of the department. In 1956 the Department of Defense listed 249 active advisory committees, not including a substantial number of committees and advisory panels that could not be named and described for security reasons. They were active in such fields as biological and chemical warfare, cryptological equipment, computers, and human resources and training. Even temporary government commissions like the Hoover Commissions have created public advisory groups to help them on such

---

[33] The number of public advisory committees is difficult to determine. In 1956 the Antitrust Division estimated that there were 5,400 advisory committees, of which 4,000 or so were established by statute. In 1957 the House Government Operations Committee, after excluding hundreds of committees working at municipal and local levels in conservation and other federal programs, estimated the number of active committees to be 1,700 to 1,800. See H.R. REP. No. 576, 85th Cong., 1st Sess. 4 (1957). In 1958, the Cabinet Secretariat in the White House Office calculated that there were 1,093 public advisory committees in twenty of the largest federal agencies.

issues as the reorganization of government agencies and changes in international economic policies.[34]

Consultants and experts may serve without compensation as WOCs. Frequently, however, experts and consultants are paid for the days on which they actually work, "when actually employed," and are thus called WAEs. Their pay may be on a time basis or at a fixed rate per day. Sometimes they receive only out-of-pocket expenses; sometimes they receive a flat per diem allowance in lieu of expenses.

The government's increasing use of consultants and experts has periodically been debated and investigated.[35] Opponents fear that the practice exposes the government to infiltration by private interests liable to use the power of government to their own advantage. But though there are risks in not limiting the conduct of government to regular officials, the continued rise in the number of consultants and other part-time workers indicates that these people are filling a basic need, that they are the only available source of the expertise and special experience the government requires constantly today. As governmental functions and private functions overlap, government must be assured of a regular flow of information from the private sector of the economy, and vice versa. Giant government, a mixed economy, and a group-organized society entail an inevitable blurring of the line between government and non-government, between government employee and non-government employee. Increasing specialization within society and persistence of the recruiting bottleneck for full-time government executives will probably intensify this development.

The use of intermittent employees is of first importance to the regulation of conflicts of interest in the executive branch. The present statutes fail to recognize the special status and needs of the

[34] Department of Health, Education, and Welfare, Staff Paper on "Department of Health, Education, and Welfare Advisory Committees," Aug. 14, 1958; HOUSE COMM. ON GOVERNMENT OPERATIONS, 84TH CONG., 2D SESS., REPLIES FROM EXECUTIVE AGENCIES TO INQUIRY REGARDING USE OF ADVISORY COMMITTEES 5–6 (Comm. Print 1956); and ANTITRUST SUBCOMM., HOUSE COMM. ON THE JUDICIARY, 84TH CONG., 1ST SESS., INTERIM REPORT ON THE BUSINESS ADVISORY COUNCIL FOR THE DEPARTMENT OF COMMERCE (Comm. Print 1955).

[35] See ANTITRUST SUBCOMM., HOUSE COMM. ON THE JUDICIARY, 84TH CONG., 2D SESS., INTERIM REPORT ON WOC's AND GOVERNMENT ADVISORY GROUPS 1–3 (Comm. Print 1956). See also the discussion of the Celler Committee's investigations, in Chapter V *supra*.

"semi-employee." Indeed, Section 1914, forbidding outside compensation, flies straight in the face of the need of modern government for intermittent personnel.

Any amendment to the present structure of conflicts restraints must be adapted to this new major factor in the personnel system of American government.

CONTRACTING OUT

Though the government produces some of its own material needs, most of its physical supplies are purchased by outside contract. Services can also be purchased by outside contract. Building maintenance, for example, can be contracted out to a real estate management firm and the operation of government cafeterias turned over by contract to outside caterers. At a level closer to its governmental functions, the government may contract with a management consulting firm to do an organizational study of a government department. For that matter, the contracting-out arrangement can be used by the government to obtain virtually any kind of study or report or to secure the performance of almost any service.

The practice of contracting out has long been a source of controversy. In part, the differences between the Army and the Air Force in the field of missile development involved the Army's attachment to its tradition of arsenals and the Air Force's commitment to the practice of contracting out. The issue sometimes develops political ideological overtones, since some identify contracting out with private enterprise. The practice is controversial on the additional, but wholly different, ground that by definition the independent contractor is said not to be an "employee" of the United States. As a result, statutes such as the conflict of interest statutes do not regulate and control such a contractor in the absence of special contract provisions between him and the government.

The evidence is that an increasing number of important activities, particularly in the defense and science fields, are being contracted out today. The point is discussed more fully in Chapter VIII. On occasion contracting out provides a way for the government to obtain the services of an expert or consultant who would not be willing to become an "employee." The method represents another effort to put to public use the talents of the society; but it circumvents for these people the existing conflict of interest restrictions.

MISCELLANEOUS PERSONNEL

To complete this catalog of the modern structure of the federal personnel system a final miscellaneous category is needed.

There are large numbers of special employees and semi-employees of the United States government today. With each of these groups the question arises whether the general conflict of interest statutes and regulations apply to them. A few examples may be given. District of Columbia employees are employees of the federal government but quite separate from the government in its federal function. Members of the National Guard serve under state control except when mobilized by the President in times of national emergency. In an international era, the United States hires thousands of overseas nationals of other countries. Retired military officers remain "officers" for many purposes. County farm agents are paid in part by the federal government and in part locally.

These and similar special groups in part or at times employed by the United States must be kept in mind in assessing any proposed restraints on conflicts of interest in federal employment.

MODERN ADMINISTRATIVE PROCESS

The revolution that has taken place in the government's internal administrative procedures is conceivably of no less significance than the changes in its functions and its personnel system. Much modern discussion of conflicts of interest in government seems better suited to the circumstances of the nineteenth century than to the operations of modern government.

When administrative procedures were weak or almost unknown, no way could be seen to cope with the conflict of interest issue other than to swing the broad axe of criminal prohibition. As modern agency regulations illustrate, skillful use of administration devices such as reporting, disclosure, disqualification, advisory bodies, and variable sanctions makes it possible to deal with the conflict of interest problem with greater refinement.

In addition, imaginative use of the techniques of the modern administrative process can, through totally different devices, reduce the risks that the conflict of interest rules were originally devised to meet. A good illustration is provided by modern procedures for prosecuting claims against the government. Much conflict of interest legislation was born of abuses surrounding such claims. Claims are no longer a serious conflict of interest problem, not because the latter was attacked, but because the former were brought under order.

Similarly, modern contracting procedures may have outdated much of our inherited concern over conflict of interest risks in government procurement. Competitive bidding is common today. The General Services Administration annually handles billions of dollars of purchases in a highly routinized way, with internal checks, audits, and controls reducing the risks of official favoritism to the vanishing point. Negotiated contracts are less obviously secure against improper conduct, but large scale procurement of this kind is limited to a few agencies (mainly Defense, the AEC, and the NASA), and it should be possible to set up special administrative protections for particular areas where the problem is real. At present the procurement procedures of these agencies, particularly those of the Department of Defense, are so complex, so subject to committee decisions, dispersion of responsibility, checks and cross-checks, and auditing controls, and so decentralized that the national risks deriving from delay and red tape very likely outweigh the risk that any individual officer can swing the procurement machinery to the company of his choice. In any case, effective administrative control of the contracting process can indirectly make rigid conflict of interest restrictions less necessary.

This chapter has sought to survey the main factors at work in the federal government today that bear upon conflicts of interest and should be taken into account in designing a set of legal restrictions against them. The federal executive establishment does not, at its critical points, look the way it did when most of the present statutory restraints were enacted. Its size, relative scale, functions, contacts with the private economy, personnel needs, staffing, recruitment, and administrative procedures, and, most of all, the character of the social-economic environment in which it operates, have all changed almost beyond recognition.

Of these, the point that deserves most stress is the interpenetration of the public and private segments of the society. Here lies the key to the modern problem of conflict of interest, as will appear more clearly in succeeding chapters.

Effects on Recruitment

To what extent do existing conflict of interest restraints deter recruitment of government personnel? The issue has never been adequately explored or debated. Except to a minor extent in the case of Section 1914, Congress gave no consideration to the recruitment problem in any recorded legislative history of the conflict of interest statutes. Mid-nineteenth century political debate could not be expected to concern itself seriously with the problem. Not until World War I, and not again until World War II, did Congress face up to the emergency shortage of executives by authorizing the use of WOCs and relaxing certain of the conflict of interest restrictions. The statutes and the episodic concern of senatorial confirming committees with the conflict of interest problem are properly seen as a disconnected string of events, not as part of any over-all program balancing the need for ethical protection against the need for qualified government personnel. The effects the present system has on recruitment are largely accidental.

CIVIL SERVICE PERSONNEL

Conflict of interest restrictions bear upon civil service employees in a variety of ways. If the civil service employee is a lawyer or accountant or other specialist, he may occasionally find himself affected by the statutory bars on assisting outsiders in claims against the government. Once in a while, he may be required to disqualify himself under Section 434 because of conflicting interests. He may, though it is less likely in the case of a permanent employee, have to forego certain outside compensation because of Section 1914. And when he leaves government service, he may be substantially restricted in his relations with the government — and consequently in his job choice — by the post-employment restrictions of his agency's regulations and by Sections 99 and 284.

But the problems most often encountered by the civil service worker involve either outside employment related to his agency or the acceptance of small gratuities, neither of which is covered by the statutes. A relatively short work week makes it possible for thousands of government employees to carry an outside job to supplement their income. The employee with a special skill or experience that he uses in his government work may want to make use of it in outside work as well. But an employee of the Federal Housing Administration who conducts an outside real estate business, for example, may seriously embarrass the agency, and regulations commonly prohibit such related activity.[1] These regulations mainly affect career personnel rather than the executive employees in Washington on temporary appointment. The other most frequent conflict of interest problem of the civil servant is the small gratuity — the dinner out, the Christmas ham, or the bottle of whiskey at New Year's, paid for by a company or individual dealing with the employee's agency. This annoying problem, calling for constant line-drawing and tact in dealing with others, is nearly always a subject of agency regulations.[2]

The recurrent problem to the agency, if not to the individual employee, is the flow of civil service employees into private companies and organizations doing business with the agency. Other, and more important, aspects of this problem are discussed in a following chapter.[3] It is enough to note here that during negotiations for such transfers, the employee will often be disqualified by regulation from dealing for the agency with his prospective employer.[4]

[1] Federal Housing Administration, *Your Job in FHA, a Handbook for Employees* 48–50 (1955); see discussion, Chapter IV *supra*, under "Outside employment."
[2] See discussion, Chapter IV *supra*, under "Gratuities."
[3] Pages 223–235 *infra*.
[4] S.E.C. 17 C.F.R. § 203.5 (Supp. 1959) (negotiation for private employment).

Conflict of interest restraints thus touch upon the civil service in many ways. Nothing in the available evidence suggests, however, that the present pattern of restraints in any way deters the recruitment of civil service employees.

POLITICAL EXECUTIVES

In the federal government today approximately 1,100 executive positions are filled on a full-time but temporary basis by political appointment of the President or the heads of agencies.[5] Less than half of these require senatorial confirmation. These 1,100 jobs are the top policy-making jobs in the executive establishment. They have become increasingly difficult to fill.

The last chapter reviewed briefly some of the major factors likely to influence a government appointee as he weighs whether to accept or reject the appointment offered him. Somewhere in the course of these considerations and counterconsiderations, the subject of conflict of interest restraints will usually crop up. The prospective appointee learns in one way or another that he may have to make some adjustments in his personal economic interests while he is in Washington and for a period after he leaves Washington, and that these adjustments may entail substantial personal sacrifice. Out of the welter of influences pressing upon him, the political appointee himself often cannot after the event assess to what extent his decision to decline was attributable to the burdens of the conflict of interest restraints, or to what extent his decision to accept was delayed, or made conditional, or otherwise limited by them. Available evidence supports the conclusion, however, that the conflict of interest restrictions have substantially contributed to the government's difficulties in recruiting executives.

APPOINTMENTS SUBJECT TO SENATE CONFIRMATION

The positions most affected have been Defense Department posts subject to confirmation by the Senate. The rigid attitude of the Senate Armed Services Committee on stock divestment has been the source of the difficulty. In at least two cases since 1953, presidential appointees who had already appeared before the Committee

[5] See BERNSTEIN, THE JOB OF THE FEDERAL EXECUTIVE 10–11 (1958).

withdrew their names when the Committee insisted upon its stock sale requirement.[6] The evidence is that many prospective appointees to Department of Defense positions have declined in advance to be considered, in large part because of the Committee's practice of forced divestment. The Secretary of Defense is reported to have written to Senator Russell on April 5, 1956, that it had been factually demonstrated in the Department's efforts to recruit outstanding people for top posts that the policy of the Senate Armed Services Committee had made it extremely difficult — even impossible — to secure the best qualified persons for particular positions.

In discussing obstacles to executive recruitment in the Department of Defense, a leading official in 1957 went even further:

> The conflict of interest statutes cause us more trouble in recruiting than any other single thing, including inadequate salary. Some time ago, several executives in the department divided up a list of 57 names to fill an important executive post. We felt that any one on the list would be all right. We were not successful. In about half of the cases, conflict of interest under the statutes kept us from getting men who otherwise would have been willing to come to Washington for two or four years. We have to find a better solution to this problem to enable the department to get its fair share of executive talent.
>
> We recently had a difficult job in research development to fill. Person after person declined the job because of conflict of interest. One fellow we wanted badly had several thousand shares of stock in a company he had worked in for 35 years. He is good for at least a few more years of executive work. He would love to come to Washington, but will not sell his stock in order to do so.[7]

Interviews with Defense Department officials and former officials, and with persons declining executive appointments to the Department, provide further support for the conclusion that confirmation policies of the Senate Armed Services Committee and the existing

---

[6] Robert Sprague was nominated as Assistant Secretary of the Air Force in January 1953. The Senate Armed Services Committee opposed his confirmation because he refused to sell his shares in his family firm, The Sprague Electric Company. His nomination was thereupon withdrawn, on February 11, 1953. In 1957 Willard F. Rockwell served as Acting Chairman of the Army-Navy Munitions Board after being nominated as Assistant Secretary of Defense for Logistics and Supply. He served several months before the Senate Committee refused to confirm his nomination because he declined to sell stocks in two family concerns, the Rockwell Manufacturing Company and the Rockwell Standard Corporation. On August 4, 1953, he requested the President to withdraw his nomination, and he resigned his government post on September 24, 1953.

[7] Quoted in BERNSTEIN, THE JOB OF THE FEDERAL EXECUTIVE 158–59 (1958).

conflict of interest restraints have hampered recruitment of depart-mental personnel.[8]

Although top executives of large publicly held companies are among those deterred from government service by the stock divest-ment requirement, it appears that the persons hardest hit by the Committee's rule are not of this group. The man most affected is the executive who owns and operates a family business. For such a man, sale of his company's stock is more than the sale of an invest-ment or the sale of shares in an employing company; it is the disposition of the family company itself to outsiders, and the relinquishment of a future career for himself and for his children.[9]

The evidence of hindrance to recruitment arising out of the Committee's rule on stock divestment relates mainly to business executives. This is in part because stock ownership is common among this group and in part because business executives are those most apt to be appointed to the Defense Department. The Com-mittee's rule, however, applies to all occupations and has an equal effect on any appointee holding stock. For example, lawyers ap-pointed as General Counsel of the Defense Department have been required to dispose of small and incidental stock investments in companies with which they had no other business affiliation.[10]

As discussed earlier, no Senate Committee other than the Armed Services Committee has shown in its confirmation proceedings a sustained concern with the conflict of interest issue. Correspond-ingly, no evidence available suggests obstacles to executive recruit-ment arising from the conduct of these Committees. And no evidence has been seen that any appointee who was willing to accept the standards imposed by a Senate confirming committee boggled at the requirements of the conflict of interest statutes or regulations.

OTHER FULL-TIME APPOINTMENTS

Less clear are the deterrent effects of the conflict of interest restraints on recruitment for posts not requiring Senate confirma-tion.

[8] For example, interviews indicate that in a recent year thirty-five persons refused to take research and development posts in Defense, and that some critical research and development posts had remained vacant for as long as six months. See Appendix C.

[9] Both Messrs. Sprague and Rockwell were in this category. Mr. Stevens' strong resistance to sale of his stock was based on the same considerations.

[10] *Hearings Before the Senate Committee on Armed Services on Nominations of Robert Dechert [and others],* 85th Cong., 1st Sess. (1957).

It will be recalled that there is nothing in the statutes themselves that requires divestment of stockholdings. As a 1958 study stated, instances of forced stock divestment "undoubtedly received tremendous publicity all out of proportion to their significance in terms of numbers of jobs affected since only 5% of the responding present or former B[usiness] M[en in] G[overnment] stated that they were required to relinquish their investments. This problem appears to be limited to a very small number of businessmen who serve, probably those in the most important positions. On the other hand, it could mean that a considerable number of businessmen declined government jobs because they refused to dispose of their investments." [11]

Except in the case of lawyers, discussed below, the most troublesome statute is Section 1914, prohibiting outside compensation. Its deterrent effect is undeniable. Inadequate salary scales are among the major stumbling blocks to government recruitment efforts.[12] Many employers are willing to grant a leave of absence to an employee while he is on a temporary government assignment, and to continue his former salary, or supplement his government salary. Section 1914 prevents this, though the employer has no business relations of any kind with the employee's agency or with the government generally. Many people who would otherwise be willing to accept government appointment are prevented by this section from doing so.

The deterrent effect of Section 1914 does not primarily fall on the highest ranking executives of the largest companies, or upon the senior men at the peak of their business careers; for these men salary is often of secondary consequence. The group most affected by Section 1914 is the middle rank of executives. These younger men usually have heavy continuing financial commitments in the form of house mortgages and school bills. To them immediate and regular cash salary payments at a steady or rising level are essential. A voluntary slash in salary, at this critical stage of their careers, especially when coupled with the increased expense of a move to Washington, is out of the question.

The full effect of Section 1914 is blurred by its uncertain mean-

---

[11] HARVARD BUSINESS SCHOOL CLUB OF WASHINGTON, D.C., BUSINESSMEN IN GOVERNMENT, AN APPRAISAL OF EXPERIENCE 26 (1958).
[12] See Chapter VI, note 13 *supra*.

ing. As noted earlier, opinions vary widely on the extent to which it prevents government employees from continuing their participation in retirement, insurance, and other such security plans common today in all institutions. If a strict construction of Section 1914 is followed, a prospective appointee faces an abandonment of his long-range retirement and insurance plans. Even if the plan permits the employee to go on leave of absence and the employer stops making payments under the plan, it is arguable that the section does not permit the employee to continue even his status as a qualified member of the plan. In any case, the amount of the payments required to be made into the plans is normally beyond the reach of the middle-ranking executive, especially if he is simultaneously facing a salary cut and increased living expenses in accepting government appointment. Altogether, Section 1914 is a serious obstacle to recruitment of men for government office at an age when they are apt to be most vigorous and productive.

Probably this effect of Section 1914 is most marked in the business community. Logically Section 1914 would be thought to have the same effects on men recruited for government service from the universities, especially if one recalls the origin of the section as a bar to prevent nonprofit institutions from supplementing the salaries of men in the Bureau of Education. But the Attorney General has expressed the opinion that a university professor might work for the government on a leave of absence, even while continuing compensation from his university, since the university was not paying him "in connection with" his government work.[13] And it is quite unlikely that a teacher's continued participation in a university insurance or retirement plan would be held to violate the section. The situations of the university employee and the business company employee are different in some degree, and a distinction in result under Section 1914 might be justified in most circumstances. There are situations, however, such as allocation of research grants, in which the university man and the businessman in government can raise exactly the same problems of conflicting interests, and here a disparity in the law applicable to them is hard to explain. Since Section 1914 is an over-all prohibition against outside compensation, it leaves no room for refined rules adapted

[13] See 39 Ops. Att'y Gen. 501 (1940).

to the employee's particular government assignment or to the particular source of his outside compensation.

Section 434, requiring disqualification of the government employee, appears to have only incidental effect on the recruitment of personnel. Occasionally an individual spot job may absolutely require the holder to deal with a particular company. An aluminum resources administrator could hardly avoid dealing with Alcoa, and an appointee with an interest in that company would have to disqualify himself so often that he could not perform his government job; he would in effect be faced with declining the appointment or disposing of the interest. Instances of this kind can occur, and have occurred, but are rare.

Section 216, forbidding payments to government employees for aid in securing government contracts, is almost a bribery statute and has no observable effect on recruitment of personnel.

The position of lawyers under the conflict of interest statutes is unique. The point was made earlier that the four statutes dealing with prosecution of "claims" mainly affect lawyers since they limit exactly the kind of representational services normally performed by their profession. In addition it happens that a combination of three extrinsic circumstances spectacularly steps up the voltage of these statutes for lawyers.

For centuries the law has said that a partner is responsible for the acts of his partners and that the acts and knowledge of one partner will be "imputed" to the others. This is an assertion of a legal policy, useful in many contexts; it is a proposition often uttered and accepted, however, as though it were a description of a fact, a proposition springing in some mysterious way from the word "partnership," but not from other words of organizational form such as "corporation." Second, the law, mainly for historical reasons, forbids lawyers to practice in the organizational form we call the corporation and requires all joint practice to be cast in the form of partnerships. Finally, the growth of the federal government, the development of a mixed public-private economy, and the increase in tax levels have brought every enterprise into abrasive contact with the government. As a result, a significant part of almost every lawyer's practice is the representation of his clients in matters in which the federal government is or may be an adverse party.

The combination of these three factors — the doctrine of imputation of partners' acts, the compulsory use by lawyers of partnerships, and the growth of private contacts with the government — dramatically increase the effect of the conflict of interest statutes on lawyers. If a lawyer becomes a government employee, not only is he forbidden to undertake representations that fall within the statutes, but by the doctrine of imputation he may be in violation if his partners undertake such representation.[14] Conversely, rigorous application of the imputation doctrine imputes to his partners knowledge of facts the employee may have learned in his government service, whether or not his partners are in fact aware of them.[15] As a consequence the lawyer who enters government service is usually forced to resign from his law partnership or impose on the firm the severe handicap of staying out of legal matters involving the government. Further, under Sections 99 and 284 he must usually, as a practical matter, not rejoin the firm for a period of two years after he leaves employment.

With the main fire of the conflict of interest statutes trained squarely on the lawyer and his practice, it would be thought that the government would encounter particular difficulty from this source in its efforts to recruit lawyers into full-time governmental service. But in spite of the restrictive conflict of interest restraints, and in spite of the fact that lawyers recruited for a particular post will often decline it because of the conflict of interest statutes, the government has consistently been able to find others willing to accept a full-time government appointment likely to last two or three years. The profession's tradition of government service accounts for much of this. Possibly law firms are more sympathetic than most employers to the lawyer's desire to serve a stint in government, and are more ready to permit him to go without losing ground in the firm. There are important practical considerations as well. Unlike the corporate executive, the lawyer finds his loss measured primarily by the reduction, if any, in his current income, since most deferred compensation plans and stock options, deductible pension plans and other fringe group-benefits, are, under the

14 See Chapter III, note 33 *supra* and accompanying text. The language of section 281 referring to services performed by the employee "or another" probably achieves the same result directly.

15 See United States v. Standard Oil Co., 136 F. Supp. 345 (S.D.N.Y. 1955).

tax laws, limited as a practical matter to business in corporate form, and are not therefore characteristic of the lawyers' partnership. Moreover, the lawyer has more incentive to enter government service: his work there will usually be more directly applicable to and related to his professional work, and his experience and contacts gained there more directly usable in his practice after leaving government. Unlike the businessman, he is apt to add to his professional stature as a result of his government service. It is true that when, after some two or three years, he leaves government employment and returns to private practice, he is subject to the post-employment restrictions of Sections 284 and 99, and these can be troublesome. Nevertheless, for whatever reasons, the conflict of interest restrictions do not appear seriously to embarrass the government's efforts to recruit lawyers for full-time government appointment. As will be seen, recruitment of lawyers for intermittent government service is quite another matter.

INTERMITTENT EMPLOYEES

Present conflict of interests restraints affect intermittent personnel differently from regular full-time personnel. In some respects their deterrent effect on recruitment of intermittent personnel is even greater.

Intermittent employees have seldom if ever come before the Senate for confirmation. The compulsory stock divestment practices of Senate committees therefore are not a factor in their recruitment.

The businessman who may be deterred by the conflict of interest restrictions from accepting full-time appointment is relatively free to serve in an advisory capacity. Asked to be a consultant one day a month, the businessman generally accepts unhesitatingly insofar as the conflict of interest restrictions are concerned. He seldom, if ever, considers himself a government "employee" by virtue of his advisory services, and he makes little or no adjustment in his private affairs on accepting the assignment. Section 1914 may raise problems, but they are usually ignored by intermittent employees.[16] If properly advised, the consultant would be aware that he is subject to Section

16 See discussion on page 66 *supra*.

434 and would avoid self-dealing situations when he is actually on
the job in Washington. But this restraint is a comparatively easy
one for a consultant to comply with, since he is seldom representing
the government in a direct transaction of business with outside
entities. The other statutes affect the businessman consultant almost
not at all.

When one turns to advisory or other intermittent services by
the lawyer, however, the teeth of the statutes cut the other way, and
the situation alters abruptly. The evidence is overwhelming that
conflict of interest restraints effectively block the government's
efforts to secure the services of lawyers to serve on its hundreds of
advisory committees.

More aware of the statutes and more professionally concerned
about the legality of his position, the lawyer sees the advisory
appointment to bristle with problems. He will recognize that, as a
consultant, he is an "employee" of the United States and that while
he is an employee, whenever that may be, he and his partners are
subject to the restrictions of the statutes. Section 1914 will raise
interesting, and insoluble, intellectual puzzles for him. But, far
more important, as soon as he becomes a United States employee
of any kind, the full weight of Sections 281, 283, 284, and Section
99 crashes down upon him and his partners. That means that his
law firm can do no tax work or patent work or antitrust work
involving the United States without exposing him to prosecution.
And even after he formally resigns as a consultant or his appointment is terminated, he faces the statutory two-year bar. His only
safe recourse is to resign from his firm. But he cannot and will not
resign from his law practice and his firm in order to stand by,
awaiting an occasional call to spend a few hours in consultation with
the government.

The result is inevitable. Lawyers with special experience or skill
— often acquired while on an earlier full-time tour of duty with
the government — are regularly requested by government agencies
to serve as continuing consultants to help the government. They are
usually forced to refuse for no reason whatever except the conflict
of interest statutes.

UNCERTAINTY AS A DETERRENT

An unmeasurable but unmistakable impetus is given to the deterrent effect of the conflict of interest statutes by their uncertainty. At many critical points they defy understanding or prediction. The lawyer asked to advise his client on the applicability of the statutes to his particular circumstances is in a difficult position. In the matter of personal conflicting interests, the political appointee occupies the most exposed position imaginable. There is no better political ammunition than the charge of conflict of interest; the party out of power will spare no efforts to smoke out the rascals; and like the foreign agent disowned by his own government if discovered, the executive appointee detected in a questionable conflict of interest position can expect little protection or defense from his own party or the administration that appointed him. Some elements of the press, radio, and television stand ever ready to raise the hue and cry. All but one of the statutes provide criminal penalties — felony penalties, comparable to those for theft or bribery — and, while prosecutions have not been frequent, no one can predict when the next prosecution will occur, perhaps not totally free of partisan overtones. Conviction, prosecution followed by acquittal, or even indictment under one of these statutes can disgrace a man for life. And so when the prospective appointee asks his lawyer for counsel on the application of the conflicts statutes to his particular situation, the careful lawyer tends to be especially cautious. The more strict the lawyer's interpretation, the more likely that the appointee will decide that the personal costs of compliance with the statutes are too great and that he had better decline the appointment.

RELATED ADVERSE EFFECTS

Existing conflict of interest restraints have other adverse effects that are related to their deterrent influence on recruitment. Many of the same forces that tend to deter people from going into government service tend to induce them to leave it. Much of the government's recruitment problem derives from its difficulties in retaining staff already on the job. In many situations it is even more important to the government to retain trained men than it is to be able to recruit untrained replacements. The conflict of interest restraints, particularly in their prohibitions on outside compensation, add to the other factors that make it difficult for the government to keep its staff.

A second consequence is that as a result of the impact of the conflict of interest restraints, government officials tend to develop informal channels for securing the assistance of men deterred from accepting formal appointment. An expert who will not come to the office as an employee once a month can frequently be reached for informal consultation in his home on the weekend. From the standpoint of the government's need for his services, this informal advice is better than nothing. Yet if there are risks in the use of outside consultants, they are surely magnified where there is no record of the consultation, no method of controlling the agenda, and no institutional arrangement for general supervision. Consultation should be as overt a matter of public record as possible, to prevent the very risks against which the conflict of interest restraints are directed. Misdirected restrictions defeat their own purposes.

Finally, the general tendency of the conflict of interest restraints is to erect a barrier around the government through which it is difficult for information to move in one direction or the other. This blockage of information flow may be the most dangerous consequence of all, judged by the demands that the twentieth century has placed upon American government. The government's programs for scientific development probably offer the best illustration of the point. They are the subject of the next chapter.

VIII

The Scientist:
A Contemporary Case Study

Earlier chapters have described some of the major forces at work in present-day America affecting conflict of interest problems in federal service. The position of modern American science and the modern American scientist graphically exemplifies these changes. As stressed earlier, the distinction between that which may be called "governmental" and that which may be called "private" has grown increasingly evanescent in American society of the mid-twentieth century. Nowhere are the mixed economy, the growth of government, and the increase in governmental functions better seen than in the field of scientific development and research.

In 1959 the United States government spent nearly $5 billion on research, engineering, and development, including procurement funds for research and development.[1] This was more than the government spent for that purpose in the four decades between 1900 and 1939 — and more than the total federal budget a generation ago. Today about one-half of all scientific research, engineering, and development carried out in the United States is paid for by federal money.[2] For 1960 about $5.5 billion has been budgeted for scientific

[1] THE PRESIDENT'S SCIENCE ADVISORY COMMITTEE, A REPORT ON STRENGTHENING AMERICAN SCIENCE 1 (1958).

[2] The dependence of some fields of scientific research upon government financing is even greater. According to the same report the government-financed share of such work in 1958 was over 85 per cent in the aircraft industry, and 60 per cent in the electrical equipment industry. *Id.* at 19. See generally NATIONAL SCIENCE FOUNDATION, FEDERAL FUNDS FOR SCIENCE, VII: THE FEDERAL BUDGET FOR RESEARCH AND DEVELOPMENT FISCAL YEARS 1957, 1958, AND 1959 (1958).

research and development programs.[3] The expense of modern scientific installations, unavoidable international pressures demanding one crash program after another, the size of the research projects required, the exponential rate of technological break-through — all combine to draw the federal government irresistibly into the field of science on an enormous scale.[4]

American scientific research today is the product of a sprawling and uncoordinated partnership of industry, foundations, universities, and government. In 1958, only 44 per cent of the federal research and development budget was spent in government laboratories; 38 per cent was allocated to laboratories owned and operated by profit-making organizations, 15 per cent to universities and other educational institutions, and 3 per cent to other groups.[5] Research and development are conducted by government laboratories, by private laboratories, by industrial laboratories, by universities on government grants, by commercial laboratories on government contracts, by nonprofit research organizations operating on government contracts, and by an endless variety of instrumentalities through which governmental and private sources share financing, administration, and direction. Private research groups contract with the government to help direct the programming of government research, and of government-financed private research. The consequence is an interpenetration of operations that defies separation.[6]

Perhaps, like the statue to the boll weevil in Enterprise, Alabama,

---

3 BUREAU OF THE BUDGET, THE BUDGET OF THE UNITED STATES GOVERNMENT FOR THE FISCAL YEAR ENDING JUNE 30, 1960, 989–99 (1959).

4 The largest sponsors of federal research and development are the Department of Defense, the Atomic Energy Commission, the Department of Health, Education and Welfare, the National Science Foundation, the Departments of Agriculture, Interior, and Commerce, and the National Aeronautics and Space Administration. Together these eight departments and agencies administer over 95 per cent of the total federal research and development budget. See THE PRESIDENT'S SCIENCE ADVISORY COMMITTEE, A REPORT ON STRENGTHENING AMERICAN SCIENCE 1 and passim (1958); NATIONAL SCIENCE FOUNDATION, op. cit., supra note 2, at 4.

5 Id. at 8–9.

6 For a thorough review of the interpenetration of university research and federal programs, see KIDD, AMERICAN UNIVERSITIES AND FEDERAL RESEARCH (1959). For insights on the relations between government and industry in research, see FIFTH ANNUAL CONFERENCE ON INDUSTRIAL RESEARCH, PROCEEDINGS [June 1954], COORDINATION, CONTROL, AND FINANCING OF INDUSTRIAL RESEARCH (1955), especially Brozen, The Economic Future of Industrial Research, and Quarles, What Military Research and Development Mean to Industry. See also Machlup, Can There Be Too Much Research? 128 SCIENCE 1320–25 (1958); King, Science and the Changing Face of Industry: The Social Phase, in 7 IMPACT OF SCIENCE ON SOCIETY (1956).

American scientists should memorialize Sputnik in marble. With the opening of the atomic age the scientist had begun to emerge from the obscurity of the laboratory, and after 1950 his public appearances increased. But he did not burst into full view until Sputnik began to swing overhead every 95 minutes; suddenly everyone heard what a few had been preaching for years. The United States was being seriously challenged in the field where it had smugly assumed itself superior. The nation was committed to a technological struggle for existence, and scientists had become very important people.

The impact upon the personal position of the scientist has been remarkable. The scientist's actions have become news. Frequently interviewed on television, on the radio and in the press, he sits in the seat of the mighty, or at least beside it, and the world of affairs and statesmen attend seriously his opinions. The old caricature of the scientist as a kind of combined Dr. Frankenstein and Mr. Chips has been replaced by a public image of the scientist as a hard working citizen of learning and probity, engaged in vital tasks and worthy of great respect.

The long-deserved shift in public attitudes is gratifying. Doubtless it will be an important factor in attracting more of the young into the field. But the flattery of public attention has not been the sole reward of eminence. The scientist and his work product are in demand; he has discovered that he can make money; and he has found as an administrator that he can man the control tower of institutions that give him a voice and community power. It is all very new, very fluid, and far from shaken down, but within the scientific community some members have found themselves adept at and interested in the new commercial and administrative side of their profession. Not infrequently today a small group of young scientists start their own company in a frontier research and development area — and hit the entrepreneurial jackpot. Larger companies, partially to prevent staff evaporation and partially because it is necessary to their operations, create the new position of Vice President for Research and Development. And some scientists can look forward to even higher corporate office. In universities, in foundations, in the nonprofit research companies, in promotional and coordinating committees, in government, and in industry, some scientists have shed the smock of intellectual wage slave and assumed the toga of executive. And then there are the consultancies. Esoteric is the specialty of the physical scientist today who has not been asked to be someone's consultant. Those scientists who have stayed in university or other institutional laboratories find consultants' fees a welcome supplement to an institutional salary — and their institutions generally permit or encourage such outside work. Thus even those who have not leaped into the commercial or administrative arena find themselves economically involved in it far more than before.

The upshot of this new status and demand is that, relatively speaking, many scientists have become men of property. They are frequently shareholders in several small high-risk, high-return ventures. When their ship comes in, or if they are with larger corporations as key employees, they have stock options, retirement and pension benefits, and the other deferred-compensation mechanisms of the modern executive. As outside consultants they may be on several payrolls at once. Even as university teachers, they are participants in security, insurance, and welfare plans of every description. In an extreme and sudden form, the scientist provides a speeded-up example of the social development of America in the last generation.[7]

Limited in number, modern scientists are in demand from all sides.[8] The most important clamorer for their talents is the federal

---

[7] All the usual qualifications must be made. Some scientific specialties have not experienced the post-1950 surge of public interest; some scientists stay in their laboratories and scorn commercial temptations; some few scientists have always gone into administrative positions; a few serious scientists have been commercially successful in the past — James Watt, for example. But the challenge of dominion over atom, space, and cell has opened whole new vistas for the scientist today, just as the challenge of sea dominion opened new ranges of opportunity to the Drakes and Hawkinses.

[8] The shortage of scientists has been a dominant concern in recent years. The National Science Foundation since 1955 has conducted annual conferences on scientific manpower, the papers of which have been published. See especially Siegel, *The Influence of Government on the Demand for Scientists and Engineers*, in SCIENTIFIC MANPOWER — 1958 (1959); Wickens, *The Shortage of Scientists and Engineers* in SCIENTIFIC MANPOWER — 1956 (1957); Feiss, *New and Changing Activities of Scientists and the Implications*, in SCIENTIFIC MANPOWER — 1957 (1958). For economic analyses of the manpower market, see BLANK & STIGLER, THE DEMAND AND SUPPLY OF SCIENTIFIC MANPOWER (1957); ALCHIAN, ARROW & CAPRON, AN ECONOMIC ANALYSIS OF THE MARKET FOR SCIENTISTS AND ENGINEERS (1958). The demand for scientific manpower in the context of general manpower demands is discussed in GINZBERG, HUMAN RESOURCES: THE WEALTH OF A NATION (1958). For a useful review of recent congressional activity related to scientific manpower, see S. REP. No. 120, 86th Cong., 1st Sess. (1959). See also *Hearings Before the Subcommittee on Manpower Utilization of the House Committee on Post Office and Civil Service*, 85th Cong., 1st Sess. (1957).

government, appearing directly or indirectly through countless semi-private forms. Somehow this demand must be met out of the available supply.

The government hires many scientists on a permanent and full-time basis.[9] As noted earlier, however, the bulk of the federal scientific budget is spent outside government laboratories. Directly or indirectly, therefore, many scientists who are not regular employees draw all or part of their income from government sources. And the government, in turn, uses almost every conceivable kind of working arrangement to enlist the specialists' services it so badly needs. Many scientists choose not to accept permanent government employment because of relatively low salaries, a more regulated environment, and other factors. But they may be available as independent contractors, hired to do a spot research project; or if the contract is given to an existing research company, or a new one, they may be willing to go on the payroll of the contracting company. Many research contracts are granted to universities, and to the new nonprofit research corporations, in which case the scientists remain, or enter, on the private institutional payroll. Research contracts themselves show great variation in their terms and form, and in the degree of contact, supervision, and working relationship between the contracting agency and the men doing the work.

Some of an agency's particular needs can often be met by part-time consultative assistance from experts in the field. It is therefore commonplace for each of the eight major federal agencies in the science field to draw to itself clusters of advisory committees of scientific specialists. Consultative assistance of this kind is of par-

---

9 According to the National Science Foundation, federal, state, and local governments employed about 50,000 scientists of all types in 1954, 18,600 of whom were engaged in research and development work. Most of these scientists were federal employees. See NATIONAL SCIENCE FOUNDATION, TRENDS IN THE EMPLOYMENT AND TRAINING OF SCIENTISTS AND ENGINEERS (1956). Data on scientists employed in the government and elsewhere must be examined closely. In 1957 Paul D. Foote, testifying as Assistant Secretary of Defense Research and Engineering, stated that there were then 840,000 scientists, engineers, and technically trained persons in the United States, of whom 250,000 were engaged in research and development work. He added that about 100,000, or 35 to 40 per cent, of the latter were employed by the Department of Defense or Defense contractors, and that the Department of Defense alone employed 44,000 engineers, scientists, and technicians. See *Hearings Before the Subcommittee on Manpower Utilization of the House Committee on Post Office and Civil Service*, 85th Cong., 1st Sess. 223 (1957). These data obviously include many technically trained persons not included in the totals of the National Science Foundation.

ticular importance in the planning and programming of research. Often the hardest problem is not how to carry out a program; it is to decide wisely what program to carry out. What avenues should be explored next? Where is the state of the art falling behind and likely to create tomorrow's bottleneck? How is the work product of different research groups and institutions to be assessed? What balance is to be struck between the priorities of basic and applied research, between the anticipated lead times of competing approaches to solutions of a problem, between equipment and manpower allocation, between present needs and training needs for the future? No one is smart enough, or informed enough, to make these judgments alone with any hope of a reasonable batting average. Only a committee approach will do — and it cannot be limited to committees of scientists on the permanent government rolls. The science agencies inevitably turn to part-time advisory committees for help. In 1959, for example, the National Aeronautics and Space Administration had fifteen such committees.

The agencies apparently have not had a difficult time in staffing these advisory committees. Scientists from industry and the universities are generally willing to serve on them for a variety of reasons, and some specialists serve as consultants to more than one agency.[10] A major motivation is the sense of direct contribution and participation in frontier areas of scientific development. Of nearly equal significance is the opportunity to exchange information with others in related work, to learn in advance of normal publication what progress has been made or is pending, and to acquire insight into the course that research is apt to take in the future. The relatively small compensation paid to these scientific consultants apparently does not significantly affect their willingness to participate.

The range and scope of the contacts and relationships that can be mobilized on behalf of the government through the operation of scientific advisory committees is demonstrated most dramatically

[10] "While the precise number of advisers is not known, they probably number well above a thousand." Probably more than 60 per cent of the scientific advisers come from the universities. See KIDD, AMERICAN UNIVERSITIES AND FEDERAL RESEARCH 193 (1959). See also PRICE, GOVERNMENT AND SCIENCE ch. 5 (1954); NATIONAL SCIENCE FOUNDATION, ADVISORY AND COORDINATING MECHANISMS FOR FEDERAL RESEARCH AND DEVELOPMENT, 1956–57 (1957); Mainzer, *Science Democratized: Advisory Committees on Research*, 18 PUB. ADMIN. REV. 314–23 (1958).

by the President's Scientific Advisory Committee.[11] One or more members of this committee would have some contact with virtually every scientific issue or interest in those fields of science and technology currently important to the government. Its first chairman, James R. Killian, Jr., explained that the function ". . . of the Committee is to provide answers to questions raised by the President, to undertake assignments for him of an advisory kind, to mobilize the best scientific advice in the country, and make recommendations to him in regard to ways by which U.S. science and technology can be advanced, especially in regard to ways by which they can be advanced by the Federal Government and on how they can best serve the Nation's security and welfare." [12]

Apart from the dozens of technical advisory committees serving the government's scientific agencies, new semipublic, semiprivate institutions have begun to develop in response to the government's urgent need for scientific talent.[13] Examples include the Institute

[11] In December of 1958 the membership of the President's Scientific Advisory Committee included the following: Dr. Robert F. Bacher, Professor of Physics, California Institute of Technology; Dr. William O. Baker, Vice President (research), Bell Telephone Laboratories; Dr. Lloyd V. Berkner, President, Associated Universities, Inc.; Dr. Hans A. Bethe, Professor of Physics, Cornell University; Dr. Detlev W. Bronk, President, Rockefeller Institute for Medical Research, and President, National Academy of Sciences; Dr. James H. Doolittle, Vice President, Shell Oil Co.; Dr. James B. Fisk, Executive Vice President, Bell Telephone Laboratories; Dr. Caryl P. Haskins, President, Carnegie Institution of Washington; Dr. George B. Kistiakowsky, Professor of Chemistry, Harvard University; Dr. Edwin H. Land, President, Polaroid Corporation; Dr. Edward M. Purcell, Professor of Physics and Nobel laureate, Harvard University; Dr. Isidor I. Rabi, Professor of Physics and Nobel laureate, Columbia University; Dr. H. P. Robertson, Professor of Mathematical Physics, California Institute of Technology; Dr. Paul A. Weiss, Rockefeller Institute for Medical Research; Dr. Jerome B. Wiesner, Director, Research Laboratory of Electronics, Massachusetts Institute of Technology; Dr. Herbert York, Chief Scientist, Advanced Research Projects Agency, Department of Defense; Dr. Jerrold R. Zacharias, Professor of Physics, Massachusetts Institute of Technology; Dr. James R. Killian, Jr., Chairman, Special Assistant to the President for Science and Technology, the White House.

The Committee is organized into a group of panels that include both regular members and others from outside the ranks of the Committee. The panels draw into the councils of the Committee a wider range of scientific experience and expert advice than can be provided by a single committee.

[12] Address by Dr. Killian on Science and Public Policy, delivered before the American Association for the Advancement of Science, Dec. 29, 1958, in S. REP. No. 120, 86th Cong., 1st Sess. 7 (1959).

[13] Much government-sponsored research has been undertaken by a few large research centers loosely affiliated with universities. A partial list includes the Jet Propulsion Laboratory at the Johns Hopkins University (Navy); Project Lincoln at the Massachusetts Institute of Technology (Air Force); the Los Alamos Scientific Laboratory and the Radiation Laboratory of the University of California (Atomic Energy

for Defense Analyses (IDA), the RAND Corporation, the Jet Propulsion Laboratory (JPL), the Radiation, Brookhaven, and Knolls
Laboratories.[14] These and the other similar entities working in the
field of science on the fringe of government differ from each other
in history, structure, and operation, but they are alike in their
fundamental character; concerned with scientific research and development, they represent new and ingenious operational and contractual amalgams of governmental and nongovernmental elements.
Most important, judged by their basic objective of making scientific
talent available to the government, they work.

What emerges, therefore, out of the government's urgent demand
for scientific manpower and out of the shortage of such manpower,
is a subtle spectrum of economic and employment relationships. At
one end is the scientist who works as a full-time government employee. At the other is the scientist who has no personal contact
with the government and whose employer and work project have
no contact with the government. Between these extremes there are
enough stops for Zeno's tortoise. Closest to full-time government
employment is part-time employment, with pay "when actually
employed" (WAE). The WAE may be an expert in a short-term
spot job over which he has operating responsibility and on which he
works for a few weeks consecutively. Or the scientist may serve
under special statutory dispensation as a WOC (without compensa-

---

Commission); the Argonne National Laboratory at the University of Chicago (AEC);
and the Ames Laboratories at Iowa State College (AEC). These research centers
employ as many as 4,000 persons each and over 15,000 in total. In 1959 the federal
government spent over $200 million for the operation of these centers. "As much
federal money is spent for the operation of a few research centers as for all support of
individual faculty members, and all other research organizations associated with universities." KIDD, AMERICAN UNIVERSITIES AND FEDERAL RESEARCH 185 (1959).

14 The Institute for Defense Analyses (IDA) is a private corporation managed by
four universities; its research activities are performed under contract with the Department of Defense. The RAND Corporation, whose headquarters are in Santa
Monica, California, is an independent research corporation operating under Air
Force contract. The Jet Propulsion Laboratory, an inheritance from World War II,
was built and is owned by the federal government but is managed on a private, civilian,
non-civil-service basis by the California Institute of Technology. The Radiation Laboratory of the University of California, beginning as a private academic organization that
was financed later from government funds, has been described as "a sort of subuniversity
for the study of atomic physics." (KIDD, op. cit. supra note 13, at 184.) Brookhaven
Laboratories, a separately incorporated research organization owned by the AEC,
is managed by Associated Universities, Inc., representing nine universities. Similarly
the Knolls Laboratory is managed by the General Electric Company for the AEC.

tion), working either in an operating capacity or as a consultant.

The scientist may take an individual contract or group-project contract to do a particular job as an independent contractor for the government. Similar contracts may, on the other hand, be drawn up between his legal employer and the government, with wide variations in the provisions on supervision and control. The government may give a grant to the scientist's institution or nonprofit research company, with the proviso that the particular scientist will work on the project or that the institution will temporarily lend the scientist to the government's project. The scientist may be simply hired by a company or institution that received the grant or the research contract. The scientist, or his own company, or his employer, may take a subcontract from the primary contractor. Or the scientist's contact with the government may be even more indirect. Perhaps he works for a company that has no research grant as such, but relies primarily on its defense production contracts for economic survival. Or his company may be a defense supplier that has been partially financed through a V-loan or some other form of government financial support. Or he may work for a university on a project wholly unrelated to the government, which, however, the university could not support if the government did not support other of its projects.

It is apparent that the present pattern of conflict of interest restraints bears little relation to the actualities of working relationships between the scientist and modern government. As a result of this maladaptation of nineteenth-century restrictions, and since they are largely irrelevant to needs, the statutes are simultaneously ineffective to curb real risks and crippling wherever they are enforced according to their terms. The many scientists who work on a contract basis, or on government-financed projects in universities or other institutions, are not "employees" and are not covered by the statutes at all. Full-time civil servant scientists are as little affected as other civil servants. The statutes that deal with prosecuting "claims" affect mainly the representational professions, and seldom if ever would apply to a scientist, except perhaps in some sort of technical contract or patent dispute in which he might be called as an expert witness. Section 434, calling for disqualification of the government official, has an impact on regular employees in operational positions,

but those employees are not apt to have significant outside commitments, while the scientist serving as consultant, on the other hand,
is seldom in the kind of business-transacting situation to which
Section 434 applies. Then too, Section 434 is thought not to apply
to transactions with nonprofit entities, often the employers of scientists. The post-employment statutes, again dealing with the prosecution of claims, have little effect on the scientist, in view of the nature
of his job.

For the scientist asked to serve the government as a consultant,
the provisions of Section 281 and of Section 1914 could be extremely
troublesome. The former, forbidding the government employee to
provide compensated services to another "in relation . . . to any . . .
matter" in an executive forum can, in view of the absence of limits
to this broad language, make almost any consulting work dangerous.
The government, the concern employing the scientist, and the scientist himself are all at all times working simultaneously on "matters"
that are "related." As for Section 1914, the problems of applying it
to intermittent employees generally have special force for the scientific consultant, typically a corporate or institutional employee.[15]
Indications are that as yet there is little general awareness in the
scientific community of these statutes, though some company counsel
have become conscious of the problem. Section 1914 in particular,
fundamentally unworkable in the case of intermittent employees,
appears to be unknown to and ignored in practice by the consultant,
though not by the full-time appointee.[16]

[15] See Chapter III *supra*, "Preliminary Evaluation."

[16] In November 1959 an incident occurred that has some relevance to the question
of recruitment of scientists and outside compensation. The Secretary of Defense
proposed the name of Charles L. Critchfield to be director of the Advanced Research
Projects Agency (ARPA), an important office in the Department of Defense for the
coordination of research and development programs, and an office that has been un-
usually difficult to fill. Mr. Critchfield was director of scientific research of a major
supplier to the Defense Department. He was to be appointed as one of the ten specially appointed WOCs permitted by the Second Supplemental Appropriations Act
of 1951. See Chapter III, note 98 *supra*. As soon as it was announced that the new
appointee would continue to receive his salary from his company, however, public
criticism arose from some members of the House of Representatives. Feeling that his
usefulness had been impaired, and declining to resign his affiliation with his company,
Critchfield requested that his name be withdrawn. See N.Y. Times, Nov. 5, 1959, p. 1,
col. 3; N.Y. Times, Nov. 7, 1959, p. 23, col. 1; N.Y. Times, Nov. 13, 1959, p. 11, col. 4;
N.Y. Times, Nov. 15, 1959, p. 33, col. 1. Since the appointment was fully authorized
by law, the case does not show that the conflict of interest statutes as such deprive
the government of the services of needed men. But it does illustrate the deterring

Administrative attention to the conflict of interest position of the temporary or consultant scientist varies from agency to agency. The regulations of the AEC on conflicts of interest of its employees are worked out in some detail, and the agency makes an effort to give all employees, full-time and consultant, a direct introduction to these regulations.[17] In some agencies, on the other hand, while the full-time scientific employee is recognized as subject to the statutes and regulations, the periodic consultant seems not to have been made fully conscious of his legal status as an "employee" for this purpose.

Yet it is inevitable, under the circumstances of modern science and modern government, that the scientific appointee, full-time or part-time, should sometimes find himself in situations of conflicting interests. Consultants must be called in to advise the National Institutes of Health and the National Science Foundation on the allocation of research grants and contracts; inevitably they will, and should, include some people from among the universities or other institutions that will receive the grants. The outside interest of such a consultant may not be simple. Even though he will seldom have a direct cash interest in the grant, in the sense that he will receive a higher pay check if the grant goes to his institution than if it goes to another, he is apt for many reasons to have a personal preference in the matter. Institutional pride, the specialist's desire to work on the problem for which the grant is given, the scientist's yearning to add to the scientific equipment available for use at his institution, the hope of attracting other scientists and students to come to stay at the institution — all the normal and healthy aspirations that go with keen interest in his work, ambition for professional standing and success, and loyalty to his institution — operate to give such a consultant expert a stake in one allocation as against another. This preference may be successfully counterbalanced in the consultant's mind. It may show up in his arguing or voting for his own institu-

---

effect of the principle of Section 1914, and indicates that more basic attitudes and political forces may bar some appointments even where the statutes would permit them.

[17] The Atomic Energy Commission has been notably sensitive to the problem of preventing conflicts of interest from arising in the work of its consultants. See discussion Chapter IV *supra;* Atomic Energy Commission, AEC Manual, ch. 4124, "Conduct of Employees" (1956).

tion, or against another, or in his leaning over so far backwards that he deprives both the government and his institution of his sound professional judgment. Among scientific advisers called in from industry to assist in making decisions on new development programs there will at times be some whose companies will receive the development contracts. Private, industrial, and institutional representatives serving within the public-private institutions such as the Institute of Defense Analyses are apt to have more than one concern in the issues under consideration.

The problem is not limited to the making of grants or contract awards. Consider, for example, the university scientist who serves as consultant to a government agency and who also serves on other days of the month as consultant to a private company, or who has an economic stake in a company of his own — all within his field of specialization. There is no conceivable way in which technical ideas or information acquired by him in the course of his three activities can be tagged and compartmented in his mind as reserved solely for use in one. He cannot, under the circumstances, avoid serving to some extent as an information conduit. And of course one of his greatest values to all concerned is precisely that he is an information conduit.

It is not the purpose of this chapter to point with alarm. No indication has been seen of improper conduct on the part of any scientific advisers; every evidence is of dedicated professional men continuously giving of themselves to their profession and to the government. Still several useful lessons may be learned from a consideration of the special conflict of interest problems of the scientist who works with, if not in, the government.

First, the scientist offers a concrete example of the working of the general factors discussed in the last chapter. His skills are in short supply, and his services are in great demand by government and others, in part as a consequence of the Cold War. He increasingly has a stake in corporate retirement and stock plans, and substantial personal economic commitments. He works in a field most dramatically illustrating the unique mixed private-public economy of contemporary America, and often cannot be classified either as a government "employee" or a "nonemployee." He demonstrates in a modern and complex form the exposure of government employees to

potential and real conflicts of interest. The desirability and work-
ability of almost any general proposal for new regulation in the field
can be successfully measured by testing it against its effect on the
situation of the scientist.

Second, the position of the scientist, particularly the intermittent
consultant, illustrates how very far from targets of modern reality
the conflict of interest statutes are for those who are not in one of
the representational professions. Suppose there were an unprin-
cipled scientist, serving as a government consultant, who wished
to profit on the outside, or add to the resources and glory of his
home institution through the improper use of his government connection and inside information. Except in certain instances where
Section 281 would apply, it is hard to find anything in any of the
conflict of interest statutes to prevent such misconduct. As for administrative regulation, the scientist's case is typical in the uneven-
ness with which regulations apply and are enforced. Taken as a
whole, the case of the scientist demonstrates the unworkability of
sweeping flat statutory rules, the necessity for flexibility and for
close tailoring of conflict of interest restraints to fit the exact need
at hand.

Finally, the scientist's situation underscores how difficult it is
to work out satisfactory solutions to modern conflict of interest
problems. Simple reiteration of the injunction against serving two
masters will not do. It is now clear, as it was not in the last century,
that any pattern of restrictions, however admirable in purpose,
must be carefully measured against its possible negative effect
upon the government's efforts to meet its urgent need for personnel
and information. Restraints on conflicts of interest in the mixed
economy of today can no longer be geared to sharp distinctions between government and non-government. Rigorous application of
even the existing conflict of interest statutes could severely cripple
governmental recruitment in a most critical area — scientific development. In the case of the consultant, one of the major potentials
for risk lies in the commercial usefulness of information acquired
out of the consultancy. Yet it is an administrative and psychological
impossibility to enforce a rule that technical information learned
in one place be forgotten in another; and the interacting flow of
ideas and information from many sources is exactly what is called

for from the scientific consultants. Government officials must disqualify themselves from participating in situations of conflicting
interests, but as the scientist's case shows, it proves very difficult to
say how far this disqualification should go. It is futile to try to draw
a sharp line separating decisions on policy matters (whether the
rocket program should emphasize liquid or solid propellants, for
example), where personal disqualification is presumably unnecessary, from decisions on immediate operating questions (whether an
award for propellant research should go to company X or company
Y), where any official interested in either company must disqualify
himself. The decision on the policy question will necessarily affect,
if not totally determine, whether future programs lie with company
X or company Y — or perhaps company Z — or with totally different
industry groups made up of different companies. Must the government, under this logic, hear no word of counsel from any industry
scientist on any issue related to the question of liquid versus solid
fuels? The evidence is that many scientific consultants, acting sometimes by agency rule and sometimes out of personal scruples, disqualify themselves from a final vote on contract and grant awards
to their own institutions. But should they even participate in the
discussion preceding the vote? On the other hand, how can the
government be denied their expert judgment when judgment in
these matters is of the highest public importance and is substantially
available nowhere else? [18]

These are the kinds of problems that must be faced today in
working out conflict of interest restraints. The scientist's situation
throws clear light on their complexity if not their solution.

As a final comment on the scientist's role in the conflict of
interest field, it would not be amiss to fly a small storm warning.
The scientist has not been long in the public arena, nor long in the
marketplace. Scientist Alpha, pure in heart, knowing himself dedi-

18 The rule of the National Science Foundation represents an effort to guard
against conflicts of interest on the part of its board members without depriving itself
of valuable counsel. Board members are not required to disqualify themselves from
participation in projects supported by the Foundation merely because of membership
on the board. On the other hand, members do not participate in board decisions
involving their own institutions, nor do they personally participate in the support
of any application of their institutions for Foundation funds. Resolution Adopted by the
National Science Board at its Fifty-fifth Meeting on September 16–17, 1958, *Participation of NSB Members in NSF Projects.*

cated only to the advance of scientific knowledge regardless of who has title to the laboratory or pays for the research, and with never a thought of conflicting interests, is likely one day to undertake a set of multiple counseling commitments that will suddenly explode into political charge, countercharge, investigation, and conceivably even indictment. Or perhaps scientist Beta, with less pure motive than Alpha, and more conscious of the economic possibilities of his government advisory position, may turn his opportunity to good account, be discovered — and again trigger the political chain reaction. The results of either of these events would be most unfortunate. The new and shining public symbol of the scientist would be tarnished; the scientists' traditional suspicion of the political process would be further darkened; and the arbitrary restraints clamped down by a politically sensitive Congress upon the use of outside scientific advice might critically hinder the government's scientific development program.

Whether or not changes are made in the conflict of interest statutes, the agencies concerned with the nation's science program could do much to head off an unnecessary explosion. Regulations could be reviewed and revised with the special problem of the scientific consultant in mind. More could surely be done to inform all consultants of the existence of the conflict of interest statutes and regulations; and beyond the range of legal regulation, some avuncular advice about the political risks of conflicting commitments could easily be passed along. If no more were done than to raise and emphasize the problem with the consultants, it would help to make them more conscious of it and to forestall trouble.

I X

Summation

No one disputes the harmful potential of conflicts between an official's duties and his personal economic advantage. Where such conflicts exist some men will succumb and favor their private over their public instincts. Concern for appearances and the absolute need to maintain the government's reputation for integrity inspire periodic legislative statements of principle on this matter. The problem is therefore not whether to have a system of legal restraints on conflicts of interest, but how to design a system that achieves the maximum protection with a minimum of undesirable collateral results. The preceding chapters provide a basis for evaluating the existing pattern of conflict of interest restraints. Out of a summary evaluation there should also emerge an outline of objectives to be sought, and hazards to be avoided, in designing a new and better program.

The existing pattern of conflict of interest restraints is in major part a failure. It falls short of its stated objectives, and it produces undesirable side effects.

Most of the conflict of interest statutes were and are pointed at areas of risk that are no longer particularly significant, mainly government claims procedures. The practices that agency regulations have found it necessary to control are largely unmentioned in the statutes. The serious problems of conflict of interest raised under modern governmental conditions are largely untouched by the statutes. Congress has done a useful and constructive job in its capacity as investigator. But the Senate confirming committees have either done little about the issue or, in the case of the Armed Services Committee, have applied a wavering standard of stock divestment, useful for certain purposes of appearances but largely ineffective in controlling official behavior. The regulations, frequently more modern in content, lack the administration to make them effective.

The most damaging result of the present system is its deterrent effect on the recruitment and retention of executive and some kinds of consultative talent. The restrictions tend to block the interflow of men and information at the very time in the nation's history when such an interflow is most necessary. As developed in earlier chapters, the undesirable effects of the present system of restraints are traceable to three basic causes: faulty drafting, inadequate administration, and the obsolescence of the statutes.

Anyone reading the conflict of interest statutes recurrently finds his way blocked by their opaque drafting, their degree of overlap, and their lack of coordination. A major contribution to the field would be made even if no more were done than to consolidate and unify this patchwork of one hundred years of fitful legislation.

The administration of the conflict of interest restraints has always been weak, especially in its want of coordination and leadership from the Chief Executive. In part this lack of executive aggressive pursuit of the topic is a product of a failure of the statutes. If they presented an integrated whole — a program — and if they imposed direct responsibility on the President to carry out that program, there can be little doubt that the central coordination and leadership found wanting in the past would improve.

Administration of the restraints also includes the application by the Senate confirming committees of their own standards in the field. Though this is not an area in which legislation is an appropriate vehicle, any comprehensive program for improving the operation of the present system of restraints should include suggestions for more efficient conduct of the confirmation process.

In any event, no program is any better than its administration. One of the items highest on any agenda for revising the present pattern of conflict of interest restraints is improvement of their administration. A well administered program could, and should, guide the thousand good men as well as snare the one bad man.

By far the greatest defect in the present system is the obsoleteness of the statutes. In most significant respects the statutes are talking about a world that has ceased to exist; they are not talking about the world that does exist in American government today. Their focus of interest is upon a class of lower-ranking politically appointed clerks that has disappeared.

The personnel system of the mid-nineteenth century, dominated by the spoils system, has given way to a complex personnel system of totally different character. The government today obtains its manpower through a vast civil service, a top revolving group of political appointees, an increasing group of temporary and intermittent employees, and an unlimited variety of contracting-out arrangements. Each of these groups is performing a vital part in the governmental process, and is here to stay. The present system of restraints treats this spectrum by lopping off one end entirely and jamming all the balance into one rigid category appropriate to full-time government clerks appointed under the spoils system. A system of conflict of interest restraints designed for today must be more flexible in recognizing the different categories of employment.

The statutes are obsolete in their narrow concentration upon government claims and government contracts. Big modern government and its citizens have many more contacts than those of claim and contract, and with these, new areas of substantive risk have arisen. A system of conflict of interest restraints should include regulation in some substantive areas not now restricted by the statutes.

The present body of restraints is obsolete in its assumptions about government procedures. These assumptions lead again to overemphasis on the anachronistic problem of claims, now under administrative control. In the case of government contracts, no account is taken of internal administrative protections against corruption of modern contracting procedures. Correspondingly, the statutes overemphasize the utility of sanctions based on the criminal law. Conflict of interest restraints should place initial emphasis on the responsibility of the executive branch to maintain discipline in its own establishment through the administrative process.

The present outdated restrictions have come into effect one by one without a consideration of their consequences upon the government's need for personnel. This probably did little harm so long as government was relatively small, its functions were not ramified, and its need for expertise was not great. But twentieth-century American government is charged with heavy international responsibilities, deeply involved in running the domestic economy and committed to a technological race for survival. It must be able to equip itself with trained talent and to provide itself with information and the judgments of the most skilled. A chronic shortage of executives and technicians makes this difficult; international semi-warfare makes it imperative.

The statutes and, to a lesser extent, the practice of the Senate Armed Services Committee do not show an awareness of the realities of economic life in the United States today. America has become a society of group participations and commitments. One evidence is the spread throughout the economy of institutional insurance, retirement and similar employee welfare plans. Many citizens will accept lower pay on a government assignment, but few will, in the name of conflict of interest, throw away their future security plans to accept government appointment. To require such a sacrifice compounds the recruiting difficulties of the government arising from low salaries, the generally low prestige of government service, the availability of favorable opportunities in the private economy, and the trend toward less mobile careers. Permanent government employees, on the other hand, can hardly be attracted or kept in government service if they are treated as second-class citizens forbidden to share, in their private lives, in the growth of the nation's economy. People no longer seek government office as a source of income — a plum for which the political game is played. Government instead is a competitor in the marketplace, bidding for temporary executive talent, and handicapped on almost every count in that competition. No adequate system of conflict of interest restraints designed for today's needs can ignore these economic facts.

Most of all, the present structure of conflict of interest restraints is obsolete philosophically — obsolete in the central idea of what it is trying to do.

In the United States today we cannot hope to build a system of restrictions that will keep all persons connected with the government from acting in any matter in which they have a personal interest. Such a system is a mirage. In part it is a mirage because these persons and their views are often needed by the government. Much more important, it is a mirage because it is an ideal founded upon the premise that there *is* a distinction between government and non-government. Because, in our mixed economy, this distinction has grown tenuous, we can no longer hope to keep our interests in neat identifiable compartments. The blending of public and private endeavor must bring with it some reassessment of the position of the men involved. For example, government, industry, and educational institutions are operating full blast on a partnership basis in the science field. It has become archaic, impractical, and inconsistent in such a situation to say that a scientist may not work "for" government unless he ceases to work "for" industry or "for" an educational institution.

The point — not an easy one, but basic — is not a naive assertion that the nature of man has improved his capacity to resist the temptation to further his own interests. It argues only that cake eating and having are incompatible. We could insist upon a strict standard of separation between our government employees and the private economic world *if* we kept government and non-government operations clearly separate and if we knew at all times who a government man was. We do neither of these. We staff our top positions with temporary in-and-out appointees. We contract out big government jobs — and then must find liaison men to tell both sides what is going on. Or, as the science field best illustrates, we merge public and private operations and call upon the services of many in an ambiguous public-private capacity.

We feel that this is the right way, the American way, to proceed, and are content with it. But one of its costs lies in the erosion of the basis for any easy solution to the conflict of interest problem. We are deliberately constructing institutions of dual, or blended, loyalties, and must be prepared to live with the conflict of interest consequences. The result is that any program of restraints for the United States must be content with approximation. Plato's philosopher kings could isolate themselves from private interests; America's democratic government cannot.

Part Three
A Proposed Remedy

X

The Program

The program proposed here is for all employees of the executive branch, but of that branch only. Existing law and practices respecting conflict of interest problems of Congress and the judiciary are unaffected by the program.

The proposed program embodies several different components. It calls first for a single integrated statute to replace the present seven conflict of interest statutes and the various exemptions under them. After a preamble, the statute contains a section defining some basic terms, which are then used consistently throughout. The next six sections prescribe a statutory code dealing with six different substantive areas of conduct involving risks of conflicts of interest in the case of executive branch employees. Administration and enforcement are the subject of four sections of the statute.

The program contemplates a code of regulations supplementing the substantive provisions of the statutory code. Responsibility for the administration of the program is vested in the President, who is then authorized to delegate most of the job to a small coordinating office. Through the work of this office, the President will issue general regulations on conflict of interest problems susceptible of such general treatment. A portion of the discussion in this chapter concerns the content of these regulations. More particularized regulations will be issued on an agency-by-agency basis. A number of procedures are recommended to promote the day-to-day administration of the program. The program includes recommendations for improved procedures in Senate confirmation hearings on executive appointees.

The proposed program makes the following key changes or clarifications in present law and practice:

— Consolidates the scattered conflict of interest laws into one unified act, with a common set of definitions and consistent approach.

— Broadens the scope of the conflict of interest laws to cover the full range of modern governmental activities.

— Differentiates in some respects between regular and intermittent employees and accommodates itself to the modern use of intermittent personnel.

— Generally strengthens the restraints against conflicts of interest, and elevates to statutory level some important restraints now in regulations or not covered, particularly relating to gifts and use of office to obtain something of value from persons doing business with the government.

— Recognizes the legitimate private economic interests of government employees, and permits employees to retain certain security-oriented economic interests, particularly continued benefits in outside pension plans.

— Places greater emphasis on administrative remedies.

— Creates the framework for an effective regulatory and administrative structure, with responsibility centered in the President.

— Moves toward improvement of procedures for, and coordination of, conflict of interest inquiries in Senate confirmation proceedings.

A number of miscellaneous proposals complete the program offered here. One such proposal is a recommendation for a study of the conflict of interest problem in Congress.

Chapter XI contains the full text of the proposed statute, accompanied by a formal commentary relating it to existing law. In this chapter the program is discussed in more general terms.

The components of the proposed program are discussed in the following order: administrative structure; substantive provisions in the statutory code; substantive provisions in the projected general regulatory code; administrative procedures; confirmation procedures; and miscellaneous recommendations.

ADMINISTRATIVE STRUCTURE

The President

In all matters within the executive branch, the key figure must be the Chief Executive. Much of the difficulty characterizing the present pattern of conflict of interest restraints is traceable to the lack of an established role to be played by the Presidency. Present restrictions in the field are the product of sporadic congressional action and scattered agency energy. The voice that should be most heard in the administration of executive-branch personnel is that of the chief of the executive branch.

The President should play the main role in two entirely different ways. The first is by power of example. The President must set the general tone of the administration — the standard of sensitivity to ethical problems that will govern the conduct of millions of subordinates. The behavior of department heads, and of their juniors, will be powerfully influenced by the standards of behavior set by example in the White House. For example, although the flow of gifts, most of them symbolic in nature, to 1600 Pennsylvania Avenue probably cannot and should not be stemmed, the matter of how the White House disposes of these gifts is very delicate. The soundest approach to this problem appears to be an invariable practice of passing such gifts along to charity or to the national museums. In all other aspects of personal behavior in relation to those who may be regarded as seeking to advance their particular economic interests, the greatest circumspection should be used by all Presidents.

The President's other major function relevant here is to govern and administer the personnel of the executive branch.

The role of administration

As seen in the executive branch of the government, the conflict of interest problem is essentially a day-to-day problem. It is not a single dragon to be slain and then enshrined in song; it is a nagging harpy constantly near at hand.

The present structure of statutory restraints as a body of criminal statutes is essentially off focus. Criminal penalties for certain kinds of serious breaches of conduct or willful violation of the law are undoubtedly needed and should be retained. But, unlike the policy-makers of the nineteenth century, we no longer are forced to cope with subtle problems of personal conduct bearing only a potential of harm with the same legal poleax we use against murder, arson, and treason. The modern administrative process gives us a whole new storehouse of refined and more useful tools with which to supplement the criminal process.

There are several reasons for strengthening the administrative process relative to the criminal process in the handling of conflict of interest problems. One reason is that as a practical matter the criminal laws in this field have been, and predictably will be, seldom used. Overreaching statutes are usually left unenforced. Further, the necessity of relying exclusively on criminal remedies has led draftsmen to the further necessity of drawing the statutory restrictions with an unfortunate, narrow rigidity. This kind of concreteness is essential for criminal enforcement. When it is attempted in an area of broad ethical regulation, it may be expected to produce exactly what it has produced — restrictions that are in some areas so narrow as to miss the problems, and are in other areas so vague and ill-defined as to be criminally unenforcible as a practical matter. Emphasis on the criminal aspect of administration necessarily focuses the restrictions and administration upon the cops and robbers aspect of the conflict of interest problem. Correspondingly it makes the statutes of little substantial assistance in the important job of providing guidelines for proper behavior for government employees. Finally, criminal penalties are out of keeping with the character of many of the offenses prescribed in the conflict of interest statutes. This is true because conflicts of interest uniquely raise the problem of "evil in embryo." Legislation against conflicts of interest is prophylactic in its nature; it seeks to head off evil before it comes. This is a legitimate and indeed necessary thing to do, but it means that in such regulation we are operating at one remove away from actual substantive offense. In such a case the law's ultimate weapons should be used sparingly.

Any new over-all program to deal with conflict of interest problems in the executive branch should therefore give first emphasis to administration. Day-to-day enforcement, in turn, should look primarily, though not entirely, to administrative sanctions.

It is of the utmost importance that the new program impose specific responsibility on the President for the administration of conflict of interest restraints. The nature of the problem will forever make it impossible for generalized statutory rules to cope effectively with it. Yet Congress, confronted with executive inaction or desultory action, has responded with proposals for more detailed and extensive legislative controls. In the long run, however, the answer cannot lie in the direction of congressional action. Legislation in the field should be limited basically to those situations where criminal penalties are appropriate and to those situations where general rules applicable to all divisions of the executive branch can be enunciated with reasonable clarity and permanence. Beyond this, Congress should do what it has often done in other areas but has never done in the conflict of interest field — impose express responsibility upon the President to develop and carry out a program for policing the executive establishment. The proposed statute so provides.[1]

Central coordinating office

The President would obviously delegate to a particular official or office full over-all responsibility for an effective personnel program coping with the conflict of interest problem. A modern conflict of interest program should envision a three-tiered structure. The first tier consists of Congress and its statutory enactments in the field. The second tier — which does now not exist at all — should be made up of the President and a central coordinating office. The third tier is the departmental or agency level where all existing administrative regulations are now prepared and promulgated.

The coordinating office would have much to do. It would be specifically responsible for developing and preparing for promulgation by the President general regulations on conflict of interest problems applicable throughout the executive branch — regulations less detailed than the more particular regulations at the lower tier of the agencies and departments themselves. It would provide a coordinating and unifying center for the development of standards applicable in the separate agencies, and would directly assist the agencies in preparing their own regulations and their enforce-

[1] See Chapter XI, § 10.

ment procedures. It would, it is hoped, develop machinery for sharing its experience on conflict of interest questions with heads of agencies and departments. It would collect information and experience under the agencies' regulations and under its own government-wide regulations, and provide a continuing source of information and legislative suggestion in the area. It would develop and maintain the necessary administrative machinery for the implementation of the statutory scheme and standards set by Congress. It would follow through on directives issued from the White House to agencies and departments in this area, and see to it that such directives were in fact put into effect. It would lend continuing assistance to the White House, to Congress, and to executive appointees in respect of their conflict of interest problems and in respect of the confirmation process discussed later. And it would provide a central focus of public and congressional attention whenever conflict of interest issues arose, and would demonstrate the seriousness with which the problem is viewed by the executive branch.

No giant super-bureau is in any sense contemplated here; at most a small office would be adequate to provide a point of central location of responsibility. The problem today is not that conflict of interest administration needs more manpower; what has been lacking has been focus, centralization of responsibility, and the designation of an official for whom the conflict of interest problem is not just another task on an endless list of operational responsibilities.

The precise location of the office is not important so long as it is directly responsible to the President. The task should not be allocated to the Civil Service Commission or to the Department of Justice. The Civil Service Commission has little contact with the appointed group of political executives with whom many of the problems arise; the role of the Department of Justice as criminal enforcement agency makes it inappropriate for this assignment. Perhaps the most obvious candidate for the job is the office of the administrative assistant to the President for personnel. Wherever the responsibility may be centered, the important thing is that it be centered in such a way as to lend continuity, initiative, and carry-through to the administration of the program.

Other functions relating more broadly to general personnel ethics could also be assigned to this office.

The recommendation for a central coordinating office responsible to the President in no way suggests that the actual administration of conflict of interest regulations should be centralized. Present patterns of regulation, agency by agency, illustrate the need for a flexible system permitting agencies to conform their regulations to their particular situations. This sort of flexibility and variation at the agency, departmental, and even bureau level is healthy and indeed essential to an effective administration. The regulatory function of the central coordinating office should be limited to the setting of across-the-board minimal standards for presidential promulgation. The office would also provide coordinated interpretations of the statutes themselves, in consultation with the Department of Justice. Subject to the statutes and subject to the general regulations issued by the President, day-to-day regulation and administration should lie with the respective departments and agencies. Corresponding responsibility and power should be clearly settled upon them by presidential action with the authority of Congress. The proposed statute provides for this authority specifically.[2]

STATUTORY CODE

It is frequently proposed as a remedy to the conflict of interest problem that Congress adopt a general Code of Ethics for all executive branch employees. The program proposed here adopts a somewhat different approach, but an approach that encompasses most of what the proponents of codes of ethics have had in mind.

There are several objections to the adoption by Congress of an over-all code of ethics. From the standpoint of this immediate study, a code of ethics covering only conflicts of interest would be incomplete, since the general problem of ethics in government is far broader than the topic under consideration here. A second objection is that, necessarily, any code adopted by Congress must be applicable on a broad scale and must therefore be couched in very general terms. The actual provisions of proposed codes of ethics have tended to be primarily hortatory. Probably the most important consideration, however, is that any such congressional action would perpetuate one of the fundamental defects that has historically characterized

2 Chapter XI, § 10.

this field — absence of a focus of clear responsibility upon the President to police the ethical practices of the executive branch. The view taken here is that, in essence, Congress should lay down general policy, enact those provisions that are of sufficient concreteness to require and permit criminal enforcement, and impose specific responsibility on the President to put the administration of ethics in the executive branch into order and keep it there.

There is therefore proposed here a statutory code of six major substantive provisions. It contemplates that the President, acting through the coordinating office described earlier, and through the individual agencies, would over a period of time develop a carefully worked out supplementary code, or codes, of conduct. It is thought that this combined technique is preferable on all scores. Prepared close to the daily workings of administration, it will produce a more workable and relevant set of rules of conduct than could ever be put together at a statutory level. Correspondingly, the statute is enabled to avoid the twin risks of platitude and rigidity.

The preparation of a statutory code governing conflicts of interest involves a two-step process: development of a general body of salutary rules of conduct, then selection from this group of those rules that are suitable for statutory statement. The first step calls for a clear identification of the objects of these rules — of the dangers to be warded off. The general issues of public policy at stake in matters of conflict of interest were discussed in Chapter I. It may now be proposed more specifically that conflict of interest restraints are aimed primarily at three general kinds of misconduct, real or apparent, and that any rule that contributes to the control of these may be considered an appropriate candidate for inclusion in a code of conflict of interest restraints. The premises are:

1. Persons occupying a position inside government must not be allowed to tamper with the wheels of government to the special advantage of themselves or any entity on the outside in which they have a personal economic interest.
2. Persons occupying a position inside government must not be allowed to help an individual or entity on the outside, where the latter is seeking to make the wheels of government move in a particular way.
3. Persons occupying a position inside government must not be allowed to use their office as a source of power or of confidential information for purposes of advancing their personal economic interests.

The periphery of regulation for these purposes is of course blurred. It may be necessary to include, under the regulations, those who are no longer in office but retain a residual capacity to influence government action, deriving from their former government position. Similarly, in view of the critical importance of maintaining public confidence in governmental integrity and of preventing trouble before it occurs, it may be advisable to include rules to deter outsiders from offering government employees undue inducements or incentives to behave contrary to these propositions. In any event, any useful conflict of interest regulation should be based on the premises mentioned.

As the second step, out of the total number of possible rules that might be suggested, the statutory code proposed here determines upon six. These six have been carefully selected for inclusion in the statute, as opposed to administrative regulations, because they can be made to meet three basic tests.

The first test is universality. A conflict of interest restraint should not be included in this integrated conflict of interest statute if it does not appropriately apply across the board to all agencies of the executive branch.

The second criterion is that the provision be capable of concrete expression. Can the proposed rule be stated with sufficient clarity to guide an employee who wants to know what he can do; to provide an adequate basis for criminal penalty; and to make it possible for lawyers to give reasonably reliable opinions on conflict of interest problems?

The final criterion used in selecting the six restraints listed here is that of history — the government's past administrative experience. The substantive restraints proposed here are in some respects more stringent than those of the present conflict of interest statutes. But they are not conjured up to head off hypothetical horrors. Some of the restrictions are adaptations of those contained in the present statutes; some of them find parentage in the body of agency regulations relating to conflicts of interest; some will be recognized as fitting particular historical incidents.

Each of the proposed six substantive rules is thought to be generally applicable, clearly statable, and grounded in governmental experience.

Before commencing the review of the substantive provisions of the proposed statute, it is useful to point out three general concepts that pervade the statute as a whole, running horizontally, so to speak, through the individual provisions.

"Intermittent Government employee" and "regular Government employee"

The first of these concepts is the distinction between the regular full-time government employee on the one hand and the intermittent government employee on the other. Attention has been drawn in the course of this book to the increasing use by the federal government of intermittent employees as consultants and experts; it has been emphasized that the demands placed upon modern government absolutely compel their use. The point has also been emphasized that the personal position of these intermittent employees differs from that of full-time employees, and that the factors affecting their recruitment differ from those affecting full-time appointees to government service. Repeatedly in this book the existing conflict of interest restrictions have been criticized for their failure to recognize the government's special need for intermittent personnel, as well as the special conflict of interest position of these men.

The statute proposed here for the most part applies the same rules to intermittent employees and to regular employees. But in several situations a distinction in treatment is drawn. The terms "regular Government employee" and "intermittent Government employee" are technically defined.[3] In substance, an intermittent government employee is a government employee who has performed services as such on not more than 52 working days out of the preceding 365 days. The consultant who comes to Washington an average of one day a week therefore remains within the category of an intermittent employee; similarly a short-term assignment not exceeding 52 days, even if consecutive, does not alter the employee's status as an intermittent employee. In special situations, the President may extend this 52-day period to 130 days upon a finding by him that the national interest requires it. The definition

3 Chapter XI, § 2(f), (g), (j), and commentary thereon.

of "employee" under the proposed statute excludes reserves of the
armed forces when not on active duty and classifies them as intermittent employees when they are on active duty solely for training.

"Government action"

A second concept appearing throughout the statute appears in
the phrase "Government action." The statutory definition of this
term is given in section 2 (e). In correspondence to nineteenth-century needs, the present conflict of interest statutes bear down
heavily on situations in which the economic relationship involved
is either a claim against the government for money or property, or
a contract with the government. This narrow focus of interest is
quite unsatisfactory in the circumstances of modern government,
as has been earlier observed in this book. Today the executive
branch can dispense not only contracts and claim awards, but
television franchises, merger clearances, urban development loans,
and tax rulings, to name but a few examples of "government action."
The purpose of this broad definition is to extend the application
of the proposed conflict of interest statute to the fullest range of
executive-branch activity.

The importance of the new concept of "government action" is
very great. It works to expand the coverage of the conflict of interest
statute far beyond the existing structure of restraints. It is a fundamental and radical change required by the circumstances of modern
government. Its full significance will become clearer as the substantive restrictions are discussed.

"Transaction involving the Government"

The third general concept deserving prior mention appears in
the recurrent phrase, "transaction involving the Government." This
too is a defined term of art under the statute. It is given in section
2(n). Somewhat more technical in nature than the concepts of the
"intermittent employee" and "government action," the idea of the
"transaction involving the government" plays an important substantive role in a variety of places throughout the statute. A major
criticism of existing conflict of interest statutes is that they are
hopelessly open-ended in defining the outer limits of the sensitive
transactions with which they are concerned. The reader may recall,

for example, the difficulty in deciding under Section 284 whether a former employee was employed or performed duty directly connected with a "subject matter" involved in the claim against the United States. The new concept of a "transaction involving the government," rigorously defined, is designed as a substitute for such boundless phrases as "subject matter" that today recur in the conflict of interest provisions. While, of course, no more self-executing than any provision can ever be, the definition of the phrase "transaction involving the government" lends a degree of concreteness to the statute that, at one of the most critical points of their interpretation, the present statutes do not have. In actual application, the firm definition of "transaction involving the government" will be found to be of great use.

The contribution of "transaction involving the government" is more a matter of clarity than of expansion or contraction of the existing law. No one knows what the proper scope of the existing laws may be.

With these three working tools in hand, it is possible to turn to a substantive review of the six rules of conduct for executive branch employees laid out in the proposed statute.

STATUTE SECTION 3: ACTS AFFECTING A PERSONAL ECONOMIC INTEREST

The central conception of conflict of interest regulation is that an official should not act for the government where his private economic interests are involved. The most direct attack upon this objective is to require the official to disqualify himself from participating in transactions involving the government in which he has a substantial personal interest. This rule of disqualification is the first substantive restraint in the new statute.

Present Section 434 is unsatisfactory in several respects. One of its striking inadequacies is that it is limited to business transactions with profit-making entities in which the employee has an interest. This rule is entirely too narrow. Today the federal executive branch acts in countless ways that have immediate economic impact on individuals. An effective conflict of interest rule on disqualification must reach out to compel disqualification of the interested official not only in respect of business transactions with business entities, but in respect of all federal executive action that substantially affects his personal economic interests, whether or not a profit-making organization is involved. A second inadequacy of Section 434 is that it applies only to one acting as an officer or agent of the government in dealing with the outside concern. The statute, as written, therefore, reaches only the front, or contact, man, and has no apparent application to require an interested official to disqualify himself from participating in the transaction in other ways, as by advice or investigation. This is obviously an unsatisfactory situation, and the proposed statute therefore spells out a much broader concept of "participation," as is noted below.

The principle of disqualification is considerably easier to state than to apply. In many cases an employee will, in worrying whether to disqualify himself from acting, consider many and varying subsidiary questions. How large must his personal economic interest in the transaction be to raise the disqualification question? Is the size of the interest to be judged relative to his personal economic worth, or by any of various other possible standards of comparison? What if the interest is held not by him but by his wife or another member of his family? How close a relationship is required between the official's government act and his personal interest in the consequences of the act? Suppose, for example, the government action, if decided one way, has no effect on his interests but if decided the other way might possibly have an effect on his interests depending on certain other contingencies? What exactly is an economic interest? Is the official, for instance, to be disqualified from dealing with his landlord on the ground that he has an economic interest in the landlord's terminating (or not terminating) his lease? What of unsalaried but highly prestigious offices held in an organization? If a government official holds one of these, may he deal with the organization for the government? What if the official's only conflicting interest in dealing with a particular person is that the official is trying to get into a country club of which the other person is currently president? And, once it is decided that the official has an "interest," or someone else in a close relationship to him has an interest, when must he disqualify himself in his official role, and from what? If, for example, there are two applicants for a license and he holds an interest in one, may he disqualify himself in respect of that one but vote against the other applicant? From what range of activities should he disqualify himself? Does it make a difference, for example, that his only connection with it is in the signing of a routine paper, or that his recommendations on the matter will be independently reviewed by others? This line of questions can be continued almost without limit.

The present Section 434, facing the same issues, answers them very narrowly. It is cast in terms of business transactions only, and there must be another business entity involved in the pecuniary profits of contracts in which the official has an interest. When, under the proposed new statute, these limiting conditions are withdrawn, the scope of the disqualification requirement is dramatically expanded. At the same time, the necessity for working out limits for the disqualification process becomes even greater. For this reason the disqualification section of the new statute, section 3, seeks to provide answers to some of these questions, guides to others, and authorization for administrative resolution of the rest.

Size and remoteness of interest

Probably the most difficult problems arise in deciding how great and how direct the official's interest in a matter must be to trigger the disqualification requirement. The problem must be met by regulations increasingly particularized as they approach the particular jobs in question. The program proposed here contemplates that the new coordinating office would start at once to develop regulations and standards for defining interests that disqualify.

Efforts to spell out these standards in terms of fixed formulae of holdings or in dollar amounts have so far proved fruitless. The most important principle is that the interest should be a substantial one — meaning that the circumstances of personal interest should raise the possibility that a reasonable man (not necessarily the particular official) would in fact be affected in his official judgment. Unlike Section 434, the proposed statute specifies the requirement of substantiality.

The most absurd challenge to common sense on this point has in the past arisen in connection with stockholdings. There seems to be at large a misconception that stock ownership is in some way different from other forms of economic holdings, and that even the smallest stockholding in an affected concern demands the official's disqualification. The concern of congressional committees, commentators, the press, and public spokesmen over stock ownership has probably had its worst effects in directing attention away from other kinds of economic interest, often of much greater importance. Any kind of contract, whether a contract of debt, of employment, of loan, of lease, of option, of purchase, of sale, of mortgage, of insurance, or of anything else, can squarely raise the conflict of interest issue in an extreme form. The disqualification rule should treat economic interests, whether in form of stock, land, employment contract, partnership interest, inheritance, or something else, on the same level.

At least two kinds of personal interests of officials should *not* be considered a basis for necessary disqualification. It is an easy demonstration that all citizens have some economic interest in everything the government does — and indeed in everything that each individual does. Like every other issue, the problem is one of judgment, not of recourse to verbal formulae producing automatic responses. Government officials do, and must, act on all kinds of things in which they have *some* private economic interest, if only in their private capacity as taxpayers. Room must be left for the kind of personal interest that is widely shared by the public at large, or a significant segment of the public, such as farmers. Similarly the official must be left free, for example, to sign his own papers with reference to his promotion in office, though he has a personal interest in his official act when he does so. Section 3(d) specifically excuses the official from the disqualification requirement in these two situations — where the official's interest is widely shared, and where it derives only from his position as an employee of the government.

The statute proposed here also resolves certain other open questions about the kind of interest that will call for disqualification. It specifies, for instance, that the official can be disqualified by the interest of his child or spouse or of an employer, or of any person who is able, through contractual relationship, to affect the official's economic interests directly and substantially. A good example of the last category would be the holder of a demand note payable by the government official; the bargaining position of such a note-holder over the employee puts the employee in a difficult conflict of inter-

est position if he is required to act for the government in any transaction involving the note-holder. In these cases, of course, it is a
prerequisite that the employee *know* of the interest of the other
party. For his own personal interests the standard of knowledge
required is somewhat different under the statute, since he is generally presumed to know what his own holdings and economic interests are.[4]

In a particular situation, identification of a disqualifying interest
must hinge on all the facts, including the agency, the job, the
government action, the impact of that action, the kind and amount
of the official's personal interest, its relation to his job, and, in some
instances, the kind and amount of his other interests. It is hard to
imagine a subject better suited for the administrative processes of
regulation and advisory ruling and less adapted to criminal sanctions. Section 3(d) explicitly places responsibility in this field upon
the President and the agencies below him.

Participation

From what should the interested official be disqualified? The
question is left quite unanswered under present law. The proposed
statute, however, says that the disqualified official shall not "participate" in the transaction involving the government; and again
"participate" is a defined word. The definition, set forth in section
2(h), will be seen to be very broad, covering, for example, "advice."
On the other hand, it requires personal affirmative action by the
official — mere "responsibility" (another defined term) is not equivalent to "participation." The definition will not answer all questions,
but it offers a guide to an answer where now there is none.

Administration of disqualification requirement

Only a very few government agencies have taken serious steps to
administer the disqualification principle. To make it fully effective,

---

4 Problems lie concealed behind the problems here. There may be persons with
significant economic leverage over a government employee who have no contract with
him; but the line must be drawn somewhere, else every potential donor to the employee
would be included. On the question of knowledge of interests, there is the possibility
that the employee will not know what his economic interests are, as where, for example,
shares unknown to him are held in trust for his benefit. The language of § 3(a) is
drafted to take account of this possibility.

some positive administration is necessary. The rules should be impressed upon employees. Employees should be encouraged, not discouraged, to transfer a sensitive matter to another official of correlative rank and responsibility, or, in some cases, to delegate the job to other officials. In some instances special agency regulations calling for a degree of personal economic disclosure may be in order. For example, all employees of the Securities and Exchange Commission are today required to maintain a current file with the agency of all concerns in which they hold securities. In such a case, the amount of the security holding would not be a critical factor. But in some situations and in some agencies, disclosure of information on the amount of a particular holding, or on other kinds of economic contracts or interests held, might be desirable.

The need for a counseling procedure or ruling process in the conflict of interest field has been mentioned earlier. Often this process could be successfully invoked in connection with disqualification. An employee who has some kind of contingent or remote interest in a matter should have some place to turn for a judgment on the necessity for his disqualification.

Disqualification is not a total instrument of protection. The most serious problems in its application arise in the case of officials of the highest rank, where statutes sometimes require particular decisions to be made by particularly high officers such as the secretary of a department. The secretary, in such a case, cannot well disqualify himself from making a decision for which he is expressly legally responsible.

And yet it is quite possible to exaggerate the importance and the significance of this argument. In the first place the conflict between the non-delegable duty and the statutory requirement to disqualify already exists under Section 434. One way or another, the federal establishment has lived with this legal neurosis for a long time. The more significant point is that when two such statutes conflict, the fault may lie not in the disqualification statute but in the statute forbidding delegation of a responsibility. The normal and better rule is that the disqualification principle should be applied for its own sake and officials should be able to delegate their duties to subordinates in most situations. At the top of any large organization the need for delegation is urgent. As the government has grown in size and complexity, the burdens of individual responsibility imposed by law on high government executives have become almost unbearable. The most extreme instance, of course, is the President, who must in some way be relieved of some of the mounting assignments continually being piled on his shoulders.

In any case, undelegable responsibilities within the federal executive establishment are comparatively rare, and where they exist they are almost invariably at the highest levels and involve matters of substantial public interest. At these heights the winds of publicity blow hard. The political power of disfavored competitors can be relied upon to produce explosive reactions if there is a suggestion that a high-ranking government official is favoring a concern in which he has an economic interest. Altogether, the disqualification rule is sound, and the principle to be followed. Non-delegable responsibilities should be kept to a minimum. Where Congress concludes to require the personal action of a particular official, it should recognize the conflict with the disqualification rule; for clarity, it should either provide the official with an exemption from the disqualification requirement of the conflict of interest statute, or provide an exception in the non-delegability rule when the official is in a position of conflicting interests.

Given a sufficiently serious and tough administrative enforcement, personal disqualification can be a major bulwark against the dangers of conflicts of interest.

Presidential exemption power

To say that an official has some personal interest in a government matter is not necessarily to say he should be disqualified from participating in it. As has been pointed out, situations frequently arise in less industrially developed countries or in smaller communities where the community loss from an expert's disqualification far exceeds community risk arising out of his personal interest in the matter up for governmental action. It is not difficult to imagine similar cases in the federal government, particularly in the field of science. The United States might, for example, need expert representation at an international conference on the peaceful uses of atomic energy. In all likelihood the most qualified men to represent the nation in such negotiations would be top scientific officials with private American companies engaged in atomic development. Yet these might be the companies that would most clearly be directly affected by any international policy decisions reached on future atomic development. Where such situations arise, a balance must be struck between the national interest in using its best — perhaps its only — experts and the national interest in protecting the public against dangerous conflicting personal interests. In some cases, presumably, the balance will be struck in favor of using the best qualified men available. For these cases, some carefully circumscribed leeway should be left for partial relaxation of the disqualification principle.

Consequently the statute offered here provides, in section 3(e), that the President be given a partial exemptive power for this purpose. The power is closely hedged about. The exemption should go only to a particular employee, not to a position. It should be used only after full disclosure of the employee's economic position producing the conflict of interest, and, except where national security is involved, that information should be put on the public record. Moreover, the President should be required to make an express determination that the national interest in the employee's participation exceeds the public interest in his disqualification. This special exemptive power should rarely be used. But where it is needed, it is badly needed. It would be foolish to impose a disqualification rule so inflexible that we have to cut off our arm to avoid the risk of breaking it.

STATUTE SECTION 4: ASSISTING IN TRANSACTIONS INVOLVING THE GOVERNMENT

The second substantive provision of the new statute states in modern form the biblical injunction against serving two masters.

In the FHA investigation in 1955 it appeared that some employees of the agency had been employed by builders to help prepare plans for submission to the agency; the same employees were then to clear the plans for the agency.[5] The case was in many ways the counterpart of one aspect of the government claims problems of the mid-nineteenth century. In each case, government employees were serving two masters — working both sides of the street, being paid by both sides in economic transactions between the

[5] See Chapter I, note 3 *supra*.

government and outsiders. The 1955 situation was instinct with the potential of fraud on the government, shake-down of the contractors, unfairness to other contractors, and threat to public confidence.

Sections 281, 283, and 216 of Title 18 presently deal with this classic conflict of interest problem.[6] In several respects, however, they are unsatisfactory and produce undesirable side effects. Sections 281 and 283 have been the main forces (along with Section 284) deterring lawyers from accepting consultative and temporary appointments with the government.

Section 4 of the new statute proposed here restates the principle of these older sections more broadly, more clearly, more in concert with modern conditions, and, hopefully, in a form that will not hinder the government's recruiting efforts.

Section 4 applies to both regular and intermittent employees. While neither may be left free to work on both sides of a transaction, the position of the regular full-time employee calls for a stricter standard and a rule of wider scope. The regular employee is the government's man, identified in the public eye as such. He can be, and should be, held to a posture of basic commitment to the government's cause, and outside activities should be curtailed if they raise doubt in the public mind about his undivided commitment. By contrast, the intermittent expert or consultant is the government's man only part of the time. He always works both for the government and for outsiders. He cannot be required to sever his relations with the nongovernmental world, and the public does not expect that he will. Sections 281 and 283 draw no distinctions in restricting the outside activities of different classes of employees. The consequence of this mechanical application of a single rule for all is to make it harder for the government to obtain the advisory services it so badly needs. Section 4 of the new statute does not repeat this error. While holding both regular and intermittent employees to a high standard, it distinguishes between them in certain respects in response to their special situations. In general, under section 4, the regular employee is required to stay out of all government matters, while the intermittent employee is required to stay out of government matters with which he has contact in his official capacity.

[6] See Chapter III *supra*.

Under section 4(a), all government employees are subject to the following rule: "Except in the course of his official duties or incident thereto, no Government employee shall assist another person, whether or not for compensation, in any transaction involving the Government — (1) in which he has at any time participated; or (2) if such transaction involving the Government is or has been under his official responsibility at any time within a period of two years preceding such assistance."

In vital respects, this rule is stiffer than either Section 281 or 283, and plugs the holes in those sections. It covers any "transaction involving the government," as that term is broadly defined in the new statute, and is not limited to "claims" as is Section 283. Similarly, it is not limited to compensated services, and thus it reaches beyond Section 281. But, unlike the present sections, this provision is aimed squarely at the real and personal conflict of interest situation, not an imputed, hypothetical one. It forbids the government employee to assist the outsider in any matter in which the employee participated, or for which he was responsible within the preceding two years, in his capacity as a government employee. Under this section, therefore, unlike Sections 281 and 283, a lawyer serving part time with the State Department would be barred from representing outsiders in connection with matters on which he worked or for which he was responsible there, but neither he nor his law partners would be forced to withdraw from other representations involving other government departments or issues such as income tax claims. The rule protects the government in all situations by forbidding the employee to work on both sides of a matter, but it makes it possible for government to obtain the part-time or temporary services of a man without forcing him to abandon his business or profession. It thus eliminates the main objectionable elements of Sections 281 and 283.

It is very likely that the rule quoted above from section 4 of the act is enough to protect the government, and that no rule is required keeping employees from assisting outsiders in *all* transactions involving the government. Modern government is so large, its activities so diverse, its chains of command so separated, that in many circumstances the influence that one government official can bring to bear upon another government official is minimal or nonexistent.

If a phocologist from the Pribilof Islands appears on behalf of a company in the New York office of the Small Business Administration, it is unlikely that his position as a government employee threatens the moral integrity of the Republic. But when it comes to government employees of high rank, a general disqualification is undoubtedly expected by the public. No matter how the early nineteenth century may have viewed it, it will not do today to have the Secretary of Commerce representing clients in tax claims before the Treasury Department. Since some full-time government employees should be broadly prohibited from assisting outsiders in government matters, and since no administrable line of distinction among regular employees can be found, the proposed new statute imposes, in section 4(b), the following additional restriction on all regular government employees: "Except in the course of his official duties or incident thereto, no regular Government employee shall — (1) assist another person for compensation in any transaction involving the Government; (2) assist another person by representing him as his agent or attorney, whether or not for compensation, in any transaction involving the Government."

Like present Section 281, this rule for the full-time employee is not limited to matters in which he was actually involved on behalf of the government. The rule is based mainly on the preservation of appearances, and partly on the potential improper influence that some employees, by virtue of their office, might have on some other employees under some circumstances. Built up of suppositions based on suppositions, the rule leans far in the direction of over-cautiousness, and should perhaps be limited in application to high-ranking officials only. In view of its inclusive application to *all* transactions involving the government regardless of the agency involved, the provision confines the proscribed activity to compensated assistance, again as in Section 281, and to assistance as agent or attorney.

Several minor points about section 4 deserve mention. "Assist," like "participate," is a defined term under section 2. The definition adds a new degree of concreteness, and seeks to answer the questions that have most often been raised in the past about the scope of the prohibitions of Sections 281 and 283. The government employee's own claims against the government, such as personal tax claims or claims for back pay, are not affected by the new statute, since only assistance to others is prohibited.[7]

Whether an employee is intermittent or regular, his political and other organizational affiliations and activities will not be affected by the section except in the most unusual situations. An employee who is a member of an organization to protect wildlife, for example, will not run afoul of section 4, even if he actively helps the organization in its efforts to influence federal policy in the direction of better wildlife protection. The efforts of such an organization would seldom produce "transactions involving the government," as defined. In those cases in which it did, the employee would not encounter a bar under the section unless his government job involves the same transactions, or he is paid by the organization to assist it in the transactions, or he acts in the capacity of agent or attorney in the transactions.

Subsection (c) of section 4 forbids the government employee to share in compensation for assistance if he is prohibited from rendering such assistance under the section. The provision is closely related to the next subsection, forbidding a government employee's partners to render assistance that he himself could not legally render because he participated in the transactions, or was, within two years, responsible for them as a government employee. This rule applies to partners of both regular and intermittent employees. It permits a regular employee to belong to a partnership handling transactions involving the government only under narrowly limited circumstances: provided the employee himself does not "assist" in the transactions; he has not participated in the transactions for the government and they have not been under his responsibility for two years; and he does not share in any of the compensation received for such assistance. Clarification of the present legal murk surrounding the status of partnerships under the conflict of interest statutes is much to be desired.

Finally, some exceptions must be carved out of the generality of the rule against assistance to outsiders. Under section 4(e) a government employee may assist another government employee who

---

[7] Assignment of a part of a claim as compensation for services does not, however, bring the assignee under this exception. For a related problem, see "Military procurement and employment of retired officers" *infra*.

is acting on behalf of the United States in the course of or incident to his official duties. Similarly, a government employee may assist an independent contractor on a government project where the employee's agency head feels that it is in the best interest of the government that the employee provide such assistance. He may assist his spouse or child in any transaction involving the government, or may assist another person for whom he is serving as guardian, executor, administrator, trustee, or other personal fiduciary. He may assist another government employee involved in disciplinary, loyalty, or other proceedings pertaining to personnel administration. And he is not prevented by the section from giving testimony under oath or from making statements required to be made under penalty of perjury or contempt. In some instances, these exceptions are subject to conditions and limitations set by regulations, and in addition are limited in various technical ways by statutory requirements such as noncompensation, disclosure, and personal disqualification.

The general principle of not serving two masters is sound, and must be firmly enforced. But in the context of modern American government, undiscriminating application of a single rule is unfeasible, and will serve only to deprive the government of needed personnel — especially advisory personnel. As section 4 illustrates, the number of difficult subsidiary problems involved is surprising. Almost none of them is adequately met by present law.

STATUTE SECTION 5: OUTSIDE COMPENSATION

It will be recalled that Section 1914 of Title 18 prohibits an employee from receiving outside compensation "in connection with" his official services, and forbids outsiders to make any contribution to or supplement the salary of an employee "for the services performed by him for" the government. The rule is related to the general rule that in the absence of special legislation an employee of the government may not serve without being paid by the government — may not be a WOC. Section 1914 is the most difficult of the conflict of interest statutes to interpret, and, where rigorously applied, the section most obstructive to the government's efforts to get and keep personnel.[8]

8 See Chapters III and VII *supra*.

It is important to recognize what the government gives up by adopting the principle of Section 1914. Many more men would be willing to work for the government if they felt they could take the pay cut involved; many employers would, with the most patriotic and civic motivations, help a former employee maintain his living standards while on a government assignment. Section 1914 makes motivations irrelevant, and curtly rejects any proffered hand extended to help it finance its staff requirements.[9] In the opinion of many, especially those first encountering it, the rule seems unnecessary, insulting, costly, and absurd. Yet, though the issue is not easy, the act proposed here retains the rule against receiving outside compensation for government services.

The rule is really a special case of the general injunction against serving two masters. Three basic concerns underlie this rule prohibiting two payrolls and two paymasters for the same employee on the same job. First, the outside payor has a hold on the employee deriving from his ability to cut off one of the employee's economic lifelines. Second, the employee may tend to favor his outside payor even though no direct pressure is put on him to do so. And, third, because of these real risks, the arrangement has a generally unwholesome appearance that breeds suspicion and bitterness among fellow employees and other observers. The public interpretation is apt to be that if an outside party is paying a government employee and is not paying him for past services, he must be paying him for some current services to the payor during a time when his services are supposed to be devoted to the government. In part the fear is that the government employee will not keep his nose to the grindstone; in part the fear is close to the fear of bribery; in part the fear is that outside forces will subvert the operation of regular policy-making procedures in the government (the historical source of Section 1914);

9 An exception has been made to permit employers to supplement the income of men called under Selective Service. 62 Stat. 608 (1948), 50 U.S.C. App. § 454(f) (1952). And recently Congress softened the rigor of the rule to permit employees to accept contributions and awards from private foundations for training purposes. 72 Stat. 336 (1958), 5 U.S.C. § 2318(a) (1958). Under section 2(g) of Executive Order 10800, the agency head may approve acceptance of contributions, awards, or payments to employees when the purpose, amount, and type of contribution, award, or payment would not place or tend to place the recipient under any improper obligation to the grantor. Civil service regulations spell out in greater detail additional factors to be considered in authorizing employees to accept such awards. United States Civil Service Commission, Federal Personnel Manual, ch. T-1, 23–25, March 25, 1959.

and in part the rule is grounded in considerations of personnel administration.

Thus the rule against outside compensation is salutary. But it would be desirable for many purposes to refine it further — to make it apply to dangerous kinds of outside compensation rather than all outside compensation. As noted earlier, the present statute forbids the compensation even if the payor has no dealings or relations whatever with the government and no special interest in its policies. Many of the problems raised by Section 1914 could be resolved if the outside compensation rule, for example, forbade outside compensation only if paid by a source in a sensitive relationship with the government employee's agency — a supply contractor dealing with the agency, for example. Regrettably, this more sharply focused approach is not workable. While it will work reasonably well in a unifunctional agency such as the Federal Communications Commission — where the class of concerns dealing with the agency is known in advance — it will not work in agencies like the Justice Department or the Small Business Administration — where there is no way to know what kind of concern will next appear at the door. If the outside compensation rule is to add anything to the general rule requiring personal disqualification, it must apply to outside compensation from any source, not just a sensitive source. A more basic objection to this approach, however, is that it simply does not go far enough to head off the unsavory public impression given when government officials are known to be on an outside payroll. The storm over gifts to White House aides in the 1950's would have been a hurricane if regular salary payments to them had been made by the donors. The new statute, therefore, retains the broad general approach of Section 1914 in its restriction upon outside compensation.

It has been exceedingly difficult to judge under Section 1914 what outside payments to government employees are illegal because received "in connection with" the employee's government services.[10] The new statute represents a serious effort to provide for a clearer and more predictable standard linking the payments and the employee's job. The device used to achieve this end is to set up in section 5(b) and (c) not only a restrictive rule on compensation from outsiders for services to the United States, but an additional rule on

10 A similar ambiguity afflicts the "for's" in the second paragraph of § 1914.

compensation from outsiders for services to others than the United States.

The first element of this two-barreled rule provides: "No regular Government employee shall receive any thing of economic value, other than his compensation from the United States, for or in consideration of personal services rendered or to be rendered to or for the United States." Compensation that the employee receives for services performed before he entered government service is, of course, his own property and does not violate the statute. Similarly, property he receives after his government employment and not for his government services is also unchallengeable. But occasionally an outside source may try to make a payment to a government employee before he becomes an employee or after he terminates his government employment, with the intention and purpose of compensating the employee for the work done while in Washington. Whenever received, such a payment violates the statute. The possibility of such efforts at evasion cannot be ignored; but neither should it lead to a statutory rule throwing a shadow of possible illegality over the entire employment record of every government employee prior to and after his government service.

Section 5(b) faces the dilemma and provides that property transfers made before or after the employee's government service will be presumed, in the absence of evidence to the contrary, not to have been made for his government work. This presumption normally accords with the facts, lends predictability to the section, and leaves the way open for the government to show the illegality of a payment where the facts so indicate. From the standpoint of appearances, the most objectionable situation is that in which the employee receives outside payments while actually in government service. Often, however, for tax and other legitimate reasons, a man leaving private life to go into government service will dispose of his private business or professional holdings, but arrange for a pay-out spread over several years into the future. Though this practice is proper and must be permitted, its surface appearance may resemble outside compensation for government work, and the employee receiving such outside payments while in government service must, without benefit of the presumption just described (but without a contrary presumption), show that they are for past services. A separate subsection (d) flatly forbids payments to be made to a government employee for services to be performed in the future, since this device offers a patent method for evading section 5.

A contract irrevocably granting to another the optional right to purchase property on particular terms in the future — a so-called option contract or option — is a "thing of value" under the statute. If paid to a government employee for or in consideration of his government services, an option is illegal under section 5; if not paid for such services, the option is legal under that section. As seen above, however, the interplay of the rules under section 5 places some emphasis on the time when the employee receives the compensation payments from the outside source. Because three or four legal "events" usually occur at different times under an option contract — the grant, the maturity of the right to exercise, the exercise, and the sale of the property — a question of interpretation could arise under section 5 as to which event should be considered the receipt of the compensation and which time the relevant time under the section. The statute therefore provides for the point specifically in section 2(m), making it clear that the date the option contract is irrevocably granted is the date of receipt. This is the date on which economic value is effectively transferred. Like any convertible security or other convertible contract right, the value of the option contract, if it has any value, is dependent entirely upon the value of the property subject to purchase under it. If land is transferred to a government employee before he enters government service, neither a subsequent increase in the value of the land, nor a sale by him of the land, constitutes a new transfer of economic value to him. The situation is exactly the same where the employee receives an irrevocable option contract respecting the same land. His rights to the land are fixed on the date he receives the contract; the date he converts the contract right into the equivalent land sees no further transfer of economic value to him, nor does such a transfer take place on the day he ultimately sells the land.[11]

---

[11] An option is a hedge. The distinction between the grant of the option and the grant of the land becomes important only if the market price of the land goes down. If the party holds the land he stands to lose when the market drops, but if he holds an option to purchase the land and the price drops below the option price, he simply does not exercise the option. The option holder does not get the land; neither does he lose on the transaction any more than the amount he paid for the option contract itself.

Increasing use of stock options and other options in the modern economy has recurrently raised the question of their status under present Section 1914. Section 5 of the new statute resolves the issue explicitly and correctly: wherever a government employee can legally receive and retain any property for services under section 5, he can legally receive and retain options on such property. Thus, if a government employee, before becoming such, was granted a bona fide irrevocable stock option exercisable in installments over a period of years, he would not be barred from exercising it in installments as they mature during his government employment.

Subsection (c) of section 5 in some respects restricts compensation to government employees for services to others than the government. These restrictions have two different purposes. They assist in the interpretation and enforcement of the general rule of section 5. And, for the first time, they express in general statutory form the sound policy often expressed by agency regulations proscribing outside employment that is embarrassing to the agency. In substance the new statute provides that if a regular government employee receives compensation for outside work during the term of his government employment, the services must be bona fide, actually performed, not within the course of his official duties, not prohibited by other laws or regulations concerning outside employment, and, except in extraordinary approved circumstances, not for or on behalf of a sensitive employer — basically, one who deals with or is subject to the regulatory jurisdiction of the employee's agency. Altogether this means, for example, that if other laws or agency regulations do not prevent it, a Civil Aeronautics Board employee may teach at a university on the weekends, but only under the most extraordinary circumstances of disclosure and special approval could he do any work for or in connection with an airline.

This rule works to reinforce the rule against outside compensation for government services. A government employee who is found receiving regular payments from an outside source is virtually forced into showing the legitimacy of the payments. If he argues that the payments are compensation for his government services, they are illegal under the general rule of section 5. If he argues that they are compensation for past services, he must be able to prove the case without the help of a presumption. If he argues that they are compensation for current services to the outsider, they will be illegal if he cannot prove that they meet the specific limitations of the third subsection of section 5(c). And if he argues that they are gifts, he will not only have to prove donative intent, but will have to show them to be legal gifts under the gift regulations of section 6, discussed later. These interworking parts are thus closely machined to achieve an administrable and discriminating regulation of outside compensation.

As in the case of present Section 1914, the new statute contains an exception for certain payments to federal employees paid out of state, county, or municipality treasuries. The provision is necessary to cover certain established categories of jointly paid employees, such as county farm agents.

WOCs

A definitional subsection of section 5 excludes from the coverage of the section all government employees who, in accordance with the terms or conditions of their appointments, are serving without compensation or are receiving only reimbursement for expenses — in other words, all WOCs. Although present Section 1914 does not contain a corresponding exclusion, the provision makes no change in policy or coverage.

As a practical matter, the WOC must always be excluded from the rule against outside compensation.[12] If he is to serve without going on the government's payroll, he must be allowed to remain on a private payroll. Past practice has been for Congress to create a spot exemption from Section 1914 whenever it authorizes WOCs to be used. A major objective of the proposals here is to set up an over-all plan that will not require constant amendment, adjustment, and *ad hoc* exceptions. Since all WOCs receive an exemption under the outside compensation rule, it is better to exclude them as a class.

The intermittent employee

The intermittent employee is also excluded from the operation of section 5. He is excluded for substantially the same reasons as

12 See the discussion of WOCs in Chapter III.

the WOC, though past practice has been considerably less clear in the case of the periodic adviser than the full-time WOC.

In some cases legislative authorizations of intermittent personnel have included exemptions from Section 1914. Far more often, advisers and experts are employees to whom Section 1914 is applicable on its face. As discussed earlier, however, the section is totally unworkable as applied to the occasional employee, and in practice is largely ignored.

Limiting section 5 to regular employees does no more than recognize that an intermittent employee who spends only part of his time in Washington is obviously on someone else's payroll, and that there is no purpose served in requiring his employer to make bookkeeping entries showing that he was not paid "for" the day he was in Washington.

Employee security and welfare plans

Section 1914 throws into doubt whether a government employee may continue his participation in a private pension, insurance, or other such welfare plan. The question is raised especially acutely where a former employer makes contributions to the plan. Earlier discussion has emphasized that such plans are increasingly characteristic of modern America, that they are of enormous importance to the long-range economic security of those under the plans, and that any rule requiring incoming government employees to throw away their future pension rights drastically deters appointees from accepting government office.[13]

It is quite possible, for certain purposes of analysis, to describe participation in these plans as "compensation" and to conclude by verbal logic that it should be prevented by the rule against outside compensation. But the function of law is to make sense, not logic. Sense here means that the government's staffing needs must be recognized as paramount to verbal logic. Section 5 of the new statute meets the issue head on and permits government employees to continue their membership in private security plans under some circumstances with certain safeguards.

This subsection, 5(f), is necessarily quite technical. It first permits

13 See Chapters VI and VII *supra*.

the government employee to remain under a former insurance, pension, or welfare plan where the former employer makes no contribution in respect of the employee during his government service. It further permits the employee to continue under a plan to which the former employer does make contributions, but only in the case of certain insurance plans and of pension or retirement plans qualified under the Internal Revenue Code, and only for a five-year period. Employees are permitted to continue under profit-sharing or stock bonus plans maintained by former employers — but only if no contributions are made based on profits attributable to any part of the period of the employee's government employment. All these provisions of the subsection are subject to further regulatory limitations. The central consideration is that the employee's rights accruing during his government service should accrue automatically and as part of the general plan, not at the whim of his former employer on an *ad hominem* basis.

Under the protective provisions of section 3 of the new statute, of course, the employee's continued participation in a pension or insurance plan would generally, if not always, constitute a substantial economic interest requiring him to disqualify himself from acting on behalf of the government in transactions involving his former employer.

Certain other suggestions appear later in this book with respect to pension and other welfare plans. But at a minimum the conflict of interest laws should be amended to make it clear that, subject to appropriate safeguards, government employees may continue to hold on to their rights under these plans for reasonable periods of government service. The problem is not a serious one for the government in attracting career people, because its own security programs are attractive. But when it comes to recruiting temporary full-time appointees, particularly for demanding executive, professional, and technical jobs, we cannot afford to impose upon the recruiting efforts of the executive branch the crippling requirement that all security rights be scrapped.

STATUTE SECTION 6: GIFTS

Much of the public controversy that has arisen in the field of conflict of interest has centered upon the problem of gifts to government officials. Such gifts may well provide a source of illicit influence over the government official; in any case they create a suspicious and unhealthy appearance. The regulations of most agencies contain provisions relating to the question of gifts, but there has been nothing in the general conflict of interest statutes on the matter. Because the problem is widespread, indeed universal, gifts are an appropriate topic for legislative treatment.

Manifestly some gifts to officials, such as family gifts, are of a personal nature and unobjectionable. The problem is how to distinguish gifts that may be dangerous from those that are not. The new statute establishes two basic criteria: one is quite concrete, and applicable to regular government employees only; the other is a broad criterion applying to all government employees.

An important factor that may taint a gift to an official is the relationship of the donor to the official's agency. Section 6 of the new statute prohibits gifts, favors, or gratuities to a regular government employee where the employee has reason to believe that the donor has a business relationship with the official's agency, or is seeking one, or where the donor has interests that may be substantially affected by the official's performance or nonperformance of his duty. For most agencies and in most situations these three objective standards define with reasonable particularity the area of sensitive donors.

In certain other situations, however, an additional standard of judgment is required. Some officials like top staff assistants to executives have essentially roving commissions; they have a broad range of functions and no direct operating responsibility to any agency. In such a situation it is difficult to apply the sensitive donor standards just listed. The statute therefore sets an additional standard. No official may accept any gift that he has reason to believe would not have been given "but for" his office or position in the government.

This second broad criterion, forbidding gifts directly linked to the official's office-holding, applies to all government employees. The first criterion, based on a sensitive relationship between the donor and the employee's agency, cannot be applied as a practical matter to the intermittent consultant or expert. A scientist who regularly works for a private company but serves as a consultant with the

Atomic Energy Commission once or twice a month is likely to have close friends of the same profession who may also be involved in one way or another with the AEC; gift interchanges among them could easily fall within the statutory prohibition on gifts from sensitive donors. But the consultant usually has no way to check who does business with the agency, and cannot be expected to upset his whole personal life for the sake of his sporadic consulting contacts with the agency. This undesirable result is avoided, and the government still protected, by the general "but for" criterion applicable to all government employees, intermittent as well as regular.

Regulations

These are the basic outlines of the proposed statute forbidding gifts to officials. Considerable regulatory flexibility is required, however, for some gifts in particular situations meet these criteria but nonetheless should be permitted. Gifts within a man's immediate family, for example, should not be barred. Special problems may also arise in the case of inheritance. Some gifts are essentially ceremonial, others, like the banquet speaker's free dinner, unimpeachable.

Perhaps the crankiest, most annoying problem of all is the question of the small business gratuity. Almost every official in almost every agency is constantly beset by offers of small favors and gratuities. An official business conference between a company and the agency runs on into the lunch hour; the official and the private company representative go to lunch; the representative offers to pick up the check. Or the official is invited for the weekend to the company representative's summer place to complete work not completed on Friday. Or it may be just an invitation to a cocktail party or reception. The possibilities range from the obviously insignificant offer of a cigarette to the obviously improper offer of a gold cigarette case. Shall the official accept or reject the dollar cigar after lunch, the lunch tab at the government cafeteria, the advertising desk set, the ham at Christmas, the night club dinner, the honorarium for a speech, the night at the theater, the airline's inaugural flight party that turns into a several-day paid vacation? The problem, as usual, is one of drawing lines between things that look very much alike at one point on the spectrum and look very different at opposite ends of the spectrum.

Present regulations wrestle with these questions and answer them in various ways. This variety is constructive. Much discretion should undoubtedly be left to the individual agencies, for the significance of the problem of small gifts can vary radically from agency to agency. Consider, for example, the difference between the position of the Small Business Administration official invited to dinner at the home of a loan applicant, and that of the State Department official invited to dinner at the embassy home of a foreign ambassador whose country is a loan applicant.

Because of the broad language of the general statutory prohibition on gifts, and the need to have varying rules in the different agencies, section 6 contains a separate provision authorizing regulations to make exceptions to the statutory prohibitions as long as there is no reason to infer that the official judgment or action of the employee is intended to be influenced by the gift. The topic of gifts, and ways of controlling them, is a good illustration of a subject that the Administrator should explore in detail, toward the end of isolating problem areas, developing general minimum regulatory standards, and assisting the individual agencies in working out their own regulations.

In general the rules on these small gifts and gratuities should be as tight as they can be drawn without chasing gnats or impeding some other affirmative policy such as diplomatic exchange and protocol. In many respects a rigid rule of no gifts whatever from sources dealing with the agency is the most attractive administrative solution. It answers all questions, it avoids all problems of explanation, it heads off in advance what may be embarrassing apparent discourtesies. Some agencies have tried it and have been well satisfied with the results. Considerable sentiment apparently favors it among employees of some other agencies.

It is essential that whatever rules are established in the agency be adhered to as closely as possible by the top political executives as well as the career people. There may be some need for special flexibility at the top positions, but it should be kept constantly in mind that each deviation at the top will greatly increase the difficulty of enforcement.

Government expense accounts

A point deserving stress is the relationship of the gift problem to inadequate governmental expense allowances. For legitimate and important reasons of policy, it is frequently useful for an agency to have a representative attend a meeting or convention, or deliver a lecture at a school. The government representative in such a case will receive the clearance, or perhaps the order, of his agency head to attend the function on behalf of the agency. The official goes as instructed, and then finds that while his government expense account has a flat ceiling of $12.00 per day, his actual expenses at the meeting place will run $15.00 or $20.00 for his room alone. In such a situation the official's choices are (1) not to go at all, to the government's loss, (2) to accept the host association's offer to pick up the hotel bill, or (3) to pay for the difference in cost out of his own pocket. Each answer is obviously unsatisfactory. The only real solution is to set per diem rates at realistic levels, either generally or on a particularized basis, and in proper cases to provide government officials with realistic expense accounts. The way to cure the risks of padded accounts is by the use of close accounting policing — not by the imposition of a per diem limitation that practically forces conscientious employees to accept gifts from outside groups having business relations with the agency.

STATUTE SECTION 7: ABUSE OF OFFICE

Since time immemorial, holders of state power have found that they can use their position to fatten their own purses. The classic form is the shakedown — the extraction of payoff money from someone vulnerable to the official's power, backed up by the direct or implied threat that the official will use his government authority in a manner that the donor might not enjoy. While the shakedown is closely akin to bribery, since the payment is made with the hope of influencing official action, it may fall short in various minor and technical ways of being fully matured bribery. In its more subtle form, the official merely acquiesces in or induces the payment to him, but with no promises involved. Thus these payments slide over into bribery on one side and into the area of improper gifts on the other.

Where the employee actively induces some kind of special advantage, we are presented with a situation that is undesirable and should be regulated but is not now covered by law. The official is creating his own conflict of interest as he goes along when he misuses his official office and turns it into an instrument for private gain.[14]

The subject of misuse of office does not call for elaborate statutory treatment or regulation. The offense and the pay-off may take a million forms. The essential concept is that the government employee should not, in his dealings with persons who have a direct relationship with his job and his agency, use the power or authority of his office to induce them to provide him or another with something of economic value. This is the substance of section 7 of the statute.

STATUTE SECTION 8: POST-EMPLOYMENT

Congress has shown a recurrent interest in the dealings with government of former government employees. Sections 99 of Title 5 and 284 of Title 18 forbid former employees to assist in prosecuting certain claims against the government for two years, and several special provisions restrict former military officers in assisting in prosecuting government claims and in the sale of goods to the government.[15]

As noted earlier, there are several reasons for these efforts to control the former employee in the name of conflict of interest. One is the fear that the former employee has acquired special inside information that gives him an improper advantage in subsequent dealings, either as against the government or as against other private parties dealing with the government. Probably the greatest concern is that the former employee, especially if he held high rank, may carry over a special influence from his former office, and, in representing a private party, may work to the prejudice of the government and other competing private parties. Some find the basis for post-employment restraints in a general disapproval of switching sides — working on a transaction first on one side and then on the other.

Taken together, these arguments are of sufficient force to lead most people to object when a government official in charge of a matter vacates his office on Friday and on Monday morning reappears representing a private party in the same matter. All agree that some regulation of post-employment activities is necessary. There is much

---

[14] This has been a major concern of congressional committees investigating the activities of individual officials. See, *e.g.*, Chapter V, note 71 *supra* and accompanying text.

[15] See Appendix B.

less agreement on the proper scope of these restrictions: from what transactions should the former employee be excluded, and for how long?

Before discussing the statutory proposal made here, something must be said of the effect of post-employment restraints on the government itself. It is not sufficiently recognized that post-employment restrictions can be overly stringent, hurting the government more than they help it. This is most easily seen in the deterrent effect of such regulation upon the government's recruitment of manpower; no man will accept government appointment — especially temporary government appointment — if he must abandon the use of his professional skills for several years after leaving government service. The adverse effect of such restrictions on the government's efficient use of skills and information is probably even greater. The knowledge of an experienced former official may be made to operate against the government, but it may also contribute to the ends of the government. In the case of scientists, whose knowledge of governmental technical needs can speed up the service of private industry to the government, the point is obvious; but the argument is as sound in almost every other area. It is directly to the government's interest to have the skills of the tax specialist put to use in the solution of tax problems. When a former employee of the Urban Renewal Administration helps a city prepare an application to that agency, his experience is being used directly to further and speed up a program of the federal government. Federal government policies such as antitrust policy or pure food and drug protection are clearly advanced by the presence in the private segment of the economy of men steeped in government experience.

In short, the problem of post-employment restrictions must be weighed in the context again of the interpenetration of the private and governmental segments of the economy. In an earlier day, government and the private economy were regarded as opposed or at least completely separate, and no need was recognized for having men outside government with experience gained inside government. With the growth of government and the technological explosion of the twentieth century, such a view has become unthinkable. Today we desperately need a maximum flow of information between the government and the outside, and post-employment restraints tend to build a wall between them. It is a source of comfort to no one in this country if an experienced military scientist or technical expert is forced by conflict of interest rules to take up truck farming or sell life insurance when he leaves the government.

Except for the special provisions concerning the military, present statutory restraints on post-employment activities are of primary, though not exclusive, concern to lawyers.[16] The reason is that the restraints are framed entirely in terms of assistance in prosecuting claims against the government. Under modern circumstances this narrow rule cannot be justified, especially since the courts have by construction linked the term "claim" to a claim for money or property.[17] If a former employee worked on a particular transaction, whether involving a claim or not, he should not engage in any later dealings with the government arising out of that transaction. All commentators and studies on the conflict of interest statutes have agreed with the Justice Department proposal of 1954 to expand the word "claim" to include any kind of dealing with the government.[18] The Act proposed here adopts this approach in its post-employment provision: if the former employee had the necessary degree of contact with a transaction while he was in government service, he is subsequently barred from assisting in any way in conjunction with that transaction. This change makes a vast horizontal expansion in the scope of the post-employment provisions, for it brings the restriction to bear upon all former employees, not just lawyers and those in a representational capacity, and upon all transactions with the government, not just claims. Under these circumstances, even more attention must be paid to the problem of adverse side effects, and special care taken to circumscribe the scope of the prohibition by other means.

Section 8 of the new statute deals with the post-employment problem. It should be read with and compared with section 4 relating to government employees' assisting outsiders in their dealings with the government. The problems are almost identical, and the

[16] Non-lawyers may on rare occasions encounter these restrictions. For example, a vice president of a defense contracting firm, recently resigned from an assistant secretaryship in Defense, may find himself unable to assist in developing the employer's case for a claim under a cost-plus government contract.

[17] See United States v. Bergson, 119 F. Supp. 459 (D.D.C. 1954), discussed in Chapter III *supra.*

[18] See Chapter III, note 76 *supra.*

sections are in many respects parallel. Much of the earlier discussion of section 4 is also relevant here, including the discussion of defined terms, particularly "transaction involving the government."

The general rule of section 8 is direct and brief. It provides in the case of all employees, regular or intermittent: "No former Government employee shall at any time subsequent to his Government employment assist another person, whether or not for compensation, in any transaction involving the Government (1) in which he at any time participated during his Government employment; or (2) if such transaction involving the Government was under his official responsibility as a Government employee at any time within a period of two years preceding such assistance." Several special features of this simple rule are to be observed, in addition to its extension beyond "claim" to cover all transactions involving the government.

Section 8, like section 4, alters present law by setting up two different rules depending upon the former employee's degree of association with the transaction concerned. The post-employment restrictions in matters the former employee personally worked on are more stringent than those for which he was only administratively responsible. The bar in respect of transactions in which he "participated," as defined, is made permanent, unlike the two-year restriction under present law; the bar as to transactions for which he was "responsible," as defined, is left at the present two-year level. Any transaction involving the government that comes up *after* the day the former employee leaves office cannot have been subject to his "responsibility" or "participation," and therefore falls, as at present, outside the post-employment restriction.

As discussed earlier, a key conception in the application of this and other sections is the scope of the term "transaction involving the government." There will inevitably be problems of interpretation arising from this term, despite its concrete statutory definition in section 2. For example, only in the particular situation can it be determined whether a routine fact-gathering of the Antitrust Division of the Justice Department has become a formal investigation, and the investigation has become a "proceeding" or "other such particular matter" and therefore a "transaction involving the government," triggering the post-employment restriction. But this problem is inherent in the task at hand. The new act goes as far as the draftsmen's ingenuity permits in specifying the standard, and represents an enormous improvement over the unmanageably vague or unduly limited terms stabbing at the point in the present statutes.[19]

In creating a permanent bar on switching sides in matters on which the former government employee worked, the new section 8 dramatically strengthens the present conflict of interest statutes. And for the lawyer, this change in the statutory rule accords substantially with the requirements of the Canons of Ethics.[20]

Another change from the present statutory restrictions is that the two-year bar in respect of matters the former employee was "responsible" for but did not "participate" in dates from the time of his responsibility, not from the date of his termination of employment. Earlier it was pointed out that the present post-employment statutes are extremely difficult to apply to employees who have shifted jobs within the government or who have come in and out of government service. This uncertainty has been a significant factor contributing to the deterrent effect of the post-employment restrictions. The rule adopted by section 8 is the sound one. If an employee of agency X has responsibility over matter A, subsequently leaves the government and then later undertakes advisory work for agency Y on matters unrelated to A, there is no reason whatever for starting a new two-year ban on matter A upon his assuming the new advisory post. It may be that in some cases an employee will not be certain of the date his responsibility for a particular matter ceased, but in such a case he can always be safe in dating the two-year bar from the date of his termination of employment. The new rule is thus more workable and protects the government against the major risks posed by the inside position of the former employee.

[19] Compare, on the point, the language of the new § 8(a), and corresponding definitions, with the term "subject matter" appearing in 18 U.S.C. § 284, the term "transaction of business with [a] business entity" appearing in 18 U.S.C. § 434, and the term "program" appearing in the proposed new § 281(b) on former military officers suggested at page 21 of SUBCOMM. FOR SPECIAL INVESTIGATIONS, HOUSE COMM. ON ARMED SERVICES, 86TH CONG., 1ST SESS., REPORT ON EMPLOYMENT OF RETIRED COMMISSIONED OFFICERS BY DEFENSE DEPARTMENT CONTRACTORS (Comm. Print 1960).

[20] The language of the Canon is "investigate or pass upon" rather than "participate," as defined, and is thus actually somewhat less restrictive than the proposed statutory rule of section 8. The text of the canon is quoted in the discussion of § 284 in Chapter III *supra*.

Like the present post-employment provisions, section 8 of the proposed act does not require compensation as an element of the offense.

For the first time, section 8 sets up a post-employment rule that can apply to all kinds of employees. Fundamentally, it keeps former employees out of government dealings in matters with which they had contact while in the government — matters wherein they have true conflicts of interest. It adopts and makes workable the basic approach of Section 284 on this central point, and rejects the shotgun technique of Section 99.

The balance of section 8 implements the basic rule quoted above, and meets some points of interpretation often raised but never settled in the past. As in section 4, the former employee is forbidden to share in compensation paid for assistance he is forbidden to render under the section. A special section on partnerships is included: "No partnership of which a former Government employee is a partner, and no partner or employee of such a partnership, shall, for a period of two years following the termination of his Government employment, assist another person in any transaction involving the Government in which such former Government employee at any time participated during his Government employment."

As may be seen, this rule on partnerships is not identical to the rule for the former employee himself. It is built upon re-examination of the actual risks involved, rather than on an automatic formula that the partnership must in the nature of things be barred wherever a partner is barred. Government employees must be permitted on leaving government service to go to work where they can use their professional skills. If a high-ranking tax lawyer formerly employed by the Treasury will contaminate any law firm he joins, and bar the whole firm from tax work, almost no law firm can accept him as a partner when he leaves government. This is the result the present rule may be read to require. Grossly unfair in effect, and based primarily on a theory of constructive or vicarious responsibility, it has resulted in formal compliance only. The former employee typically goes to work for the partnership as an "employee" and becomes a "partner" only on the second anniversary of his separation from government. Or he resorts to the formation of two "partnerships" made up of the same partners, with one of the "partnerships" doing no government work — though the same men do the work.

The rule under section 8 protects the government where it needs realistic protection. The former employee cannot assist in the forbidden transactions. He cannot assist his partners in them and may not provide information about them, either for two years or permanently, depending upon the degree of his prior association with the forbidden transactions. The former employee cannot share in any compensation received out of the services from which he is barred, including any slice of partnership profits. And in spite of the fact that the partner cannot at any time transmit any information to his partners concerning transactions on which he actually worked while in government, the partnership and its partners are still barred — mainly for reasons of public appearances — from assisting in such transactions for a period of two years.

The Canons of Ethics of the bar have been interpreted to impose a more stringent rule than the statutory rule on partnerships set forth in section 8. Canon 36 is apparently viewed to bar the law firm in any situation where any member is barred.[21] Even as applied to lawyers, there is good reason for the statute to go somewhat less far than this canon in this respect. The proposed post-employment statute goes farther than the canon in applying to any transaction in which the government employee "participated"; it is broader than any present statute in providing a permanent bar in some cases; and it is the first such statute to apply explicitly to partnerships. And it is entirely possible that current interpretations of ethical practice in the legal profession may adjust with time and with the evolution of modern conditions of law practice, especially the growth of the large, departmentalized, and even inter-city law firm. Similarly no reason appears for setting a different rule for legal departments of corporations from that set for "partnerships" — since the legal form of organization hardly determines whether the former government employee does or does not pass along information to the man at the next desk or to his superiors. But whatever the rules of one profession and whether or not they are sound, the stat-

21 See AMERICAN BAR ASSOCIATION, CANONS OF PROFESSIONAL ETHICS, Canons 6, 36, 37 (1959) as construed in United States v. Standard Oil Co., 136 F. Supp. 345 (S.D.N.Y. 1955), and cases cited therein, discussed in Chapter III *supra*, text accompanying note 77.

utes must be written for all government employees and based on the
general merits of the situation. This is true of the new post-employment statute proposed here, which reaches out beyond the historical
narrow concern of its predecessors with the representation of claims
and the single profession of the lawyer.

Military procurement and employment of retired officers

A uniquely difficult problem is offered by the private employment of commissioned military officers following termination of
their active status.[22] We have seen in Chapter III the extent to
which the present conflict of interest restraints were founded on
abuses involving military procurement. Not only are the historical
facts of procurement abuses responsible for a number of the general
conflict of interest statutes; they also account for a group of special
provisions applicable to the post-active-service activities of commissioned military officers.

The oldest of the existing statutes on post-employment conduct
of former military officers originated in 1896, as a part of an appropriations act for the pay of the Navy.[23] The pertinent portion,
for present purposes, bars retired officers of the regular Navy or
Marine Corps from engaging "in selling, or contracting or negotiating to sell, naval supplies or war materials to the Department of
the Navy." Loss of retirement pay is the sanction. No parallel provision exists for the retired officers of the Army or Air Force. The
ban has no time limit; it applies for life. A second provision in the
field is more realistic, in that it imposes only a two-year ban. It is
also less discriminatory, since it applies to commissioned officers of all
the armed forces, plus the regular Coast Guard, the Coast and Geodetic Survey, and the Public Health Service.[24] The section forbids
the officer to engage "in the selling of or contracting for the sale
of or negotiating for the sale of to any . . . [of the agencies in which
commissioned officers serve] any supplies or war materials." A third
relevant provision is an exception to an exception, tucked into Section 281 of Title 18. In 1940 the Congress adopted an amendment
writing retired officers out from under Section 281. However, a sec-

[22] See Appendix B.
[23] 10 U.S.C. § 6112 (1958).
[24] 67 Stat. 437 (1953), 5 U.S.C. § 59(c) (1958).

ond clause of the amendment forbids "any retired officer to represent any person in the sale of anything to the government through the department in whose service he holds a retired status." This, too, is a permanent ban, and is phrased in terms of representing others. A somewhat similar amendment was made to Section 283 in 1949, confined to prosecuting or assisting in the prosecution of claims. Thus there are on the books today three provisions imposing broad prohibitions upon certain former officers in their dealings with government in procurement matters.

During the congressional session of 1959 the special problems of post-active-service employment of military officers erupted in a new controversy. On the floor of the House an amendment to a military appropriation bill was offered that would have had the effect of preventing military officials from going to work for Defense Department contractors. It was defeated by one vote; and the defeat was achieved only by the promise of the congressional leadership that a study would be undertaken of the extent to which military officers, following their service in uniform, were accepting positions as corporate executives with defense contractors and using their influence in the Pentagon improperly. During the summer of 1959 the study was undertaken by a subcommittee of the House Committee on Armed Services, known as the Hebert Subcommittee.

As is proposed here, the Hebert Subcommittee in its report recommended that the coverage of Sections 283 and 284 be extended to include most governmental relationships rather than just "claims." The Committee also recommended a sweeping concept of "selling" to the government; a ban on former officers prohibiting them for two years after termination of their active service from selling through any branch of the armed forces; and a *permanent* bar against selling to the government "in connection with any program for which he performed procurement, maintenance or supply duties." [25] The Hebert proposals also recommended inclusion of civilian employees of the Defense Department within the scope of the bar.

The essential difference between the general post-employment statutes and provisions and proposals applicable to former com-

---

[25] SUBCOMM. FOR SPECIAL INVESTIGATIONS, HOUSE COMM. ON ARMED SERVICES, 86TH CONG., 1ST SESS., REPORT ON EMPLOYMENT OF RETIRED COMMISSIONED OFFICERS BY DEFENSE DEPARTMENT CONTRACTORS (Comm. Print 1960). See Appendix B *infra*.

missioned military officers is that the commissioned-officer statutes carry a ban based on former relationship to the *department or agency,* without reference to the particular *matter* in question. The fundamental approach of section 8 of the proposed act recommended here is a post-employment ban based on relationship to a particular matter. In other words, under the proposed act there is no ban on new matters first arising after the employee has left the agency, and he may assist in any way he sees fit in furthering such matters before his former agency.

The congressional viewpoint, as expressed in statutes over the years, appears to be that special relationships in the case of commissioned officers demand a more stringent rule. The pattern of special statutes suggests a congressional conviction that the commissioned officer must be closed off from his former agency in a whole class of matters, whether or not he had anything to do with them while in government and whether or not they arose after his departure from government service. This kind of "relationship" bar must depend, for its rationale, upon an assumption that there are unique factors inherent in the situation of commissioned officers dealing with their former fellows in the armed forces. Perhaps the distinction between commissioned officers and others has been historically overestimated; as we move into an era of a more civilian-oriented defense establishment and scientific weapons-system, the distinction lessens; and the service academies themselves are perhaps not as tightly knit units as they once were. On the other hand, years of experience in dealing with these matters appear to have convinced Congress that reason exists to justify treating the problem of the former officer differently, and it cannot be stated with assurance that there has been sufficient change to warrant retreat from the very substantial body of law on the subject that now exists.

A fundamental principle underlying the act proposed here is to permit agencies or the President to issue special regulations adapted to the special needs of the individual agencies. Strict consistency in the application of this principle would call for regulations of the Defense Department to meet whatever special problems are raised by the status of former commissioned officers. It is arguable, however, that this approach is not realistic in the light of the unique pressures on the Secretary of Defense from the armed forces themselves. Moreover, weight must be given to the recurrent congressional determination that special controls are needed with regard to former commissioned officers.

Accordingly, the act proposed here adopts a compromise approach. It imposes on the President not an optional power but an obligation to issue regulations in this area. Section 8(e) requires the President to issue regulations prohibiting former commissioned officers, for the period specified in the regulations, from personally dealing with personnel of the Department of Defense, or of such units thereof as may be specified in such regulations, in procurement and other transactions spelled out in the regulations. In other words, Section 8(e) etches out the proposed coverage of the Presidential regulations. By the phrase "personally dealing," it puts emphasis on the officer's actual personal relationship to his former agency. Most important, it leaves the President some flexibility in specifying the duration of the prohibitions following termination of active service by the commissioned officer in question, and the breadth of the ban in terms of what divisions, technical services, branches, or other organizational units or sub-units of the Department of Defense the former officer is to be banned from dealing with. This flexibility is vital, since the ban should be no broader than is necessary to meet the real problems. The ban should be carefully tailored, and not blindly cut along the lines of an outmoded pattern. The vital services that these highly trained former military officers can continue to contribute to the defense effort as civilians must not be overlooked.

Under the proposed section 8 the retirement pay of a retired commissioned officer is terminable for a violation of the applicable regulations. This is a useful and effective sanction, consistent with the present body of statutory law in this area.

The proposed statute would repeal the present special provisions applicable to commissioned officers. Two of the statutes would be repealed only as of the effective date of the Presidential regulations.

A general comment on post-employment restrictions

Three dangers relating to conflict of interest are usually cited in support of post-employment restrictions: disclosure of inside government information; undue and unfair influence of former employees

on those who remain; and the immorality of switching sides. Yet
it is possible that these have all been exaggerated in significance,
while another risk connected with post-employment activities may,
in some circumstances, be of greater seriousness than any of them.

Interviews revealed a substantial body of opinion that government employees who anticipate leaving their agency someday are
put under an inevitable pressure to impress favorably private concerns with which they officially deal. Conceivably, an offer of a
later job might be used as the pay-off for favors done while in office,
but this is rank bribery, subject to criminal prosecution, and not
the point here. The risk is not bribery through the device of job
offers; the risk is that of sapping governmental policy, especially
regulatory policy, through the nagging and persistent conflicting
interests of the government official who has his eye cocked toward
subsequent private employment. To turn the matter around, the
greatest public risks arising from post-employment conduct may well
occur *during* the period of government employment, through the
dampening of aggressive administration of government policies.

It is essential that this problem be isolated and recognized; but
it is virtually impossible to prescribe any fully effective remedy for
it. Section 3 of the proposed act calls for disqualification of the employee from participating in government action in which there is
a substantial economic interest of "any person with whom he is
negotiating or has any arrangement concerning prospective employment." This parallels a present requirement of the Securities
and Exchange Commission on disqualification of the employee in
respect of any employer with whom he is negotiating. But these
rules do not affect situations in which there is not even a preliminary
offer or informal understanding. In limited contexts where there is
no problem of stifling particular skills, temporary bars might be laid
down by regulation forbidding a company to hire an agency employee where the employee acted on the government's behalf in a
transaction with the firm. But such rules could easily grow dangerously broad and should be limited to special situations, as in direct
lending agencies like the Small Business Administration, where the
rule is now in effect.[26] For example, a flat five-year ban on former
Civil Aeronautics Board personnel forbidding them to work for an

26 Small Business Administration, Manual No. 100, § 903.014(i) (1956).

airline would not be a wise rule. It would make government recruitment much more difficult, especially since, as was earlier observed,
one attraction to government service is the prospect of acquiring a
transferable skill.

But not all problems are soluble. One of the costs of a flexible
and interflowing penetration of the private and public economy is
that people will often have an eye ahead for the next move. We
derive many benefits from the process of personnel flow in and out
of government. If we are to continue to enjoy such benefits of our
system — and they are very great — we must be prepared to pay
some small price. Most of all, we must not unthinkingly throw away
these benefits in overreaction to an occasional instance of misconduct by one of the government's five million civilian and uniformed
employees.

REGULATIONS

Not all areas of conduct calling for controls on conflicts of interest can be treated by statute. The program advanced here assumes
particularized regulation at the agency level. It also calls for presidential promulgation of a body of general regulations under the
statute.[27] One of the main functions of the proposed Administrator
would be study and preparation of such regulations; but the subject
and range of some of these regulations can be foreseen.

General interpretation

Several critical phrases in the statute have been drafted in anticipation that interpretative regulation will fill in detail.

Under section 3, an official is required to disqualify himself
from action where he has a "substantial economic interest." Supporting regulation should be drawn setting minimum standards,
built upon the principle that an economic interest is not "substantial" unless it is such as to be likely to influence the action of a
reasonable man — or to cause the public to think that it would.
It is not likely that the regulations could set up standards in dollar
or other numerical terms, but guidance could be provided by listing
factors to be considered and indicating something of the weight

[27]Chapter XI, § 10.

to be given to different factors. The difficulty of drawing lines in this field should not lead the Administrator to yield to the temptation to interpret every economic interest, however trivial, as ground for necessary disqualification. The statutory use of the term "substantial" is important and deliberate.

Pension and group security plans

Technical implementing regulations must be promulgated under subsection (f) of section 5, the outside compensation section, to spell out the details of the statutory scheme for permitting retention of certain pension, insurance, and other rights under security plans. The necessary general criteria are set forth in the statute.

Joint claims

A technical problem under sections 4 and 8 that has received no attention in the past should be mentioned as appropriate for regulatory action. These sections prevent an employee and former employee from assisting others in certain adversary situations vis-à-vis the government, but preserve to the employee himself his personal rights to protect his own interests and claims against the government (subject, of course, to the disqualification rule of section 3). The employee must be able to fight out his own income tax problems with the Internal Revenue Service, for example. In some situations, however, certain conduct on the employee's part in support of his personal rights may not be acceptable. Consider, for instance, a government employee who owns a small part of a large tract of land being condemned by the government. Clearly he can press his claim for damages with full vigor. But ought he to assume a position of leadership in organizing all the other landholders and financing their activities to try to block the entire project — by court action, administrative process, and legislative lobbying? Or, to shift the example, consider a government employee with a real though relatively small interest in an oil company that is pressing for transfer of federal off-shore oil rights to state control. To what extent may he participate in the effort to bring about the transfer? Such questions cannot be answered in the statute. It is important to be aware that the necessary and legitimate statutory exclusion of personal claims of employees can, in some circumstances, be abused. Regulatory recognition of the problem in advance could do something to head it off.

Gifts

Section 6 of the statute expressly calls for regulatory exceptions, and without such supplementation is unworkably stringent. These regulations are of special importance and should be accorded top priority by the Administrator. In particular, the recurrent problem of the business lunch and the small gratuity should receive prompt regulatory attention.

Sale of information and speculation

Much of the private law on the question of the fiduciary loyalty of an employee to his employer has revolved about two situations. In the first, the employee acquires a useful piece of business information, such as a trade secret or a list of customers, and then either sells this information to a competitor or sets up business across the street on the basis of the information. In the second, the employee in the course of his work learns of information that can be turned to his personal economic advantage, whereupon he makes off with the business opportunity and does not turn it over to the employing company. For centuries the courts have been seeking to work out the proper limits of the scope of duty of different kinds of employees in different kinds of situations to their employers.

These situations are not exactly analogous to the situation of most government employees, though in some cases the circumstances overlap. The reason is that normally the government is not itself looking for business opportunities. But closely similar problems can arise. When they do, they are severely aggravated by the ingredient of public confidence that is involved when the parties are the government and an official. Suppose an employee of the Air Force learns that an air base is to be built in a particular location, and promptly runs out to buy up land in the area. Or suppose he sells this information to some other person who buys up the land. He has clearly violated a confidence, used his office to line his own pocket, and probably cost the government money. Or consider another somewhat different case. An employee of the Agriculture Department learns that the Department will soon announce that much of the wheat crop is infected with hay fever fungus, and with this advance knowledge that the price of uninfected wheat will skyrocket, he plunges into wheat futures. Here the government is not directly, economically, and adversely affected by the employee's action. Nonetheless this is clearly intolerable behavior and inconsistent with the fundamental injunction not to mix up public and conflicting private interest.

Existing conflict of interest statutes do not treat either the sale or misuse of government information or speculation, though there are special statutes dealing with protection of agriculture statistics, trade secrets, and income tax data.[28] No separate statutory provision on information sale is included in the new statute, primarily because of drafting problems.[29] Some agencies have general regulations respecting speculation,[30] but more carefully drawn and wider-ranging regulation is needed on this point.

Fundamentally, regulation should make it clear that no government employee shall sell or use for the purpose of personal economic advantage any information which he acquired solely by virtue of his official position and which is not public information. But serious difficulties arise from such broad restrictions. The distinction between legitimate long-term investment and speculation on the basis of a hot tip is frequently hard to detect. Furthermore, information has a way of resisting compartmentation, and we often cannot avoid using information to which we have been exposed as it melds into what we call "experience." In the case of the scientist who learns, while in government employment, something of a new technique, or a government lawyer who acquires extensive knowledge of the tax laws, what begins as information becomes fused into a body of professional knowledge and skill, and conflict of interest regulations must not be so broadly drawn as to prevent the use of such professional skill. Finally, regulations on sale of information pose delicate questions of freedom of speech, freedom of inquiry, and the importance to the public of keeping information channels open from inside government to the public outside. For example, the public interest requires that, subject only to security require-

28 See, *e.g.*, 18 U.S.C. §§ 1902, 1905, 1906, 1907, 1908 (1958).
29 Note, however, that under § 2, providing information can constitute "assistance" and be barred under §§ 4 and 8.
30 See Chapter **IV**, notes 6, 28, and 32 *supra*.

ments, autobiographies, memoirs, and other writings of men who have retired from government be open to the public eye. Many observers feel that there are already too many muffles on the release of information from inside government.

Information control is difficult, but the difficulty of the job does not mean that the job itself must be abandoned. The principle is certainly clear: a government employee should not be able to use inside government information as a commodity for sale or as a device to hold up the government or as a basis for speculation.

Contracting out

Earlier chapters have pointed out the extent to which the government looks to independent contractors for the performance of services. Such contracting out is essential to the government's operations. Specialists — whether for operating cafeterias, developing an engine, setting up a filing system, or designing war games — can, through the contracting-out arrangement, be brought in on an *ad hoc,* short-term basis to help the government where it needs help. These specialists are sometimes individuals; more often they are specialized professional or semi-professional institutions or companies. Often the contracting-out arrangement makes it possible to attract the services of specialists who would not be willing to serve as direct employees of the government, mainly because of low salary scales, but also because of the generally more regulated environment.

The relationship of conflict of interest regulation and the contracting-out practice is ticklish. Legally the party contracting to perform the services is an "independent contractor" and not an "employee." As such, he is not subject to the existing statutes and regulations respecting government employees. Yet in particular cases the work being performed by the specialist-contractor can be identical with that which he would perform if the legal arrangement between him and the government were that of employee and employer. In these functionally identical situations all the conflict of interest problems of one are mirrored in the other. The only significant exception to this statement arises from the fact that there is less of an identification in the public's eye between the contractor and the government. And thus in the public's view of appearances,

the contractor is not in as sensitive a position with respect to conflicts of interest as the employee.

An over-all statutory solution is impossible. As described earlier,
the variety of different kinds of contractual relationships between
outsiders and the government is endless. Especially in the case of
the specialist organization, there can be no workable general rule
defining the reach and scope of the possible particular conflict of
interest restrictions. To use an admittedly extreme example, if
General Motors contracts to design and develop a new rocket, which,
if any, of the conflict of interest rules discussed in these chapters
should be applied to which employees of General Motors? the
limitations on outside compensation? or the restrictions on assisting
outsiders? Would the rules include employees of subcontractors?
General Motors as a corporation? all employees of General Motors?
only those working on the project? only executive personnel working
on the project? The questions multiply easily.

Again, the service contract, in which a private concern and
government work closely together, illustrates the interpenetration
of public and private characteristic of this century. Yet the normal
and useful contracting-out arrangement can be abused for the
purpose of evading conflict of interest regulation. How this can be
prevented — in what circumstances and by what techniques — is
another important problem facing the Administrator.

Until the basic pattern of regulation of employees is settled
and until many more facts are in hand respecting the conflict of
interest risks arising from contracting out, any effort to spell out
rules applicable beyond the category of employees is premature. The
statute therefore stops at the point of recognition of the problem, but
specifically calls upon the Administrator to undertake and conduct,
in conjunction with agency heads, a study of the extent to which
principles of the statute should be made applicable to persons having
contracts, subcontracts, licenses, or the like with or from the United
States, and to their employees.[31]

Advisory committees

As the use of advisory committees has increased, pressure to
regularize the procedures of these committees has mounted. In Chapter IV it was noted that the Attorney General has been motivated

[31] Chapter XI, § 10(b)(1)(G).

by antitrust considerations to promulgate a government-wide code on the procedural practices to be followed by such committees. Similarly legislation was introduced in the Congress in 1957 proposing an over-all set of procedures designed to put more direct responsibility in the regular-employee members sitting with the committees.[32]

The problem, as usual, is easier to state than to resolve. Advisers should advise and the decisions should be made by the regular government employees: this in general is the right formula for the new era of government-private cooperation. Realistically, however, it is often a most difficult standard to apply. It assumes that the government has in its regular service men of a professional competence that enables them, regardless of the circumstances, to make a reasonable choice among several alternatives presented to them by the private members of the advisory committee. Frequently, particularly in areas of the most advanced technology, the number of men able to deal with the particular problem is so limited, and the likelihood that one of them will be a permanent employee of the United States Government is so small, that as a practical matter the advice tendered by the private advisory committee can resolve the issue on the table, regardless of the form in which the meeting is conducted. Nonetheless, there are clear protections to the government in keeping the chairmanship of these committees in government hands, in requiring fixed agenda, and in making serious efforts to obtain several sides of controversial decisions.

One of the more difficult, and more interesting, tasks that would confront the Administrator under the proposed statute would be a study of procedures of these advisory committees from the point of view of conflicts of interest. In the preparation of regulations, great effort must be made not to impose upon all agencies an identical pattern that may work well in some but be ill-adjusted to the needs of others. Flexibility at the agency level is essential.

ADMINISTRATION AND ENFORCEMENT

Emphasis throughout this book has been placed upon the need for effective administration of any program of conflict of interest regulation. The anticipated administrative structure has been

32 See H.R. 3378 and H.R. 7390, 85th Cong., 1st Sess. (1957).

sketched in, with the statute, the general presidential regulations, and the individual agency regulations creating three tiers, administered by the President through the Administrator, through the heads of agencies and bureaus, and through the Department of Justice in matters of criminal offense. A few comments about its actual operations are in order.

Interpretative advice

The conscientious employee, while anxious to comply with applicable regulations, understandably does not wish to act adversely to his personal economic interests when it is not necessary. He deserves a reliable prior answer to the question whether his own circumstances will violate the conflict of interest statute and regulations. Except in a handful of agencies, there has been no procedure in the past under which an employee can secure such an advance ruling. Uncertainty and lack of coordination are major problems in the area. It would be a major step forward in administration if procedures were available for employees to refer conflict of interest questions to the general counsels of their agencies and to their agency heads, and if agency heads could turn to the central coordinating office for precedents in other agencies and for advice, especially regarding Presidential regulations. There are difficulties in such an arrangement in situations where penalties are criminal and where the enforcing agency, such as the Department of Justice, is asked to put itself on record in advance stating that there will be no prosecution. Perhaps there is no full solution to this difficulty, though some guidance should be possible, limited to particular disclosed facts. At least where the question is one of the proper interpretation of general regulations issued by the central coordinating office, or of agency or departmental or bureau regulations, advance rulings should be possible.

The statute expressly authorizes official advice by the Administrator in consultation with the Attorney General where requested by the President or agency heads.[33] Under appropriate circumstances such advice given in advance, limited to its facts, could operate as evidence of a state of mind negativing the existence of the state of

[33] Chapter XI, § 10(b)(1)(F).

mind required for criminal penalties under the act.[34] In any case, close coordination among agency personnel officials, responsible administrative officials of the General Accounting Office, and officials of the Department of Justice, all working with the Administrator, would make a substantial contribution toward the equitable administration of conflict of interest restraints.

Orientation

Much can be done to fight the conflict of interest problem by preventive measures. Until very recently no significant effort had been made by any administration to provide orientation to its appointed executives. In 1959, however, the administration undertook such an orientation effort through a one-week series of lectures, discussions, and reading assignments about life along the Potomac; one of the subjects touched upon is the conflict of interest issue. This approach to the problem has long been wanting, and is expressly provided for in the statute. If conflict of interest regulation is to be properly administered, these preventive efforts should be sustained, extended, and picked up in further detail within the appointee's own agency or department. The orientation need is particularly acute in the case of consultants and other intermittent employees.

Other preventive measures

As observed in Chapter IV, various agencies have attempted in a sporadic way to develop other preventive techniques of administration calculated to meet conflict of interest problems before rather than after the event. To provide particular incentive to agency heads to establish such procedures and follow them aggressively, the statute in section 11 specifically provides for several of them and authorizes the President, if he so chooses, to require them of the individual agencies involved. Some of these procedures are mechanical and simple, but they perform a direct function in increasing the alertness of employees to the ever present danger of conflicts of interest.

Section 11 authorizes agency heads to require employees to sign a statement that they have read an appropriate summary of the rules established by the act and the regulations issued thereunder;

[34] Chapter XI, § 21.

to require employees to report periodically as to their non-government employment, if any; to require agents or attorneys representing other persons before an agency to certify that, to the best of their knowledge, the representation will not violate sections 4 or 8 of the act or the regulations issued thereunder; and to require persons who are principals in transactions involving the government to certify that, to the best of their knowledge, they have not received assistance under circumstances that would violate sections 4 and 8 or the regulations issued thereunder.

The importance of preventive action in this field of ethical conduct cannot be overstated. There is, of course, nothing exclusive about the particular techniques listed in this section. Some agencies might, for example, wish to institute enrollment procedures for former employees, as has been proposed recently for the Department of Defense; and various other techniques of administration are promising and feasible. They may be used by agency heads to supplement those specified in the statute. General responsibility and authority is imposed and conferred upon agency heads by section 10(c).

The existing structure of restraints has been a clear failure in the area of guidance or advance warning. One of the most important themes of this book is that the catch-a-thief approach of the old statutes must yield place to a program of guidance for the majority.

Penalties

The program proposed here places its major reliance in the first instances upon administrative penalties rather than criminal penalties. For this reason, the statute, unlike any existing statute in the field, contains a lengthy section on administrative procedure.

The head of the agency is authorized to dismiss, suspend, or otherwise discipline any employee of his agency if he finds that the employee has violated the statute or regulations under the statute. The procedures prescribed are those applicable for disciplinary action for employee misconduct generally. Judicial review is provided to the extent provided by law for disciplinary action for misconduct of employees of the same category and grade.

Agency heads are also provided under section 12 with administrative sanctions directed against persons other than employees. They are, for example, authorized, upon a finding of a violation of the Act, to bar or impose reasonable conditions upon the appearance of the violator before the agency; and they are authorized to bar or impose reasonable conditions upon the conduct of, or negotiation or competition for, business by the agency on the part of the violator. This power of the agency head to bar or limit outside persons from contacts with the agency must be exercised with due caution and protected against abuse by procedural safeguards. At some length, therefore, section 12(b) spells out the applicability of the Administrative Procedure Act to findings of violations under the statute; as protection, it provides too for subpena power, attendance of witnesses, witnesses' fees and mileage, judicial review, the effect of judgments and decrees of the reviewing court, the availability of further judicial review, and other vital procedural matters. Though entirely new to the field of conflict of interest, section 12 is not in itself extraordinary, being primarily drawn parallel to the procedural sections of other statutes establishing administrative hearings and rulings.[35]

Section 216, one of the present conflict of interest statutes, authorizes the President to void government contracts where, in violation of that section, a government officer receives anything of value for aiding in procuring a government contract. Section 12(c) of the new statute develops this idea and applies it across the board to the entire statute. Unlike the blanket statement that the President may void the contract, however, the language of the new statute seeks to provide greater particularity for the procedures to be followed in such an extraordinary matter. Consistently with the rest of the statute, the rescission section is extended beyond contracts; any government action influenced by a violation of the statute is made subject to the rescission power. The finding that a violation of the act has substantially influenced government action is a prerequisite, and this finding is subject to judicial review. The matter of whether the contract should, under all the circumstances, including the position of innocent third parties, be set aside by the government, is a matter of judgment not subject to judicial review.

---

[35] See, *e.g.*, Federal Power Act, §§ 308, 309, 313, 49 Stat. 858 (1935), 16 U.S.C. §§ 825(g), 825(h), 825(l) (1958), amending 41 Stat. 1063 (1920).

A new enforcement weapon is provided to the Attorney General by subsection (d) of section 12. This weapon is a civil remedy for damages, collectible by the United States Government against any employee or former employee who shall, to his economic advantage, have acted in violation of the act. Under this subsection, the United States may recover on its behalf, in partial reimbursement for its expenses in administering the act, damages in an amount equal to three times the amount of such economic advantage to the employee. It is anticipated that there will be less hesitance in bringing actions under this subsection than has been shown in the past in case of actions brought for criminal remedies. Hopefully, too, the prospect of a triple loss, coupled with an administrative program that makes employees aware of this risk, should give employees considerable pause as they survey their outside economic affiliations.

Further civil penalties are provided in the field of civil fines applicable to any person who violates the statute by an improper payment to a government employee where the payor believed or had reason to believe that the receipt of the payment by the employee constituted a violation of certain specified sections of the act.[36] The important thing to be noted here is that the statute specifically provides for penalties upon the improper conduct of the payor as well as upon the recipient government employee.

The degree of purposeful intent required to be shown to invoke the civil penalty against the outsider is much less than the degree of intent required to be shown to invoke the criminal penalties discussed below.

Section 12 concludes with a series of general administrative points. Administrative rulings and findings under the act must be filed and published at least once a year, except where publication would be inconsistent with national security. It is anticipated that through this device over a period of time, and through the coordinating action of the Administrator, a body of guiding precedent and thought will develop relating to conflict of interest problems. A six year statute of limitations is imposed, applicable both to

---

[36] Chapter XI, § 9. The precise workings of this section are somewhat technical. Standards of knowledge necessarily vary from offense to offense, and some of the sections, such as the disqualification section, § 3, by their nature cannot be violated by payments by an outsider. See Chapter XI, §§ 9 and 12(e) and commentary accompanying these sections.

administrative and other action, and commencing from the occurrence of the alleged violation.

The statute retains criminal penalties, however. Unlike the existing patchwork of statutes, the criminal penalties provided are consistent throughout, being a fine of not more than $10,000 or imprisonment for not more than one year, or both. The key and critical difference between the proposed new statute in this respect and the existing laws is that under the new statute criminal penalties are reserved for flagrant cases of deliberate violation. The degree of intent required is inherent in the two words "purposely" and "knowingly." Definitions of these terms are incorporated verbatim from drafts of the American Law Institute's Model Penal Code. The reasons for the shift in emphasis toward administrative and civil rather than criminal sanctions have been set forth at some length earlier in this chapter.[37]

Altogether, the new statute combines in sections 12 and 21 a full armory of weapons for administration and enforcement. These range from routine and minor administrative reprimand through more serious administrative remedies such as dismissal or bar from appearance before the agency, through damages actions, civil penalties, and up to the most strict sort of criminal penalty. With a wide choice of sanctions available, administrators and enforcement officials will find it far easier to select an appropriate remedy to deal with the particular case before them, and will not be driven to forego all penalty when they are unable to make out a case for the drastic criminal sanctions now contained in the conflict of interest statutes. In short, the new statute provides a uniform and integrated system of administration and enforcement.

SENATE CONFIRMATION

Senators, executive branch officials, and commentators are unanimous in the view that it would be desirable to regularize the existing procedures of congressional confirming committees, particularly the Senate Armed Services Committee, in matters of conflict of interest. In view of the nature of the confirmation process and the unicameral prerogatives of the Senate in this field, a statutory solution to the

[37] See discussion *supra* under "The Role of Administration."

problem is inappropriate. What can be done is to develop a series of practices and procedures that will create a better atmosphere and lend a greater degree of predictability to the standards applied to the individual appointees appearing before the committees.

There is good reason to think that the enactment of the statute proposed here, and the vigorous administration of the program offered here, would itself ease the situation before the Senate confirming committees. If there were a unified body of relevant law and regulations, in keeping with the demands and risks of the twentieth century, and if the Senate were able to see an effective executive administration of that program, much of the present pressure put upon the confirming committees would be relieved. The way has already been pointed out, especially in the hearings respecting AEC Chairman McCone. This appointee appeared before the committee armed with an opinion that his position would not violate the conflict of interest laws and, furthermore, armed with a general plan for the disposition of his personal properties that had been approved by the Attorney General. With relatively little difficulty the Senate committee went along with this well worked out arrangement.

It should not be necessary so to provide by statute, but the anticipation is that the Administrator will, on the basis of his continued consideration of conflict of interest questions, develop a familiarity that no one has at present with the law and regulations in the field, and become a continuing source of advice to all government officials concerned with the conflict of interest problem. The Administrator will have files, records, and transcripts immediately available to him in one centralized place — all dealing with the same recurring problems. He will have an intimate familiarity with the statutes and the presidential regulations. He will further have available in his files all regulations of individual agencies relating to the problem. He will have experience gained both in working with the Attorney General in cases of prosecutions and in rendering advice in day-to-day situations when called upon by the President and agency heads. Most likely, under these circumstances, when an appointee is selected for a particular agency, the appointing authority or his representative, the coordinating Administrator, the general counsel of the agency, perhaps a representative of the Department of Justice, and often counsel to the appointee, will sit down together to appraise the appointee's situation under the Conflict of Interest Act and the regulations and to devise an over-all plan shaped to the appointee's individual economic position and to the office he is being appointed to. Where such a plan has been worked out, a full analysis of the appointee's situation can be prepared by the Administrator; this analysis, together with its conclusions developed in consultation with the Department of Justice, will be sent over with the appointee to the Senate confirming committee.

Though of course the Senate committee would at all times retain its full constitutional power to confirm or not to confirm as it chooses, the likelihood is that in time this conflict of interest procedure would become institutionalized and would substitute for the present haphazard situation. A substantial improvement in the workings of government would have been brought about, and a substantial factor deterring many from accepting high-ranking government position would be mitigated.

Because the circumstances surrounding each appointee and his appointment differ markedly from those of other appointees to other positions, any substantive proposals or standards are difficult to set here. One point does, however, deserve special emphasis.

All the examples of conflict of interest difficulties before the Senate committees have involved stock. This overconcentration on one particular kind of property holding is clearly misplaced. The overconcern with stockholdings has two unjustifiable aspects. There is no reason and much unfairness in putting the government employee into the position of a second-class economic citizen unable to participate in the growth of the American economy through the holding of stock. Second, in no situation does stockholding as such entail any greater or more special risk of improper conflict of interest behavior than any other form of property holding, whether a land leasehold, or a boat title, or a partnership interest.

The type of trust used by Mr. McCone, with the clearance of other officials, in itself offers an excellent vehicle for solving many of the stockholding conflicts that have arisen in the past. Under this arrangement the appointee entering government puts the securities into a trust held by an independent trustee, the trust to terminate on the appointee's completion of his tour of government service. The appointee is not informed what securities are held by the trust, nor has he any power of control or distribution or disposition over the properties in the trust so long as the trust continues. Properly set up and policed, and followed in good faith, this sort of plan offers an attractive adjustment between the frequently serious economic loss sustained by the appointee if he is required to divest himself of his securities and the public's need to protect itself against the use of public office for private gain. A similar kind of trust arrangement was established by President Eisenhower before he assumed office. The trust mechanism is healthy in appearance, protects the government since the trust beneficiary does not even know what securities he holds an interest in, and yet permits the appointee to enter government service without a complete disruption of his personal estate.

It may be hoped that here the procedural use of the Administrator and the Administrator's opinions, coupled with circumscribed and bona fide use of the trust device, will lead to a steady improvement in confirmation proceedings. However, it may be expected that the Senate's continuing interest in the issue will not abate until such time as the executive branch demonstrates that it is adequately and aggressively handling its own conflict of interest problems.

MISCELLANEOUS

Amendments and repealers

The program advanced here constitutes a substantial effort to create a continuing and comprehensive plan sufficiently flexible internally to make it unnecessary to carve out hosts of spot exemptions.

The proposed act amends six of the seven basic conflict of interest laws analyzed in Chapter III so as to make them inapplicable to executive branch employees after the effective date of the proposed act. The form of the amendments has the effect of leaving these present statutes in full force and effect as to any persons not covered by the proposed act. Such persons would include, in the case of particular statutes, congressmen, legislative branch employees, and any employees of the judiciary branch, or other persons to the extent covered by one or more of the present statutes, but not coming within the definition of "employee" in the proposed act.

The seventh basic conflict of interest statute in effect today, 5 U.S.C. Section 99, would be repealed outright. This statute covers only persons who are within the definition of "Government employee" in the proposed act, and hence there would be no reason for preserving the section.[38]

Another proposed repeal is that of an ambiguous statute dating from 1791 and containing a jumble of conflicts restraints for "clerks" in the Treasury Department.[39] The general provisions of the proposed act provide ample basic protection in the case of Treasury Department employees as well as other employees and any peculiar or specialized needs of the Department should be met by regulations. The proposed act leaves untouched, however, a number of narrow statutes that outlaw particular economic interests for particular employees or categories thereof. Examples are the prohibition against certain business interests of the Secretary of the Treasury,[40] and the prohibition against investments in civil aeronautics enterprises by members of the Civil Aeronautics Board.[41]

Reserves of the armed forces while on active duty for training are classified under the proposed act as "intermittent Government employees," irrespective of the duration of their training period in any year. A corresponding repealer implements this provision.

Two other statutes repealed by the proposed act pertain to (a) certain employment of officers and retired officers of the Regular Navy and Regular Marine Corps, 10 U.S.C. Section 6112; and (b) the selling activities of retired commissioned officers with respect to "any supplies or war materials," 5 U.S.C. Section 59c. The basis for these repeals is discussed in connection with the post-employment provisions of the proposed act, *supra*.

The remaining repealers deal with laws now in effect that provide exemptions from one or more of the seven basic conflict of interest statutes. The principle followed is that an exemption to a statute that

---

[38] Quite apart from its relation to the new affirmative program offered here, this sanctionless anachronistic section should be repealed, as many sources have proposed.

[39] REV. STAT. § 244 (1875), 5 U.S.C. § 254 (1958).

[40] REV. STAT. § 243 (1875), as amended, 5 U.S.C. § 243 (1958).

[41] 52 Stat. 981 (1938), as amended, 49 U.S.C. § 1321(b) (1958). Other instances are the prohibition against interests in public lands on the part of employees of the General Land Office, REV. STAT. § 452 (1875), 43 U.S.C. § 11 (1958), and the prohibition against interests in mail contracts on the part of employees of the Postal Service, 18 U.S.C. § 440 (1958).

will no longer itself be applicable to the exempted class of persons is meaningless, and should be deleted. It should be noted that many of the exemptions that are repealed are not total exemptions, but are only partial in nature. The substantive restraints that these exemptive provisions either leave in effect or impose by special language are usually designed to meet the special situation of a consultant or expert. As such, they are frequently very close in their approach, and even their wording, to the provisions of the proposed act applicable to "intermittent Government employees." A generalized statutory principle reflecting the special situation of consultants and experts is preferable to a proliferation of exemptive provisions applicable to particular consultants and experts. No rationale to the present lack of uniformity in exemptive provisions for consultants and experts can be perceived. The present hodge-podge of exemptions and semi-exemptions yields only discrimination among departments and agencies, and even among consultants and advisers to the same department or agency. This discrimination is eliminated by the proposed act.

Other recommendations

Much can be done toward attracting top talent to government service through the reform of the conflict of interest restraints. But much more needs to be done. If government is not to be priced out of the talent market, it must pay salaries commensurate to the scales required to attract able men. At the lower and middle levels, government salaries compare favorably with those of the private segment of the economy; at the executive and technical levels this is increasingly less true. It is dangerous and short-sighted policy for the government to deprive itself by low salary scales of the services of the key personnel it needs.

A part of the problem of compensation is the problem of the growing use of security plans. Several important developments are needed if these plans are not to operate as an impediment to the government's recruiting efforts. The first kind of action needed is action by employers. It would be of immense assistance to the government if employers could be persuaded to be more liberal and constructive about employees' leaving for periods of government service. It is possible to hope for a day when most employers can be persuaded to save the employee's place on the promotional ladder during his absence. But without going this far, employers can at least move in the direction of ameliorating the government's recruitment needs by providing in their security and welfare plans that an employee who is on leave of absence for government service will continue to be eligible and a participant under the plan. It asks a great deal of an employee of a private company to throw away his pension rights and health insurance in order to serve in the federal government for a few years. Changes in the law can help eliminate part of the necessity for this. But such changes will be useless unless the employers, the unions, the lawyers, and those who participate in the preparation and establishment of these plans also provide that the employee may remain a participant under the plan while in government service. Widespread adoption of this viewpoint is urgently needed and recommended.

At the same time, adjustments in the law are required to make effective this more liberal view on the part of employers. Probably of greatest importance is the necessity for the Internal Revenue Service, or perhaps Congress, to make it perfectly clear that the tax status of an employee security or welfare plan will not be impaired if it does provide for government-service leaves of absence with a retention of participating status. At the state level, amendment of local insurance laws may be required to ensure the validity of group insurance programs containing similar provisions. Perhaps in the long run, despite the frightening administrative problems involved, we may arrive at some sort of clearing house or other coordination or exchange arrangements for pension and other plans so as to free the general economy from the immobilizing effect of an atomistic welfare system based on individual companies, unions, universities, governments, and other institutions.

A lesser point than the preceding two is the need for a thoroughgoing consolidation of all legislation on the books dealing with federal government personnel. At present it is a congeries of special provisions and special exemptions, badly in need of general overhauling. In recent years the Civil Service Commission has been in the process of preparing such an over-all compilation, and legislation on the point was introduced in 1959.[42] If the material were

42 H.R. 8748, 86th Cong., 1st Sess. (1959).

pulled together and integrated, it would reveal that there are a substantial number of spot statutes hidden in unsuspected corners of the United States Code expressing in varying ways the underlying policies against conflicts of interest. Until this consolidation takes place, it will remain difficult for lawyers and administrators to work in this field.

Finally, in view of the close relationship between the executive and legislative branches, a recommendation made in Chapter II may be reiterated, that a full-scale study be undertaken of the special conflict of interest problems of members of Congress.

A comment on disclosure

In the past few years, several committees and commentators have made suggestions of various kinds for improvement of the conflict of interest laws. In some instances the substance of some of the points supported here has appeared in other quarters. Examples include the repeal of 5 U.S.C. Section 99 and the extension of the "claims" statutes to cover a broader category of dealings with the government. In other instances, however, the program advanced here differs from the proposals of others, particularly in its integration. In all cases except one, the argument in this study explains why the position recommended here has been thought to be the better one. The arguments against other proposals have been implicit in the arguments advanced here.

This statement cannot be made of one proposal, however. A number of legislators have periodically pressed for a solution to the conflict of interest problem based on compulsory full disclosure by officials of all their personal assets and sources of income. Legislation to this effect was introduced in 1958.[43] There is, of course, a case to be made for disclosure as an approach to the conflict of interest problem. The more light the better, it can be argued. To the extent that the conflicts problem is one of public confidence, it is probable that full personal disclosure by officials of their personal economic affairs would make a favorable public impression and a contribution to public confidence. Yet, on balance, a statute requiring full disclosure does not seem to be the best route to pursue.

Perhaps impeding of recruitment is the first objection. The ten WOCs now permitted to be appointed in the Department of Defense

43 See H.R. 10631, 10780, 13295; S. 1057, 3346, 3979, 4223, 85th Cong., 2d Sess. (1958).

with partial exemption from the conflict of interest laws are required to file information of their financial holdings for publication in the *Federal Register*. Most of the time, several of these important jobs are vacant. Interviews indicate that among the obstacles encountered in efforts to fill them, the disclosure requirement stands high. Americans are loath to reveal their personal assets and income, for many reasons, and many will resist bitterly any efforts to make them do so.

Apart from the recruitment question, the full disclosure approach raises substantial risks of another kind. It is an almost certain invitation to demagogic political attack of one kind or another — upon the poor man as one who cannot manage even his own economic affairs, and upon the rich man as one who is privileged and has lost contact with the mass of the citizenry.

But, most important, disclosure alone will not do the job. The basic rules spelled out in the program advanced here are still needed — disqualification, bars on assisting outsiders, limits on gifts, post-employment control, and so forth. Disclosure as a remedy suggests that the main problems of conflict of interest arise out of asset holdings. As this entire book seeks to make clear, this is too simplified a view of the problem. At best disclosure would help to *police* the kind of substantive restrictions that are needed.

Some elements of disclosure are worked into the program recommended here. Where this is done, however, it is for an express purpose, and to meet a particular problem; for example, disclosure of the particular conflicting interest is required as a substitute protection in the limited case of exemptions from the disqualification rule of section 3 of the proposed act. But unless and until it can be shown that an integrated and aggressive program on all fronts has been a failure in relying upon a combination of rule and policing devices, the severe unfortunate side effects of the all-out disclosure requirement argue overwhelmingly against its adoption.

CONCLUSION

The program advanced here will not "solve" the problem of conflict of interest in federal employment. Like most real problems, this is one we must live with permanently, strive to mitigate, and adjust to.

Governmental ethical standards can only be seen as a part of the society's general moral atmosphere. This is especially true under the American system of continual interflow of men and information between government and the private segment of the society. We can, and must, expect a somewhat higher standard of moral performance from government officials than from other citizens, but demands for super-standards for government personnel are out of touch with reality and on occasion demagogic.

The program proposed, however, will do several things. It meets the triple flaws of the present pattern of conflict of interest restraints — obsolescence, weakness of administration, and faulty drafting. It will greatly further the main aim of the conflict of interest statutes — preservation of the integrity of government. It will provide for an integrated and comprehensible system of standards and sanctions together with an effective machinery for administering that system. It is shaped to modern conditions, and is flexible enough to permit further developments as new problems arise. It is grounded upon a realistic conception of the problem of conflicting interest as it appears in the modern setting of American government and society.

And it will make a significant contribution toward staffing the federal government for world leadership.

Proposed Act
with Technical Commentary

It is one thing to make general policy recommendations. It is frequently quite another to convert these recommendations into usable legislative form. Not all the program proposed in the last chapter is statutory, but much of it is. This chapter contains in fully worked out bill form an Executive Conflict of Interest Act designed to put the proposed program into effect, together with a section-by-section technical commentary to accompany the act.

The act consolidates the existing law on conflict of interest for federal executive-branch employees into one unified statute with a single set of definitions and a consistent approach. The heart of the act is Title I, in which key terms are defined and the basic forms of conflict of interest are treated in a logical progression. The six major substantive restraints deal with action by a government employee in his official capacity in a matter in which he has a personal interest, and in his private capacity in furtherance of an interest adverse to the government; with receipt of pay from outside sources, and of gifts; with action designed to induce payments from outside sources; and with post-employment activities adverse to the government's interest. The proposed administrative structure and the civil remedies are also set forth in Title I. Title II establishes the criminal penalties by creating a new chapter to Title 18 of the United States Code. Title III amends and repeals various laws presently applicable to executive-branch employees. Title IV sets forth the short title and effective date of the proposed act.

The act follows.

S. (H. R.)—

IN THE SENATE OF THE UNITED STATES
(IN THE HOUSE OF REPRESENTATIVES)

A BILL

To supplement and revise the criminal laws prescribing restrictions against conflicts of interest applicable to employees of the executive branch of the Government of the United States, and for other purposes.

Be it enacted by the Senate and House of Representatives of the United States of America in Congress assembled,

TABLE OF CONTENTS

Sec. 10. Administration.

Sec. 11. Preventive measures.

Sec. 12. Remedies; civil penalties; procedures.

TITLE I — PROHIBITED CONDUCT, ADMINISTRATION AND PROCEDURE

§ 1. Preamble; declaration of policy and purpose

(a) The proper operation of a democratic government requires that officials be independent and impartial; that government decisions and policy be made in the proper channels of the governmental structure; that public office not be used for personal gain; and that the public have confidence in the integrity of its government. The attainment of one or more of these ends is impaired whenever there exists, or appears to exist, an actual or potential conflict between the private interests of a government employee and his duties as an official. The public interest, therefore, requires that the law protect against such conflicts of interest and establish appropriate ethical standards with respect to employee conduct in situations where actual or potential conflicts exist.

(b) It is also fundamental to the effectiveness of democratic government that, to the maximum extent possible, the most qualified individuals in the society serve its government. Accordingly, legal protections against conflicts of interest must be so designed as not unnecessarily or unreasonably to impede the recruitment and retention by the government of those men and women who are most qualified to serve it. An essential principle underlying the staffing of our governmental structure is that its employees should not be denied the opportunity, available to all other citizens, to acquire and retain private economic and other interests, except where actual or potential conflicts with the responsibility of such employees to the public cannot be avoided.

(c) It is the policy and purpose of this Act to promote and balance the dual objectives of protecting Government integrity and of facilitating the recruitment and retention of the personnel needed by Government, by prescribing essential restrictions against conflicts of interest in the executive branch of the Government without creating unnecessary barriers to public service.

§ 2. Definitions

Unless the context of this Act otherwise clearly requires, for purposes of this Act the terms defined in this section shall have the respective meanings hereinafter set forth. The terms defined in this

---

§ 1. Preamble; declaration of policy and purpose

The preamble emphasizes two objectives: (a) protecting Government integrity and promoting confidence in Government; and (b) facilitating the recruitment and retention of the personnel needed by Government. The preamble states that it is the "policy and purpose of this Act to promote and balance" these dual objectives. Existing statutes in the field

section include:
  "agency"
  "agency head" and "head of an agency"
  "assist"
  "compensation"
  "Government action"
  "Government employee"
  "intermittent Government employee"
  "participate"
  "person"
  "regular Government employee"
  "responsibility"
  "State"
  "thing of economic value"
  "transaction involving the Government"

(a) "Agency" means —
  (1) the Executive Office of the President;
  (2) an executive department;
  (3) an independent establishment within the executive branch; and
  (4) a Government corporation.
  For purposes of this subsection (a) —
  (i) the executive departments are the Departments of State; Defense; Treasury; Justice; Post Office; Interior; Agriculture; Commerce; Labor; and Health, Education, and Welfare; and
  (ii) "independent establishment within the executive branch" means any establishment, commission, board, committee or other unincorporated instrumentality of the United States which is

----

of conflict of interest give no express recognition to the need for this balancing of policies.

§ 2. Definitions

Section 2 sets forth definitions of the basic terms used throughout the Act. Existing scattered conflict of interest statutes make no effort at consistent usage.

not —

(A) part of an executive department or Government corporation; or

(B) part of the legislative or judicial branches of the United States.

(iii) "Government corporation" means any corporation which is either defined as a "wholly owned Government corporation" in the Government Corporations Control Act of 1946, as the same may be amended from time to time, or is designated as a Government corporation for purposes of this Act by the President by regulations issued pursuant to section 10.

(a) "Agency": The definition of "agency" is an adaptation of the definition found in H.R. 8748, 86th Congress, 1st Session, introduced by Congressman Celler on August 20, 1959. The definition is an important link in marking out the scope of application of the Act, and in other respects. It includes:

(1) the Executive Office of the President, which consists of the White House Office, the Bureau of the Budget, the Council of Economic Advisers, National Security Council, Operations Coordinating Board, Central Intelligence Agency, National Aeronautics and Space Council, Office of Civil and Defense Mobilization, President's Advisory Committee on Government Organization;

(2) the ten Executive Departments;

(3) each "independent establishment" within the executive branch (this is in itself a defined term which includes the independent agencies and miscellaneous Government commissions and committees); and

(4) each "Government corporation." "Government corporation" is defined to include, first, every corporation that is defined as a "wholly owned Government corporation" in the Government Corporations Control Act, 59 Stat. 597 (1945), as amended, 31 U.S.C. § 846 (1958), section 101 of which specifically enumerates these corporations. Second, it includes other corporations designated by the President as a "Government corporation" for purposes of the Executive Conflict of Interest Act. The President's designation must be in the form of a regulation issued pursuant to section 10 of the Act. The President could, under this authorization, designate as a "Government corporation" one that is within the classification of "mixed ownership Government corporations" under section 201 of the Government Corporations Control Act. 59 Stat. 600 (1945), as amended, 31 U.S.C. § 856 (1958).

(b) "Agency head" and "head of an agency" mean the chief executive officer of an agency, who shall be the chairman in the case of an independent establishment which is a commission, board, or committee. The Secretary of Defense may delegate to the Secretaries of the Army, the Navy, and Air Force such of his responsibilities as an agency head as he may deem appropriate.

(c) "Assist" means to act, or offer or agree to act, in such a way as to help, aid, advise, furnish information to, or otherwise provide assistance to, another person believing that such action is of help, aid, advice, or assistance to such person and with intent so to assist such person.

Thus, the definition of "Government corporation" has flexibility in two respects:

(A) the Congress may from time to time add to the list of enumerated "wholly owned Government corporations" under the Government Corporations Control Act; and

(B) the President may designate additional corporations by regulation.

(b) "Agency head" and "head of an agency": The first sentence of the definition needs no amplification.

The second sentence authorizes the Secretary of Defense to delegate "such of his responsibilities as an agency head as he may deem appropriate" to the service Secretaries. In all probability the Secretary of Defense would want to make such a delegation, particularly since each of the three military services now has its own conflict of interest regulations promulgated by its own Secretary.

(c) "Assist": The term "assist" is a key term in section 4 (assisting in transactions involving the Government) and in section 8 (post-employment). The concept has antecedents in several of the basic statutes presently in effect. These existing statutes, and the pertinent language in each, are as follows (emphasis added):

18 U.S.C. § 281: ". . . any *services* rendered or to be rendered, either by himself or another, in relation to any proceeding, . . ."

18 U.S.C. § 283: ". . . acts as an agent or attorney for prosecuting any claims against the United States or *aids or assists* in the prosecution or support of any such claim . . ."

5 U.S.C. § 99: ". . . act as counsel, attorney, or agent for prosecuting any claim against the United States . . . nor in any manner, nor by any means, to *aid in* the prosecution of any such claim . . ."

Commentary on "Assist," continued:

These critical provisions in existing conflict of interest laws have caused much difficulty in their vagueness. The definition in the Act meets a variety of points not answered at all by these provisions.

The definition of "assist" in the Act is more inclusive than any of the foregoing, in that it includes "to act, or offer or agree to act, in such a way as to help, aid, advise, furnish information to, or otherwise provide assistance to . . ." The language "offer or agree to act" makes the actual rendering of services irrelevant, so long as the Government employee or former Government employee indicates, by offer or agreement, his willingness to perform the services. In this respect the definition precludes a holding such as that in *United States v. Reisley,* 32 F. Supp. 432, 35 F. Supp. 102 (D.C.N.J. 1940), in which the court concluded that section 281 was not violated where the purported services were not actually performed by the officer who received compensation for them.

It should be noted that assistance may take the form merely of furnishing information to another person. The information need not be confidential in any sense, or even have been acquired in the course of Government employment. In this respect, "assist," as used in the Act, goes beyond the various limited regulations and the specific spot statutes prohibiting sale of certain kinds of Government-acquired information. To constitute a violation of either section 4 or 8, however, the employee or former employee must assist in a "transaction involving the Government," as defined.

It may be noted that the language "acts as counsel, attorney, or agent," which appears in 18 U.S.C. § 284 (and a variant of it in 5 U.S.C. § 99) does not appear expressly in the definition of "assist." Such language is unnecessary, since serving as counsel, attorney, or agent for another person would clearly be encompassed by the words "help, aid, advise." See, however, the special rule of section 4(b), where regular employees are forbidden to assist by representing another as his agent or attorney even where no compensation is involved.

Other important features of the definition of "assist" are the requirements that the employee believe that the action is of assistance to the other person and that he intend to assist the other person. Thus, for example, if a Government employee publishes an article that in fact provides another person with valuable assistance in furthering a proceeding he has pending in a Government agency, but the Government employee had no knowledge of such person and no intent so to assist him, the definition of "assist" would not be met.

On this question of the state of mind of the Government employee, the definition of "transaction involving the Government" in sections 4 and 8 is also pertinent. As will appear, that term requires belief, or reasonable ground for belief, that the particular transaction does or will involve the Government.

(d) "Compensation" means any thing of economic value, however designated, which is paid, loaned, granted, or transferred, or to be paid, loaned, granted, or transferred for, or in consideration of, personal services to any person or to the United States.

(e) "Government action" means any action on the part of the executive branch of the United States, including, but not limited to —

(1) any decision, determination, finding, ruling, or order, including the judgment or verdict of a military court or board; and

(2) any grant, payment, award, license, contract, transaction, sanction or approval, or the denial thereof, or failure to act with respect thereto.

(d) "Compensation": The term "compensation" appears in several places in the Act, particularly throughout section 5 and as a key element in the broad prohibition of section 4(b)(2).

This definition incorporates another defined term: "thing of economic value" (see section 2, subsection (m)).

The definition of "compensation" is confined to payments and other transfers made "for, or in consideration of, personal services to any person or to the United States." Thus the term does not include a payment or other transfer made bona fide either as a gift or as the purchase price of property sold. But a *loan* of money or goods in consideration of personal services may constitute compensation.

Similar terms, but undefined, appear in 18 U.S.C. §§ 281, 1914, and 216, and have, on occasion, raised questions of interpretation. See especially the discussion of section 5 *infra*.

(e) "Government action": The definition of "Government action" expresses a new concept. Existing statutes, with the exception of 18 U.S.C. § 281, are narrowly limited to particular kinds of Government matters, particularly claims and contracts. The definition of "Government action," however, taken together with the term "transaction involving the Government," extends the coverage of the conflict of interest provisions well beyond the existing structure of restraints, and adds greatly to the scope of their protection. No present conflict of interest statute contains a similar concept. See the discussion on page 197 *supra*.

The second paragraph of the definition merely enumerates certain specific manifestations of the items in the first paragraph. The two paragraphs of the definition thus overlap, since it is hard to conceive of a "grant, payment, award, license, contract," etc. (paragraph (2)) which is not also a "decision" (paragraph (1)).

(f) "Government employee" means any individual who is —

(1) appointed by one of the following acting in his official capacity —

(A) the President of the United States, or

(B) a person who qualifies as a Government employee under this definition; and

(2) engaged in the performance of a Federal function under

- -

(f) "Government employee":

(1) *General Comment.* This definition like that of "agency," is an adaptation of a similar term found in H.R. 8748, 86th Congress, 1st Session (1959). To be within the definition of "Government employee," one must meet all three of the tests prescribed by paragraphs (1), (2), and (3) of the definition.

The term "Executive act" used in paragraph (2) is not intended to be limited to Executive orders, but encompasses other types of official and duly authorized action by the executive branch.

"Authority" used in paragraph (3) is broad enough to cover consultants and experts who might not be acting under the "supervision" of another official in the normal sense of the term "supervision."

The reason for the fairly elaborate definition of "Government employee" lies in the desire to achieve a much greater certainty than presently exists as to who is subject to the restraints of the conflict of interest laws. The definition in the Act clearly excludes, for example, the man who is informally telephoned by a Government official for consultation, or who may even come to the office of the Government official and confer with him for a few hours or a day. On the other hand, the definition clearly includes any consultant who obtains consulting pay or reimbursement for travel and/or a per diem expense allowance, pursuant to a "WAE" (when actually employed) designation. Any such designation would constitute a sufficient appointment to meet the test of paragraph (1). While it is conceivable that the requirement of an "appointment" may permit some informal consultants to escape application of the conflict of interest laws, the same is true today, and is inevitable. It would be impossible to try to draw lines, for example, between (1) an experienced friend whose views are sought during a social evening, (2) a Bernard Baruch on a park bench, to whom a Cabinet Secretary goes for advice, (3) a Washington lawyer called over to a private lunch with a Cabinet Secretary to discuss a problem, and (4) the representative of a civic organization who spends two days participating in a small Departmental conference or "seminar." Who among these is an "employee," assuming none of them has received an "appointment" of any sort? The only difference between

authority of the Constitution, an Act of Congress, or an Executive act; and

(3) under the supervision or authority of one of the persons listed in (A) or (B) under (1).

Notwithstanding the foregoing, the term "Government employee" shall not include any of the following —

(i) officers and employees in the legislative and judicial branches

----

the third and fourth cases is that in the fourth a written invitation may have been issued, and the time spent at the Department may have been a little longer.

An alternative possible approach to the definition of "Government employee" would be to enumerate criteria analogous to the common law tests of employee vs. independent contractor, such as whether or not a place to work is provided for the individual. But these criteria are difficult to apply, the weighting of criteria pointing to opposite conclusions is indeterminable, uniformity could not be expected; and, in the last analysis, the approach proves impractical.

(2) *Relationship to "agency"; exclusions.* Since the Act is intended to apply only to employees of the executive branch, and since the three tests for a Government employee would sweep in legislative and judicial branch employees, an exclusion for "officers and employees in the legislative and judicial branches of the United States" is set forth in the second part of the definition. Similar reasoning calls for the express exclusion of employees of the District of Columbia and of corporations other than Government corporations, as defined. In other words, the basic intent is that only employees of an "agency" be included within the definition of "Government employee." However, to state the matter that simply assumes prior knowledge of who is an "employee" of an agency. But since this is the issue, the Act proceeds by first defining who is an "employee" of the Federal Government and then by narrowing the class by exclusion to executive branch employees.

(3) *Reservists.* Under present law, a reservist of the Armed Forces is not considered an "employee" when on active duty for training. 70A STAT. 632 (1956), 5 U.S.C. § 30r(d) (1958). Under the definition in the Act, the reservist who is not on active duty is similarly excluded from the category of "employee." But the Act does not contain an exclusion for reservists on active duty; so they are "employees" for purposes of the Act.

As will be seen in later discussion, however, reservists on active duty for training only are classified as "intermittent Government employees." See also the corresponding technical amendment at sec-of the United States;

(ii) employees of the District of Columbia;

(iii) employees of corporations other than Government corporations as defined in subsection (a)(iii) of this section; and

(iv) a reserve of the Armed Forces, when he is not on active duty and is not otherwise a Government employee.

An individual shall not be deemed an employee solely by reason of his receipt of a pension, disability payments, or other payments not made for current services, or by reason of his being subject to recall to active service.

Every Government employee shall be deemed either "intermittent" or "regular," as determined by the definitions contained in subsections (g) and (j), respectively, of this section.

---

tion 35 of the Act conforming 5 U.S.C. § 30r(d) to this approach. The more carefully refined restrictions of the Act distinguishing between intermittent and regular employees make it no longer necessary to undergo the risks of a blanket exemption for reservists on active duty for training.

(4) *Retired Personnel.* In *Morgenthau v. Barrett,* 108 F.2d 481 (D.C. Cir. 1939), *cert. denied,* 309 U.S. 672 (1939) it was held that a retired Army officer was an "officer" for purposes of section 281. Subsequent amendments to sections 281 and 283 expressly exempted retired officers but incorporated new provisions restricting sales to, and prosecution of claims against, the Government by retired officers.

Under the Act, however, the next to last paragraph of the definition of "employee" excludes retired persons, including military personnel, who merely receive Government pensions or similar payments, not for current services. In respect of retired military officers, this provision has the effect of overruling the *Morgenthau* case. The retired officer or employee, of course, is still a "former employee" under the Act and subject to all restraints applicable to persons in that class. See section 8. And the retired military officer is also subject to whatever special rules are set by the President pursuant to section 8(e). See the discussion in Chapter X *supra,* under "Military procurement and employment of retired officers."

(5) *"Intermittent" or "regular."* The definition expressly provides that every Government employee will be deemed "intermittent" or "regular," as determined under the definitions of subsections (g) and (j) of section 2.

(g) "Intermittent Government employee" means any Government employee who has performed services as such employee on not more than fifty-two working days (which shall not include Saturdays, Sundays, and holidays) out of the preceding three hundred and sixty-five calendar days: *Provided, however,* That —

(1) the President may issue an order increasing to not more than one hundred and thirty days the number of working days within a three hundred and sixty-five calendar day period on which a particular Government employee may perform services while still being classified as an intermittent Government employee for purposes of this Act: *Provided,* That the President shall make a determination that the national interest requires the issuance of such order. A statement of the pertinent facts and of

----

(g) "Intermittent Government employee": The explicit expression of the concept of an "intermittent" employee represents an innovation for purposes of conflict of interest statutes. On the other hand, it is not unknown to federal personnel administration (see, *e.g.,* 36 DECS. COMP. GEN. 351 (1956)), and in a real sense the concept is already built into the conflict of interest laws. So many statutory exemptions and special provisions now appear with respect to advisory boards and consultants, it is apparent that Congress has recognized the necessity of treating them differently from regular, full-time employees. The necessity is real, for it is obvious that by his very nature an intermittent employee will have outside economic interests on which he is primarily dependent. In many cases, these economic interests (primarily, his private employment) provide the intermittent employee with the very expertise that makes Government seek his advice.

The sections of the Act that in some degree differentiate in treatment between the intermittent employee and regular employee are:

Section 4 (assisting in transactions involving the Government);
Section 5 (compensation for regular Government employees from non-Government sources);
Section 6 (gifts).

In general, an intermittent Government employee is one who has performed services as such on not more than 52 working days in the preceding 365 days. The rationale of a 52-day test is that it permits the intermittent employee one day of Government service per week each year; it is thus a minimum practical figure. The figure of 52 days happens to be exactly 20 per cent of the 260 days adopted by the Civil Service

the President's determination of national interest shall be published in the Federal Register;

(2) a Reserve of the Armed Forces, unless otherwise a regular Government employee, shall be classified as an intermittent Government employee for purposes of this Act while on active duty solely for training, irrespective of the number of working days of such training;

(3) irrespective of the fact he has performed services on less than fifty-two working days, a Government employee shall be deemed a regular Government employee, as defined in subsection (j) of this section, and not an intermittent Government employee, if —

(A) he was appointed to a position calling for regular and continuing full-time services, and

----

Commission for certain purposes as the basic working year.

(1) *Application of the "time test."* Under the Act, working days do not include Saturdays, Sundays, and holidays, in conformity with present practice of the Civil Service Commission in computing the number of days a "temporary" employee has worked. See 36 DECS. COMP. GEN. 351 (1956).

The date for counting up the 365-day year is the date as of which it is important to know whether an employee is intermittent or regular. If a person serving as a Government consultant wants to know on May 15 whether on that date he is an intermittent rather than a regular employee, he counts backward 365 days from May 15 and ascertains whether, during that period, he has worked on more than 52 working days.

Work performed on any part of a working day would be treated as work for the full day. It would make no difference whether or not the work is performed on Government premises.

(2) *The Presidential power as to intermittent employees.* The proposed Act provides some flexibility in the "time test" by permitting the President to increase from 52 days to not more than 130 days the number of working days within a year on which a particular Government employee may perform services while still being classified as an intermittent employee for purposes of the Act. The 130-day figure represents one-half of the working year adopted by the Civil Service Commission, and is also the same figure used by the Civil Service Commission in distinguishing between intermittent and other employees. In order to grant this additional time to a part-time employee to continue to serve the Government under the less stringent rules

(B) his appointment did not evidence an intent that his services would be for a period of less than one hundred and thirty working days in the three hundred and sixty-five calendar day period following such appointment.

An intermittent Government employee shall be in such status on days on which he performs no services as well as days on which he performs services.

The termination of any particular term of employment of an intermittent Government employee shall take effect on the day when the earliest of the following events occurs:

(i) He becomes a regular Government employee, as defined in subsection (j) of this section;

(ii) He resigns, retires, or is dismissed, or the termination of his

---

applicable to intermittent employees, the President must make a specific determination that the "national interest requires the issuance of such order." This determination requires in effect a balancing of the need for the services against the undesirability of continued Government association not subject to all the laws applicable to regular employees. This determination and a statement of the pertinent facts must be published in the Federal Register.

While the element of flexibility described above would probably be used rarely, it seems essential. There are numerous instances of special studies which last for six months or even more, and even assignments to represent the United States at important international conferences frequently run well over 52 working days. The complete severance of a private employment relationship, or the dissolution of a partnership, because of undertaking a relatively short-term assignment such as these, will probably be unnecessary in 99 per cent of the cases to protect the Government from conflict of interest risks.

(3) *Reservists on training duty.* As has been noted, the Act would bring within the scope of the conflict of interest rules all Reserves of the Armed Forces on active duty solely for training (a change in present law). But it is essential that they have the status of "intermittent employees" under the Act, and the Act so provides. While most Reserves will not exceed 52 days of training in a year, a one-day-per-week trainee who takes two full additional weeks of training each year would exceed 52 days and therefore special provision is made for such reserves on training duty to retain their intermittent status past the 52-day limit.

(4) *Full-time employees in the first 52 days of their service.* There

status is otherwise clearly evidenced; or

(iii) Three hundred and sixty-five calendar days shall have elapsed since the last working day on which he shall have performed services as an intermittent Government employee, unless his appointment was expressly for a longer period.

. -

is no reason to classify as an "intermittent employee" a new regular, full-time employee who has simply not yet served 52 days in his job. Subsection (3) of the definition of "intermittent employee" prevents such a classification. The critical elements are (A) the nature of the position, and (B) the intent evidenced by the appointment, *i.e.*, whether it was for a temporary assignment of less than 130 working days in the year.

If the intent evidenced by the original appointment was for less than 130 working days of service, the employee would become a regular Government employee if he worked over 52 days without Presidential extension of his intermittent status.

(5) *Cessation of status.* An intermittent employee is subject to the conflict of interest rules on days on which he performs no services for the Government as well as on days on which he performs services for the Government.

An intermittent Government employee may become a regular Government employee by working on more than 52 working days in the preceding 365 calendar days. He may also resign, retire, or be dismissed; or his appointment may be (and often is) for a specified period of days, after which it runs out and he automatically ceases to be an employee.

A special and probably rare situation must also be considered: that of the consultant who is appointed to serve when and as needed for an unspecified period. He may be called, let us say, to serve on January 2, 1960, but is not called again. Under the rules of the definition, he is an intermittent employee all during 1960 and on January 1 and 2 of 1961. However, under the rule of paragraph (iii) a needed cut-off is provided. When 365 calendar days has elapsed since the last working day on which he performed services as an intermittent Government employee, he ceases to be a Government employee of any kind (unless his original appointment was expressly for a longer period).

It should be noted that an intermittent employee in the special situation just described can always end his state of suspended animation by submitting a resignation. And in the one case where the proposed Act contains a provision that is geared to time elapsed since the termination of employment (section 8(c)), the Act also contains a

(h) "Participate," in connection with a transaction involving the Government, means to participate in Government action or a proceeding personally and substantially as a Government employee, through approval, disapproval, decision, recommendation, the rendering of advice, investigation, or otherwise.

----

special provision in section 8(d) that prevents the "unused" consultant from being penalized for not having been told by the Government that his services were no longer needed. Thus, the fact that the technical termination of his employment for conflicts purposes may not come until a year after he last performed services for the Government will not put the "unused" consultant in a worse position, for purposes of applying the post-employment rule of section 8(c), than that of the consultant who resigns immediately after the last day of his services.

(h) "Participate": The term "participate" is used with reference to Government employees acting (or purporting to act) in matters for the Government. It has essentially two functions, neither of which is adequately performed by the vague provisions of existing law.

(1) In section 3 of the Act, the concept is used in a prohibitory sense, prescribing what a Government employee may *not* do with respect to a transaction involving the Government in which he has a personal economic interest; and

(2) in sections 4 and 8 it is used to express that degree of association with a transaction involving the Government that will invoke the rules prohibiting the participating employee from assisting private persons in furthering that particular transaction involving the Government.

The definition gives several examples of what may constitute "participating," namely: "approval, disapproval, recommendation, decision, the rendering of advice, investigation, or otherwise." These words are analogous to but broader than the language of Canon 36 of the Canons of Professional Ethics of the American Bar Association, which provides: ". . . A lawyer, having once held public office or having been in the public employ, should not after his retirement accept employment in connection with any matter which he has investigated or passed upon while in such office or employ."

Again, in an effort to add concreteness of meaning, each of these types of participation is qualified by the words "personally and substantially." Under this qualification, a Civil Aeronautics Board official would presumably, for example, not have "participated" in a proceeding for a route certificate if his sole relationship to the case was to affix his signature to a list of assignments of hearing examiners, one of which was

(i) "Person" means any —

    (1) individual;

    (2) partnership, association, corporation, firm, institution, trust, foundation, or other entity (other than the United States or an agency), whether or not operated for profit;

    (3) State or municipality of the United States or any subdivision thereof, including public districts and authorities; and

    (4) foreign country or subdivision thereof.

(j) "Regular Government employee" means any Government employee other than an intermittent Government employee, as defined in subsection (g) of this section. The termination of any particular term of employment of a regular Government employee shall take effect when he resigns, retires, or is dismissed, or the termination of his status is otherwise clearly evidenced.

---

for the proceeding in question. On the other hand, if the same CAB official affixed his initials to the decision of the hearing examiner in a manner connoting substantive approval or disapproval, or made a recommendation to the Board concerning the case, he would have participated "personally and substantially," even if he in fact had done no more than glance at the final sentence of the decision. In other words, the qualifying phrase "personally and substantially" is intended to rule out participation by purely ministerial or procedural acts, but not to create a loophole for the lazy executive in the chain of command who may have not bothered to dig into the substance of the case.

Drawing the line for the "personally and substantially" test will not always be easy; but it is a vast improvement over existing ambiguity. Substantiality is a familiar legal distinction and is vitally needed for sensible administration of conflict of interest principles.

(i) "Person": The definition of "person" requires no special comment other than to note that neither the United States nor an "agency" is a "person" within the definition. Other political entities, including foreign countries, States of the United States, and municipalities are "persons."

(j) "Regular Government employee": The definition here is a simple one, in that it includes all Government employees not classified as intermittent Government employees under subsection (g).

The second sentence of the definition establishes criteria for the date of termination of any particular term of employment. For a related technical point, see section 8(c)(1) of the Act. Presidential regulations issued under section 10 should amplify these criteria to provide guidance as to whether, for example, a period of terminal leave would be treated as a part of the term of employment for purposes of the Act.

(k) "Responsibility," in connection with a transaction involving the Government, means the direct administrative or operating authority, whether intermediate or final, and either exercisable alone or with others, and either personally or through subordinates, effectively to approve, disapprove, or otherwise direct Government action in respect of such transaction.

(k) "Responsibility": This term, along with "participate," constitutes a key test for the invocation of certain rules under sections 4 and 8 prohibiting a present or former Government employee from assisting private persons in furthering a particular transaction involving the Government.

"Responsibility" is designed to express "chain of command" operational authority. For example, with respect to a decision made by a field representative of the Bureau of Public Assistance in the Department of Health, Education and Welfare, at least the following would have "responsibility": (1) The Director of the Bureau of Public Assistance; (2) The Commissioner of Social Security; and (3) The Secretary of Health, Education and Welfare. The field representative himself not only was "responsible" but "participated," and is therefore subject to more stringent rules.

Others might have "responsibility," depending on the circumstances, such as the Regional Director of the Department in the region in which the decision was made, and one or more of the sub-Cabinet officers of the Department or the Director of Administration.

Personal aides and assistants to officials having "responsibility" would not have responsibility solely by virtue of their positions. But they might acquire responsibility by delegation, and also could at any time shift into the category of persons who "participate" if the particular transaction reached their desks within the Department.

The fact that an official's decision is subject to approval, disapproval, or modification by higher authority does not negate his "responsibility." Otherwise the only "responsible" official would be the agency head. The word "intermediate" is intended to connote this point.

The fact that a higher authority never has any personal contact with a particular transaction involving the Government, and does not even know of its existence, does not negate his "responsibility" if he could theoretically exercise it. A complete delegation of authority to a subordinate does not relieve the higher authority of "responsibility" if he could revoke the delegation of authority.

Where a commission or board has final authority, each member has "responsibility."

On the question of the scope of responsibility, see *United States v. Standard Oil Co.*, 136 F. Supp. 345 (S.D.N.Y., 1955), Chapter III *supra*.

(l) "State" means any State of the United States and the District of Columbia, Puerto Rico, Guam, and the Virgin Islands.

(m) "Thing of economic value" means any money or other thing having economic value, and includes, without limiting the generality of the foregoing —

(1) any loan, property interest, interest in a contract, or other chose in action, and any employment or other arrangement involving a right to compensation;

(2) any option to obtain a thing of economic value, irrespective of the conditions to the exercise of such option; and

----

(l) "State": No special comment is needed.

(m) "Thing of economic value": This term is analogous to similar phrases used in various statutes. For example, 18 U.S.C. § 216 uses the phrase "money or thing of value."

A loan is expressly included in the concept of "thing of economic value," as is a business contract or a job which carries with it a right to compensation. In other words, the fact that a loan is arm's length and bears full interest; the fact that a contract is arm's length with full consideration on both sides; and the fact that bona fide services are performed in a job: none of these facts would remove the loan, contract, or job from the concept of "thing of economic value."

An option to obtain a thing of economic value is itself a thing of economic value. The same is true of a promise or undertaking to deliver or procure a thing of economic value.

For purposes of section 5 of the Act it is important to know the time when a thing of economic value is received. Accordingly, the definition itself establishes rules as to time of receipt in the case of an option or promise. In the case of an option, the time of its receipt is declared to be "the time the right to the option becomes fixed." Thus, an option to acquire a share in an oil lease in six months by payment of a stated sum is deemed to be a thing of economic value received at the time the option terms and rights are fixed. Similarly, an option to acquire stock of a corporation in five blocks of 100 shares each over a five-year period, upon payment of the stated purchase price at the time of exercise as to each block of shares, is a thing of economic value received at the time the option terms and rights of the parties are fixed. See Chapter X, note 10 and accompanying text.

In the case of a promise or undertaking, the time of receipt is the time the promise or undertaking is made.

(3) any promise or undertaking for the present or future delivery or procurement of a thing of economic value.

In the case of an option, promise, or undertaking, the time of receipt of the thing of economic value shall be deemed to be, respectively, the time the right to the option becomes fixed, irrespective of the conditions to its exercise, and the time the promise or undertaking is made, irrespective of the conditions to its performance.

(n) "Transaction involving the Government" means any proceeding, application, submission, request for a ruling or other determination, contract, claim, case, or other such particular matter which the

----

(n) "Transaction involving the Government": This term is of major importance in the Act and is used in numerous places, particularly sections 3, 4 and 8. Its definition approximates the series of words in 18 U.S.C. § 281: "any proceeding, contract, claim, controversy, charge, accusation, arrest, or other matter in which the United States is a party or directly or indirectly interested." It is much broader in scope than the corresponding provisions of the other conflict of interest statutes. See, for example, 18 U.S.C. § 434 ("transaction of business") and *Ingalls v. Perkins,* 33 N.M. 269, 263 Pac. 761 (1927), narrowly construing this already narrow term.

Section 281 and the Act's definition of "transaction involving the Government" are sufficiently similar to permit close legal comparison between the drafting of the two. Some of the differences between the language of 18 U.S.C. § 281 and the definition of "transaction involving the Government" are these:

(1) The words "controversy, charge, accusation, arrest" in 18 U.S.C. § 281 have been dropped in favor of words more expressive of the nature of most modern Federal Government action, *i.e.:* application, submission, request for a ruling or other determination."

(2) The modifying word "particular" has been inserted before the word "matter," so as to read "or other *particular* matter."

(3) Whereas 18 U.S.C. § 281 appears to require that the proceeding or other particular matter actually be "before" an agency, *i.e.,* already pending, "transaction involving the Government" could include a proceeding or other particular matter at a pre-filing stage.

(4) "Transaction involving the Government" requires a belief (or reason to believe) on the part of the individual whose conduct is being considered that the proceeding or other particular matter does in fact or will in fact involve the Government. This element of state of mind

Government employee or former Government employee in question believes, or has reason to believe —

(1) is, or will be, the subject of Government action; or

(2) is one to which the United States is or will be a party; or

(3) is one in which the United States has a direct and substantial proprietary interest.

----

is a necessary addition. Suppose, for example, that a Government employee with certain technical skills assists a friend to perfect a machine. The Government employee thinks he is only helping his friend to get a contract with Corporation X. In fact, the friend is in negotiation with the Government as to a contract for the purchase of the machine, and the work the Government employee is doing is a critical element in furthering the friend's efforts to obtain the Government contract. As such, it might well, without the state of mind clause in the definition, violate section 4 (which prohibits assistance to outsiders in transactions involving the Government).

(5) The words "directly or indirectly interested," which appear in 18 U.S.C. § 281, have been dropped. The Federal Government's range of interest today is so limitless that the need in the Act is to find a way to circumscribe its application in this respect, not to extend it further.

The relationship of "transaction involving the Government" to "Government action" is worth noting. The latter is a far broader phrase, serving only to express the concept of what Government does. "Transaction involving the Government," on the other hand, expresses a particular relationship between Government and a private person. It seeks to bring the nongovernmental party into focus, and to express a concrete relationship between him and the Government.

See also the discussion in Chapter X *supra,* under "Transaction involving the Government."

§ 3. Acts affecting a personal economic interest

(a) ECONOMIC INTERESTS OF A GOVERNMENT EMPLOYEE. — No Government employee shall participate in a transaction involving the Government in the consequences of which he has a substantial economic interest of which he may reasonably be expected to know.

(b) ECONOMIC INTERESTS OF PERSONS IN WHICH A GOVERNMENT EMPLOYEE HAS AN INTEREST. — No Government employee shall participate in a transaction involving the Government in the consequences of which, to his actual knowledge, any of the following persons has a direct and substantial economic interest:

---

§ 3. Acts affecting a personal economic interest

The purpose, rationale, and main features of section 3 of the Act are discussed under the corresponding caption in Chapter X *supra;* the comparable section in existing law is 18 U.S.C. § 434, discussed in Chapter III.

Subsection (a) states the general prohibition against participation by a Government employee "in a transaction involving the Government in the consequences of which he has a substantial economic interest of which he may reasonably be expected to know."

The test of "reasonably be expected to know" is new, but necessary. It exculpates the Government official who, for example, is the beneficiary of a trust of securities, who has instructed the trustee not to advise him of the specific securities held by the trust, and who in fact is wholly unaware that a given security is held by the trust. Another example is the case of an employee who is the residuary legatee under the will of a person who has just died. The Government employee may well be unaware of (1) the death; (2) the terms of the will; or (3) the assets held by the estate. On the other side of the line of "reasonably be expected to know" is the case, for example, of an official who claims he simply forgot that his portfolio of ten securities included 20 per cent of the shares of a major construction company. While his state of mind would be relevant in a criminal prosecution, it would not (absent other special facts) excuse him from the disqualification requirement of section 3.

Subsection (b) lists a series of persons whose economic interest will be treated for disqualification purposes as though it were the employee's. There are two qualifications to this statement:

(1) the employee must have "actual knowledge" of the existence of the economic interest; and

(2) the economic interest must be "direct" as well as substantial.

(1) his spouse or child; or

(2) any person in which he has a substantial economic interest of which he may reasonably be expected to know; or

(3) any person of which he is an officer, director, trustee, partner, or employee; or

(4) any person with whom he is negotiating or has any arrangement concerning prospective employment; or

(5) any person who is a party to an existing contract with such Government employee or an obligee of such Government employee as to a thing of economic value and who, by reason thereof, is in a position to affect directly and substantially such employee's

- -

While the word "direct" cannot be given a precise content, it rules out remote interests in those cases where the interest is already once removed from the employee himself.

By including the spouse or child in paragraph (1), subsection (b) aims squarely at a form of subterfuge not usually covered by statutory or regulatory language.

Paragraph (2) covers, for example, the case of ownership of shares of a holding company that has a major subsidiary in a particular line of business; of being a partner in a partnership that has a major interest in a particular business.

Paragraph (3) covers certain situations where there may be difficulty in proving a substantial economic interest but where a special relationship gives rise to strong policy reasons for invoking the prohibition against participation as a Government employee. The most obvious example is that of an employee who is the director of a company but who owns only a few of its shares.

By analogy to present Department of Commerce regulations, it might be suggested that paragraph (3) should include any person by whom the employee "has been employed within the last two years." This is too broad, however, to adopt as a statutory general rule. There are many cases where an individual who has worked in a given industry most of his adult life will enter Government service for the latter portion of his career. A mining engineer, for instance, might accept a top position in the Bureau of Mines. It seems wholly unrealistic to disqualify him from regulating the last company he worked for (and from which he has severed all connections) when he must issue regulations for the mining industry as a whole. It also seems pushing matters too far to insist upon a Presidential exemption for such a case. Accordingly, the Act relies on regulations to cover any special situations which may arise in a particular

economic interests.

(c) DISQUALIFICATION. — Every Government employee shall disqualify himself from participating in a transaction involving the Government when a violation of subsection (a) or (b) would otherwise result. The procedures for such disqualification shall be established by regulations issued pursuant to section 10.

(d) SUBSTANTIAL ECONOMIC INTEREST. — The term "substantial economic interest" may be defined by regulations issued by the President pursuant to section 10, but the term shall not include —

(1) the interest of a Government employee in his grade, salary, or other matters arising solely from his Government employment;

----

agency and which demand disqualification of recent employees of private concerns from acting with respect to their former employers. Middle grounds are possible. Presidential regulations might, for example, prescribe that recent employees expressly "on leave of absence" from former employment should be deemed employees of their former employers for purposes of section 3(b)(3).

Paragraph (4) covers a most important situation: that of the employee who is negotiating with respect to, or has any arrangement concerning, prospective employment. This situation has been covered in some of the more complete agency regulations. For example, the Department of Commerce prohibits official action affecting any private person or organization "with whom he has arranged or is negotiating for subsequent employment or business relations." (See Section 6 of the Dept. of Commerce Regulations on Conflicts of Interest.) General discussion of the need for prohibitions in this area appears at the end of Chapter X *supra*, under "A general comment on post-employment restrictions."

Paragraph (5) states the principle of economic interest by reason of contractual relationship or debt obligation. See the discussion in Chapter X *supra*, under "Size and remoteness of interest."

Subsection (c) merely enunciates the requirement of disqualification from participation in cases where the prohibitions of subsections (a) and (b) are applicable.

Subsection (d) in effect creates two exceptions to the disqualification requirement:

(1) where the employee's interest derives only from his position as an employee of the Government; and

(2) where the employee's interest is shared by a broad segment of society such that it ceases to be personalized.

While the second of these exceptions will present some difficulties in

(2) the interest of a Government employee, or of a person referred to in subsection (b) solely as a member of the general public,
or of any significant economic or other segment of the general
public.

(e) PRESIDENTIAL EXEMPTION. — The President may issue an order
suspending the operation of subsections (a) and (b), in whole or in
part, as to a particular employee with respect to transactions involving the Government of a particular category or in connection with a
particular assignment, provided that the President shall make a determination that under all the circumstances the national interest in
such employee's participation exceeds the public interest in his disqualification. A full statement of the pertinent facts and of the
President's determination of national interest shall be published in
the Federal Register.

----

application, it is an essential concept and merely reflects a principle that
a court would undoubtedly read into any statute drafted to achieve the
general purposes of the present 18 U.S.C. § 434 and section 3 of the
Act. No one would say that a Treasury official must disqualify himself
from working on a general tax reduction program because he will benefit
along with millions of other taxpayers. But one might well conclude that
a Treasury official should disqualify himself from recommending retro-
active application of a special rule as to tax treatment of stock options if
he were a member of a relatively narrow class of people who would benefit. Subsection (d)(2) is designed to express this distinction.

Subsection (e) sets forth the power of Presidential exemption; a section
of Chapter X is devoted to this subject. It should be noted that the
recipient of a Presidential exemption is still subject to the restraints of
the other sections of the Act. In this connection, see particularly the
discussion of section 4, *infra*.

As is noted in Chapter X, section 3 is substantially broader than 18
U.S.C. § 434 in the scope of its protection, while being more precise in
its application. The elements of broadening are chiefly these:

(1) section 3 is not confined to economic interests in business entities;

(2) it expressly reaches certain important forms of indirect economic
interest; and

(3) it covers any participation by a Government employee (such as
advising the Government official who must make the decision), rather
than being confined to cases where the employee "acts as an officer
or agent of the United States for the transaction of business with"
the private party.

§ 4. Assisting in transactions involving the Government

(a) GENERAL RULE FOR ALL EMPLOYEES. — Except in the course of his official duties or incident thereto, no Government employee shall assist another person, whether or not for compensation, in any transaction involving the Government —

(1) in which he has at any time participated; or

(2) if such transaction involving the Government is or has been under his official responsibility at any time within a period of two years preceding such assistance.

(b) ADDITIONAL GENERAL RULE FOR REGULAR EMPLOYEES. — Except in the course of his official duties or incident thereto, no regular Government employee shall —

(1) assist another person for compensation in any transaction

----

§ 4. Assisting in transactions involving the Government

The purpose, rationale, and main features of this section of the Act are discussed under the corresponding caption in Chapter X *supra;* comparable existing provisions are 18 U.S.C. §§ 281 and 283, discussed in Chapter III.

The general rule of subsection (a), applicable to all employees, is precisely the same in scope as section 8, applicable to the post-employment status of former Government employees. As a result of this exact meshing, the intermittent employee, for purposes of the prohibitions against assistance to private parties in their governmental matters, is in substantially the same position as the recent former Government employee. The one exception to this principle, the difference in scope between sections 4(d) and 8(c), is treated in the discussion of section 8, *infra.*

Subsection (b) is in many respects a merger of the present 18 U.S.C. §§ 281 and 283, but is confined to regular Government employees. Paragraph (1) adopts substantially the rule of the present 18 U.S.C. § 281; services *for compensation* are barred in respect of any matters before any agency. (It should be noted that this is a Government-wide prohibition). Paragraph (2) adopts the concept of 18 U.S.C. § 283, that compensation is not an essential element of the offense in some situations. The situations selected by paragraph (2) are those where the Government employee acts in a *representative capacity* for the private party — "representing him as his agent or attorney." The rationale is, of course, that the weight of the factor of appearances is greatly increased where the Government employee "fronts" for the private party in a transaction involving the Government.

involving the Government;

(2) assist another person by representing him as his agent or attorney, whether or not for compensation, in any transaction involving the Government.

(c) No SHARING IN COMPENSATION. — No Government employee shall share in any compensation received by another person for assistance which such Government employee is prohibited from rendering pursuant to subsection (a) or (b).

(d) PARTNERSHIPS. — No partnership of which a Government employee is a partner, and no partner or employee of such a partnership, shall assist another person in any transaction involving the Government if such Government employee is prohibited from doing so by subsection (a).

(e) PERMITTED EXCEPTIONS. — (1) Nothing in this section shall prevent a Government employee, subject to conditions or limitations set forth in regulations issued pursuant to section 10, from assisting, in a transaction involving the Government —

(A) his parent, spouse, or child, or any thereof for whom he is

----

Among the "permitted exceptions" of subsection (e), the only one requiring special note here is paragraph (1)(D). This exception permits an employee, with special advance approval by the head of his agency, and with certification as to the national interest (see paragraph (G)), to assist a Government contractor or subcontractor in the performance of his work for the Government. The need for this exception is closely related to the need for the Presidential exemption under section 3. A scientist employed by a private company and serving on an advisory board under a section 3 exemption is cleared to advise the Government despite his outside employment — but he is still not cleared under section 4. His responsibilities with his company may practically compel him to assist his company in the performance of work under a Government contract. And it is undoubtedly in the interests of the United States that he should so assist. In such a case, the "permitted exception" of paragraph (1)(D) of section 4 is needed and available. The protections surrounding the granting of an exception under section (1)(D) are sufficient to guarantee against abuses.

It is pertinent to note that section 4 is similar to a number of the exemption provisions in present law for advisory boards and consultants in that it applies a more narrowly focused body of restraints upon intermittent employees. For example, 68 Stat. 859 (1954), as amended, 22

serving as guardian, executor, administrator, trustee, or other personal fiduciary;

(B) a person other than his parent, spouse, or child for whom he is serving as guardian, executor, administrator, trustee, or other personal fiduciary;

(C) another Government employee involved in disciplinary, loyalty, or other personnel administration proceedings; or

(D) another person in the performance of work under a contract with or for the benefit of the United States:

Provided, however, That —

(E) in the case of clauses (A) and (B), such Government employee shall not have at any time participated in such transaction, nor, in the case of clause (B), shall such transaction have been under his official responsibility; and

(F) in the case of clauses (A), (B), (C), and (D), the circumstances of the assistance shall have been disclosed to the head of the employee's agency and approved by him in advance of the assistance; and

---

U.S.C. § 1792(a) (1958), a provision of the Mutual Security Act, exempts intermittent employees appointed under that Act from "the provisions of sections 281, 283 or 284 of Title 18, or of section 99 of Title 5 . . . except insofar as such provisions of law may prohibit any such individual from receiving compensation in respect of any particular matter in which such individual was directly involved in the performance of such service." The Mutual Security Act language: "any particular matter in which such individual was directly involved," and the language of the proposed Executive Conflict of Interest Act: "in any transaction involving the Government in which he has at any time participated," are extraordinarily similar in their impact. Thus, Congress has already recognized and responded to the need for a different rule for the intermittent employee, in exactly the same manner as the proposed Executive Conflict of Interest Act. In a very real sense, the proposed Executive Conflict of Interest Act would merely make uniform for *all* intermittent employees in Government the present differentiation in conflict of interest principles already adopted under the numerous acts of Congress.

Altogether, section 4 in some respects broadens present 18 U.S.C. § 281, clarifies it in almost all respects, and adapts it to modern Government by applying somewhat different rules for the intermittent Government employee.

(G) in the case of clause (D), the head of such employee's agency shall have certified in writing that in his opinion the national interest will be promoted by permitting the special knowledge or skills of such Government employee to be made available to assist such other person in connection with such performance.

(2) Nothing in this section shall prevent a Government employee from giving testimony under oath or from making statements required to be made under penalty of perjury or contempt.

§ 5. Compensation for regular Government employees from non-Government sources

(a) UNCOMPENSATED EMPLOYEES. — For purposes of this section the term "regular Government employee" shall not include any Government employee who, in accordance with the terms of his appointment, is serving without compensation from the United States or is receiving from the United States only reimbursement of expenses incurred or a predetermined allowance for such expenses.

(b) PAYMENTS FOR SERVICES TO THE UNITED STATES. — No regular Government employee shall receive any thing of economic value, other than his compensation from the United States, for or in consideration of personal services rendered or to be rendered to or for the United States. Any thing of economic value received by a regular

----

§ 5. Compensation for regular Government employees from non-Government sources

The purposes, rationale, and main features of section 5 are discussed under the corresponding caption in Chapter X *supra;* the comparable section in existing law is 18 U.S.C. § 1914, discussed in Chapter III.

Subsection (a) states the non-applicability of the section to employees who are serving without compensation ("WOC") in accordance with the terms of their employment. See the discussion under the caption "WOCs" in Chapter X.

The first sentence of subsection (b) states the prohibition against supplementation of Government salary "for or in consideration of personal services rendered or to be rendered to or for the United States." In other words, if all the employee does is to work for the Government,

Government employee prior to or subsequent to his Government employment shall be presumed, in the absence of a showing to the contrary by a clear preponderance of evidence, not to be for, or in consideration of, personal services rendered or to be rendered to or for the United States.

(c) COMPENSATION FOR SERVICES TO OTHERS. — No regular Government employee shall receive any thing of economic value (other than his compensation from the United States) for or in consideration of personal services rendered, or to be rendered, to or for any person during the term of his Government employment unless such services meet each of the following qualifications:

(1) The services are bona fide and are actually performed by such employee;

(2) The services are not within the course of his official duties;

(3) The services are not prohibited by section 4 or by applicable laws or regulations governing non-Government employment for such employee; and

(4) The services are neither performed for nor compensated by any person from whom such employee would be prohibited by section 6(b) from receiving a gift; or, alternatively, the services and compensation are fully disclosed in writing to the head of the employee's agency and are approved in writing by him.

---

he may not receive payments from others as supplementary compensation. The second sentence raises a presumption that payments received prior to entry into Government service are not "for, or in consideration of, personal services rendered or to be rendered to or for the United States." See the discussion of subsection (b) in Chapter X.

Up to this point, Section 5 largely reflects present law, although "for, or in consideration of," is a concept substantially more precise than the "in connection with" appearing in the present U.S.C. § 1914.

Subsection (c), discussed in Chapter X *supra,* goes well beyond present law by building a strong protective barrier as to payments *not* for or in consideration of Government services. The four conjunctive tests of the legitimacy of particular payments for non-Government services are self-explanatory.

(d) PAYMENTS FOR FUTURE SERVICES TO OTHERS. — No regular Government employee shall receive, directly or indirectly, any thing of economic value during the term of his Government employment in consideration of personal services to be rendered to or for any person subsequent to the term of such employment. Nothing contained in this subsection (d) shall be deemed to prevent a Government employee from entering into a contract for prospective employment during the term of his Government employment.

(e) COMPENSATION FROM LOCAL GOVERNMENTS. — Nothing contained in this section shall prevent a Government employee from receiving compensation contributed out of the treasury of any State, county, or municipality if —

(1) the compensation is received pursuant to arrangements entered into between such State, county, or municipality and such employee's agency; or

(2) the compensation and the services for which it is received are fully disclosed in writing to the head of the employee's agency and are approved in writing by him.

(f) CONTINUATION IN CERTAIN PENSION AND OTHER PLANS. — (1) Nothing contained in this section shall prevent a Government employee's continuation in a bona fide pension, retirement, group life, health, or accident insurance, or other employee welfare or benefit plan maintained by a former employer but to which such former employer makes no contributions on behalf of such employee in respect of the period of his Government employment.

Subsection (d) precludes evasion of the principles of subsections (b) and (c) through the subterfuge of making present payments for services to be rendered in the future. The second sentence of subsection (d), however, expressly authorizes contracts for future employment. (Here a reference back to section 3(b)(4) is in order. That provision requires a Government employee to disqualify himself in a transaction involving the Government which affects a person with whom the Government employee "is negotiating or has any arrangement concerning prospective employment.")

Subsection (e), as in the case of the present 18 U.S.C. § 1914, contains

(2) Nothing contained in this section shall prevent a Government employee's continuation in a bona fide plan, maintained by a former employer and to which such former employer makes contributions on behalf of such employee, in the case of —

(A) a pension or retirement plan qualified under the provisions of the Internal Revenue Code, or

(B) a group life, health, or accident insurance plan: *Provided,* That the contributions by such employer are not made for a period longer than five consecutive years of Government employment (or an aggregate of five years out of the preceding ten).

(3) Nothing contained in this section shall require the termination of the rights of a Government employee acquired under a bona fide profit-sharing or stock bonus plan maintained by a former employer and qualified under the provisions of the Internal Revenue Code: *Provided,* That no contributions are made by such former employer on behalf of the Government employee based on profits attributable to any portion of the period of his Government employment.

(4) The provisions of this subsection (f) shall be subject to any additional conditions or limitations, including limitations on maximum amounts, set forth in regulations issued pursuant to section 10.

(g) TRAVEL AND RELATED EXPENSES. — Travel and related expenses received other than from the United States shall be deemed to be for or in consideration of personal services rendered to or for a person only to the extent provided in regulations issued pursuant to section 10.

---

an exception for certain payments to Federal employees paid out of State, county, or municipal treasuries. The provision is necessary to cover certain established categories of jointly paid employees, such as county farm agents.

Subsection (f) sets forth the wholly new provisions as to pension, retirement, group insurance, and other employee welfare and benefit plans, and also as to profit-sharing and stock bonus plans. See the discussion under "Employee security and welfare plans" in Chapter X *supra.*

The handling of travel and related expenses is expressly left to regulations, under subsection (g).

§ 6. Gifts

(a) GENERAL RULE FOR ALL EMPLOYEES. — No Government employee shall receive, accept, take, seek, or solicit, directly or indirectly, any thing of economic value as a gift, gratuity, or favor from any person if such Government employee has reason to believe the donor would not give the gift, gratuity, or favor but for such employee's office or position within the Government.

(b) ADDITIONAL GENERAL RULE FOR REGULAR EMPLOYEES. — No regular Government employee shall receive, accept, take, seek, or solicit, directly or indirectly, any thing of economic value as a gift, gratuity, or favor from any person, or from any officer or director of such person, if such regular Government employee has reason to believe such person —

(1) has or is seeking to obtain contractual or other business or financial relationships with such employee's agency; or

(2) conducts operations or activities which are regulated by such employee's agency; or

(3) has interests which may be substantially affected by such employee's performance or nonperformance of official duty.

- -

§ 6. Gifts

The purposes, rationale, and main features of this section are discussed under the corresponding caption in Chapter X *supra;* there is no comparable section in existing law. See, for regulations in the field, Chapter IV *supra* under "Gratuities."

Subsection (a) states the general prohibition against receipt or solicitation of a gift from any person who the Government employee "has reason to believe" would not give the gift, gratuity, or favor "but for such employee's office or position within the Government." While this is essentially a subjective test, this kind of a standard is not inappropriate for the difficult and necessarily personal area of gifts.

The rule of subsection (a) is applicable to both regular and intermittent employees. An illustration of the application of the section to an intermittent employee may be helpful. A labor relations consultant who also serves on a Labor Department advisory board may lawfully receive a gift from a labor union client even though the client is regulated in certain respects by the Department of Labor, provided that the relationships between donor and donee make it evident that the gift is not being made primarily *because of* the consultant's position on the advisory board. If, on the other hand, another union with which the consultant has never had dealings makes a gift to him, the circumstances may suggest

(c) PERMITTED EXCEPTIONS. — Exceptions to subsections (a) and (b) may be made by regulations issued pursuant to section 10 in situations where the circumstances do not lead to the inference that the official judgment or action of the Government employee receiving, directly or indirectly, the gift, gratuity, or favor was intended to be influenced thereby.

§ 7. Abuse of office

Except in the course of his official duties or incident thereto, no Government employee shall, in his relationships with any person specified in the succeeding sentence, use the power or authority of his office or position within the Government in a manner intended to induce or coerce such other person to provide such Government employee or any other person with any thing of economic value, directly or indirectly. This section shall apply to relationships with any person, or any officer or director of such person, from whom such Government employee, if he were a regular Government employee, would be prohibited by section 6(b) from receiving a gift.

----

that the donor "would not give the gift, gratuity, or favor but for such employee's office or position within the Government."

Subsection (b) prescribes three reasonably objective tests as to when a regular Government employee may not receive a gift. As is pointed out in Chapter X, these tests could not realistically be applied to the intermittent employee, since the typical consultant or adviser could not then, under section 6, receive a gift from the same employer or client by whom he could lawfully be paid under section 5.

Subsection (c) authorizes exceptions by regulations. The need for such exceptions is discussed fully under "Regulations" in Chapter X.

§ 7. Abuse of office

The purposes, rationale, and main features of section 7 are discussed under the corresponding caption in Chapter X *supra;* there is no comparable section in existing law. Little amplification is needed here.

It is to be noted that the same class of "sensitive" persons listed in the second of the gift prohibitions in section 6 is brought by reference into section 7. This is the class of persons for whom the power of the particular Government employee's office is significant.

Section 7 breaks essentially new ground; no statutes or regulations clearly embrace the concept of the section.

§ 8. Post-employment

(a) GENERAL RULE. — No former Government employee shall at any time subsequent to his Government employment assist another person, whether or not for compensation, in any transaction involving the Government —

(1) in which he at any time participated during his Government employment; or

(2) if such transaction involving the Government was under his official responsibility as a Government employee at any time within a period of two years preceding such assistance.

(b) NO SHARING IN COMPENSATION. — No former Government employee shall share in any compensation received by another person for assistance which such former Government employee is prohibited from rendering by subsection (a).

(c) PARTNERSHIPS. — (1) No partnership of which a former Government employee is a partner, and no partner or employee of such a partnership, shall, for a period of two years following the termination of his Government employment, assist another person in any transaction involving the Government in which such former Government employee at any time participated during his Government employment. For purposes of this subsection (c)(1), the termination of the former Government employee's employment with the agency by which he was employed when he so participated shall be deemed

----

§ 8. Post-employment

The purpose, rationale, and main features of section 8 are discussed under the corresponding caption in Chapter X *supra;* comparable existing provisions are 18 U.S.C. § 284 and 5 U.S.C. § 99.

Subsection (a) states the general post-employment rule: (1) a permanent bar against assisting in matters in which the former Government employee "participated" during his Government employment; and (2) a two-year bar against assisting in matters which were under his official "responsibility." The parallelism of this subsection to subsection (a) of section 4 has been pointed out in the discussion of that section.

The rule of section 8 is the same for both regular and intermittent employees. However, most consultants and experts will not have "responsibility," since they are not given line operating authority. Accordingly, their primary concern will be with matters in which they have "participated."

to be the termination of his Government employment.

(2) Whenever subsection (c)(1) would be applicable but for the expiration of the period of two years referred to therein, the circumstances of the former Government employee's participation in the transaction during his Government employment, if the individuals acting for the partnership are aware of such participation, shall be disclosed to the agency principally involved in the transaction involving the Government, and an affidavit of such former employee to the effect that he has not assisted in such transaction involving the Government shall be furnished to such agency.

(d) SPECIAL RULE FOR COMPUTATION OF TWO-YEAR PERIOD FOR CERTAIN FORMER INTERMITTENT EMPLOYEES. — For purposes of subsection (c), a former intermittent Government employee whose employment terminated under clause (iii) of section 2(g) shall be deemed to have terminated such employment on the last working day on which he performed services as an intermittent Government employee.

(e) PERSONS FORMERLY ON ACTIVE DUTY AS COMMISSIONED OFFICERS OF ARMED FORCES. — The President shall, in furtherance of this section 8, issue regulations of the nature herein described applicable to persons who have been commissioned officers on active duty in one of the armed forces of the United States. Such regulations shall have the effect of prohibiting such persons, for the periods therein specified, from personally dealing with personnel of the Department of

---

It should be kept in mind that the scope of the post-employment bar can be expanded by particular agencies in relation to their special needs. Some of the present post-employment regulations are discussed in Chapter IV, under "Post-employment dealings." Regulations such as these would continue under the proposed Act.

The present 5 U.S.C. § 99 would be repealed outright by section 36(a) of the proposed Act. Such repeal has often been proposed.

The point of time for measuring the two-year ban on assistance in "responsibility" transactions is discussed in Chapter X.

Subsections (b) and (c) relating to sharing in compensation and the activities of partnerships, are also discussed in Chapter X. Subsection (c)(2) requires a full disclosure of a partner's former participation in a matter (more than two years earlier), if the partners handling the case are aware of his participation. Furthermore, the permanent personal bar against assistance by the partner who did participate is highlighted

Defense, or of such units thereof as may be specified in such regulations, with the purpose of assisting in the sale of anything, including services to the United States through the Department of Defense or such units thereof as may be specified in such regulations. The retirement pay of any retired commissioned officer who violates such regulations shall be terminated pursuant to the regulations issued hereunder for the periods therein specified.

(f) PERMITTED EXCEPTIONS. — The permitted exceptions applicable to Government employees under section 4(e) shall also be applicable to former Government employees under this section 8, subject to conditions or limitations set forth in regulations issued pursuant to section 10. For purposes of this section 8, references in such section 4(e) to the Government employee providing assistance shall be deemed to be to the former Government employee, and references to his agency shall be deemed to be to his former agency.

----

by the requirement of an affidavit by him that he has not in fact "assisted" in the particular transaction. When the broad scope of the word "assist" is considered, it becomes clear that the partner who participated must stay completely out of the matter in order to be able to give the affidavit. "Assist" is applicable to information and other help given to his partners as well as to the client.

Subsection (d) states a special rule, applicable in the case of certain former intermittent employees, for computing the two-year partnership bar of section 8(c). The particular former intermittent employees are those whose employment ended solely by reason of the expiration of a 365-day period following the day on which they last performed services. This is the case of the "unused" consultant, discussed in connection with subsection 2(g)(iii) above. The special rule of subsection (d) serves to eliminate any extension of the two-year period in the case of the "unused" consultant beyond the period applicable to the consultant who resigns at the end of his last day of service.

Subsection (e) is fully discussed under "Military procurement and employment of retired officers" in Chapter X.

Subsection (f) incorporates all of the exceptions of section 4(e). Thus, for example, the former Government employee could obtain permission from his former agency to work on a Government contract as a private citizen even though he participated in the same contract as a Government employee, if the agency head makes the certification required by section 4(e)(1)(G). Thus again section 8 is made parallel to section 4. There is no reason to apply a tighter rule to a former employee under section 8 than to a current employee under section 4.

§ 9. Illegal payments

(a) PAYMENTS AS COMPENSATION, ETC. — No person shall give, pay, loan, transfer, or deliver, directly or indirectly, to any other person any thing of economic value believing or having reason to believe that there exist circumstances making the receipt thereof a violation of section 4, 5, or 8.

(b) GIFTS. — No person shall give, transfer, or deliver, directly or indirectly, to a Government employee any thing of economic value as a gift, gratuity, or favor if either —

(1) such person would not give the gift, gratuity, or favor but for such employee's office or position within the Government; or

(2) such person is in a status specified in clause (1), (2), or (3) of section 6(b).

Exceptions to this subsection (b) may be made by regulations issued pursuant to section 10 in situations referred to in section 6(c).

----

§ 9. Illegal Payments

A frequent criticism of conflict of interest restraints, both at the Federal level and other levels of government, is that they fall most heavily on the Government employee and rarely catch the "outsider" who may have induced the offense. Of the present basic Federal conflict of interest statutes, only 18 U.S.C. §§ 216 and 1914 expressly apply to payments made by others to a Government employee. While it is true that the general conspiracy section, 18 U.S.C. § 371, and the prohibition against aiding and abetting, 18 U.S.C. § 2(a), may serve to reach payors of compensation illegally received, the outsider's offense should be an independent one.

Section 9 of the Act is aimed at bringing about a better balance between the impact of the conflicts statutes on the Government employee, or former employee, and the person who causes the wrong by making the payment.

Subsection (a) prohibits the transfer of anything of economic value by any person "believing or having reason to believe that there exist circumstances making the receipt thereof a violation of section 4, 5, or 8." These enumerated sections cover, it will be recalled,

assisting in transactions involving the Government (section 4) ;
compensation for regular Government employees from non-Government sources (section 5) ;
post-employment (section 8) .

Subsection (b) creates a parallel offense for the donors of gifts. Section 6 of the Act, the section prohibiting receipt of certain gifts by Govern-

§ 10. Administration

(a) RESPONSIBILITY OF THE PRESIDENT. — (1) Subject to the provisions of this Act, and other laws, the President shall be responsible for the establishment of appropriate standards to protect against actual or potential conflicts of interest on the part of Government employees and for the administration and enforcement of this Act and the regulations and orders issued hereunder.

(2) The President may, and shall do so when required by this Act, issue regulations carrying out the policies and purposes of this Act. Such regulations shall take precedence over any regulations issued by agency heads pursuant to subsection (c).

(3) The President shall have particular responsibility for the enforcement of this Act as applied to employees of the Executive Office of the President and to agency heads, and for this purpose the President shall have all the powers of an agency head.

(4) The President may conduct investigations of facts, condition or conditions, practices, or other matters in carrying out his responsibilities and powers under this subsection (a) and in obtaining information to serve as a basis for recommending further legislation related to the purposes of this Act. In connection with any such investigation the President shall have all the powers with respect

- -

ment employees, contains several provisions as to what the donee believes to be the donor's intent. But the donor knows his own intent. Accordingly, the offense as to donors is restated in section 9, as a separate subsection (b), in direct terms, rather than in the indirect terms of subsection (a), *i.e.* believing that there "exist circumstances" which would make the transfer a violation of section 6.

The same exceptions as to gifts that appear in regulations under section 6 will reappear in regulations under section 9(b).

Section 9 is by its nature inapplicable to the restrictions of section 3 (disqualification) and 7 (abuse of office), since the offenses proscribed there are committed by the Government employee acting alone.

§ 10. Administration

The purpose, rationale, and major features of section 10 are discussed under the corresponding caption in Chapter X *supra*.

to oaths, affirmations, subpenas, and witnesses as are provided in section 12(b)(2). The President may delegate any or all of his powers under this subsection (a)(4) to the Administrator referred to in subsection (b) or to others, either generally or in particular instances.

(b) EXECUTIVE CONFLICT OF INTEREST ACT ADMINISTRATOR. — (1) The President shall designate an official from within the Executive Office of the President or create an office within the Executive Office of the President (such official or the head of such office being hereinafter referred to as the "Administrator") to perform the following functions:

(A) To assist the President in carrying out his responsibilities under subsection (a);

(B) To receive copies of all regulations issued by agency heads pursuant to subsection (c), to analyze the same and make recommendations to agency heads with respect thereto;

(C) To receive reports from agencies and to collect information with respect to, and conduct studies of, personal conflicts of interest of Government employees within the executive branch;

(D) To consult with the Attorney General, the Chairman of the Civil Service Commission, the Comptroller General and other appropriate officials with respect to conflict-of-interest matters affecting more than one agency;

(E) To consult with agency heads, and with appropriate officers designated by them, as to the administration of this Act within their respective agencies and the regulations issued hereunder applicable to their respective agencies;

(F) To give advice, in consultation with the Attorney General, with respect to the application of this Act and regulations issued hereunder, when so requested by the President or agency heads;

(G) To undertake and conduct, in conjunction with agency heads, a study of the extent to which any of the principles of this Act should be made applicable to persons and to the employees of persons having contracts, subcontracts, licenses, or similar relationships with or from the United States; and

(H) To provide reports and information to the President and

the Congress concerning the administration of this Act and conflict of interest matters generally.

(2) The Administrator is authorized to employ personnel and expend funds for the purposes of this Act, to the extent of any appropriations made for the purposes hereof.

(c) RESPONSIBILITY OF AGENCY HEADS. — (1) Each agency head shall be responsible for the establishment of appropriate standards within his agency to protect against actual or potential conflicts of interest on the part of employees of his agency, and for the administration and enforcement within his agency of this Act and the regulations and orders issued hereunder.

(2) Each agency head may, subject to the regulations issued by the President under subsection (a)(2), issue regulations carrying out the policies and purposes of this Act as applied to his agency. He shall file copies of all such regulations with the Administrator.

(3) Each agency head may conduct investigations of facts, conditions, practices, or other matters in carrying out his responsibilities and powers under this subsection (c). In connection with any such investigation the agency head shall have all the powers with respect to oaths, affirmations, subpenas, and witnesses as are provided in section 12(b)(2). The agency head may delegate any or all of his powers under this subsection (c)(3) to any officer designated by him, either generally or in particular instances.

§ 11. Preventive measures

The head of an agency may, and shall do so if so provided in regulations issued by the President, establish by regulation pro-

----

§ 11. Preventive measures

The purpose, rationale, and main features of section 11 are discussed under the corresponding caption in Chapter X *supra*. See also the discussion of agency regulations covering certification, review of outside employment, and reporting, under the corresponding captions in Chapter IV.

Recent proposals for enrollment of retired officers employed by defense contractors would be squarely within the purposes and authority of section 11. Other types of reporting will be devised by agencies from time to time, all serving to reduce the risks of actual conflicts of interest.

cedures for the purpose of preventing violations of this Act, including, but not limited to, regulations requiring —

(a) individuals entering Government employment with such agency and, periodically, the employees or particular categories of employees of such agency, to sign a statement that they have read an appropriate summary of the rules established by this Act and the regulations issued hereunder;

(b) employees of such agency, or particular categories thereof, to report periodically as to their non-Government employment or self-employment, if any;

(c) representatives of other persons before an agency to certify that, to the best of their knowledge, their representation will not violate section 4 or 8 or the regulations issued thereunder; and

(d) persons who are principals in transactions involving the Government to certify that, to the best of their knowledge, they have not received assistance under circumstances which would violate section 4 or 8 or the regulations issued thereunder.

§ 12. Remedies; civil penalties; procedure

(a) ADMINISTRATIVE ENFORCEMENT AS TO CURRENT GOVERNMENT EMPLOYEES. —

(1) Remedies and Civil Penalties: The head of an agency may dismiss, suspend, or take such other action as may be appropriate in the circumstances in respect of any Government employee of his agency upon finding that such employee has violated this Act or regulations promulgated hereunder. Such action may include the imposition of conditions of the nature described in sub-

----

§ 12. Remedies; civil penalties; procedure

The rationale and main features of section 12 are discussed under "Penalties" in Chapter X *supra;* there are no comparable existing provisions.

Subsection (a) is confined to present Government employees. Its main function is to establish a firm statutory base for application of the full range of employee disciplinary procedures to conflict of interest situations.

Subsection (b) sets up a structure of procedures for enforcement as to former Government employees and persons who are neither former nor

section (b)(1).

(2) Procedure: The procedures for any such action shall correspond to those applicable for disciplinary action for employee misconduct generally, and any such action shall be subject to judicial review to the extent provided by law for disciplinary action for misconduct of employees of the same category and grade.

(b) ADMINISTRATIVE ENFORCEMENT AS TO FORMER GOVERNMENT EMPLOYEES AND OTHERS. —

(1) Remedies and Civil Penalties: The head of an agency, upon finding that any former employee of such agency or any other person has violated any provision of this Act, may, in addition to any other powers the head of such agency may have, bar or impose reasonable conditions upon —

(A) the appearance before such agency of such former employee or other person, and

(B) the conduct of, or negotiation or competition for, business with such agency by such former employee or other person, for such period of time as may reasonably be necessary or appropriate to effectuate the purposes of this Act.

(2) Procedure:

(A) Hearings. — Findings of violations referred to in subsection (b)(1) shall be made on the record after notice and hearing, conducted in accordance with the provisions governing adjudication in title 5, United States Code, secs. 1005, 1006, 1007, 1008, and 1011 (Administrative Procedure Act). For the purposes of such hearing any agency head, or any officer designated by it, is empowered to administer oaths and affirmations, subpena witnesses, compel their attendance, take evidence, and require the production of any books, papers, correspondence, memoranda, contracts, agreements, or other records which the agency head finds relevant or material to the inquiry. Such attendance of witnesses and the production of any such rec-

----

current Government employees. The Administrative Procedure Act is relied on as to hearing procedures, and provision is made for judicial

ords may be required from any place in the United States at any designated place of hearing. Witnesses summoned by the agency head to appear shall be paid the same fees and mileage that are paid witnesses in the courts of the United States.

(B) Judicial review. — (i) Any party to a proceeding under this subsection (b) aggrieved by an order issued by the agency head pursuant hereto, may obtain a review of such order in the court of appeals of the United States for any circuit wherein said party is located or has its principal place of business, or in the United States Court of Appeals for the District of Columbia, by filing in such court within sixty days after the order of the agency upon a written petition praying that such order be modified or set aside in whole or in part.

(ii) A copy of such petition shall forthwith be transmitted by the clerk of the court to the agency head involved, and thereupon such agency head shall file with the court the record upon which the order complained of was entered. Upon the filing of such petition, such court shall have jurisdiction, which upon the filing of the record with it shall be exclusive, to affirm, modify, or set aside such order in whole or in part.

(iii) No objection to the order of the agency head shall be considered by the court unless such objection shall have been urged before the agency or there is reasonable ground for failure to do so.

(iv) The findings of the agency head as to the facts, if supported by substantial evidence, shall be conclusive. If any party shall apply to the court for leave to adduce additional evidence, and shall show to the satisfaction of the court that such additional evidence is material in that there were reasonable grounds for failure to adduce such evidence in the proceedings before the agency, the court may order such additional evidence to be taken before the agency and to be adduced upon the hearing in such manner and upon such terms and conditions as to the

---

review. "The findings of the agency head as to the facts, if supported by substantial evidence, shall be conclusive."

court may seem proper.

(v) The agency head may modify his findings as to the facts by reason of the additional evidence so taken and shall file with the court such modified or new findings which, if supported by substantial evidence, shall be conclusive, and his recommendation, if any, for the modification or setting aside of the original order. The judgment and decree of the court, affirming, modifying, or setting aside in whole or in part, any such order of the agency head, shall be final, subject to review by the Supreme Court of the United States upon certiorari or certification as provided in sections 346 and 347 of title 28. The commencement of proceedings for review under this subsection shall not, unless specifically ordered by the court, operate as a stay of the agency head's order.

(c) RESCISSION OF GOVERNMENT ACTION. — The President or any agency head may, in addition to any other available rights of rescission, cancel or rescind any Government action without contractual liability to the United States where —

(1) he has found that a violation of this Act has substantially influenced such Government action; and

(2) in his judgment the interests of the United States so require under all of the circumstances, including the position of innocent third parties.

The finding referred to in clause (1) shall be made in accordance with the procedures set forth in subsection (b)(2) and shall be subject to judicial review in accordance with the provisions of subsection (b)(2)(B): *Provided*, That the President or such agency head may suspend Government action pending the determination, pursuant to this subsection, of the merits of the controversy. The exercise of judgment pursuant to clause (2) of this subsection shall not be subject to judicial review.

Subsection (c) provides a statutory base for the common law principles of rescission. The provision is discussed in Chapter X.

Subsections (d) through (h) are characterized briefly in Chapter X.

(d) CIVIL REMEDY FOR DAMAGES AGAINST EMPLOYEES AND FORMER EMPLOYEES. — The Attorney General of the United States may bring a civil action in any district court of the United States against any Government employee or former Government employee who shall, to his economic advantage, have acted in violation of this Act, and in such action may recover on behalf of the United States, in partial reimbursement of the United States for its expenses of administering this Act, damages in an amount equal to three times the amount of such economic advantage.

(e) CIVIL PENALTIES FOR ILLEGAL PAYMENTS. — The Attorney General of the United States may bring a civil action in any district court of the United States to collect from any person who shall violate section 9 a civil penalty of not more than $5,000, in partial reimbursement of the United States for its expenses of administering this Act. The Government employee or former Government employee involved shall not be subject to prosecution under title 18, United States Code, section 2, or title 18, United States Code, section 371, or any other provision of law dealing with criminal conspiracy, by reason of the receipt of any such payment.

(f) PUBLICATION OF CERTAIN FINDINGS AND DECISIONS. — Whenever the head of any agency, or the President, exercises the authority conferred by subsections (a), (b), or (c) of this section, copies of the findings and decision therein shall be filed with the President and shall be published at least once each year as part of a volume collecting such findings and opinions. Such volumes shall be made available for public inspection and shall also be made available for distribution or sale to interested persons.

(g) INTERESTS OF NATIONAL SECURITY. — When any provision of this Act requires publication of information and the President finds that publication of part or all of such information is inconsistent with national security, he may suspend the requirement of such publication to the extent and for such period of time as he shall deem essential for reasons of national security.

(h) STATUTE OF LIMITATIONS. — No administrative or other action under subsections (b), (c), (d), or (e) of this section to enforce any provision of this Act shall be commenced after the expiration of six years following the occurrence of the alleged violation.

TITLE II — CRIMINAL PENALTIES

§ 21. Acts in violation of Executive Conflict of Interest Act

Title 18 of the United States Code is amended by adding a new chapter thereto, to be designated chapter 16 and reading as follows:

"CHAPTER 16 — CONFLICTS OF INTEREST

"§ 301. Acts in violation of Executive Conflict of Interest Act

"Any person who shall purposely or knowingly violate any provision of the Executive Conflict of Interest Act shall be fined not more than $10,000, or imprisoned for not more than one year, or both. For purposes of this section, the terms 'purposely' and 'knowingly' shall have the respective meanings set forth in subsections (a) and (b):

"(a) 'Purposely': A person acts purposely with respect to a material element of an offense when —

"(1) if the element involves the nature of his conduct or a result thereof, it is his conscious object to engage in conduct of that nature or to cause such a result; and

" (2) if the element involves the attendant circumstances, he knows of the existence of such circumstances.

"(b) 'Knowingly': A person acts knowingly with respect to a material element of an offense when —

"(1) if the element involves the nature of his conduct or the attendant circumstances, he knows that his conduct is of that nature or he knows of the existence of such circumstances; and

"(2) if the element involves a result of his conduct, he knows that his conduct will necessarily cause such a result."

----

§ 21. Acts in violation of Executive Conflict of Interest Act

The criminal penalties of the Act are described under "Penalties" in Chapter X *supra*. The criminal penalties are, of course, equally applicable to "outsiders," *i.e.,* those who violate section 9, as they are to Government employees and former Government employees.

In the case of the existing statutes, the criminal penalties are contained in the individual substantive sections and differ substantially from one another.

TITLE III — AMENDMENT AND REPEAL
OF EXISTING LAWS

§ 31. Amendment of title 18, United States Code, sections 216 and 1914

Section 216 of chapter 11 and section 1914 of chapter 93 of title 18 of the United States Code are each amended by adding the following as a new paragraph to precede the present text of each such section:

"From and after the effective date of the Executive Conflict of Interest Act, this section shall not apply to (1) any person who is a Government employee as defined in section 2(f) of that Act, and (2) any act of another person which is directed toward such a Government employee."

§ 32. Amendment of title 18, United States Code, sections 281, 283, and 434

Sections 281 and 283 of chapter 15 of title 18 of the United States Code are each amended by deleting the second paragraph thereof. Each of such sections is further amended and section 434 of chapter 23 of title 18 of the United States Code is amended by adding the

----

§ 31. Amendment of title 18, United States Code, sections 216 and 1914

The amendments make these two sections inapplicable both to employees covered by the Executive Conflict of Interest Act and to "outsiders" dealing with them. These two sections of present law are in a special category since (as noted in the commentary on section 9 of the Act) they are the only ones containing express prohibitions against payors.

§ 32. Amendment of title 18, United States Code, sections 281, 283, and 434

The amendments make these three sections of present law inapplicable to employees covered by the Executive Conflict of Interest Act.

In addition, the special provisions of 18 U.S.C. §§ 281 and 283 applicable to retired officers of the armed forces of the United States are deleted. See the discussion under "Military procurement and employment of retired officers" in Chapter X *supra*.

following as a new paragraph to precede the present text of each such section:

"From and after the effective date of the Executive Conflict of Interest Act, this section shall not apply to any person who is a Government employee as defined in section 2(f) of that Act."

§ 33. Amendment of title 18, United States Code, section 284

Section 284 of chapter 15 of title 18 of the United States Code is amended by adding the following as a new paragraph to precede the present text of such section:

"From and after the effective date of the Executive Conflict of Interest Act, this section shall not apply to any person who has been a Government employee as defined in section 2(f) of that Act."

§ 34. Amendment of title 22, United States Code, section 1792(a)

Section 532(a) of the Mutual Security Act of 1954 (68 Stat. 859), as amended by section 10(d) of the Act of July 18, 1956 (70 Stat. 561; 22 U.S.C. 1792(a)), is amended to read as follows:

"(a) Service of an individual as a member of the Board established pursuant to section 308 of this Act or as an expert or consultant under section 530(a) shall not be considered as employment or holding of office or position bringing such individual within the provisions of section 6 of the Act of May 22, 1920 (5 U.S.C. 715), or section 212 of the Act of June 30, 1932 (5 U.S.C. 59a), or any other Federal law limiting the reemployment of retired officers or employees or governing the simultaneous receipt of compensation and

----

§ 33. Amendment of title 18, United States Code, section 284

The amendment makes this section of present law inapplicable to former Government employees covered by the Executive Conflict of Interest Act.

§ 34. Amendment of title 22, United States Code, section 1792(a)

This amendment deletes the present exemption provisions of the Mutual Security Act as to advisers, experts, and consultants. The substance of the deleted language is quoted above in the commentary on section 4. The rationale of the amendment is set forth under "Amendments and Repealers" in Chapter X.

retired pay or annuities. Contracts for the employment of retired military personnel with specialized research and development experience, not to exceed ten in number, as experts or consultants under section 530(a), may be renewed annually, notwithstanding section 15 of the Act of August 2, 1946 (5 U.S.C. 55(a))."

§ 35. Amendment of title 5, United States Code, section 30r(d)

Section 29(d) of the Act of August 10, 1956 (70A Stat. 632; 5 U.S.C. 30r(d)), is amended to read as follows:

" (d) When he is not on active duty, or when he is on active duty for training, a reserve is not considered to be an officer or employee of the United States or a person holding an office of trust or profit or discharging any official function under, or in connection with, the United States because of his appointment, oath, or status, or any duties or functions performed or pay or allowances received in that capacity: *Provided, however,* That a reserve on active duty for training shall be deemed an employee of the United States for purposes of the Executive Conflict of Interest Act."

§ 36. Repeal of particular substantive restraints

The following sections are repealed:

(a) Section 190 of the Revised Statutes (5 U.S.C. 99) (relating to post-employment prosecution of claims by employees in departments); and

(b) Section 244 of the Revised Statutes (5 U.S.C. 254) (relating to certain business interests of clerks in the Treasury Department).

----

§ 35. Amendment of title 5, United States Code, section 30r(d)

This amendment has the effect of bringing reserves of the armed forces who are on active duty for training within the scope of the Executive Conflict of Interest Act. The new language is the proviso at the end of the sentence. See the commentary on section 2(f)(3).

§ 36. Repeal of particular substantive restraints

The repeal of 5 U.S.C. §§ 99 and 254 is discussed under "Amendments and Repealers" in Chapter X. Many commentators have recommended the repeal of the former section, while the latter section is obviously an anachronism.

§ 37. Repeal of particular substantive restraints applicable to retired officers

The following sections are repealed:

(a) Section 1309 of the Act of August 7, 1953 (67 Stat. 437; 5 U.S.C. 59c) (relating to loss of retirement pay by retired commissioned officers engaged in certain selling activities).

(b) Section 6112 of chapter 557 of title 10 of the United States Code (relating to the loss of pay or retirement pay by certain officers who sell naval supplies to the Navy Department).

§ 38. Repeal of exemptions from particular conflict-of-interest statutes

The following sections are repealed:

(a) Section 173(c) of chapter 7 of title 10 of the United States Code (providing certain conflicts exemptions for advisers to the Secretary of Defense).

(b) Section 1583(b) of chapter 81 of title 10 of the United States Code (authorizing conflicts exemptions for persons employed by the Secretary of Defense to serve without compensation).

(c) Section 5153(d) of chapter 513 of title 10 of the United States Code (providing certain conflicts exemptions for members of the Naval Research Advisory Committee).

(d) Section 807 of the Act of August 2, 1954 (68 Stat. 645; 12 U.S.C. 1701h) (providing certain conflicts exemptions for members of advisory committees of the Housing and Home Finance Agency).

(e) Section 5 of the Act of June 4, 1956 (70 Stat. 243; 16 U.S.C. 934) (providing certain conflicts exemptions for commissioners and

----

§ 37. Repeal of particular substantive restraints applicable to retired officers

The repeal of 5 U.S.C. § 59c and 10 U.S.C. § 6112 is discussed under "Military procurement and employment of retired officers" in Chapter X, and is referred to again under "Amendments and Repealers" in Chapter X.

§ 38. Repeal of exemptions from particular conflict of interest statutes

The various repealers set forth herein are discussed under "Amendments and Repealers" in Chapter X.

members of advisory committees appointed under the Great Lakes Fishery Act of 1956).

(f) Section 5 of the Act of September 7, 1950 (64 Stat. 778; 16 U.S.C. 954) (providing certain conflicts exemptions for commissioners and members of advisory committees appointed under the Tuna Conventions Act of 1950).

(g) Section 5 of the Act of September 27, 1950 (64 Stat. 1068; 16 U.S.C. 984) (providing certain conflicts exemptions for commissioners and members of advisory committees appointed under the Northwest Atlantic Fisheries Act of 1950).

(h) Section 5 of the Act of August 12, 1954 (68 Stat. 698; 16 U.S.C. 1024) (providing certain conflicts exemptions for commissioners and members of advisory committees appointed under the North Pacific Fisheries Act of 1954).

(i) Section 1003 of the Act of September 2, 1958 (72 Stat. 1603; 20 U.S.C. 583) (providing certain conflicts exemptions for members of advisory committees and information councils appointed under the National Defense Education Act of 1958).

(j) Section 14(f) of the Act of May 10, 1950 (64 Stat. 154, 155; 42 U.S.C. 1873(f)) (providing certain conflicts exemptions for members of the National Science Board and committees and commissions appointed under the National Science Foundation Act of 1950).

(k) Section 163 of the Atomic Energy Act of 1954 (68 Stat. 951), as amended by section 2 of the Act of September 21, 1959 (73 Stat. 574; 42 U.S.C. 2203) (providing certain conflicts exemptions for members of the General Advisory Committee and advisory boards appointed under the Atomic Energy Act of 1954).

(l) Section 1(t) of the Act of June 19, 1951 (65 Stat. 87; 50 U.S.C. App. 463(a)) (providing certain conflicts exemptions for particular Selective Service officials).

(m) Section 113 of the Renegotiation Act of 1951 (65 Stat. 22), as amended by section 13 of the Act of August 1, 1956 (70 Stat. 792; 50 U.S.C. App. 1223) (providing certain conflicts exemptions for employees of departments and agencies to which the Renegotiation Act of 1951 is applicable and of the Renegotiation Board).

(n) Section 7(b)(4) of the Act of August 9, 1955 (69 Stat. 582; 50 U.S.C. App. 2160(b)(4)) (providing certain conflicts exemptions for persons serving without compensation under the Defense Production Act of 1950).

TITLE IV — MISCELLANEOUS PROVISIONS

§ 41. Short title

This Act shall be known and may be cited as the "Executive Conflict of Interest Act."

§ 42. Effective date

This Act shall take effect ninety days after the date of its enactment, except that section 37 shall not take effect until the effective date of the regulations issued by the President pursuant to section 8(e).

Appendixes

APPENDIX A

A Note on State, Local, and Foreign Government

State and local regulation

State and local regulation of the conflict of interest problem is beyond the scope of this book. The issue has frequently arisen at this level, however. Many states have legislation on the subject, though little of it is carefully worked out. For a collection of examples of state legislation, see Eisenberg, *Conflicts of Interest Situations and Remedies,* 13 RUTGERS L. REV. 666 (1959). In 1954 New York enacted a relatively fully developed set of statutes. These statutes include a code of conduct, grant broad enforcement powers to the Attorney General, and establish an advisory committee on ethical standards for state employees. See N.Y. PUBLIC OFFICERS LAW §§ 73, 74; N.Y. EXECUTIVE LAW §§ 63, 74.

Large municipalities have been increasingly active in the field. New York City in 1959 enacted a detailed Code of Ethics covering all employees, including Councilmen. See N.Y. Times, Aug. 21, 1959, p. 10, cols. 2–5. Similarly, Philadelphia has recently enacted a comprehensive ordinance dealing with conflict of interest problems. See Note, *Conflict-of-Interests of Government Personnel: An Appraisal of the Philadelphia Situation,* 107 U. PA. L. REV. 985 (1959); see also BUREAU OF MUNICIPAL RESEARCH AND PENNSYLVANIA ECONOMY LEAGUE (EASTERN DIVISION), PHILADELPHIA GOVERNMENT (1959).

In the state and local field, litigation of conflict of interest questions has been substantial. Charges of conflict of interest have often been used to attack the validity of local government action, particularly in cases where the alleged offender was an elected official. See 3 YOKLEY, MUNICIPAL CORPORATIONS § 439, at 13–17 (1958). The charge has also frequently been used as a ground for removal of employees. See 4 McQUILLIN, MUNICIPAL CORPORATIONS § 12.237, at 265–66, and accompanying notes (3d ed. 1949).

For a modern study of the topic at the state level, see NEW JERSEY LEGISLATIVE COMMISSION ON CONFLICTS OF INTERESTS, REPORT TO THE SENATE AND GENERAL ASSEMBLY (1957); MINNESOTA GOVERNOR'S COMMITTEE ON ETHICS IN GOVERNMENT, ETHICS IN GOVERNMENT (1959). See also DALHOUSIE UNIVERSITY INSTITUTE OF PUBLIC AFFAIRS, MUNICIPAL OFFICIALS AND PUBLIC CONTRACTS 32–35 (1958); Eisenberg, *supra*. On the problem of conflict of interest on the local level, see also Kaplan & Lillich, *Municipal Conflicts of Interest: Inconsistencies and Patchwork Prohibitions*, 58 COLUM. L. REV. 157 (1958); Lenhoff, *The Constructive Trust as a Remedy for Corruption in Public Office*, 54 COLUM. L. REV. 214 (1954); Note, *The Doctrine of Conflicting Interests Applied to Municipal Officials in New Jersey*, 12 RUTGERS L. REV. 582 (1958); Annot., 40 A.L.R. 344 (1942).

Close enforcement of conflict of interest restrictions in small communities is often impossible and frequently not even desirable. In a small town almost every citizen has a personal interest in every decision on road and school location, or on zoning, for example. Yet this very interest is the primary qualification for, rather than a disqualification from, sitting on a local deciding body.

Little is known of the impact of existing restrictions on recruitment for local government office.

Foreign experience

In England, national civil servants are governed by a Code on Establishment Matters called "Estacode." Portions of Estacode relate to conflict of interest. In response to an inquiry made to the British Civil Service Commission, the following extract from Estacode was received from J. J. S. Shaw, Treasury Chambers, Great George Street, London, S.W. 1, under cover of September 30, 1959:

CONDUCT AND DISCIPLINE

General This sub-section sets out the rules which govern the conduct of civil servants. No attempt has ever been made to prepare a complete list of matters which, because of the particular character and duties of the Civil Service, require regulation, nor has it ever been thought necessary to lay down a precise code of conduct because civil servants jealously maintain their professional standards. In practice the distinctive character of the British Civil Service depends largely on the existence and maintenance of a general code of conduct which, although to some extent intangible and unwritten, is of very real importance. There are however a number of things on which it has been found expedient from time to time to issue general instructions, and these are to be found in the subsequent paragraphs of this sub-section.

The Civil Service carries out many and varied functions each of which may require special standards of its own, so that the application of a general principle will vary with the circumstances of different departments and call for special rules for particular staffs. There are however certain general principles which apply to all members of the Service. Departments are advised to incorporate these principles in their own staff rules and instructions, and in particular to bring them to the notice of each new entrant, temporary as well as permanent. They are as follows:

(a) The first duty of a civil servant is to give his undivided allegiance to the State at all times and on all occasions when the State has a claim on his services.

(b) A civil servant must not subordinate his duty to his private interest, neither is he to put himself in a position where his duty and his private interests conflict and he must not make use of his official position to further those interests.

(c) Though the State is in general not concerned with its servants' private activities, they must not be such as might bring discredit on the Service — for example, heavy gambling and speculation are to be avoided, particularly in departments which have access to information which could be turned to private gain.

(d) The high standard which the Service sets itself goes beyond the normal standards of personal honesty and integrity — the civil servant must not only be honest in fact, but also he must not lay himself open to suspicion of dishonesty.

(e) Civil servants who advise Ministers and carry out Ministers' policies (and thus come within the "politically restricted" group as defined in paragraph 36(c) below) are bound to retain a proper reticence in matters of public and political controversy, so that their impartiality is beyond suspicion. It follows that they should not normally take an active part in any matter which is, or could be, one of public and political controversy, whether or not it is one with which they are officially concerned. If for any reason they feel impelled as private citizens to do so in relation to some particular issue, they should first consult their official superiors and should, if necessary, seek an interview with the permanent head of the department.

Handling of contracts No Government contract may be let to a Government servant in the contracting department, or to any partnership of which he is a member (except to a corporation in which he is a shareholder), or to any company of which he is a director (except as a nominee of the Government) unless he has disclosed fully the measure of his interest in the contract and the head of department has given permission for the letting of the contract to proceed. No Government servant may accept a directorship, except as a nominee of the Government or with the express permission of the head of his department, in any company holding a contract with his department. An officer who

comes into official contact with any matter concerning a business
organization in which he has an interest must disclose his interest to
the head of the department and ask that some other officer may deal
with the matter.

Outside occupations Full time civil servants, whether established or
unestablished, are not allowed to accept any post in the management of
any society, or any trading, commercial, industrial or financial firm or
company which would require their attendance at any time during
normal official hours. The following general principles apply:

(a) No officer may at any time engage in any activity which would
in any way tend to impair his usefulness as a public servant.

(b) No officer may engage in any occupation or undertaking which
might in any way conflict with the interests of his department
or be inconsistent with his position as a public servant.

An officer who has any doubt about the propriety of undertaking any
particular work should consult the head of his department or his
Establishment Officer.

*Private occupations including part-time employment by a Government
department* In considering applications from staff for permission to
undertake any private occupations, departments should ensure that the
activity does not conflict with the particular duties on which the officer
is employed, or with his primary duty to the State. The general principles of the code of conduct which applies to all members of the
Service are set out in paragraph 2. In addition departments may find it
desirable to draw up special codes of conduct naming outside activities
which owing to the nature of the department's work are incompatible
with the official duties of the staff. It should also be borne in mind that
departments have a right to call on staff at any time. An officer must
not, therefore, bind himself to regular outside employment during
normal working hours and permission to undertake a private occupation should be granted only on the understanding that the department's claims on the officer's services take priority over those of any
outside employer. As far as possible, differences in treatment based
solely on the medium of the activity should be avoided.

Subject to these considerations no general restriction should be
placed on the private occupations of civil servants beyond those necessary to ensure that official work does not suffer, and a department
should not concern itself with the activities in which a civil servant may
engage outside his official duties (always provided no question of propriety arises) unless they involve official time, official information or
experience acquired in the course of official duties, or payment from
a Government department.

In this century infrequent instances have occurred of alleged misconduct on the part of high-ranking British government officials. In 1957

a question was raised whether the Directors of the Bank of England had prematurely disclosed an impending increase in the discount rate. See N.Y. Times, Sept. 27, 1957, p. 8, col. 7; N.Y. Times, Oct. 5, 1957, p. 36, col. 1; N.Y. Times, Nov. 14, 1957, p. 10, col. 5; N.Y. Times, Nov. 15, 1957, p. 16, col. 1; N.Y. Times, Dec. 7, 1957, p. 3, col. 2; N.Y. Times, Dec. 21, 1957, p. 2, col. 3. See also THE TRIBUNAL APPOINTED TO INQUIRE INTO ALLEGATIONS OF IMPROPER DISCLOSURE OF INFORMATION RELATING TO THE RAISING OF THE BANK RATE, REPORT (COMMAND PAPER 350, 1958).

In 1914, charges of improper speculation based on inside information were made against the Chief Whip of the House of Commons. A Select Committee, with the Earl of Halsbury presiding, decided that the accused had not actually put himself in a position of conflicting economic interest, but he had engaged in a speculative transaction that was improper. Lord Halsbury pronounced a general rule that stands still as the governing principle: "In conclusion, we think it is within our province to express our strong opinion that there should be henceforth an inflexible rule to preclude those who hold any public office from entering upon any speculative transactions in stocks or shares in any circumstances whatsoever, and that this rule should be by them inculcated on their subordinates both by precept and example. The evils that may arise from a violation of this principle are incalculable." REPORT FROM THE SELECT COMMITTEE OF THE HOUSE OF LORDS ON THE CHARGES AGAINST LORD MURRAY OF ELIBANK (1914). See N.Y. Times, Feb. 9, 1914, p. 3, col. 2; N.Y. Times, Feb. 18, 1914, p. 4, col. 2. See also N.Y. Times, Jan. 13, 1914, p. 4, col. 6.

In 1948 a case arose in England involving a professional influence peddler who collected sums from clients to pass along in the form of hospitality and gifts to government officials. Some gifts were given, though the peddler apparently simply pocketed much of what he collected. A Member of Parliament was charged with receiving gratuities and with showing favor to the donors in certain applications before the Board of Trade; attempted bribery was alleged, but not found by the investigating tribunal. The Tribunal of Inquiry was asked to give guidance to officials who have to deal with applications from personal friends, but in its report did not lay down general rules on acceptance of gratuities. REPORT OF THE TRIBUNAL APPOINTED TO INQUIRE INTO ALLEGATIONS REFLECTING ON THE OFFICIAL CONDUCT OF MINISTERS OF THE CROWN AND OTHER PUBLIC SERVANTS, COMMAND PAPER 7616 (1949). See N.Y. Times, Nov. 16, 1948, p. 15, col. 1; N.Y. Times, Nov. 18, 1948, p. 9, col. 6; N.Y. Times, Nov. 30, 1948, p. 14, col. 8.

Pertinent local legislation in Canada, the United Kingdom, Australia, New Zealand, the Netherlands, Norway, Sweden, and Switzerland is described in DALHOUSIE UNIVERSITY INSTITUTE OF PUBLIC AFFAIRS, MUNICIPAL OFFICIALS AND PUBLIC CONTRACTS (1958). A helpful bibliography on the foreign problem is UNITED NATIONS, INTERNATIONAL BIOGRAPHY OF PUBLIC ADMINISTRATION (1957). Other references include Callard, *On the*

Ethics of Civil Servants in Great Britain and North America, in 4 PUBLIC POLICY, HARVARD UNIVERSITY GRADUATE SCHOOL OF PUBLIC ADMINISTRATION YEARBOOK 134 (1953); New Jersey Law Revision & Legislative Services Commission, Division of Legislative Information & Research, Memorandum prepared for Conflict of Interests Study Commission, Conflicts of Interest among Government Officers and Employees in Great Britain (Nov. 4, 1957); U.S. News & World Report, Sept 2. 1955, p. 321, on the British method of treating the conflict of interest problem.

A Note on Retired
Military Officers

The conflict of interest problems of retired military officers have long been the subject of special legal treatment. Conflict of interest statutes, one civil statute without penalty, statutes restricting officers' rights to retirement pay, and regulations of the military departments all play a part.

CRIMINAL STATUTES AND 5 U.S.C. § 99

The two criminal statutes aimed directly at the problem of retired officers are 18 U.S.C. § 281 and 18 U.S.C. § 283. Certain other statutes which are not directed primarily toward retired military officers may also affect them.

18 U.S.C. § 281 (1958)

In 1940 the predecessor to Section 281 was amended to provide: "Retired officers of the armed forces of the United States, while not on active duty, shall not by reason of their status as such be subject to the provisions of this section. *Nothing herein shall be construed to allow any retired officer to represent any person in the sale of anything to the Government through the department in whose service he holds a retired status.*" (Emphasis supplied.)

The history of this amendment indicates that it was adopted in response to the court's holding, in *Morgenthau v. Barrett,* 108 F.2d 481 (D.C. Cir. 1939), that a retired Army officer, not on active duty, was still an "officer" subject to the prohibitions and sanctions of Section 281. The court in the *Barrett* case felt compelled by the words of the statute and weight of authority to make this decision. But it expressed its opinion that the policy behind the law, and common sense, would dictate an opposite result. The Committee on Military Affairs agreed with the court's general view. In its report accompanying the 1940 amendment the Committee stated:

> The only effect of this bill will be to extend to retired officers not on active duty the same exemptions from the operation of Section . . . [281] as were extended to Reserve officers by the Act of July 1, 1930 (46 Stat. 841). . . .
> . . . Though a part of the Military Establishment, retired officers not on active duty — the only class to which this bill applies — are more nearly in a civil than a military status. They have no military duties to perform, and though in time of war they may be called to duty without their consent, this is a contingency to which every citizen is subject. In time of peace their status is no different from that of citizens, generally. [*sic*] and, as said by the court of appeals, their "activities are wholly separated from official life." It is absurd, therefore to think that retired officers, particularly while not on active duty, as such, can exert any undue influence in the departments or bureaus, or with commissions, agencies, or instrumentalities of the Government, or with any officers therewith connected. The time of retired officers not on active duty is their own. There is no loss of time to the Government, through their employment by private interests, as there is in the case of officers and employees on active duty whose whole time belongs to the Government. As the primary purposes of the statute seem to be to discourage the use of undue or sinister influence by those in a position to exert it, and to prevent the loss to the Government of time for which officers and employees are paid by the Government, and neither of these reasons can have any application to retired officers not on active duty, there appears to be no good reason why they should not be exempted from the provisions of Section [281] . . . as proposed in this bill.

See H.R. REP. No. 2330, 76th Cong., 3d Sess. 1–2 (1940).

Thus retired officers are in general exempted from the prohibitions of Section 281. But the built-in exception to this exemption is broad and has caused trouble. The force of the exception is to forbid a retired officer to "represent any person in the sale of anything to the Government through the department in whose service he holds a retired status." This language has never been judicially construed.

The Navy Judge Advocate General has pointed out some of the ambiguities of this language:

> The statute most frequently referenced in this field is 18 U.S.C. 281. The Preparedness Investigating Subcommittee of the Senate Committee on Armed Services has recently stated that this section "prohibits retired officers * * * from representing — 'any person in the sale of

anything to the Government through the department in whose service he holds a retired status.' " Under this interpretation, the phrase "to represent any person in the sale of anything" is sufficiently comprehensive to include not only the sale of materials and supplies but also the sale of various types of services. The phrase "to represent any person" seems adequate to include situations where a retired officer sells for himself as well as those where he sells for or on behalf of another person or organization. The "department in whose service" a retired Navy or Marine Corps officer holds his retired status is the Department of the Navy, not the Department of Defense. Accordingly, this law does not prohibit a retired Navy or Marine Corps officer from selling to the Army, to the Air Force, or to other Government agencies.

The Government viewpoint is well expressed by the quotation from the Senate Committee. A careful reading of Section 281, however, raises some doubt about the validity of that interpretation. Notice that the first sentence of the second paragraph in Section 281 in general terms exempts retired officers (not on active duty) from the prohibitory provisions of the first paragraph of Section 281. The second sentence of the second paragraph does not specifically prohibit retired Navy and Marine Corps officers from selling to the Navy. Rather it states that "nothing herein shall be construed to allow" any retired Navy or Marine Corps officer to sell to the Navy Department. Because of the awkward and somewhat vague manner in which this exception has been written, it is arguable that the second sentence in the second paragraph of Section 281 is not intended to subject a retired naval officer to criminal prosecution if he sells to the Navy Department but is designed only to make certain that the exception contained in the prior sentence is not construed as a defense to criminal charges (or a loss of pay) under other laws. Admittedly, a retired officer who acts on this assumption would be taking a calculated risk in regard to criminal prosecution, particularly in the present conflict of interest climate.

Navy Judge Advocate General Journal, November 1957, pp. 8–9.

18 U.S.C. § 283 (1958)

In 1949 retired officers were exempted by amendment from the conflict of interest prohibitions of 18 U.S.C. § 283 respecting prosecution of claims. Thus after nine years of inconsistency, Section 283 was harmonized in this respect with Section 281. Again, however, a substantial exception was carved out of the exemption. The exception reads: "Nothing herein shall be construed to allow any such retired officer within two years next after his retirement to act as agent or attorney for prosecuting or assisting in the prosecution of any claim against the United States involving the department in whose service he holds a retired status, or to allow any such retired officer to act as agent or attorney for prosecuting or assisting in the prosecution of any claim against the United States involving any subject matter with which he was directly connected while he was in an active duty status." The two year limitation period does not carry over to the phrase following the comma, and the statutory language therefore imposes upon retired officers a lifetime disqualification from prosecuting claims involving any "subject matter" with which they were connected while on active duty. Except for the permanence of the bar, the language of the second clause obviously parallels that of the general post-employment statute, 18 U.S.C. § 284.

The Navy Judge Advocate General Journal has stated: "The emphasis of this section in relation to retired Navy and Marine Corps officers is a prohibition (1) upon acting 'as agent or attorney for prosecuting or assisting in the prosecution of any claim against the United States involving' the Department of the Navy and (2) upon the prosecution of any claim against the United States involving any subject matter with which the retired officer was directly connected while on active duty. A retired Navy or Marine Corps officer is restricted for only two years in regard to claims involving the Department of the Navy; he is forever restricted in regard to matters with which he was directly connected while on active duty." Navy Judge Advocate General Journal, November 1957, p. 9.

Other Criminal Statutes

The prohibitions of 18 U.S.C. §§ 434 and 1914 by their nature have no application to retired personnel. 18 U.S.C. § 216 probably does not apply to retired personnel, though the contrary opinion was apparently formerly held by the Judge Advocate General.

Whether general conflict of interest statutes on post-employment conduct apply to retired personnel is a special problem, since by definition retired employees are already in a post-employment stage. 18 U.S.C. § 284, the general criminal conflicts statute on post-employment, is applicable to military personnel in active service. Thus, by its provisions, such persons are forbidden for two years after termination to prosecute or act "as counsel, attorney, or agent for prosecuting, any claims against the United States involving any subject matter directly connected with which such person was so employed or performed duty." But retired military personnel are probably not considered as such to be "officers" under Section 284, and the statute therefore does not in all likelihood continue to apply to them indefinitely past the two-year period. The net result is that in the case of retired military personnel, Section 284 runs as a concurrent bar with the special two-year post-employment provision in Section 283.

22 U.S.C. § 1764 prohibits any Government employee for two years subsequent to the termination of his government service from receiving any pecuniary reward in connection with the procurement of goods or

services under the Mutual Security Act as amended in 1958. Retired military officers are not infrequently involved in the procurement of supplies and services for the Western allies, and may to this extent find themselves subject to this statute.

5 U.S.C. § 99 (1958) (Civil Statute)

5 U.S.C. § 99, the civil statute dealing with post-employment activities of former employees of the government, applies to employees of a "department" only, and the Attorney General has taken the view that it does not automatically apply to retired military officers by virtue of their status as such, since they are not members of a "department." Military officers who held certain posts in the Defense Department might fall within the scope of the section, however. 31 Ops Att'y Gen. 471 (1919). Compare, however, the special exemptive provisions contained in Section 113 of the Renegotiation Act of 1951, as amended. 65 Stat. 22 (1951), as amended, 70 Stat. 792, 50 U.S.C. § 1223 (1958); cf. 40 Ops Att'y Gen. 289 (1943).

STATUTES RESTRICTING RETIREMENT PAY

Three conflict of interest statutes, instead of imposing criminal sanctions, call for forfeiture of the retired officer's retirement pay. These statutes are 5 U.S.C. § 59c, 10 U.S.C. § 6112 (b), and 5 U.S.C. § 740c.

The first two of these statutes prohibit the sale by former military personnel of various supplies and war materials; Section 740c is more general. It provides that anyone convicted under certain bribery or conflict of interest sections will be precluded from receiving federal retirement pay.

67 Stat. 437 (1953), 5 U.S.C. § 59c (1958), and
70A Stat. 381 (1956), 10 U.S.C. § 6112 (b) (1958)

5 U.S.C. § 59c provides: "No payment shall be made from appropriations in any Act to any officer on the retired lists of the Regular Army, Regular Navy, Regular Marine Corps, Regular Air Force, Regular Coast Guard, Coast and Geodetic Survey, and Public Health Service for a period of two years after retirement who for himself or for others is engaged in the selling of or contracting for the sale of or negotiating for the sale of to an agency of the Department of Defense, the Coast Guard and Geodetic Survey, and the Public Health Service any supplies or war materials." Significant aspects of this section include coverage of all retired military personnel, a two-year limitation, its limited coverage prohibiting only "sales" or contracting or negotiating for "sales" of "supplies or war materials," and application of the bar throughout the entire Defense Department.

10 U.S.C. § 6112(b) applicable to retired naval and marine officers only, provides: "If a retired officer of the Regular Navy or the Regular

Marine Corps is engaged for himself or others in selling, or contracting or negotiating to sell, naval supplies or war materials to the Department of the Navy he is not entitled to any payment from the United States while he is so engaged." Important features of this section include the limitation of its coverage to naval and marine officers, a perpetual bar, limitation to "selling, or contracting or negotiating to sell, naval supplies or war materials," and its limited scope in prohibiting sales to the Department of the Navy only.

A general comment on the scope of these two sections has been supplied by the Navy Judge Advocate General:

> The distinction between these two statutes should be carefully noted. [10 U.S.C. § 6112(b)] . . . applies (a) only to retired officers of the Regular Navy and Regular Marine Corps, (b) as long as they hold their retired status, (c) who, for themselves or others, sell, contract or negotiate for the sale of naval supplies or war materials to the Navy Department. [5 U.S.C. § 59c] . . . applies (a) to retired regular officers of all Armed Forces (and other listed government departments), (b) only for a period of two years after retirement, (c) who, for themselves or others, sell, contract or negotiate for the sale of any supplies or war materials to the specified government departments (including the Department of Defense). Neither statute applies to reserve officers; and it appears that neither statute applies to retired permanent enlisted personnel, advanced to commissioned rank on the retired list under the provisions of 10 U.S.C. 6151 (1956). (Comp. Gen. dec. B-129273 of 12 October 1956). . .
>
> *What activities constitute "selling, contracting for sale or negotiating for sale"?* The quoted terms have been interpreted to include virtually all activities surrounding the selling process. The signing of a government contract by the President of a Corporation, although that is his only relationship to a particular transaction, has been held "contracting for sale" within these laws. (JAG:II:2:JAC:sh of 13 August 1956.) Preliminary negotiations preceding a contract or sale constitute "negotiating for sale." [See 38 Decs. Comp. Gen. 470, 472–73 (1959).] The precise extent to which activities related to a sale to the government are within the quoted phrase cannot always be delineated with any degree of certainty. However, wherever possible and where all relevant facts are available, the Office of the Judge Advocate General will supply an advisory opinion to retired personnel concerning their proposed activities. As noted in the introduction, any such opinions will not bind the government.
>
> *What are "naval supplies or war materials"?* The words "naval supplies or war material" have been interpreted to include almost any conceivable [property] item. Pocket combs and soft drinks are naval

supplies within the quoted statute. (JAG:II:2:JAC:mks of 5 March 1956; JAG:II: :mmt of 15 September 1949, pub. in CMO 3–1950, 98) [The Comptroller General has sanctioned this broad construction of the phrase "naval supplies and war materials." See DECS. COMP. GEN. B-140581 (1959), reported in 28 U.S.L. WEEK 2234 (Nov. 9, 1959). 38 DECS. COMP. GEN. 470, 474–75 (1959) also interprets broadly this phrase and other ambiguous portions of 5 U.S.C. § 59c and 10 U.S.C. § 6112(b).] There is, however, an important exception to this term. Persons or firms who "are commonly understood as being engaged in the furnishing of professional services . . . [such as plans, specifications, designs, or drawings]" are not engaged in selling "naval supplies or war material" to the government, since "clearly professional services are not "naval supplies or war materials" within the accepted meaning of that term." (Comp. Gen. Dec. B-12238 of November 7, 1940) The term "supplies or war materials" . . . should be similarly interpreted.

What is the "Navy Department"? This term . . . has been construed to include not only the Navy itself, but Agencies and instrumentalities, such as Navy Exchanges, ships' stores and commissaries of the Navy. (JAG:II:2:JAC:mks of 5 March 1956; see CMO 3–1950, 98; JAG:II: JWB:mmt of 31 March 1950) [See 38 DECS. COMP. GEN. 470, 475–76 (1959).] This is an indication of the construction which will be placed upon the comparable phrase, listing various government departments, in [5 U.S.C. 59c]. . . .

What is the effect of engaging in the activities listed in the quoted statutes? The quoted statutes are not criminal and do not purport to make illegal the selling, contracting for sale or negotiating for the sale of supplies or war materials to the specified government departments. They merely provide that, if a retired officer engages in any of the prescribed activities, he will not be entitled to receive retired pay for the period involved. (JAG:II:2:JAC:mks of 5 March 1956) Although a retired officer forfeits his retired pay only while he is engaged in such a manner, once the Navy Department determines that he is so occupied, he will be considered in that status until he proves that he has discontinued his selling activities.

Navy Judge Advocate General, Reference Guide to Employment Activities of Retired Naval Personnel, September 1957. *Cf.,* however, 38 DECS. COMP. GEN. 470, 473–4 (1959).

68 Stat. 1142 (1954), 5 U.S.C. § 740c (1958)

In 1954 Congress enacted the "Hiss Act" prohibiting retirement payments to any person convicted of violating various laws. These include 18 U.S.C. §§ 216, 281, 283, 284, and 434. The statute thus reinforces the conflict of interest restraints on retired military officers.

Regulations of the Department of the Air Force

The regulations of the Department of the Air Force are the most comprehensive of those of the three military departments.

Generalized Air Force regulations call for "fair play" in Air Force procurement. Section 7 of AFR 30–30 then requires all retired Air Force officers and former personnel seeking to do business with the Air Force within two years after termination to file an affidavit stating:

(1) Their former connection with the Air Force and the date of termination thereof;

(2) The subject matter of the business they are transacting and intend to transact with Air Force personnel, and whether their duties in their former connection with the Air Force related to the same subject matter;

(3) Whether they gave any personal attention to the matters under consideration or gained any personal knowledge of the facts thereof while connected with the Government.

Coming at the conflicts problem from the other side, the same Air Force regulation also expressly prohibits its personnel from dealing with any former personnel who are acting in violation of the conflicts statutes.

Finally, the Air Force seeks to paraphrase and explain existing statutory bars on retired officers. Thus, Air Force Pamphlet 34–4–3, part I, ch. VIII, para. 6.b (1), dated January 1957, sums up the post-employment prohibitions of Section 281 as follows: "A retired Regular Air Force Officer may not sell, contract or negotiate for the sale of anything to the Air Force. This prohibition applies to any activity on behalf of the prospective contractor which is directly aimed toward forming the basis of a contract with the Government. However, it is not intended to preclude a retired officer from accepting employment with private industry solely because his employer is a contractor with the Government. Therefore, it should not be construed that these prohibitions apply to activities which are only remotely connected with sales or contracts as distinguished from direct participation in obtaining a contract with the Government on the behalf of a prospective contractor."

Regulations of the Department of the Army

Department of the Army regulations are scattered among the many branches of the army establishment. Conflict of interest restrictions appear in quotations or paraphrasing of existing statutes, supplemented by code of ethics statements calling for "fair play" and "equal treatment" on the part of procurement officials. The Department of the Army has, however, sought to implement 5 U.S.C. § 59c. Section 16–65 of AR 37–104 provides: "Each officer upon retirement, or each retired officer who was recalled to active duty upon relief from assignment to such active duty, will submit to the disbursing officer who pays his retired pay [a certificate that he is not selling or negotiating for the sale of supplies of war materials to the Defense Department and that he will immediately notify the disbursing officer if he engages in such activities within 2 years after retirement]."

AR 632–35 seeks to implement the claims prohibitions of Sections 283 and 284. It prohibits all Army personnel from dealing with any retired military or civilian official as the representative of a claimant against the federal government, if he retired within the preceding two years, unless such retired official has executed a Notice of Appearance disclosing a) his former status in military service, b) whether the matter involves a military department in which a retired status is held, and c) whether it was pending in one of the departments during his active service (D.A. 1627).

Regulations of the Department of the Navy

The Navy Judge Advocate General has issued pamphlets aimed at educating retired naval officers as to conflicts prohibitions. These pamphlets paraphrase, quote, and explain existing statutory bars and thus seek to help retired naval officers. However, the actual material of the Navy Department does little more to supplement the statutory restraints than to enunciate general rules of equal treatment and fair play on the part of naval procurement officers.

Department of Defense Regulations

In the light of the present unintegrated state of conflict of interest regulations in the military departments, the Preparedness Subcommittee in 1957, the Celler Subcommittee in 1958, and the Hebert Committee in 1960 urged the Defense Department to adopt master regulations of uniform applicability throughout the military establishment. PREPAREDNESS INVESTIGATING SUBCOMM., SENATE COMM. ON ARMED SERVICES, 85TH CONG., 1ST SESS., TWELFTH REPORT ON CONFLICT OF INTEREST IN THE ARMED SERVICES 15 (Comm. Print 1957); STAFF OF SUBCOMM. NO. 5, HOUSE COMM. ON THE JUDICIARY, 85TH CONG., 2D SESS., REPORT ON FEDERAL CONFLICT OF INTEREST LEGISLATION, pt. IV, p. 63 (Comm. Print 1958); SUBCOMM. FOR SPECIAL INVESTIGATIONS, HOUSE COMM. ON ARMED SERVICES, 86TH CONG., 1ST SESS., REPORT ON EMPLOYMENT OF RETIRED COMMISSIONED OFFICERS BY DEFENSE DEPARTMENT CONTRACTORS 20 (Comm. Print 1960).

The "Dual Compensation" Statutes: A Separate Problem

The so-called "dual compensation" statutes in general forbid the United States to hire former government employees receiving retirement pay, including retired military officers. 47 Stat. 406 (1932), as amended, 5 U.S.C. § 59 (a) (1958); 28 Stat. 205 (1894), as amended, 5 U.S.C. § 62 (1958). Not actually grounded in conflict of interest considerations, these statutes are frequently mentioned in this context and have also been attacked as depriving the government of a valuable source of personnel.

APPENDIX C

A Note on
the Research Program

Legal research

In preparation for this study an extensive legal research survey was conducted on the basic conflict of interest statutes, legislative history, regulations, related judicial opinions, and secondary legal sources. The companion volume to this book will contain a detailed review of the law in this field. A bibliography prepared in the course of this research appears at 13 THE RECORD OF THE ASSOCIATION OF THE BAR OF THE CITY OF NEW YORK 323–30 (May 1958).

Factual research

A. Questions.

Apart from legal questions, the project raised two basic questions calling for accumulation of data from field research.

1. What is actually done under the conflict of interest restraints —
   a. by government administrators by way of enforcement?
   b. by private individuals in adjusting their affairs to the restraints?
   c. by government officials in the conduct of their duties?

2. What effects do these restraints have, particularly in their impact upon recruitment and retention of personnel by the government and upon the flow of information between government and the private sector?

B. The Research.

1. Administrative Agencies.

The major government agencies, for purposes of inquiry, were divided into six groups. The groups were:
   a. over-all agencies dealing with personnel and legal problems (*e.g.*, Department of Justice, the Civil Service Commission, and the Bureau of the Budget);
   b. the Department of Defense;

c. licensing agencies (*e.g.*, Federal Communications Commission, Civil Aeronautics Board);

d. regulatory agencies (*e.g.*, Securities and Exchange Commission, Federal Power Commission);

e. fund-granting agencies (*e.g.*, Housing and Home Finance Agency, National Science Foundation);

f. special agencies (*e.g.*, Department of the Interior, Export-Import Bank, Atomic Energy Commission, Department of Commerce).

Inquiry into conflict of interest experience was conducted in two or more agencies (and their subordinate departments and bureaus) from each of these six categories. Following a review of the regulations of these agencies, field research took the form of lengthy interviews by the staff, with the help of committee members, of:

a. administrative officials — particularly personnel officers and inspection and enforcement officers;

b. general counsels;

c. top administrators, political executives;

d. miscellaneous general employees.

2. General Executive Officials.

Interviews were conducted with government officials of general responsibility from the current and preceding administrations, particularly with respect to problems of recruitment of executives.

3. Congress.

On the subject of congressional committee investigations and the work of Senate confirming committees in the field of conflict of interest, full reported transcripts were reviewed in dozens of proceedings deemed to warrant such attention. All transcripts of confirmation proceedings respecting appointments to administrative commissions since 1953 were examined. In all, over seventy-five selected transcripts were studied from the point of view of conflict of interest.

Extensive interviews were then conducted with members of both houses of Congress, with staffs of many of the committees dealing with confirmations, and with the staffs of the committees that had investigated aspects of the conflict of interest field in recent years.

4. General Conferees.

A large group of persons were interviewed who were selected because of their unusual experience in and out of government service. This group included former government officials, members of the judiciary, students of government, professional administrators, lawyers, businessmen, representatives of civic organizations, and many others. A special effort was made to learn something of the position of the scientist and of the executive scientist.

5. Interviewing.

Interviewing was conducted by the staff and by members of the committee. Interviews were informal and tended to run over an hour. At many of the committee's regular two-day sessions, officials and other persons appeared before the committee to discuss their experiences and views on the conflict of interest question. All persons interviewed were assured that any information given would be held in complete confidence and no names would be given revealing sources of information.

C. Conclusions reached.

The many conclusionary assertions of fact made in this book are based upon these accumulated data; they do not purport to be based upon formal sampling technique. On the other hand, the total number of persons who might be expected to have had sustained experience with the problem of conflict of interest in federal employment is not great, and the interviews conducted numbered over two hundred. The staff and the committee believe that the factual conclusions presented here are warranted by the evidence seen.

Tribute and warm thanks are due to the scores of people who helped with the research work. Uniformly, interviewees and conferees from all branches of government and from all administrations willingly shared their time, their experiences, and even their personal financial confidences. The committee and staff are grateful to them all for their cooperation.

Index

Index